Special Edition

USING
ISAPI

D1398556

que®

Special Edition

USING
ISAPI

Written by Stephen Genusa with

Bobby Addison, Jr. • Allen Clark • Dean Cleaver • Kevin Flick
Thomas LeRoux • Martin J. Norman • Tom Parkinson
Paul P. Parrone, Jr. • Michael Regelski • Andrew D. Smith
David A. Torres

que®

Special Edition Using ISAPI

Credits

PRESIDENT
Roland Elgey

PUBLISHER
Joseph B. Wikert

PUBLISHING MANAGER
Fred Slone

EDITORIAL SERVICES DIRECTOR
Elizabeth Keaffaber

MANAGING EDITOR
Sandy Doell

DIRECTOR OF MARKETING
Lynn E. Zingraf

ACQUISITIONS EDITOR
Tracy Dunkelberger

PRODUCTION EDITOR
Judith Goode

PRODUCT MARKETING MANAGER
Kristine Ankney

ASSISTANT PRODUCT MARKETING MANAGERS
Karen Hagen
Christy M. Miller

STRATEGIC MARKETING MANAGER
Barry Pruett

TECHNICAL EDITORS
Sundar Rajan
John Smiley

TECHNICAL SUPPORT SPECIALIST
Nadeem Muhammed

ACQUISITIONS COORDINATOR
Carmen Krikorian

SOFTWARE RELATIONS COORDINATOR
Susan D. Gallagher

EDITORIAL ASSISTANTS
Jennifer L. Condon
Andrea Duvall

BOOK DESIGNER
Ruth Harvey

COVER DESIGNER
Dan Armstrong

PRODUCTION TEAM
Marcia Brizendine
Jenny Earhart
Jason Hand
Bob LaRoche
Erich Richter
Kaylene Riemen
Staci Somers

INDEXER
Tim Tate

Composed in *Century Old Style* and *Franklin Gothic* by Que Corporation.

This is dedicated to Tammy and the little one.

—*Stephen Genusa*

About the Authors

Stephen Genusa is Director of Web Development at IRdg (**http://www.irdg. com**) in Winter Park, Florida. He also works as an independent consultant and contributor to industry magazines. He lives in the Dallas, Texas area. Stephen has worked as a systems analyst, software engineer, local area network administrator, and hardware technician. He has a special affinity for database and graphical user interface design but can't seem to stay away from the system application programming interfaces for very long. He established and maintains the frequently asked questions area for the Microsoft Internet Information Server at **http//rampages. onramp.net/~steveg/iis.html** and The ISAPI Developer's Site at **http// rampages.onramp.net/~steveg/isapi.html**, IIS-Config at **http//rampages. onramp.net/~steveg/iiscfg.zip**, I-Spy at **http//rampages.onramp.net/ ~steveg/ispy.zip**, and EyeSAPI at **http//rampages.onramp.net/~steveg/ eyesapi1.zip**. He can be contacted through e-mail at **steveg@onramp.net**.

Bobby Addison, Jr., is a freelance author and programmer in Albany, Georgia. He got his start with computers 13 years ago with an Apple IIe and Applesoft BASIC, and has been hacking away ever since. Bobby can be reached at **baddison@iname.com**.

Allen Clark has been working in software development since the early eighties, beginning in high-end computer-aided design (CAD) system development. In 1996, he joined Logos Research Systems, Inc., to work on the Logos Library System, a multilingual, multimedia, electronic publishing platform.

Allen has developed numerous back-end, ISAPI-based services. He is designing ISAPI-based application and data delivery systems for the Logos Library System.

Dean Cleaver is a Visual Basic enthusiast who has worked in the computer industry for many years. His background includes six years of university studies in electrical and electronic engineering, and accounting. During the past three years, Dean has written extensive and specialized software for the transport, travel, and printing industries. He is working on corporate intranets and client-server systems in Auckland, New Zealand.

Kevin Flick is a lead developer for Norton Utilities in California. He has a double honors degree in math and computer science from Southampton University in the U.K., and a master's in advanced computer methodologies from Queen Mary College in London. Kevin is author of Luckman's Web Commander™, a Web server, and continues to influence commercial software development. He is working on new Internet research and development, and is also an independent consultant and technology advisor.

Thomas LeRoux is a senior systems analyst at a major pharmaceutical corporation. His programming experience ranges from developing telephony applications in Visual Basic to writing Win32 database services in C++. He has recently been busy programming ISAPI extensions for his company's intranet.

Tom has a B.S. in computer science from Hofstra University and lives in Morristown, NJ. He can be reached at **lerouxt@haven.ios.com**.

Martin J. Norman is a special projects manager for Network Designers Ltd., a U.K. software development and consulting company specializing in networking in the Fujitsu/ICL market. An honors graduate from Teesside University, Martin has designed and programmed customer solutions in Hong Kong, South Africa, and throughout Europe. He has implemented communications products in Windows and NT environments. Martin can be reached at **martin@ndl.co.uk**.

Tom Parkinson's dual backgrounds—librarianship and data processing—are reflected in his work on this book. Tom's research skills were polished during many years as a librarian at the collegiate level. His work as a programmer spans a continuum from PDPs to Pentiums, and emphasizes the interaction between applications and operating systems. Tom holds a Master's of Science in Information Systems and a Master's of Library Science from the University of Pittsburgh. He would like to dedicate his work on this book to his parents, Mary and Tom. Tom lives in Springfield, MA and can be reached at **tpark@voicenet.com**.

Paul P. Parrone, Jr., is a consultant based in central New Jersey. He has a B.S. from DeVry Institute of Technology in computer information systems. During the past seven years, Paul has worked on client-server development with major companies, using tools such as C and C++. His most recent effort is the development of a company-wide intranet application powered by Microsoft's Internet Information Server.

Michael Regelski is the director of software development at Lenel Systems International. Lenel Systems is one of the leaders for industrial security products, including photo ID management and access control.

Michael has an M.S. in software development and management, and a B.S. in computer engineering from Rochester Institute of Technology. He has conributed to other Que titles, including *Special Edition Using Visual Basic 4.0*, *Building Multimedia Applications with Visual Basic 4.0*, and *Special Edition Using Windows NT Server 4.0*.

Andrew D. Smith is Webmaster at Community Health Plan in Latham, New York, and has been a consultant for several Fortune 500 companies. He spends his non-work hours answering technical questions via email (**andrewsmith@hotmail. com**), keeping up with technology, dabbling with his Web page, and developing freeware for the Internet community.

David A. Torres is CIO and chief technologist with ClearMind, Inc., a Microsoft solution provider based in the Dallas area. ClearMind specializes in interactive commercial Web-site development. David is a Microsoft-certified systems engineer, Microsoft-certified solutions developer, and Microsoft product specialist. He specializes in developing interactive commercial Web sites using ISAPI, the BackOffice SDK, and other third-party tools. He is also an accomplished developer of ActiveX controls for use in the business environment and has been a featured speaker at Microsoft Developer Days, Windows World, and the New Mexico Computer Conference and Expo.

Acknowledgments

I would like to thank John Ludeman, Lester Waters, and Stan Murawski of Microsoft for answering so many questions about ISAPI and Microsoft Internet Information Server. Your contributions in the public and private forums have been invaluable.

I would like to thank Tracy Dunkelberger, Fred Slone, Judith Goode, and everyone else involved with this project at Que Corporation. Thanks for giving me the room to create a book that I'd want on my bookshelf and for helping me when I needed it.

I'd like to thank the coauthors of the book who worked so hard to provide the best reference for ISAPI developers.

Thanks to Tom Sheldon and Angela Genusa for the authoring advice. Thanks to Jeff Duntemann for introducing me to programming over 10 years ago and to Steve McConnell for *Code Complete,* a book that left a lasting mark on the quality of my software development.

I'd like to thank my dear wife Tammy for her patience and her help with so many things. Thank you to my father and mother, Vincent and Carol, for teaching me that diligence and honest labor provide a special satisfaction. Thank you to Archie, affectionately known as "Big Bad," and Betty for your patience during the long hard years of work on the career that led to this book.

Thanks to Joe Galindo for teaching me how to create a road map for life and for showing me that my options were unlimited. Thanks to Doug Walz, Mark Harwell, Kirk Lockhart, and Eric Best for your understanding while I was working on this book.

Stephen Genusa

We'd Like to Hear from You!

As part of our continuing effort to produce books of the highest possible quality, Que would like to hear your comments. To stay competitive, we *really* want you, as a computer book reader and user, to let us know what you like or dislike most about this book or other Que products.

You can mail comments, ideas, or suggestions for improving future editions to the address below, or send us a fax at (317) 581-4663. For the online inclined, Macmillan Computer Publishing has a forum on CompuServe (type **GO QUEBOOKS** at any prompt) through which our staff and authors are available for questions and comments. The address of our Internet site is **http://www.mcp.com** (World Wide Web).

In addition to exploring our forum, please feel free to contact me personally to discuss your opinions of this book: I'm **104124,3145** on CompuServe, and I'm **tdunkelberger@que.mcp.com** on the Internet.

Thanks in advance—your comments will help us to continue publishing the best books available on computer topics in today's market.

Tracy Dunkelberger
Acquisitions Editor
Que Corporation
201 W. 103rd Street
Indianapolis, Indiana 46290
USA

NOTE Although we cannot provide general technical support, we're happy to help you resolve problems you encounter related to our books, disks, or other products. If you need such assistance, please contact our Tech Support department at 800-545-5914 ext. 3833.

To order other Que or Macmillan Computer Publishing books or products, please call our Customer Service department at 800-835-3202 ext. 666. ▨

Contents at a Glance

Table of Contents

I | Introducing ISAPI

IV | ISAPI Filters

12 Using ISAPI Filters 305

V | Advanced ISAPI Topics

17 Troubleshooting and Debugging Extensions and Filters   455

18 Making Your Extensions Thread-Safe   487

VI | Appendixes

Introduction

The Internet Server Application Programming Interface (ISAPI) was introduced in early 1996 as a replacement for the Common Gateway Interface (CGI). ISAPI offers better performance than CGI and scales up quickly for high-traffic Web sites.

Other specifications were developed in the quest to replace CGI, which is slow and lacks scalability. But none of these interfaces are so widely accepted as ISAPI.

Two of the largest Web server vendors were behind ISAPI, Microsoft and Process Software, and other Web server vendors hurried to adopt the specification. The result: ISAPI is an overnight success. ■

Purpose of This Book

The first few chapters of this book lay a foundation for ISAPI by showing you how the Web's Hypertext Transport Protocol (HTTP) works. We look at dynamic Web sites and how Windows NT is becoming the accepted platform for the Web.

We move on to the theory behind ISAPI extensions and show you how to build ISAPI extensions *without* the Microsoft Foundation Classes (MFC). Then we show you how to build extensions *with* MFC.

We also look at object linking and embedding (OLE)ISAPI, and how you can use Microsoft Visual Basic (VB) to extend your Web server.

Next we discuss ISAPI filters and how the server interacts with filters. We build some filter examples to illustrate the principles behind filters.

The last few chapters of the book give you valuable information on how to debug your ISAPI dynamic link libraries (DLLs) and how to make them thread-safe.

What You Need to Use This Book

Most of the examples in this book use C++ so you'll need a 32-bit, C/C++ compiler if that's your language of choice. Also covered are the Microsoft VB OLEISAPI interface, and some examples on the companion CD to the book use Borland's Delphi 2.0.

The companion CD holds C++ and Delphi extension and filter headers, along with other tools that ISAPI developers will find useful. All the source code used in the book's examples is included on the CD.

Here is a list of what you'll need:

- Microsoft Visual C++ (or other 32-bit C++ compiler) *or* Delphi 2.0 *or* Microsoft VB for OLEISAPI extensions.
- A workstation that has an ISAPI-enabled Web server.
- A thread-safe version of any ODBC driver. You'll need this for the examples that use the open database connectivity (ODBC) interface.

How This Book Is Organized

This book is organized into six parts, with eighteen total chapters and three appendixes that cover all aspects of ISAPI development. This book assumes that you are reading the chapters in order.

But if, for example your interest is with ISAPI filters, you can read the introductory material and safely skip to Chapter 12 to learn about ISAPI filters.

Following is an overview for each of the five parts of the book.

Part I: Introducing ISAPI

Chapter 1, "Introducing ISAPI," discusses what you can do with ISAPI and lists HTTP server vendors who use some aspect of the ISAPI specification.

Part II: The Web, NT, and ISAPI

Chapter 2, "The Web and Windows NT," discusses the client-server model. It looks at HTTP, and shows you how Web servers and clients communicate. The chapter ends with a discussion of cookies and authentication schemes used on the Web.

Chapter 3, "Understanding Dynamic NT Web Sites," considers how ISAPI extensions and filters help you to develop dynamic Web sites. It looks at server interface options, including CGI, WinCGI, ISAPI, and the ActiveX. CGI and WinCGI lead into an introduction to how ISAPI works. Chapter 3 closes with a review of programming language options.

Chapter 4, "CGI vs. ISAPI: Pros and Cons," discusses the pros and cons of CGI and ISAPI. It considers the scalability and safety of each, and gives recommendations that you can use for your Internet and intranet development.

Part III: ISAPI Extensions

Chapter 5, "Using ISAPI Extensions," looks at how you can use ISAPI extensions to add dynamic capabilities to your Web site. It shows you how ISAPI extensions are executed from a Web client.

Chapter 6, "Understanding ISAPI Extensions," discusses how ISAPI extensions interface to a Web server. It explains how ISAPI extension DLLs are built and the rules a developer must follow to build extensions.

Chapter 7, "Creating ISAPI Extensions," is a tutorial that shows you how easy it is to build a simple ISAPI extension. You build a couple of simple extensions and view the output using your Web browser.

Chapter 8, "Using Extension Capabilities," shows you how to build on the function of your extensions. It discusses how data is received from a Web client, how to parse the data from the client, and what information the Web server makes available through the extension control block. It also looks at how to add redirection capabilities to your extensions.

Chapter 9, " Building Extensions with MFC," shows you how to use the Microsoft foundation classes (MFC) to build ISAPI extensions. You build an extension and use the GET and POST methods. You learn how parse maps work and how to use form elements, including text boxes and radio buttons.

Chapter 10, "Extending Your Web Server with Extensions," tells you about extending your Web server using ISAPI extensions. You build a couple of live extensions that you can easily extend and use on your Web server. Included is a token parsing extension that adds dynamic Hypertext Markup Language (HTML) capabilities right "out of the box."

Chapter 11, "OLEISAPI," discusses the Microsoft VB interface to the ISAPI server. It shows you how to use VB to extend your Web server with VB OLE extensions.

Part IV: ISAPI Filters
Chapter 12, "Using ISAPI Filters," is about using ISAPI filters to add dynamic capabilities to your Web site.

Chapter 13, "Understanding ISAPI Filters," shows you how ISAPI filters work. You learn about building an ISAPI filter, using the powerful features of ISAPI filters, and how ISAPI filters interact with Web servers. The chapter closes with the rules for developing ISAPI filters.

Chapter 14,"Creating an ISAPI Filter," shows you how to build an ISAPI filter. It discusses the server function that filters can take advantage of and tells you how to install ISAPI filters on your Web server.

Chapter 15, "Building Filters with MFC ISAPI Classes," is about using MFC to create ISAPI filters. You create a filter using MFC and learn how MFC works. You also learn how to avoid the stumbling blocks to MFC.

Chapter 16, "Extending Your Web Server with Filters," shows you how to build ISAPI filters you can use on your own Web server. You build a custom authentication filter, use thread synchronization, and connect to an ODBC data source. Then you build a custom logging filter and learn how to allocate memory in a filter.

Part V: Advanced ISAPI Topics

Chapter 17, "Troubleshooting and Debugging Extensions and Filters," shows you how to avoid common problems with building ISAPI DLLs. You learn from the mistakes of others, which saves you grief in the long run. Included are tips for writing durable, easy-to-debug extensions and creative techniques for debugging ISAPI DLLs.

Chapter 18, "Making Your Extensions Thread-Safe," explains threads and how they enhance the performance of ISAPI extensions. You learn how NT schedules threads for execution and how to use critical sections to make your ISAPI DLLs thread-safe. Using NT synchronization mechanisms to protect access to shared resources is also covered.

Part VI: Appendixes

Appendix A supplies the ISAPI 1.0 and 2.0 specifications in a reference format that's handy to consult while you're working with ISAPI. Appendix B lists additional resources for ISAPI that can be found on the Internet.

About the Companion CD

The companion CD to the book holds all the source code used in the examples, the EyeSAPI extension debugger, IISCFG, and I-SPY utilities written by the author, the HTML conversion of Que's *Special Edition Using Windows NT Server 4.0*, *Special Edition Using Visual C++,* and a sneak preview of Que's upcoming release of *Using Active Server Pages*. See "Installing from the CD-ROM" in Appendix C for more details.

Conventions Used in This Book

To make this book easier to use, the following typographical conventions are used:

A word or phrase used for the first time appears in *italics* and is usually accompanied by a definition.

Code examples appear in a `special monospace type`.

`Italic monospace` is used to indicate placeholders and variables—words that you are supposed to replace with a setting.

This book also includes these other features to increase its usability:

N O T E This is an example of a Note. Notes provide additional information that may help you avoid problems or that you should consider when using the features described in the text.

Occasionally, the lines of code that you see in this book may be too long to fit on one printed page. When this happens, you see the code continuation character shown in the following line:

```
'This is an example of a line of code that should be typed as a
➥single line but is too long to fit on one line of the printed
page.'
```

This character means that the line was broken to fit on the printed page. If you decide to type a line of code that contains this character, you should *not* use the Enter key. Just ignore the character and type both lines, as a single entry, before pressing Enter.

In addition, code listing titles help you find and use the sample code and application files in this book. All the code listing titles have the file name of the sample code or application so you can find them on the companion CD. ●

Introducing ISAPI

Introducing ISAPI

The convergence of technologies always brings exciting times. In this case, we are witnessing the convergence of technologies that were at one time available only to an elite group consisting primarily of government agencies and educational institutions.

These technologies created what we know as the Internet. When combined with the power of the personal computer, the Internet brings world-wide connectivity to everyone with access to a PC—including corporate entities, "mom and pop" businesses, entrepreneurs, individuals, and even many of society's disadvantaged.

Intellectual and economic forces are now driving businesses and individuals to exploit the power of the Internet and the newly coined *intranet*—Internet technologies used in the corporate environment.

What is ISAPI?

An overview of what ISAPI is all about.

The advantages of ISAPI over CGI

A look at why you should consider ISAPI over CGI.

How ISAPI can solve Web development problems

How ISAPI allows you to extend the Web server in ways CGI cannot.

The two types of ISAPI interfaces

Filters and extensions: two different ways to extend your Web server.

Who uses ISAPI?

Web vendors who use ISAPI.

The Internet and the rapidly growing demand for intranets have created an immediate demand for developers who understand these technologies and can use them both at the Internet and at the intranet level.

Even more exciting for many developers, though, are the changes in the software arena. Software tools and technologies have always lagged behind the advancements in the ever-increasing power of hardware. Although this trend shows no sign of abating, we can be sure of one thing: Software development technologies are finally coming of age.

Object-oriented languages that were once shunned are now commonplace in many developers' toolkits. Operating systems now provide extensive application program interfaces (APIs), allowing developers to add powerful functionality with a simple API call.

Languages such as C++, Delphi, and Java are proving to be good foundations for drag-and-drop graphical user interface (GUI) programming. This makes rapid application development (RAD) a joy. Add technologies such as COM and DCOM, which enable developers to build and use components on a local computer or on one that is halfway around the world, and developers are often limited only by their imaginations.

The Internet server application programming interface (ISAPI) is one of the new technologies available to today's developer. ISAPI is an interface to Hypertext Transport Protocol (HTTP) servers that allows developers to extend Web servers and provide an unexpected degree of functionality. ISAPI extensions (also called *server applications*) and filters allow the server to be extended in ways that Common Gateway Interface (CGI) or its competing interfaces never could.

In this chapter, we give you a high-level overview of what ISAPI is, the advantages of ISAPI over CGI, how ISAPI can extend the server in ways that CGI cannot, and the two types of interfaces to a Web server that ISAPI provides. We close the chapter by looking at the vendors and products that are currently supporting the ISAPI specification. ■

What Is ISAPI?

ISAPI (pronounced *eye-sap-ee*) was developed by Process Software in collaboration with Microsoft Corporation and other Web server vendors. ISAPI is a high-performance, scalable solution for developers who want to create dynamic Web sites. These sites have to be able to handle high request rates without degrading the HTTP server's performance.

N O T E The best source for ISAPI information on the Internet is the ISAPI Developer's Site at **http://rampages.onramp.net/~steveg/isapi.html**. ▦

ISAPI is now used by many of the most popular Web server vendors, including Microsoft, Process Software, and Spyglass.

Why Use ISAPI?

There are a number of compelling reasons to use ISAPI. ISAPI is not simply a better CGI. ISAPI is different from CGI and was designed to solve the problems of CGI.

First, ISAPI scales much better than CGI. ISAPI dynamic link libraries (DLLs) need fewer resources, such as server memory, than CGI. This means that your server can handle more concurrent requests under ISAPI than a Web site can using CGI.

ISAPI is also faster than CGI. ISAPI allows you to write extensions to the server that can outperform their CGI counterparts by as much as five times.

Finally, ISAPI allows you to extend a Web server in ways that Web server vendors may not have envisioned. ISAPI gives much more control over an HTTP connection than CGI can. It does this by providing events that an ISAPI filter handles in each step of processing during an HTTP connection.

We'll look at each of these items in more detail.

Scalability

ISAPI allows you to build Web sites that scale up from one connection to hundreds of concurrent connections per second without massive additional resources, such as server memory. Until ISAPI came along, the answer to better CGI performance was to throw more memory at the Web server until the Web server stopped memory swaps to the disk.

CGI works by creating a new process for each CGI request. The Web server responds to a CGI request by creating a new process, filling that process' environment with HTTP request variables, and starting the CGI application.

The memory needs of concurrent processes can rise quickly. ISAPI applications, on the other hand, do not need to create a new process. The ISAPI server simply creates a thread pool when the server is initialized.

Creating a thread takes much less memory than creating a new process. A free thread from this thread pool serves the incoming connection. If the threads in the thread pool are all in use, the server can create additional threads to handle the waiting connections.

Thread creation is much faster than process creation. The server must also track new CGI applications while they are running. The server may even need to do some cleanup after the application ends.

With ISAPI, the server calls the ISAPI DLL's entry point and leaves processing up to the extension or filter. Once processing is complete, the ISAPI DLL does any necessary cleanup and returns control of the thread to the server.

Figure 1.1 compares the scalability of CGI processes and ISAPI threads.

FIG. 1.1
ISAPI threads can scale up faster and more efficiently than CGI processes.

CGI Processes

ISAPI Threads

Microsoft's Web site is a testament to the scalability of ISAPI. In mid-1996 when it had one of the largest request rates on the Internet, the site was run on four Pentium computers.

This was a remarkable accomplishment. Consider the number of ISAPI DLLs that are used on the site by Microsoft to log, redirect, and provide information about Microsoft, its products, and technologies to **www.microsoft.com** users.

Faster Performance

As we mentioned in the previous section, creating a new process is expensive in terms of time—particularly when the memory-hungry process causes disk swapping. Because ISAPI threads are created in the same process as the server, and because the thread pool handles connections, there is no additional overhead with ISAPI.

In addition to this, CGI applications are I/O bound. CGI applications read from standard input (stdin) and write to standard output (stdout). The server in turn reads this output and transfers the results back to the Web client (usually a Web browser).

The in-process threads under ISAPI have access to functions on the server that instruct the server to transmit a buffer of data back to the client. This is more efficient than CGI's out-of-process method. Finally, with ISAPI, the number of context switches needed by the server software is reduced by the in-process model.

Extensibility

CGI is limited to adding functionality through extensions we typically think of as *applications*. For example, when called, an extension can query a stock quote database and return the latest NYSE figures for a list of companies the Web user is interested in.

Although ISAPI supplies the same functionality through an extension, ISAPI allows a developer to extend *the server,* adding functionality at a more basic level than CGI allows. In other words, ISAPI can do everything that CGI can and a lot more.

Figure 1.2 illustrates this concept.

FIG. 1.2
CGI extends server functionality indirectly. ISAPI extends server functionality directly *and* indirectly.

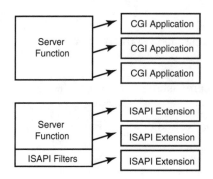

For example, every HTTP request has a logging event—an event in which data for that particular request is written to the log. ISAPI filters allow you to change the data written to the log so you can add custom logging.

At present, eight steps are exposed during the processing of an HTTP connection. Each step can be handled by one or more ISAPI filters, overriding the server functionality altogether or simply enhancing the server vendor's functionality. This kind of functionality was not possible with CGI.

Using ISAPI

We'll look at some of the things you can do with ISAPI that bring unparalleled power to the Web developer.

Managing Custom Security

One of the most important features of a Web server is the ability to manage a Web user's access to information on the server. Many Web sites need a mixed security model in which users are granted access to different areas of the Web site, based on their security level.

Anonymous users have free access to the public areas of the Web site, whereas authenticated users have access to areas of the Web site that hold private information. ISAPI filters allow developers to create custom security models that protect these private areas so that only specially authenticated users can access them.

More than that, with ISAPI, a developer can use custom encryption schemes that protect the security of the data as it is routed from the Web server to the Web client. For example, an ISAPI filter with a Web browser plug-in could make a fully secured connection using an encryption scheme such as DES or BlowFish.

The plug-in with the Web server's ISAPI filter could validate the user with a custom authentication form and supply private data that is protected through an "industrial-strength" encryption scheme understood by the plug-in.

The server's ISAPI filter would create a custom Multipurpose Internet Multimedia Extensions (MIME) type that the browser plug-in would decrypt and display on the browser's screen.

Custom URL Handling

Using ISAPI, a Web site can handle requests for specific URLs, based on different criteria. In a multiserver scenario, an ISAPI filter can monitor the server load and off-load new traffic to the site with the smallest pending workload.

The ISAPI filter can also rotate requests and redirect them to other servers, based on anything from the Web client's Internet Protocol (IP) address to the kind of browser the Web client is running.

Custom Logging

Logging Web traffic is critical for most Web sites. Early in the Web's history, the "hit count"—a count of how many Web clients retrieved a specific URL—was the only valuable information.

But Web clients now host a multitude of plug-ins, many Web sites handle multimedia, and the demands of business continue to grow. The result is a need to gather as much information about the users accessing a Web site as possible.

Today, all Web servers have logging built into the basic system. They collect information such as which URL was retrieved, the time and date of retrieval, the status code of the HTTP transfer, and a number of other items.

With most servers, you can't change or collect additional information. But you can use ISAPI to collect additional information such as browser type or the HTTP referrer.

Levels of ISAPI Use

An HTTP server can use two kinds of ISAPI DLLs. The first, *extensions,* are similar to CGI applications. The second, *filters,* offer a new way of extending the server to allow a fine-grained control over HTTP transactions.

Extensions

Like CGI applications, extensions are loaded when specifically requested by a Web client and typically stay loaded by the server until the server is shut down. The difference is that with an ISAPI extension, the server can unload extensions if necessary—for example, to manage memory. Extensions are loaded into the same memory address space as the server.

Filters

Filters offer functionality not possible with CGI. Filters break down an HTTP transaction to its basic stages of processing. This allows the developer to change how the server would normally complete each stage of the HTTP transaction.

ISAPI filters are loaded as soon as the server starts running and stay loaded as long as the server is running. Filters give developers a great way to extend the server's functionality.

If you are planning to buy a Web server and want to develop ISAPI filters, look closely at the Web server vendor's implementation of ISAPI. Microsoft is the only vendor so far to use the ISAPI filter specification.

ISAPI Specifications 1.0 and 2.0

The first ISAPI specification, 1.0, has been amended. The current ISAPI specification, 2.0, has only a few additions. Keep this in mind as you look at Web servers that may need the functionality added in the 2.0 specification.

Also, keep in mind that any Web server using the 2.0 specification should be able to communicate with extensions and filters that conform to the 1.0 specification.

ISAPI and Microsoft IIS

Microsoft's use of ISAPI is complete throughout their Web server lineup. Microsoft NT server 3.51 included Internet Information Server (IIS) 1.0, which used ISAPI 1.0, including extensions and filters.

Microsoft NT server 4.0 ships with IIS 3.0 and includes full support for ISAPI 2.0, including filters and extensions. Microsoft NT Workstation 4.0 ships with Peer Web Services, a scaled-down version of IIS, but includes full support for ISAPI 2.0, including extensions and filters.

Finally, Microsoft is incorporating a Personal Web Server into future versions of the Microsoft Windows operating system that includes full support for ISAPI 2.0, including extensions and filters. Microsoft will also be incorporating an extended ISAPI interface into their new streaming media server.

N O T E   Microsoft has released the Personal Web Server for Windows 95 users that includes full support for the ISAPI 2.0 specification. ▓

ISAPI and Process Purveyor

Process Software produced the ISAPI specification with Microsoft. Process Software uses ISAPI 1.0 for extensions in their Process Purveyor Web server software.

Other ISAPI Supporters

Table 1.1 lists other vendors that support ISAPI.

Table 1.1   Other Vendors that Support ISAPI

Company	Product	Extensions	Filters
Cyber Presence	Cyber Presence	Yes	No
Computer Software Manufaktur GmbH	Alibaba	Yes	No
Internet Factory	Commerce Builder	Yes	No
Luckman Interactive	Web Commander	Yes	No
O'Reilly	WebSite Pro	Yes	No

The Future of ISAPI

Few technologies are worth investing in if they won't be around tomorrow. We have seen how fast today's hardware and software become outdated. So how does the future of ISAPI look? Very bright—and for a number of reasons.

In less than a year, many of the major Web server vendors have used ISAPI at some level. This support will continue to grow since no other server API except the aging CGI is so widely used.

Microsoft's commitment to ISAPI was crucial in helping establish ISAPI as a standard interface to the Web server. This commitment continues in cutting-edge products such as the Microsoft Media Server, a media-streaming server.

ISAPI extensions are functionally related to CGI applications, and ISAPI filters provide a new level of functionality to Web developers.

From Here...

In this chapter, you learn what ISAPI is, why ISAPI was developed, some of the things you can do using ISAPI, the types of ISAPI interfaces, and which Web vendors support ISAPI. To find out more about how to extend your Web server with ISAPI, see the chapters listed next.

- Chapter 2, "The Web and Windows NT," tells you how the Web protocol works and gives you the history of Windows on the Web.

- Chapter 4, "CGI vs. ISAPI: Pros and Cons," discusses the pros and cons of ISAPI by comparison with CGI.

- Chapter 5, "Using ISAPI Extensions," is an introduction to extending your Web server with ISAPI extensions.

- Chapter 12, "Using ISAPI Filters," is an introduction to extending your Web server with ISAPI filters.

The Web, NT, and ISAPI

The Web and Windows NT

The Web and Windows NT are an exciting pair of technologies to be involved with today. With the rapid development of technologies for NT, such as ISAPI from Microsoft, and the strong growth of the Internet and intranets, mastering Windows NT and Web development promises to be an exciting journey. ■

The client/server model of the Web

The Web is based on a client/server model. You learn about the functions of the client and server in the client/server model.

User agents and Web servers

You see the various types of user agents and Web servers.

HTTP, the protocol of the Web

HTTP is a simple protocol to understand because it is based on a request-response paradigm.

Web browser cookies

Cookies allow the server to store small amounts of data on the client side and to have that information sent back to the server in special circumstances.

How the Web Works

As you develop ISAPI applications, you will find that it is vital to understand how the Web works. The fact is, the more you understand about Web communications, the more powerful your ISAPI programs will be.

ISAPI extensions and filters effectively become part of the Web server, as illustrated in Figure 2.1, through runtime dynamic linking. That is, at runtime, the server loads your dynamic link library (DLL) through the LoadLibrary and GetProcAddress functions.

At that point, your ISAPI programs have complete access to Web requests as they occur. They can supply the results of hypertext transport protocol (HTTP) requests, modify the results from other server extensions or static files, and log specialized information about those requests. In other words, ISAPI is a new and powerful means to an end. The end you want to achieve is efficient and dynamic Web communications.

FIG. 2.1
ISAPI extensions and filters become part of the Web server.

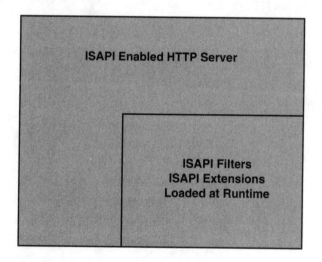

ISAPI Enabled HTTP Server

ISAPI Filters
ISAPI Extensions
Loaded at Runtime

Clients and Servers

The Web is based on a client-server model. Client-server computing distributes the basic components, user interface, program logic, and data between the client and server computers.

In a client-server model, the client

- Can request data from the server
- Can post data back to the server for storage
- Can request a process to run on the server
- May provide functional logic

In a client-server model, the server

- Can send data to the client
- Provides access to data storage
- May provide functional logic

In traditional client-server modeling, clients and servers can be "thin" or "fat." The terms indicate a functional relationship rather than a physical characteristic of the computer. The standard components of an application are a user interface, the program's logic or business rules, and data storage.

Client-server computing is a division of labor that is typically needed by most applications. The server is optimized to provide data to multiple clients, and the client application is optimized to interact with the end-user. The one task that may reside on one or both sides of the model is the functional logic.

Thin clients are generally limited to a user interface. All processing and program logic reside on a fat server. The server is called "fat" because the functional logic resides on the server. This is the most common model on the Web today. This model is illustrated in Figure 2.2.

The client in your case is typically a Web browser such as Microsoft's Internet Explorer. The Web browser is simply a user interface to many kinds of data that are retrieved from the Web server. In your case, the ISAPI applications provide the functional logic to the HTTP server and the client displays the various types of data from a specific URL.

By moving the program logic from the server to the client, you create a fat-client, thin-server model. Each client accessing the server makes program flow decisions based on the logic or business rules that reside on the client computer. The thin server acts as a gateway to data storage for clients. The fat-client, thin-server model is illustrated in Figure 2.3.

FIG. 2.2
Thin clients work with
fat servers.

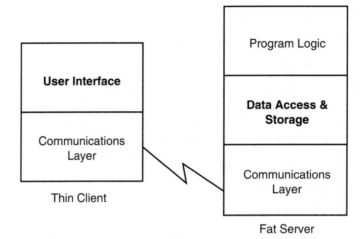

FIG. 2.3
Fat clients work with
thin servers.

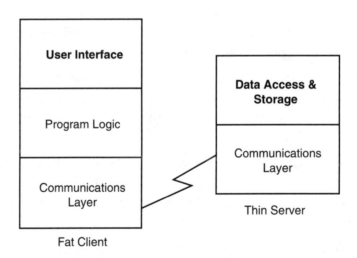

There are other models such as *distributed services* in which program functionality
is shared between clients and servers.

Clients on the Web are also called *user agents*. The server in this case is a Web
server such as Microsoft Internet Information Server (IIS). In the past, because
Web browsers were simply a user interface, the Web model was a fat server, thin
client. However, with the innovation of technologies that allow client-side programming, such as Microsoft ActiveX/COM, the browser is now rapidly being enabled
to do client-side processing.

User Agents   User agents refer to any client software that initiates a request to a Web server. As the Web increases in complexity, new types of user agents are invented to provide new functionality for Web users.

Web Browsers   The most popular type of user agent is the Web browser. By now, most readers probably have installed countless beta versions of various Web browsers. Because the Web is changing so quickly, developers often need the latest browser version using the latest HTML tags, features like style sheets, and the latest technologies like ActiveX.

Web browsers are the "human interface" to the Web. They enable you to navigate from Web site to Web site and to bookmark your favorite sites so that you can return later. On the practical side, they allow you to research subjects that interest you, to find old friends, or to read the latest news from around the world.

The first Web browser was created in November 1990 on a NeXT computer by Tim Berners-Lee, a consultant for CERN, the European Laboratory for Particle Physics (**http://www.cern.ch**). In February 1993 an alpha version of Mosaic for X (**http://www.ncsa.uiuc.edu/SDG/Software/Brochure/UNIXSoftDesc. html#XMosaic**) was released by the National Center for Supercomputing Applications (NCSA).

The lead programmer on this project at the NCSA was Marc Andreeson. Marc left the NCSA to create a company that we've come to know as Netscape Communications Corporation. Netscape Navigator is currently the most popular browser on the Web.

Microsoft entered into the browser market in early 1995 with Internet Explorer (IE) (**http://www.microsoft.com/IE**). Microsoft is aggressively marketing IE and many industry analysts expect IE to become the standard Web browser within the next year (see Figure 2.4).

Other User Agents   Other user agents have been designed to harness the resources of the Web. For example, some user agents compile information about the contents of a Web site, which are then presented for search and retrieval. Users can instantly search tens of thousands of Web pages for key words, phrases, and even concepts.

FIG. 2.4
Microsoft Internet Explorer.

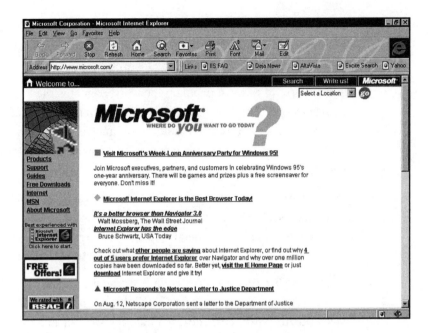

You probably know these user agents by names like Excite (**http://www.excite. com**), AltaVista (**http://altavista.digital.com**), Lycos (**http://www.lycos.com**) and InfoSeek (**http://www.infoseek.com**). Figure 2.5 shows the user interface that AltaVista provides to their Web index. This technology has been scaled down to the enterprise level in software packages such as Microsoft ActiveX Search, code-named Tripoli.

Another class of user agent has been created to find broken links on Web sites. These agents traverse a chain of document links, requesting each document from the server and ensuring that they are valid. These "spiders" note new URL links in each document that have not been verified and then follow these new chains till site verification is complete.

A new class of *intelligent agents* is being developed today to do more complicated tasks such as creating custom reports based on information located on the Web. Some of these intelligent agents even negotiate business transactions.

The Web browser will continue to serve as the human interface to the Web, but user agents such as these will help us to find the information that's really important to us.

FIG. 2.5
AltaVista: A popular
Web crawler.

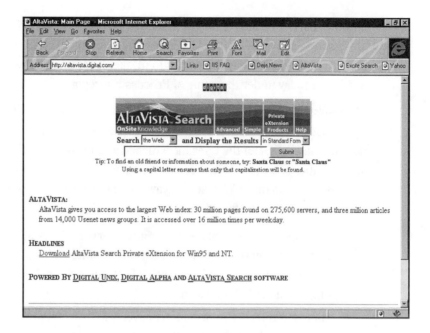

Web Servers   The other component of the client-server model is, of course, the server. Web servers are the software packages that accept connections from user agents and service the requests from those clients by sending back responses in the form of informational messages and documents.

As we mentioned before, the first Web software was developed on a computer from NeXT in November 1990. Once the Web client-server model was developed, programmers began working on stand-alone servers and rudimentary browsers.

By the end of 1992 there were 26 "reasonably reliable" servers on the Internet, and by January of the next year the number doubled. Near the end of 1993 the number had grown to 200 known Web servers. Three years later, at the end of 1996, there are hundreds of thousands of Web servers on the Internet and an unknown number of servers in use on corporate intranets.

Early HTTP Servers on Windows   One of the earliest Web servers on the Windows platform was named Win-HTTPD by Bob Denny. Denny created a true multi-threaded application that runs under Windows 3.1. The server also allowed image mapping, security, and CGI programs. Denny went on to write a Web server known today as O'Reilly Website.

Another early Web server for the Windows platform is the EMWAC HTTP server, designed to run on Windows NT. The authors of this software quit developing the free product and rewrote the server to market it commercially. This product is marketed today under the name of Process Purveyor.

Commercial HTTP Servers   At one time it was almost impossible to find HTTP servers for the Windows platform because most of the available options were focused on UNIX. But the tides have turned and these days UNIX is being dropped by a number of large software companies in favor of the Windows NT platform. In fact, there are so many Web servers available today on the Windows NT platform that we'll look at just a few of them.

- Netscape Communications Commerce Server—Netscape Communications Commerce Server was the first serious commercial contender in the HTTP server marketplace for Windows NT. At this writing, Netscape does not support the ISAPI interface.

- Microsoft Internet Information Server—Microsoft entered the Web server market in February 1996 with IIS 1.0. Microsoft IIS was clearly one of the fastest servers on the market. Microsoft released IIS 3.0 in December 1996.

  IIS 3.0 sports up to a 56 percent increase in server performance on single-processor servers and up to a 62 percent increase on dual-processor servers. In addition, Microsoft is incorporating a product called ActiveX Server Framework, code-named Denali, into the server, providing server-side scripting.

  By the fall of 1996, IIS was rapidly rising in the sales charts. Microsoft and Process Software jointly developed the ISAPI 1.0 specifications, and both IIS 1.0 and IIS 3.0 support ISAPI.

  The coming years promise to be exciting as new technologies such as Denali are released.

HTTP—the Protocol of the Web

Web servers are also commonly called HTTP servers. HTTP is the protocol used by these servers to communicate with Web clients. It is a client-server protocol designed for fast and efficient transfer of hypertext documents.

HTTP is a simple protocol to understand. It is based on a request-response para-digm.

A simple HTTP transaction looks like this:

1. The user agent opens a connection to the server, typically via TCP/IP on port 80.

2. Once the connection is established, the client sends a request to the server in the form of a text message.

3. The server responds with the requested document, document information, or error code.

4. The server closes the connection.

Figure 2.6 shows a simple but complete HTTP transaction.

FIG. 2.6
A complete HTTP transaction.

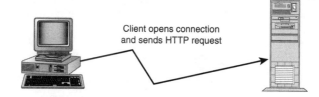

Client opens connection
and sends HTTP request

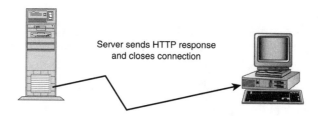

Server sends HTTP response
and closes connection

HTTP is also a stateless protocol. That is, the protocol does not maintain any infor-mation about previous requests to the server: each request is independent of all other requests. Because the protocol is stateless, each request must have complete information about the current request being made.

TCP/IP Connections   Before looking at HTTP requests, we'll cover briefly how Web clients and servers connect. HTTP connections generally use TCP/IP, which is made up of two different protocols.

- The transport control protocol (TCP) is a transport-layer protocol responsible for moving data between applications. TCP also defines the concept of port numbers. There are standard port numbers for most services, such as FTP (port 21), Gopher (port 70), Telnet (port 23), and HTTP servers (port 80). TCP creates a byte stream from the data it receives from applications.

- The Internet protocol (IP) is a network-layer protocol that creates packets out of the byte stream that TCP creates. The IP protocol also defines the Internet addressing scheme. Internet addresses are 32 bits (4 bytes) wide and typically in the form of xxx.xxx.xxx.xxx (255.255.255.0).

Before an HTTP connection can be made, the client and server computers must both be connected to the Internet. This is usually done through TCP/IP.

The other element in achieving a connection is the domain name system (DNS). Before a connection can be made with a remote host, the IP address of the host must be determined. We usually know a host's name by something like www.microsoft.com. These English descriptions are used because people can remember www.microsoft.com more easily than they can remember 207.68.137.35.

The DNS system works like this:

1. The local computer creates a request to the local DNS server for an IP address.
2. If the local DNS server does not have an entry for the host name, it sends the request up the hierarchy of DNS servers until one of them responds with the IP address.
3. The local DNS receives the IP address from the remote DNS and returns the result to the local computer.

This entire process is typically completed within a fraction of a second, although some requests may be longer because of network congestion. Once our Web browser knows the IP address of the HTTP server, it attempts to open a connection to that IP address, typically using port 80, and the HTTP request is submitted to the server.

N O T E   Using host names like www.microsoft.com also allows the remote DNS server to do some interesting tricks such as load balancing. By rotating the IP address among a number of host computers, the DNS server can manage server loads. You can see this in action by pinging www.microsoft.com a number of times. You will notice that the IP changes each time you ping the host.

Ping is a utility that comes with Windows 95 and Windows NT that can test a network connection or allow you to determine a remote host's IP address. To use ping, open a Command prompt and type **PING** to receive help using the utility. ▪

HTTP Requests   The simplest request consists of a request method, a requested URI, and the version of HTTP that the user agent can accept. A URI is a formatted string that identifies a network resource giving a name, location, or other identifying characteristic of the resource. We look at URIs and URLs in a little more detail shortly.

So what happens when you click on a link in your Web browser? If the link is a simple GET request, a request is generated by the browser, and the browser opens a connection to the server and sends the request. The request looks something like this:

```
GET /default.htm HTTP/1.0
```

This request tells the server to GET the resource named /default.htm and send it back to the user agent using HTTP version 1.0. The server receives this request and tries to find the file, and then send it back using HTTP 1.0.

If it cannot find the file, an error message is returned. Once the response is completed, the connection to the user agent is closed by the server. The user agent then displays the results of the request on your screen.

Let's look at how the server responds to this GET request in more detail.

HTTP Responses   The Web server's response consists of a *status line, response header, entity header,* and *entity body.* Here is an example of how a successful HTTP transaction would look in response to our GET request:

```
HTTP/1.0 200 OK
Server: Microsoft-IIS/2.0
Date: Fri, 16 Aug 1996 16:53:58 GMT
Content-Type: text/html
Accept-Ranges: bytes
```

```
Last-Modified: Fri, 12 Jul 1996 01:30:00 GMT
Content-Length: 4051
[blank line ended with CRLF]
<!doctype html public "-//IETF//DTD HTML//EN">
<html>
<head>
</head>
<body background="/images/backgrnd.gif">
[other information sent has been removed]
```

The first item sent back from the server is called the *status line*. The status line consists of a string identifying the HTTP version and a status code. In this case the status of our request is 200, which equates to the status description of OK. Table 2.1 lists the common HTTP status codes.

Table 2.1   HTTP Status Codes

Status Code	Response Phrase	Definition
200	OK	The request has succeeded. The information returned with the response is dependent on the method used in the request, as follows: GET, an entity corresponding to the resource requested is sent in the response; HEAD, the response must only contain the header information and no Entity-Body; POST, an entity describing or containing the result of the action.
201	Created	The request has been fulfilled and resulted in a new resource being created. The newly created resource can be referenced by the URI(s) returned in the entity of the response.
202	Accepted	The request has been accepted for processing but the processing has not been completed.
204	No Content	The server has fulfilled the request but there is no new information to send back.

Status Code	Response Phrase	Definition
300	Multiple Choices	This response code is not directly used by HTTP/1.0 applications but serves as the default for interpreting the 3xx class of responses.
301	Moved Permanently	The resource requested has been assigned a new permanent URL, and any future references to this resource should be made using that URL.
302	Moved Temporarily	The resource requested resides temporarily under a different URL. Since the redirection may be altered on occasion, the client should continue to use the `Request-URI` for future requests.
304	Not Modified	The client has made a conditional `GET` request and access is allowed, but the document has not been modified since the date and time specified in the `If-Modified-Since` field. The server must respond with this status code and not send an `Entity-Body` to the client.
400	Bad Request	The request could not be understood by the server because of malformed syntax. The client should not repeat the request without changes.
401	Unauthorized	The request needs user authentication. The response must include a `WWW-Authenticate` header field (Section 10.16) containing a challenge applicable to the resource requested.
403	Forbidden	The server understood the request but is refusing to fulfill it. Authorization will not help and the request should not be repeated.

Part

II

Ch

2

continues

Table 2.1   Continued

Status Code	Response Phrase	Definition
404	Not Found	The server has not found anything matching the Request-URI. No indication is given of whether the condition is temporary or permanent.
500	Internal Server Error	The server encountered an unexpected condition that prevented it from fulfilling the request.
501	Not Implemented	The server can't fulfill the request. This is the appropriate response when the server does not recognize the request method and can't use it for any resource.
502	Bad Gateway	The server, while acting as a gateway or proxy, received an invalid response from the upstream server it accessed in attempting to fulfill the request.
503	Service Unavailable	The server can't handle the request because of temporary overloading or maintenance of the server. This is a temporary condition that will be alleviated after some delay.

The server also sends back additional information called *response headers*. These normally include the kind of server software being used and the current server date and time. Also included is an entity header with the date the resource requested was last changed, the type of resource in multipurpose Internet mail extensions (MIME) type/subtype form, and the length of the entity body.

Once these request headers are sent, the server ends the request header with a blank line. The server then sends the entity body, which in our example is 4051 bytes of text/html data.

Request Methods   In the example above, we use the GET request method. GET is designed to retrieve information from the HTTP server. The URI designated in the GET request can be a static HTML file or it can be an ISAPI DLL that, for example, generates a dynamic HTML page from a SQL server database.

GET works fine if we want only to get information from the server. But what happens if we need to send information to the server? Web sites usually need a number of different data entry forms such as sign-up forms or feedback forms.

The POST method allows Web browsers to send data to the Web server. Forms, like the one shown in Figure 2.7, are typically used to post data to a Web server. A POST request with request headers looks like this:

```
POST /scripts/srch.dll HTTP/1.0
Accept: */*
Referer: http://199.1.154.46/isapi/srch.htm
Accept-Language: en
Content-Type: application/x-www-form-urlencoded
UA-pixels: 1024x768
UA-color: color16
UA-OS: Windows NT
UA-CPU: x86
User-Agent: Mozilla/2.0 (compatible; MSIE 3.0B; Windows NT)
Host: 199.1.154.46
Connection: Keep-Alive
Content-Length: 92
Pragma: No-Cache
[blank line ended with CRLF]
input_text=now+is+the+time+for+all+good+men+%28and+women%21%29+
➥to+come+to+ISAPI+programming.
```

As you can see, the client begins the POST request with the request method, the URI the data will be posted to, and the HTTP version. At the end of our request headers, you see the standard blank line and then the data we posted to the server.

The data encoding is denoted in the Content-Type subtype. In this case the encoding is x-www-form-urlencoded. This encoding does a number of simple data transformations such as translating spaces to a plus sign.

We have posted the data to the server. In this case the server responds to the Web browser with this:

```
HTTP/1.0 200 OK
Server: Microsoft-IIS/2.0
Date: Fri, 16 Aug 1996 16:50:02 GMT
```

Part
II

Ch
2

```
Content-Type: text/html
<head><title>Search Results</title></head><BODY
BACKGROUND="/samples/images/backgrnd.gif"><BODY
BGCOLOR="FFFFFF"><TABLE><TR><TD>
<IMG SRC="/ images/SPACE.gif"
[other html data deleted]
```

The Web browser receives the response consisting of `test/html` data. The browser removes the status line, response, and entity headers, and then displays the HTML in the browser's window.

FIG. 2.7

Forms allow Web browsers to post data to the server.

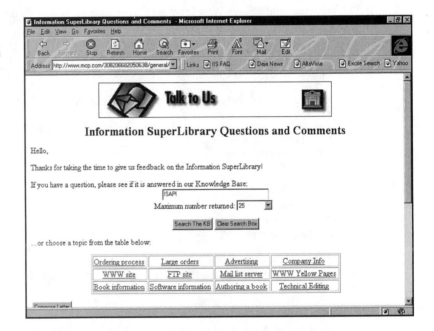

We've looked at the GET and POST request methods. The final method we'll look at is the HEAD request method. The HEAD request method allows user agents to get information about a specific URI entity without getting the entity itself. A HEAD request takes the form of

```
HEAD /default.htm HTTP/1.0
```

The server responds by returning the same response headers as it does for a GET request, but the server does not include the entity body:

```
HTTP/1.0 200 OK
Server: Microsoft-IIS/2.0
Date: Mon, 19 Aug 1996 22:22:23 GMT
Content-Type: text/html
```

```
Accept-Ranges: bytes
Last-Modified: Fri, 12 Jul 1996 01:30:00 GMT
Content-Length: 4051
```

The HEAD method is useful to find out whether a resource has changed or to find out other characteristics of the resource without actually getting that resource.

Table 2.2 summarizes the common request methods.

Table 2.2   HTTP Request Methods

Method	Definition
GET	The GET method means retrieve whatever information (in the form of an entity) is identified by the Request-URI. If the Request-URI refers to a data-producing process, the produced data and not the source text of the process is returned as the entity in the response, unless that text happens to be the output of the process.
POST	The POST method requests that the destination server accept the entity enclosed in the request as a new subordinate of the resource identified by the Request-URI in the Request-Line.
HEAD	The HEAD method is identical to GET except that the server must not return any Entity-Body in the response. The meta-information in the HTTP headers in response to a HEAD request should be identical to the information sent in response to a GET request.

Request Headers   Request headers provide the user agent and HTTP server with additional information about an HTTP transaction. For example, the Accept header field provides information about what MIME types the client can accept. The User-Agent header field provides the name of the user agent that is requesting the document. Here is our original GET request as Microsoft IE 3.0 would send it:

```
GET /default.htm HTTP/1.0
Accept: */*
Accept-Language: en
UA-pixels: 1024x768
UA-color: color16
UA-OS: Windows NT
UA-CPU: x86
User-Agent: Mozilla/2.0 (compatible; MSIE 3.0B; Windows NT)
Host: 199.1.154.46
Connection: Keep-Alive
```

The request is still a GET request for the document /default.htm using HTTP 1.0. But the Accept header tells the server that we can accept any MIME type or subtype, as shown by the */*.

Accept-Language shows that the preferred language of the client is English. The server could tailor the language response by using this header field.

UA-pixels and UA-color give information about the client's video capabilities. The server could select graphics that are created specially for various screen resolutions based on this information. UA-OS and UA-CPU show the type of operating system and hardware the client is running under, and so on.

As you can imagine, a server ISAPI application could use each of these items and tailor the output to give the user-agent the best possible presentation of the information requested.

Table 2.3 lists the common HTTP request headers. Note that some of the header fields listed are from the HTTP 1.1 specification. The reality of Web development is that the technology is changing so quickly that developers may have to use it before the specifications are final.

Table 2.3   Common HTTP Request Headers

Header	Definition
Accept	The Accept request-header field specifies certain media types that are acceptable for the response. Accept headers can be used to show that the request is limited to a small set of types, as in the case of a request for an inline image.
Accept-Language	The Accept-Language request-header field is like Accept but restricts the set of natural languages that are preferred as a response to the request.
Authorization	To authenticate itself with a server—usually after getting a 401 response—a user agent includes an Authorization request-header field with the request. The Authorization field value is the authentication information of the user agent for the realm of the resource requested.

Part

II

Ch

2

Header	Definition
Cache-Control	The Cache-Control general-header field gives directives that *must* be obeyed by all caching mechanisms along the request/response chain. The directives are meant to prevent caches from adversely interfering with the request or response. These directives typically override the default caching algorithms.
Content-Base	The Content-Base entity-header field specifies the base URI for resolving relative URLs within the entity. This header field is described as Base in RFC 1808, which is expected to be revised.
Content-Encoding	The Content-Encoding entity-header field is a modifier to the media-type. When present, its value shows what additional content coding has been applied to the resource and thus what decoding mechanism must be applied to get the media-type referenced by the Content-Type header field. The Content-Encoding allows a document to be compressed without losing the identity of its underlying media type.
Content-Length	The Content-Length entity-header field shows the size of the Entity-Body, in a decimal number of octets, sent to the recipient. Or, in the case of the HEAD method, this field shows the size of the Entity-Body that would have been sent had the request been a GET.
Content-Type	The Content-Type entity-header field shows the media type of the Entity-Body sent to the recipient or, in the case of the HEAD method, the media type that would have been sent had the request been a GET.
Date	The Date general-header field represents the date and time at which the message was originated and has the same semantics as orig-date in RFC 822.
Expires	The Expires entity-header field gives the date/time after which the entity should be considered invalid. This allows information providers to suggest the volatility of the resource or a date after which the information may no longer be valid. Applications must not cache this entity beyond the date given.

continues

Table 2.3 Continued

Header	Definition
	The presence of an `Expires` field does not imply that the original resource will change or cease to exist at, before, or after that time. However, information providers who know or even suspect that a resource will change by a certain date should include an `Expires` header with that date.
Host	The `Host` request-header field specifies the Internet host and port number of the resource requested, as obtained from the original URL given by the user or referring resource. The `Host` field value *must* represent the network location of the origin server or gateway given by the original URL.
If-Modified-Since	The `If-Modified-Since` request-header field is used with the `GET` method to make it conditional. If the resource requested has not been modified since the time specified in this field, a copy of the resource is not returned from the server. Instead, a `304` (not modified) response is returned without any `Entity-Body`.
Last-Modified	The `Last-Modified` entity-header field shows the date and time at which the sender believes the resource was last modified. The exact semantics of this field are defined in terms of how the recipient should interpret it. If the recipient has a copy of this resource that is older than the date given by the `Last-Modified` field, that copy is considered invalid.
Location	The `Location` response-header field defines the exact location of the resource that was identified by the Request-URI. For 3xx responses, the location must show the server's preferred URL for automatic redirection to the resource. Only one absolute URL is allowed.
Pragma	The `Pragma` general-header field includes implementation-specific directives that may apply to any recipient along the request/response chain. All `Pragma` directives specify optional behavior from the viewpoint of the protocol; however, for some systems, behavior has to be consistent with the directives.

Header	Definition
Referer	The Referer request-header field allows the client to specify, for the server's benefit, the address (URI) of the resource from which the Request-URI was obtained. This allows a server to generate lists of back links to resources, logging, optimized caching, and so on. It also allows obsolete or mistyped links to be traced for maintenance. The Referer field must not be sent if the Request-URI was obtained from a source that does not have its own URI, such as input from the user keyboard.
Server	The Server response-header field holds information about the software used by the originating server to handle the request. The field can have multiple product tokens (Section 3.7) and comments identifying the server and any significant subproducts. By convention, the product tokens are listed in order of their significance for identifying the application.
User-Agent	The User-Agent request-header field holds information about the user agent originating the request. This is for statistical purposes, the tracing of protocol violations, and automated recognition of user agents for the sake of tailoring responses to avoid particular user-agent limitations. Although it is not needed, user agents should include this field with requests.
WWW-Authenticate	The WWW-Authenticate response-header field must be included in 401 (unauthorized) response messages. The field value consists of at least one challenge that shows the authentication scheme(s) and parameters applicable to the Request-URI.

Part

II

Ch

2

URLs, URIs, and URNs   You'll run into the terms *URL* and *URI* often in working on the Web. We'll try to unravel the confusion about the difference between URLs and URIs.

URLs have been called *uniform resource locators* and *universal resource locators*. The current specifications use *uniform* rather than *universal*.

URLs are a form of URIs. In practice, an URL is a protocol and address that identify an "object." That object could be a document, graphic image, video movie, sound file, or host computer.

The only protocols that can be used, according to the specifications are file://, ftp://, file, http://, mailto://, news://, nntp://, telnet://, wais:// and prospero://.

Uniform resource identifiers (URIs) are a general family of resource identifiers consisting of URLs and URNs.

A uniform resource name (URN) is "any URI that is not an URL."

Figure 2.8 shows the relationship between URIs, URLs, and URNs.

FIG. 2.8
The URI family of identifiers.

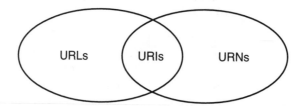

MIME Types   The MIME specification was created by a need to transfer graphics images and other binary formats in e-mail. The use of the MIME scheme was adopted by the designers of the HTTP protocol to allow these same binary documents to be transferred via the Web.

The MIME naming convention uses a type/subtype scheme in which type represents a major category such as audio, video, image, or text. The subtype specifies the application type such as wav, gif, tif, or jpeg.

You will notice in HTTP response headers that the server sends a Content-Type header denoting the MIME type of the document the GET, HEAD, or POST request results in. In the case of our GET request:

```
GET /default.htm HTTP/1.0
```

The beginning of the response header looks like this:

```
HTTP/1.0 200 OK
Server: Microsoft-IIS/2.0
Date: Fri, 16 Aug 1996 16:53:58 GMT
Content-Type: text/html
```

Note that the content-type is text/html. If the resource requested is a GIF file, the Content-Type looks like this:

```
Content-Type: image/gif
```

Table 2.4 lists some of the common MIME types.

Table 2.4 Common MIME Types

MIME Type	MIME Subtype	Application
audio	x-wav	WAV audio file
audio	x-aiff	AIFF audio file
text	html	HTML file
text	plain	TXT text file
image	gif	GIF image
image	jpeg	JPEG image
image	tiff	TIF image
video	mpeg	MPEG video
video	quicktime	Apple QuickTime video
video	x-msmovie	Microsoft AVI video

Testing HTTP Requests   From time to time you will find it useful to directly test a request against a live server. Instead of writing an application to handle this situation, you can use the Telnet application that comes with Windows 95 and Windows NT. To test this, try the following:

1. Start Telnet.
2. Select Connect and then Remote System.
3. In the Host name field, enter your computer host that is running the Web server.
4. Change the Port to 80.
5. Type **GET /default.htm HTTP/1.0** [enter][enter].

You may need to turn logging on (see Figure 2.9) to capture all the information that is returned by the server. To do this, select the Terminal menu and then select Start Logging.

You can also use the Notepad program that comes with Windows NT and Windows 95 to develop complex GET and POST requests. Once you have developed the request, you can copy and paste these requests into the Telnet session.

FIG. 2.9
Logging the Telnet sessions allows you capture the data for analysis later.

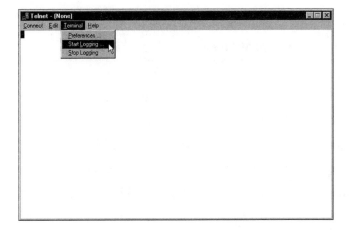

HTTP Cookies   We would be remiss not to discuss HTTP cookies. Cookies allow the server to store small amounts of data on the client side and have that information sent back to the server in specified circumstances.

Cookies are at least a partial answer to the problem of the stateless nature of the HTTP protocol. States can be preserved through the use of cookies.

A cookie is sent as part of the HTTP response header from the server. For example, if we want to store a variable named UserAccount on a client's Web browser, we can send a cookie that looks like this:

```
Set-Cookie: UserAccount=6758; path=/; domain=.abcdef.com
```

This tells the browser to send a cookie called UserAccount in all future request headers, with a value of 6758, for all documents requested under the path '/', including subdirectories.

Let's look at a few HTTP requests and see how this works. Suppose you've just started your browser and want to look at a document located at **http:// www.abcdef.com/latest_news.html**. You type in the URL, and the browser generates a request that looks like this:

```
GET /latest_news.html HTTP/1.0
Accept: */*
Accept-Language: en
User-Agent: Mozilla/2.0 (compatible; MSIE 3.0B; Windows NT)
Host: 199.1.154.46
Connection: Keep-Alive
```

The server at www.abcdef.com finds the `/latest_news.html` document and responds with this:

```
HTTP/1.0 200 OK
Server: Microsoft-IIS/2.0
Date: Fri, 09 Aug 1996 10:03:23 GMT
Content-Type: text/html
Set-Cookie: UserAccount=6758; path=/; domain=.abcdef.com
Accept-Ranges: bytes
Last-Modified: Sat, 17 Aug 1996 01:30:00 GMT
Content-Length: 2592
[blank line ended with CRLF]
<!doctype html public "-//IETF//DTD HTML//EN">
<html>
<head>
</head>
<body background="/images/backgrnd.gif">
```

Part
II

Ch
2

Now, unseen by the Web user, the browser receives a cookie named `UserAccount` with a value of `6758`. Any cookies that are valid for the given domain, path, and date-time are sent in the HTTP request header until the browser is closed. For example, the next request from the browser might look something like this:

```
GET /news/world_news.html HTTP/1.0
Accept: */*
Accept-Language: en
Cookie: UserAccount=6758
User-Agent: Mozilla/2.0 (compatible; MSIE 3.0B; Windows NT)
Host: 199.1.154.46
Connection: Keep-Alive
```

If we want to store this cookie in the client browser's cookie cache file, we can specify the `expires` attribute and set the expiration date to a time in the future. We could also set additional cookies so that the browser sends back multiple data items when a request is made. In that case, the request from the browser would look like this:

```
GET /news/world_news.html HTTP/1.0
Accept: */*
Accept-Language: en
Cookie: UserAccount=6758; Hits=3; Level=2
User-Agent: Mozilla/2.0 (compatible; MSIE 3.0B; Windows NT)
Host: 199.1.154.46
Connection: Keep-Alive
```

As you see, we have cookies set for `UserAccount`, `Hits`, and `Level`. Developers who use cookies should take note that a client can have up to 30 cookies per server or domain set at any one time.

CAUTION

A bug in Netscape Navigator 1.1 and earlier prevents cookies from being set when the path attribute is set to '/' and the expires attribute is not specified. Make sure you specify an expires attribute if you want the cookie saved when the path is set to '/'.

The current draft specifications for cookies indicate that a maximum of 300 cookies can be stored on a client computer at any given time. Cookies are limited to 4,096 bytes, including the length of the cookie names.

A list of cookie attributes is in Table 2.5.

Table 2.5   Cookie Attributes

Variable	Example	Definition
name	UserAccount=6758	This is the name of the cookie you want to work with. The cookie name is the only required attribute of a cookie.
expires	expires=Mon, 11-Nov-1996 00:01 GMT	The expires attribute sets the date that the cookie expires. Once the expiration date arrives, the cookie is destroyed by the browser and is no longer sent to an HTTP server.
domain	domain=www.abcdef.com	The domain attribute specifies which domains the cookie should be sent to. For example, a cookie with the domain of .abcdef.com is valid within the domain www.abcdef.com and search.abcdef.com. But a cookie with a domain of www.abcdef.com is only valid within that specific domain.

Variable	Example	Definition
path	path=/	The path attribute shows the subset of URLs for which the cookie is to be used. If the path is set to '/', the cookie is sent to the server for all URLs requested. If the path is set to '/foo', the browser sends the cookie to the server when documents in the /foo directory are requested. Documents requests in the /foobar directory also qualify to receive the cookie.
secure	secure	If the secure attribute is present, the cookie is only sent by the browser that is connected through a secure communications connection using Secure Sockets Layer (SSL). If the secure attribute is not present, the cookie is transmitted over secure and non-secure connections.

Cookies are useful because once a user is identified, the server can essentially have the client's browser identify itself in future HTTP transactions. State information can be passed on each transaction, including record number requests, user account information, and other information that normally would have to be stored in HTML hidden fields.

 The server could also encrypt the cookie data using strong encryption such as DES, Blowfish, or a custom encryption scheme. Because the encryption and decryption process is located on the Web server, a developer in the U.S. does not have to worry about export laws.

continues

continued

> And because the server simply wants that token data passed back to the server on each request, the Web client does not need any special software to handle encryption or decryption.

You should not put too much trust in the cookie *cache* for a number of reasons. First, the cookie file can be erased by the user at any time. If the only source of important data is the cookie cache file, you've just lost that data.

Next, if the browser receives over 300 cookies, it can delete cookies at its own discretion. There aren't any rules in the specifications about which cookies are chosen for deletion.

And finally, the user may switch browsers. The file format for the cache cookies is not specified and varies from vendor to vendor.

HTTP Authentication   Creating secure areas on a Web site is often necessary. For example, you might want to secure an area from all Web users except those who have subscribed to a premium service, or you might want to reserve an area of your site for remote business partners or employees. A few different authentication schemes are available, depending on the Web server you are using. Table 2.6 lists the schemes currently available.

Table 2.6   Authentication Schemes

Name	Details
Anonymous	The user is not authenticated. A user name or password is not requested from the user agent asking for resources from the server. Information published is available to anyone who has the URL.
Basic	The user agent must authenticate itself with a user name and password for each realm. Basic authentication encodes the user name and password with base64 encoding. This is considered a non-secure method and should be treated accordingly.

Name	Details
NT Challenge/Response	The user agent must authenticate itself with a user name and password for each realm. NT Challenge/Response (NTLM) (shown in Figure 2.10) encrypts the user name and password, providing a secure method of transferring the user name and password to the server. When possible, you should use NT Challenge/Response over basic authentication. The only HTTP server supporting NTLM is IIS.

Part

II

Ch

2

FIG. 2.10
Microsoft's Internet Service Manager allows you to configure authentication options.

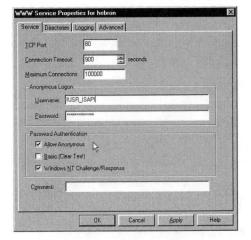

As we saw before, the HTTP protocol is stateless. Therefore, once a client has "logged onto" the HTTP server and an HTTP transaction is completed, the client is immediately "logged off." That is, the server retains no knowledge of the client or its permissions.

As you can see from Table 2.6, the Basic authentication scheme transmits the user name and password for each request. This again is because of the stateless nature of the HTTP protocol.

The server uses the user name and password in an attempt to authenticate the user and allow access to the secured areas. NT Challenge/Response works the same way but transfers the user name and password in encrypted form.

Let's take a look now at how an authenticated HTTP transaction works. We'll look
at basic authentication and then at NTLM. First, our user agent requests the default document from the /secure-docs/ directory:

```
GET /secure-docs/ HTTP/1.0
Accept: image/gif, image/x-xbitmap, image/jpeg, image/pjpeg, */*
Accept-Language: en
UA-pixels: 1024x768
UA-color: color16
UA-OS: Windows NT
UA-CPU: x86
User-Agent: Mozilla/2.0 (compatible; MSIE 3.0; Windows NT)
Host: 199.1.11.197
Connection: Keep-Alive
```

The Web server gets the request and determines that the area has been secured.
The server does not get a user name and password, so the server responds with a
401 Access Denied response message:

```
HTTP/1.0 401 Access Denied
WWW-Authenticate: Basic realm="www.abcdef.com"
Content-Length: 24
Content-Type: text/html
Error: Access is Denied.
```

Because the server has sent a 401 Access Denied message, the Web browser displays a dialog box requesting a user name and password for this secured area.
A typical authentication dialog box is shown in Figure 2.11.

FIG. 2.11

The 401 Access
Denied response
instructs the browser
to display an authen-
tication dialog box.

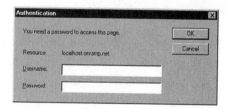

Once the user types in a user name and password, the Web client sends another
request, as follows:

```
GET /secure-docs/ HTTP/1.0
Accept: image/gif, image/x-xbitmap, image/jpeg, image/pjpeg, */*
Accept-Language: en
UA-pixels: 1024x768
UA-color: color16
UA-OS: Windows NT
UA-CPU: x86
```

```
User-Agent: Mozilla/2.0 (compatible; MSIE 3.0; Windows NT)
Host: 199.1.11.197
Connection: Keep-Alive
Authorization: Basic eW91IHZhc3RlZDp5b3VyIHRpbWUhDQo=
```

You can see that the client now includes an Authorization header that gives the realm name Basic, and the user name and password base64 encoded. Unencoded, this would reveal the user name and password separated by a colon.

The server checks its user database, determines the validity of the supplied user name and password, and sends back the requested URL if they are correct. If the user name and password are not correct, another 401 message is sent to the browser and the browser redisplays the Authentication dialog box.

This continues until the user supplies a correct user name and password combination, or the user presses the Cancel button, in which case the browser displays an Error: Access is Denied message on the Web browser screen.

NT challenge/response security works roughly the same way. The initial GET request is made with the Authorization header. The server determines that the URL is in a password-protected area and responds with a 401 error.

Because NTLM authentication is active on the server, the response header includes a WWW-Authenticate: NTLM header informing the client that NTLM authentication is the preferred method.

If the client allows NTLM, it uses NTLM to respond to the request. If it does not allow NTLM, the client falls back on the Basic authentication scheme.

```
HTTP/1.0 401 Access Denied
WWW-Authenticate: NTLM
Content-Length: 24
Content-Type: text/html

Error: Access is Denied.
```

Once we enter the information and press Enter, the Web browser reissues the request, as follows:

```
GET /secure-docs/ HTTP/1.0
Accept: image/gif, image/x-xbitmap, image/jpeg, image/pjpeg, */*
Accept-Language: en
UA-pixels: 1024x768
UA-color: color16
UA-OS: Windows NT
UA-CPU: x86
```

Part
II

Ch
2

```
User-Agent: Mozilla/2.0 (compatible; MSIE 3.0; Windows NT)
Host: 199.1.11.197
Connection: Keep-Alive
Authorization: NTLM T2ACMM7ARUAABAAAAA7IAAAABgAGAUJASTO5Ww
```

As you can see, the `Authorization` header is included in the request header. This shows the server that NTLM will be used to authenticate the user. The server decrypts the user name and password data, compares them to the database, and responds accordingly.

One other interesting thing to note about the encrypted user name and password is that under NTLM they encrypted information changes with each request, whereas the base64'd method leaves the user name and password the same, regardless of how many times it is transferred.

Where to Find More Information

The definitive source of information on Internet protocols and standards is a series of documents called *Request For Comments (RFC)*. Information on everything from HTTP to simple mail transfer protocol (SMTP) to netiquette guidelines can be found in the RFCs. Table 2.7 lists a number of RFCs that ISAPI/Web developers will find useful.

A searchable index of RFCs is available at **http://ds.internic.net/ds/ dspg1intdoc.html**.

Table 2.7 Important Internet RFCs

RFC	Location	Description
1808	**http://ds.internic.net/rfc/rfc1808.txt**	Relative Uniform Resource Locators
1630	**http://ds.internic.net/rfc/rfc1630.txt**	Universal Resource Identifiers in WWW
1738	**http://ds.internic.net/rfc/rfc1738.txt**	Uniform Resource Locators (URL)
1736	**http://ds.internic.net/rfc/rfc1736.txt**	Functional Recommendations for Internet Resource Locators

RFC	Location	Description
1866	http://ds.internic.net/rfc/rfc1866.txt	Hypertext Markup Language—2.0
1980	http://ds.internic.net/rfc/rfc1980.txt	A Proposed Extension to HTML: Client-Side Image Maps
1867	http://ds.internic.net/rfc/rfc1867.txt	Form-Based File Upload in HTML
1942	http://ds.internic.net/rfc/rfc1942.txt	HTML Tables
1945	http://ds.internic.net/rfc/rfc1945.txt	Hypertext Transfer Protocol—HTTP/1.0
1738	http://ds.internic.net/rfc/rfc1738.txt	Uniform Resource Locators (URLs)
822	http://ds.internic.net/rfc/rfc822.txt	Standard for the Format of ARPA Internet Text Messages
1341	http://ds.internic.net/rfc/rfc1341.txt	MIME (Multipurpose Internet Mail Extensions)
1896	http://ds.internic.net/rfc/rfc1896.txt	The text/enriched MIME Content-type
1872	http://ds.internic.net/rfc/rfc1872.txt	The MIME Multipart/Related Content-type
1180	http://ds.internic.net/rfc/rfc1180.txt	A TCP/IP Tutorial
1034	http://ds.internic.net/rfc/rfc1034.txt	Domain Names—Concepts and Facilities
1035	http://ds.internic.net/rfc/rfc1035.txt	Domain Names—Implementation and Specification
1794	http://ds.internic.net/rfc/rfc1794.txt	DNS Support for Load Balancing

Part II

Ch 2

continues

Table 2.7   Continued

RFC	Location	Description
1983	http://ds.internic.net/rfc/rfc1983.txt	Internet Users' Glossary
1796	http://ds.internic.net/rfc/rfc1796.txt	Not All RFCs are Standards

Web Resources   There are a number of other resources you should become familiar with. Many of these are located at the home of the Web, the World Wide Web Consortium (W3C). See Table 2.8 for a list of these resources.

Table 2.8   Web Developer Resources

Location	Description
http://www.w3.org/	World Wide Web Consortium (W3C)
http://www.w3.org/pub/WWW/Protocols/	HTTP Protocol Specifications
http://www.w3.org/pub/WWW/MarkUp/	HTML Specifications
http://www.mcp.com/306622191284704/general/workshop/	The HTML Workshop

From Here...

By now you should have a good idea how the Web works and how the HTTP protocol works. We've seen how browser cookies can help overcome the fact that HTTP is a stateless protocol, and we've looked at how the HTTP authentication process takes place.

For more information on topics covered in this chapter:

■ See Chapter 7, "Creating ISAPI Extensions," for information about how to use the concepts you've learned here with ISAPI extensions.

■ See Chapter 14, "Creating an ISAPI Filter," for information about how to use the concepts you've learned here with ISAPI filters.

Part
II

Ch
2

Understanding Dynamic NT Web Sites

This chapter is an introduction to Web programming. We look at how dynamic Web sites can provide a rich experience for Web users. Then we go behind the scenes to look at how Web servers produce these dynamic pages.

We look at the most popular server interface options and detail how CGI and WinCGI work. When you understand these two interface options, you'll be prepared to implement ISAPI, and you'll have a better understanding of how the Web works.

We close this chapter by looking at the programming language options you have. This should help you to choose the right language for your development projects. ∎

Learn about dynamic Web sites

Internet server applications and filters are the key to developing interactive Web sites.

Become familiar with the popular server interface options

CGI, WinCGI, ISAPI, and ActiveX Server are discussed.

Learn how CGI works

The Common Gateway Interface (CGI) is now the most popular interface to Web servers. We'll look at how it works.

Learn how WinCGI works

The second most popular option on the Web today is WinCGI. We'll look at how WinCGI works and cover the WinCGI specification.

Review the programming language options

Each programming language has its strengths and its weaknesses. Choose the right language for each job.

One of the exciting things about the Web is that it offers easy and instant access to so much information on so many varied topics. The ease of putting information on the Web, along with the ease of navigating it, has provided a treasure trove of information that at one time was not readily accessible.

In many cases, the information was locked away in the archives of an educational institution or corporation where few had access to it. Because the Web makes it so easy to share information, countless gigabytes of new information are published on the Web every month.

First-generation Web sites consisted of static Hypertext Markup Language (HTML) pages. *Static* means that the pages were not generated on the fly by software on the server.

Static pages are typically created and uploaded to the host Web server. There, they are served to Web users time after time until the HTML author (called the *Webmaster*) decides to make changes. The Webmaster makes the changes and reuploads the pages. The pages once again remain static until they are revised again. Figure 3.1 illustrates this concept.

FIG. 3.1

This Microsoft
Internet Information
Server FAQ is static
HTML.

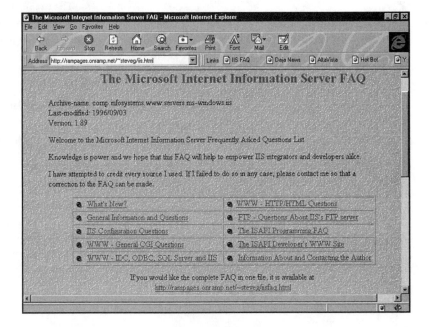

What It Means to Be Dynamic

So just what are dynamic HTML pages? Unlike a static file that resides on the server's disk and goes out to the Web user's browser without change, dynamic pages change from Hypertext Transport Protocol (HTTP) request to request.

In many cases, there is no static HTML file at all. Instead, the complete HTML file is generated when the server gets the HTTP request from a Web user.

HTML output can change in a number of ways. For example:

- A static HTML template can be modified on the fly by software on the server. A page displaying the current date might be generated using this method.
- The HTML output can be generated from a database by software on the server. Say a Web user makes a query for specific items from a database. An Internet server application would query the database and create the dynamic HTML output for the Web user.
- Software on the server can detect characteristics of the Web user's browser and customize the graphics so that the user has a better viewing experience.
- Information posted by the Web user can be used to customize the HTML output. Say a user chooses various options about what he or she wants to see. The Internet server application can customize the HTML output to match the user's request.

Through dynamic HTML, the Web user's experience is enhanced because the dynamic HTML is customized for the needs, tastes, or requests of that particular Web user.

Figure 3.2 is an example of how Microsoft Network's (MSN) MSN.com service is allowing users to customize the information they see.

Once users of MSN.com choose the information they want to see, MSN sends a client cookie to the user's Web browser. On future visits, the user is greeted with HTML tailored to that user's selections, as shown in Figure 3.3. For more information about cookies, see Chapter 2, "The Web and Windows NT."

Part

II

Ch

3

FIG. 3.2
MSN on the Web offers custom user pages based on a user's selections.

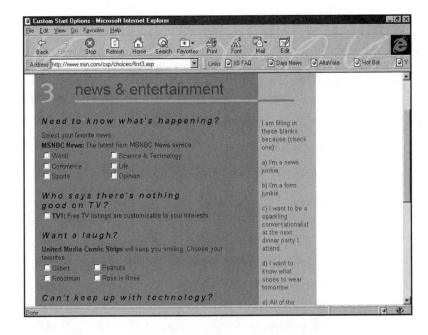

FIG. 3.3
An example of MSN's customized HTML.

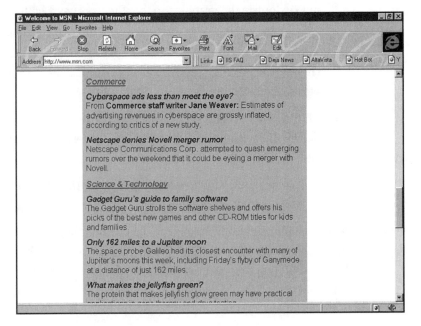

The HTML in Figure 3.3 could be the output from a database the user has searched, or the page could be tailored to take advantage of the features of the user's Web browser. And, of course, dynamic HTML allows us to create interactive pages in which Web users choose the information they get. Figure 3.4 is another example of this concept.

FIG. 3.4
Microsoft's Tripoli Search Engine produces dynamic HTML based on search information provided by the user.

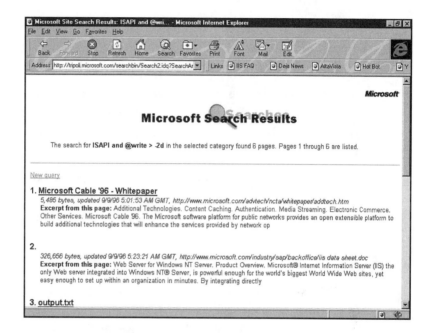

Understanding Interface Options

A number of interface options are available to deliver dynamic documents via the Web. These include the Common Gateway Interface (CGI), the Windows CGI (WinCGI), Microsoft ActiveX Server (code-named *Denali*), Internet Server API (ISAPI), Netscape's API (NSAPI), and others, such as FastCGI, Spry's BGI, and Spyglass's ADI.

CGI and WinCGI are the most commonly used interfaces to an HTTP server. We'll take a look at each of these in a little more detail.

CGI

The CGI specification was created by John Franks (**john@math.nwu.edu**), Ari Luotonen (**luotonen@ptsun00.cern.ch**), George Phillips (**phillips@cs.ubc.ca**), and Tony Sanders (**sanders@bsdi.com**), the original lead authors of the earliest HTTP server.

CGI was created because it became obvious that only certain functions were appropriate to build into the HTTP server software. Yet other server functionality was useful and even necessary.

The term *gateway* was chosen for a software program that handles information requests and returns the appropriate document, or even generates a document on the fly. The idea is that this additional program is a gateway to information that the server could not normally access.

CGI programming needs a moderate degree of technical skill. CGI programs can be written in almost any programming language, including C or C++, Practical Extraction and Report Language (Perl), Pascal, or even with a batch file.

WinCGI

WinCGI was created by Robert B. Denny (**rdenny@dc3.com**), the author of Win-HTTPD and O'Reilly's HTTP server named WebSite. Denny's Win-HTTPD server runs under Microsoft Windows 3.1 and gave the Windows world its earliest HTTP server.

With a large pool of Windows programmers created by such products as Microsoft Visual Basic (VB), Denny recognized the need to update the CGI specification for the Windows environment. WinCGI and CGI work in much the same way, as we'll see shortly.

WinCGI is like CGI in that you need a moderate degree of technical skill to create a WinCGI application. WinCGI programs can be written in almost any programming language. But the languages that work in the Windows environment are particularly suited to WinCGI. These include VB, C and C++, and Delphi.

ActiveX Server

Microsoft ActiveX Server should be shipping before the end of 1996. ActiveX will revolutionize dynamic HTML generation by scripting together ActiveX components. These components span an array of functionality, accessing data across the Web and providing content directly into the HTML stream.

These include Browser Capability objects that specify client capabilities, ActiveX Data Objects that interface with local and remote data sources, and server objects that provide a power interface to server function. The beauty of the ActiveX is that you don't need a high level of technical skill to build dynamic HTML pages.

An ActiveX application is HTML with in-line scripting. ActiveX supports an open scripting standard, interfacing with any scripting engine that meets the ActiveX scripting specification.

Part

II

Ch

3

ISAPI

ISAPI was created by Microsoft and Process Software as an answer to the deficiencies of CGI and WinCGI. The formal specification was released in March 1996 by both companies. As we saw in Chapter 1, "Introducing ISAPI," ISAPI has been embraced by a number of HTTP server vendors.

You need a relatively high level of technical skill to use ISAPI. Two examples of skills you'll need are the ability to write thread-safe DLLs and to avoid tying up server threads for long periods of time. You can develop ISAPI extensions and filters using most 32-bit C/C++ compilers and Delphi 2.0.

NSAPI

The Netscape API (NSAPI) was developed by Netscape Communications Corporation as an interface to their server software. NSAPI allows developers to extend the functionality of Netscape server products much as ISAPI does. So far, no other HTTP vendors have embraced NSAPI.

You need a relatively high level of technical skill to use NSAPI. The only compilers known to work with NSAPI are C compilers outlined in the NSAPI documentation (**http://home.netscape.com/newsref/std/server_api.html**).

Other APIs

A number of other interfaces have been developed to overcome the inefficiencies of CGI. These include FastCGI, the Spry Binary Gateway Interface (Spry BGI), and the Spyglass Application Development Interface (**http://www.spyglass. com/techspec/specs/adi_spec.html**). These interfaces have limited use in the Web development community. Table 3.1 lists the standard interface options.

Table 3.1 Standard Interface Options	
Name	**Languages**
CGI	C, C++, Pascal, Basic, Perl, Tkl
WinCGI	C, C++, Pascal, VB
ActiveX Server	VB Script, Jscript, Java, Perl
ISAPI	C, C++, Pascal
NSAPI	C, C++

Understanding CGI

CGI, regardless of the operating system, works like this:

1. A user agent requests a resource from the HTTP server. The user agent does not know if the resource is static or dynamic. It simply requests the resource and expects the server to return it.

NOTE   Remember that a user agent can be either a Web browser or another type of program, such as a robot, spider, or crawler, as discussed in Chapter 2, "The Web and Windows NT." ■

2. The server determines that the resource needs CGI and begins a new process.

3. The HTTP server fills the environment of that new process with variables indicating the specifics of the current transaction.

4. The HTTP server executes the CGI application to fulfill the request. In some cases, the HTTP server may use command-line parameters to supply additional information to the CGI application.

5. The CGI application reads the environment variables to determine the action to take.

6. The CGI application reads from standard input (`stdin`) if any information has been POSTed to the server and writes to standard output (`stdout`) the results of the processing. The server reads the data coming through `stdout` and sends that back to the client connection.

7. The server typically ends the process although some servers can be configured to reuse that new process a pre-configured number of times for more efficient operation.

Part
II
Ch
3

Figure 3.5 illustrates this sequence of events.

FIG. 3.5
CGI processing.

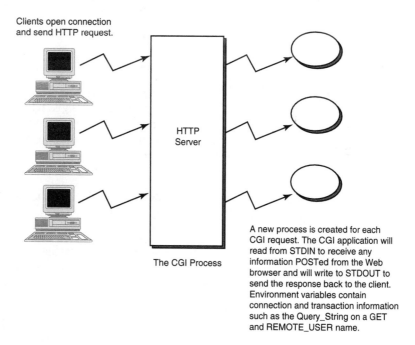

Clients open connection and send HTTP request.

HTTP Server

The CGI Process

A new process is created for each CGI request. The CGI application will read from STDIN to receive any information POSTed from the Web browser and will write to STDOUT to send the response back to the client. Environment variables contain connection and transaction information such as the Query_String on a GET and REMOTE_USER name.

CGI Environment Variables

Environment variables are used to pass information from the operating system to application software or from application to application as in the case of CGI. Table 3.2 lists the environment variables available to a CGI application.

Table 3.2   CGI Environment Variables

Environment Variable	Description
AUTH_TYPE	If the server has user authentication and the script is protected, this is the protocol-specific authentication method to validate the user.
CONTENT_LENGTH	The length of the content as given by the client.
CONTENT_TYPE	For queries with attached information, such as HTTP POST and PUT, this is the content type of the data.
GATEWAY_INTERFACE	The revision of the CGI specification to which this server complies. The format is CGI/revision.
HTTP_ACCEPT	The mail Internet extension (MIME types the client accepts), as given by HTTP headers. Other protocols may need to get this information from elsewhere. Separate each item in this list by commas according to the HTTP specifications. The format is type/subtype, type/subtype.
HTTP_USER_AGENT	The browser the client is using to send the request. The format is software/version library/version.
PATH_INFO	The extra path information, as given by the client. In other words, scripts can be accessed by their virtual path name followed by extra information at the end of this path.
	The extra information is sent as PATH_INFO. This information should be decoded by the server if it comes from a URL before it is passed to the CGI script.

Environment Variable	Description
PATH_TRANSLATED	The server provides a translated version of PATH_INFO, which takes the path and does any virtual-to-physical mapping to it.
QUERY_STRING	The information following the ? in the URL that referenced this script. This is the query information and it should not be decoded in any fashion. Always set this variable when there is query information, regardless of command-line decoding.
REMOTE_HOST	The name of the host making the request. If the server does not have this information, it should set REMOTE_ADDR and leave this unset.
REMOTE_ADDR	The IP address of the remote host making the request.
REMOTE_IDENT	If the HTTP server uses Request for Comments (RFC) 931 identification, this variable is set to the remote user name retrieved from the server. Limit use of this variable to logging only.
REQUEST_METHOD	The method with which the request was made. For HTTP, this is GET, HEAD, POST, and so forth.
REMOTE_USER	If the server has user authentication and the script is protected, this is the user name the Web client was authenticated as.
SERVER_NAME	The server's host name, Domain Name Service (DNS) alias, or IP address as it would appear in self-referencing URLs.
SERVER_SOFTWARE	The name and version of the server software answering the request (and running the gateway). The format is name/version.
SERVER_PORT	The port number to which the request was sent.
SERVER_PROTOCOL	The name and revision of the information protocol this request came in with. The format is protocol/revision.
SCRIPT_NAME	A virtual path to the script being executed, used for self-referencing URLs.

Part
II

Ch
3

CGI Script Input

For requests with information attached after the header, such as HTTP POST or PUT, the information is sent to the script on stdin.

The server sends CONTENT_LENGTH bytes on this file descriptor. Remember that it also gives the CONTENT_TYPE of the data.

CGI Script Output

The script sends its output to stdout. This output can be either a document generated by the script or instructions to the server for retrieving the output. Stdout is read by the server and sent back to the client connection.

Understanding WinCGI

WinCGI works like CGI. The difference is that Windows INI files pass information to the WinCGI application instead of through stdin and environment variables. This is how WinCGI works:

1. A user agent requests a resource from the HTTP server. The user agent does not know if the resource is static or dynamic. It just requests the resource and expects the server to return it.

2. The server determines that the resource needs CGI and creates a Windows INI file that holds many of the same variables that the CGI process would create. These variables give information to WinCGI about the current transaction.

3. The HTTP server creates a new process using the Windows API call CreateProcess() service to start the CGI program. The command line for CreateProcess() takes the form of WinCGI-exe cgi-data-file. The cgi-data-file command-line parameter is the name of the Windows INI file the WinCGI application will use to fulfill the request: START.

4. The WinCGI application reads from a file specified in the INI file if any information has been POSTed to the server and writes to another specified file the output or results of the requested processing.

5. The HTTP server uses the Win32 `WaitForSingleObject()` API call to detect when the WinCGI application terminates.

6. The HTTP server reads the data from the specified output file and sends that back to the client connection.

Figure 3.6 illustrates the WinCGI process.

FIG. 3.6
WinCGI Processing.

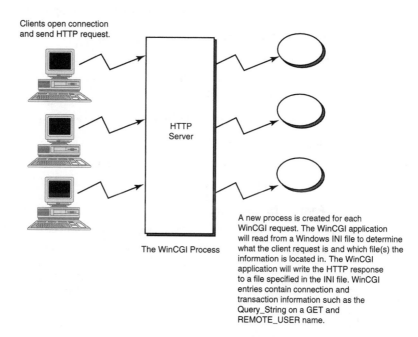

Clients open connection and send HTTP request.

HTTP Server

The WinCGI Process

A new process is created for each WinCGI request. The WinCGI application will read from a Windows INI file to determine what the client request is and which file(s) the information is located in. The WinCGI application will write the HTTP response to a file specified in the INI file. WinCGI entries contain connection and transaction information such as the Query_String on a GET and REMOTE_USER name.

Part

II

Ch

3

The WinCGI Specification

As we mentioned earlier in "WinCGI," Bob Denny was the creator of the WinCGI specification. We'll now take a look at the WinCGI specification that he created.

I/O Spooling   A key feature of Windows CGI is its spooled exchange of data between the server and the CGI program. It is essential that the server provide efficient transfer of data between the spool files and the network. This means that the server should use memory-mapped techniques and minimize the number of separate network I/O requests used.

The reasons for using spooled I/O are as follows:

- Most rapid application development (RAD) packages do not have native network (socket) I/O capabilities.

- Socket I/O techniques are relatively exotic, and efficient results need a thorough knowledge of the Win32 network interface. All input and output would require complex buffering to achieve acceptable network efficiency.

- Sockets cannot be inherited by a 16-bit program.

- Spooled input (such as POST content) can be memory mapped and thus processed far more efficiently than is possible using stream-oriented techniques.

- A reference set of spool files can be used for regression testing and debugging in the RAD development environment.

- Spool files can be retained after a CGI program runs, for "postmortem" analysis, also using the RAD environment.

HTML Form Data Decoding   Windows CGI requires that the Web server decode HTML form data if present in a POST request. The server does not have to decode form data if it appears in the *query string* portion of a request URL.

Form data can be sent by a browser to the server in two ways, explained in the following sections.

URL-Encoded   This is the most common form data format. The contents of form fields are "escaped" according to the rules in the HTML 1.0 specification, then concatenated using unescaped ampersand characters. This URL-encoded data is sent as a stream to the server with a content type of application/x-www-form-urlencoded.

Multipart Form Data   This format was introduced for efficient file uploading with forms. You can use it without explicitly including a file upload form field, however. The contents of the form fields are sent as a MIME multipart message. Each field is contained in a single part. The content type indicated by the browser is multipart/form-data. Compliant servers must decode both form data types.

Launching the CGI Program   The server uses the CreateProcess() service to launch the CGI program. The server maintains synchronization with the CGI program so it can detect when the CGI program exits. This is done using the Win32 `WaitForSingleObject()` service, waiting for the CGI process handle to become signaled, indicating program exit. The server must never use a shell to execute the CGI program. This can create serious security risks.

N O T E The CGI program's process handle becomes signaled before the process rundown is complete. Reliance on rundown to close files, inherited handles, etc., can cause obscure synchronization problems. ▓

Command Line   The server must execute a CGI program request by doing a `CreateProcess()` with a command line in the following form:

```
WinCGI-exe cgi-data-file
```

▓ `WinCGI-exe`   The complete path to the CGI program executable. The server does not depend on the current directory or the PATH environment variable. Note that the executable need not be a .EXE file. It can be a document, provided an "association" with a corresponding executable has been established.

▓ `cgi-data-file`   The complete path to the CGI data file.

Launch Method   The server issues the `CreateProcess()` so that the process being launched has its main window hidden. The launched process itself should not cause the appearance of a window nor a change in the Z-order of the windows on the desktop.

The server supports a CGI program/script debugging mode. If that mode is enabled, the CGI program is launched so that its window shows and is made active. This can help in debugging CGI applications.

Document Associations   The server must honor document associations. If the target of a Windows CGI request is a document (not an executable), the server must attempt to find the associated application for the document and launch the application so that the document is processed.

The CGI Data File   The server passes data to the CGI program via a Windows private profile file in key-value format. The CGI program can then use the standard Windows API services for enumerating and retrieving the key-value pairs in the data file.

The CGI data file contains the following sections:

- ▪ [CGI]
- ▪ [Accept]
- ▪ [System]
- ▪ [Extra Headers]
- ▪ [Form Literal]
- ▪ [Form External]
- ▪ [Form File]
- ▪ [Form Huge]

The [CGI] Section   This section contains most of the CGI data items (accept types, content, and extra headers are defined in separate sections). Each item is provided as a string value. If the value is an empty string, the keyword is omitted. Table 3.3 lists the variables found in the [CGI] section of the WinCGI INI file.

Table 3.3   The [CGI] Section

INI Variable	Description
Request Protocol	The name and revision of the information protocol this request came in with. Format: protocol/ revision. Example: HTTP/1.0.
Request Method	The method with which the request was made. For HTTP, this is GET, HEAD, POST, etc.
Executable Path	The logical path to the CGI program executable, as needed for self-referencing URLs. This may vary if the server supports multihoming with separate logical path spaces.
	The server must provide the physical path equivalent using the logical-to-physical mapping for the identity on which the current request was received.
Document Root	The physical path to the logical root /. This may vary if the server supports multihoming with separate logical path spaces. The server must provide the physical path to the logical root for the identity on which the current request was received.

INI Variable	Description
Logical Path	A request can specify a path to a resource needed to complete that request. This path can be in a logical path name space. This item holds the path name exactly as received by the server without logical-to-physical translation.
Physical Path	If the request contained logical path information, the server provides the path in physical form in the native object (such as file) access syntax of the operating system. This may vary if the server supports multi-homing with separate logical path spaces.
	The server must provide the physical path equivalent using the logical-to-physical mapping for the identity on which the current request was received.
Query String	The information following the "?" in the URL that generated the request is the query information. The server furnishes this to the back end whenever it is present on the request URL without any decoding or translation.
Request Range	Byte-range specification received with request (if any). See the current Internet Draft (or RFC) describing the byte-range extension to HTTP for more information. The server must support CGI program participation in byte-ranging to be compliant with this specification.
Referer	The URL of the document that contained the link pointing to this CGI program. Note that in some browsers, the implementation of this is broken and cannot be relied on.
From	The e-mail address of the browser user. Note that this is in the HTTP specification, but is not used in some browsers because of privacy concerns.
User Agent	A string description of the client (browser) software. Not generated by all browsers.

Part

II

Ch

3

continues

Table 3.3   Continued

INI Variable	Description
Content Type	For requests with attached data, this is the MIME content type of that data. Format: `type/subtype`.
Content Length	For requests with attached data, this is the length of the content in bytes.
Content File	For requests with attached data, the server makes the data available to the CGI program by putting it into this file. The value of this item is the complete path name of that file.
Server Software	The name and version of the server software answering the request (and running the CGI program). Format: `name/version`.
Server Name	The network host name or alias of the server, as needed for self-referencing URLs. This (in combination with the server port) could be used to manufacture a full URL to the server for URL fix-ups. This may vary if the server supports multihoming. The value of this item must be the host name on which the current request was received.
Server Port	The network port number on which the server is listening. This is also needed for self-referencing URLs.
Server Admin	The e-mail address of the server's administrator. This is used in error messages and might be used to send MAPI mail to the administrator, or to form `mailto:` URLs in generated documents.
CGI Version	The revision of the CGI specification to which this server complies. Format: `CGI/revision`. For this version, `CGI/1.2 (Win)`.
Remote Host	The network host name of the client (requestor) system, if available. This item is used for logging.

INI Variable	Description
Remote Address	The network (IP) address of the client (requestor) system. This item is used for logging if the host name is not available.
Authentication Method	The protocol-specific authentication specified in the request. If present, this is normally Basic. The server must provide this whether or not it was used by the server for authentication.
Authentication Realm	The method-specific authentication realm given in the request. If present in the request, the server must provide this whether or not it was used by the server for authentication.
Authenticated Username	The user name (in the indicated realm) that the client used to try authentication, as specified in the request. If present in the request, the server must provide this whether or not it was used by the server for authentication.
Authenticated Password	The password the client used to attempt authentication, as specified in the request. If present in the request, the server must provide this whether or not it was used by the server for authentication.

The [Accept] Section This section contains the client's acceptable data types found in the request header as:

```
Accept: type/subtype {parameters}
```

If the parameters (e.g., q=0.100) are present, they are passed as the value of the item. If there are no parameters, the value is Yes.

The accept types may easily be enumerated by the CGI program with a call to GetPrivateProfileString() with NULL for the key name. This returns all of the keys in the section as a null-delimited string with a double-null terminator.

The [System] Section This section contains items that are specific to the Windows implementation of CGI. Table 3.4 lists the variables found in the [System] section of the WinCGI INI file.

Table 3.4   The *[System]* Section

INI Variable	Description
GMT Offset	The number of seconds to be added to GMT time to reach local time. For Pacific standard time, this number is –28,800. Useful for computing GMT times.
Debug Mode	This is No unless the server's CGI/script tracing mode is enabled, then it is Yes. Useful for conditional tracing within the CGI program.
Output File	The full path name of the file in which the server expects to receive the CGI program's results.
Content File	The full path name of the file that contains the content (if any) that came with the request.

The *[Extra Headers]* Section   This section contains the "extra" headers that were included with the request, in key=value form. The server must URL-unescape both the key and the value prior to writing them to the CGI data file.

N O T E   The extra headers may easily be enumerated by the CGI program with a call to GetPrivateProfileString() with NULL for the key name. This returns all the keys in the section as a null-delimited string with a double-null terminator. ■

The *[Form Literal]* Section   If the request is an HTTP POST from an HTTP form (with content type of application/x-www-form-urlencoded or multipart/form-data), the server decodes the form data and puts it into the [Form Literal] section.

For URL-encoded form data, raw form input is of the form key=value&key=value&..., with the value parts in URL-encoded format. The server splits the key=value pairs at the &, then splits the key and value at the =, URL-decodes the value string and puts the result into key=(decoded)value form in the [Form Literal] section.

For multipart form data, raw form input is in a MIME-style multipart format with each field in a separate part. The server extracts the field named and value from each part and puts the result into key=value form in the [Form Literal] section.

If the form contains any SELECT MULTIPLE elements, there will be multiple occurrences of the same key. In this case, the server generates a normal key=value pair for the first occurrence and appends a sequence number to subsequent occurrences. It is up to the CGI program to know about this possibility and to recognize the tagged keys.

The [Form External] Section   If the decoded value string is more than 254 characters long, or if the decoded value string contains any control characters or double-quotes, the server puts the decoded value into an external temp file and lists the field into the [Form External] section as:

    key=pathname length

pathname is the path and the name of the temp file containing the decoded value string, and length is the length in bytes of the decoded value string.

> **N O T E**   Be sure to open this file in binary mode unless you are certain that the form data is text! ▒

The [Form Huge] Section   If the raw value string is more than 65,535 bytes long, the server does no decoding. But it does get the keyword and mark the location and size of the value in the Content File. The server lists the huge field in the [Form Huge] section as:

    key=offset length

offset is the offset from the beginning of the Content File at which the raw value string for this key is located, and length is the length in bytes of the raw value string. You can use the offset to do a Seek to the start of the raw value string and use the length to know when you have read the entire raw string into your decoder.

> **N O T E**   Be sure to open this file in binary mode unless you are sure the form data is text! ▒

Part
II

Ch
3

The [Form File] Section If the request is in the `multipart/form-data` format, it may contain one or more file uploads. In this case, each file upload is placed into an external temp file similar to the form external data. Each such file upload is listed in the `[Form File]` section as:

```
key=[pathname] length type xfer [filename]
```

`pathname` is the path name of the external temp file containing the uploaded file, `length` is the length in bytes of the uploaded file, type is the MIME content type of the uploaded file, `xfer` is the content-transfer encoding of the uploaded file, and `filename` is the original name of the uploaded file. The square brackets must be included. They are used to delimit the file and path names, which may contain spaces.

In the following example of form decoding, the form contains a small field, a SELECT MULTIPLE with two small selections, a field with 300 characters in it, one with line breaks (a text area), and a 230K field.

```
[Form Literal]
smallfield=123 Main St. #122
multiple=first selection
multiple_1=second selection

[Form External]
field300chars=C:\TEMP\HS19AF6C.000 300
fieldwithlinebreaks=C:\TEMP\HS19AF6C.001 43

[Form Huge]
field230K=C:\TEMP\HS19AF6C.002 276920
```

Understanding Language Options

Now we'll look at the most common language options for CGI, WinCGI, and ISAPI. Each language has its own advantages and its own disadvantages. You should carefully consider:

- The costs of development using a particular language.
- The skill level needed by programmers using a particular language.
- The maintenance costs for debugging the code.
- The performance factors of a compiled versus an interpreted language.
- The availability of third-party tools and libraries for the language.

C/C++

C and C++ need the most technical skill of the language options we'll look at, but they also give developers the most advantages. For the sake of this discussion, we'll consider C and C++ to be the same.

Using C, you can develop for any of the Internet server interface options. Developers using Microsoft Visual C++ can create CGI, WinCGI, ActiveX components, ISAPI extensions and filters, NSAPI extensions, and FastCGI-compliant applications. C is also a compiled language (versus an interpreted language) for creating small and fast binary executables.

For this reason, if speed is a concern, C should be one of your top options. The debugging facilities allow interactive debugging in some cases, which is a real development advantage not currently offered by the other language options.

Sample CGI Application Using C   This C CGI demo sets a client-side cookie and presents the user with a screen that says Greetings from CGI.

```
#include <stdio.h>

void main()
{
    printf("Content-type: text/html\n");
    printf("Set-Cookie: Lang=C\n");
    printf("<html><head><title>CGI C Demo</title></head>");
    printf("<body><h1>Greetings from CGI</h1>");
    printf("</body></html>");
    exit(0);
}
```

Sample ISAPI Extension Using C   The same program written with an ISAPI interface follows:

```
#include <windows.h>
#include <httpext.h>
#include <string.h>
#include <stdio.h>

BOOL WINAPI GetExtensionVersion( HSE_VERSION_INFO *pVer )
{
    pVer->dwExtensionVersion = MAKELONG(HSE_VERSION_MINOR,
        HSE_VERSION_MAJOR);
    lstrcpyn( pVer->lpszExtensionDesc, "ISAPI C Demo",
        HSE_MAX_EXT_DLL_NAME_LEN );
    return TRUE;
```

Part

II

Ch

3

```
        }

        DWORD WINAPI HttpExtensionProc(EXTENSION_CONTROL_BLOCK *pECB)
        {

            CHAR  buff[2048];
            DWORD dwLen=0;

            pECB->dwHttpStatusCode=0;
            wsprintf(buff,"Content-Type: text/html\r\n\r\n"
                    "<head><title>ISAPI C Demo</title></head>\n"
                    "<body><h1>Greetings from ISAPI</h1>\n");
            dwLen=lstrlen(buff);
            if (!pECB->ServerSupportFunction( pECB->ConnID,
                HSE_REQ_SEND_RESPONSE_HEADER, "200 OK",
                &dwLen,(LPDWORD) buff ))
            {
                return HSE_STATUS_ERROR;
            }
            pECB->dwHttpStatusCode=200;
            return HSE_STATUS_SUCCESS;
        }
```

Visual Basic

Microsoft VB is the premier, GUI-building RAD environment for the Windows platform. Of course, with WinCGI you can't create GUI applications, but the environment is still excellent for creating these Internet and intranet applications.

Microsoft VB 3.0 and 4.0 can produce WinCGI applications or OLEISAPI extensions. Of the products we consider here, VB is one of the easiest to learn.

VB 5.0 supports the creation of ActiveX components that can be placed on the server.

Delphi

Borland's Delphi is an Object Pascal-based visual development environment for the Windows platform. Delphi 1.0 is a 16-bit compiler and can be used to create 16-bit WinCGI applications. Delphi 2.0 is a 32-bit version that can produce 32-bit WinCGI, Windows console applications for CGI support, and can also produce ISAPI DLLs.

Delphi is a slightly more technical product than VB 3.0 and 4.0 but not quite as complicated as the Visual C++ environment. A number of libraries are available for producing Internet applications using Delphi.

Example CGI Application Using Delphi 2.0   This Delphi CGI demo sets a client-side cookie and shows the user a screen that says Greetings from CGI.

```
program DelpCGI;

    {$APPTYPE CONSOLE}

    uses
      SysUtils;

    begin
      WriteLn('Content-type: text/html');
      WriteLn('Set-Cookie: Lang=Delphi');
      WriteLn('<html><head><title>CGI Delphi Demo</title></head>');
      WriteLn('<body><h1>Greetings from CGI</h1>');
WriteLn('</body></html>');
    end.
```

Sample ISAPI Extension Using Delphi 2.0   The same program written with an ISAPI interface follows:

```
library DelpISAP;

uses
    SysUtils,
    Windows,
    ISAPI;

const
    CrLF = ^M^J;

Function GetExtensionVersion (var pVer : HSE_VERSION_INFO):BOOL;
        export; stdcall;
begin
    pVer.dwExtensionVersion := MAKELONG(HSE_VERSION_MINOR,
        HSE_VERSION_MAJOR);
    StrPCopy(pVer.lpszExtensionDesc, 'Delphi Test ISAPI DLL');
    result := True;
end;

Function HttpExtensionProc (var pECB : EXTENSION_CONTROL_BLOCK):
        DWORD; export; stdcall;

var
```

```
        Buffer    : Array[0..2047] of Char;
        Response : Array[0..8] of Char;
        dwLen     : longint;

    begin

        StrPCopy(Buffer, 'Content-Type: text/html' + CrLf +
            'Set-Cookie: Lang=Delphi' + CrLf + CrLf +
            '<html><head><title>CGI Delphi Demo</title></head>' +
            '<body><h1>Greetings from CGI</h1></body></html>');
        StrPCopy(Response, '200 OK');
        dwLen := StrLen(Buffer);
        pECB.ServerSupportFunction( pECB.ConnID,
            HSE_REQ_SEND_RESPONSE_HEADER, @Response, @dwlen, @Buffer);
        result := HSE_STATUS_SUCCESS;
    end;

    exports
        HttpExtensionProc,
        GetExtensionVersion,
        DllMain;

    begin
    end.
```

Perl

Perl was created by Larry Wall in the early 1980s. Perl is an interpreted language that is a combination of awk, C, sed, and UNIX shells. The syntax of Perl is similar to C.

Perl was originally developed to process text files. As it turned out, the Web's popularity created a sudden demand for processing HTML (text) files. Perl has rapidly become the most popular CGI language on UNIX-based systems.

Because Perl is an interpreted language, there are no known libraries for WinCGI, and developers are currently limited to writing CGI scripts with Perl.

NT developers can pick up the latest copy of Win32 Perl from **http://www.perl. hip.com/**.

From Here...

In this chapter, we explored the CGI and WinCGI server interfaces. Because ISAPI builds on the basic concepts of these interfaces, new Web developers should familiarize themselves with them.

We also reviewed the programming language options that are available and list considerations for starting Web development projects. For more information on the topics addressed in this chapter, see the following chapters:

- Chapter 4, "CGI vs. ISAPI: Pros and Cons," discusses the factors you should consider before choosing an interface to an Internet server.
- Chapter 6, "Understanding ISAPI Extensions," shows you how ISAPI can create dynamic Web applications.
- Chapter 13, "Understanding ISAPI Filters," shows you that ISAPI can do things that CGI and WinCGI can't do.

CGI vs. ISAPI:
Pros and Cons

In the past, Web sites consisted of static HTML pages. Interactivity was through external processes on the Web server, called common gateway interface (CGI) applications.

For example, if you needed to access data not stored in Hypertext Markup Language (HTML), you would use a CGI application to access the data and send the results back to the client in HTML.

You could develop the CGI application in any language. This was usually the language the developer was most proficient in.

ISAPI is a standard programming interface that can be used by both Web site developers and Web server developers. ISAPI offers faster, more efficient solutions than CGI. ISAPI also has new features such as the ability to apply additional processing to all HTTP requests.

What are the benefits of using CGI for Web development?

Since time and resources have already gone into CGI application development, maintaining these applications will provide short term productivity gains.

How do CGI and ISAPI compare for average throughput and number of simultaneous connections that each can handle?

The telling statistic in Web site performance is response time. The ISAPI architecture allows for better resource management, which yields better performance.

What are the benefits of using ISAPI?

ISAPI provides a new architecture for extending the Web server's features and performance.

The ISAPI alternative to CGI is the ISAPI extension (also called a *server application*). ISAPI extensions allow CGI- type functionality with faster performance and fewer resources.

ISAPI filters (also called *server filters)* afford additional preprocessing and postprocessing of all HTTP requests to a Web server. Filters enable developers to add custom logging, authentication, auditing, and security to their Web sites.

If you have already invested in CGI applications, your time and effort have not been wasted. ISAPI is fully compatible with CGI.

You can also supplement ISAPI by developing new ISAPI that put a mix of ISAPI and CGI on the server. For operating Web sites, it might make sense to continue CGI applications and add new functionality on the Web with ISAPI. ■

CGI Benefits

CGI has been the standard for building interactive Web sites for many years. CGI was originally conceived in the UNIX world of Internet development. The purpose was to provide a common method for handling client requests for information that didn't reside in HTML format.

A CGI application is a separate process (executable) that is invoked by the Web server to handle a specific client browser request. For example, the client browsing a company intranet might request the phone extension of an employee.

The client browser types in the name of the employee in an HTML fill-in form. The logic in the fill-in form passes the name of the employee to a CGI application on the Web server in the form of a hypertext transport protocol (HTTP) request.

The server invokes the CGI application to search for the employee name and return the phone extension in HTML to the server. The server forwards the information back to the client.

CGI has served the Internet development community well over the years. CGI uses standard input (`stdin`), standard output (`stdout`), and environment variables to communicate between a Web server and a CGI application. The rest of this section highlights CGI's benefits.

Consistency with UNIX Practices

CGI was born into UNIX, which until recently was the predominant Internet server platform. The reasons were simple.

CGI used existing operating system features for interprocess communications. Reading `stdin`, `stdout`, and environment variables were simple operations. And since UNIX was a preemptive, multitasking operating system, starting another process was easy.

Above all, the approach did not vary from traditional UNIX development or Web development practices. CGI applications are stand-alone processes that can be developed and tested independently of ancillary systems.

CGI was a manageable process for software developers and server administrators. Developers could use their existing UNIX experience to create new Internet applications using CGI. Its consistency with traditional development practices made CGI a natural choice for the Internet.

Separate Process for Server Integrity

Since CGI applications are executables, they run in a separate address space from the Web server. It is virtually impossible for a rogue CGI application to crash the Web server.

This supplies a high level of reliability to your Web site. If the CGI application crashes during an HTTP request, the Web server times out after not receiving a response and returns a server failure error to the client.

N O T E A "bad" CGI application cannot directly harm the Web server. But a bad CGI application can affect the performance of your Web site if the operating system does not clean up after the application crashes. Each instance of the CGI application that stays in memory consumes the resources of the Web site computer. ▪

This is in direct contrast to ISAPI extensions and filters, which are used as dynamic link libraries (DLLs). ISAPI extensions are loaded into the address space of the Web server. Although ISAPI extensions provide speed and resource advantages, it is also possible for an ill-behaved extension to crash the Web server.

Easier to Debug

Debugging a CGI application is relatively easy, depending on the complexity of the application. Because a CGI application is a separate process, you can run it through the debugger without intervention from external applications such as a Web server.

A CGI application gets all its data from stdin and from environment variables. During a debugging session, the parameter string that would normally be passed from the Web server can be manually entered to the CGI application as command-line parameters.

Let's say a client browser calls the CGI application with the following query:

http://scripts/foo.exe?Param1

The Web server in turn starts the foo.exe process with the Param1 parameter on the command line of the executable. During a debugging session, you can manually enter the same information. Figure 4.1 illustrates entering command-line parameters using the Microsoft Visual C++ debugger.

FIG. 4.1
Debugging a CGI application using Visual C++ to enter command-line parameters.

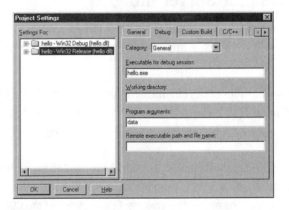

The nature of CGI applications allows traditional debugging methods. This means a CGI application can be debugged like any other application. You don't need any special tricks. Such familiarity allows developers to quickly test and debug their CGI applications.

Another feature you can use to debug CGI applications is Just-in-Time debugging. Just-in-Time debugging means executable files can be compiled and linked in debug mode.

If at any time while the application is executing a protection violation occurs, the debugging libraries take over and let the user debug the application. The debugger is loaded into memory and the source code pinpoints the spot where the error occurred.

N O T E To use Just-in-Time debugging, you have to meet the following criteria:

- Your development environment must accept Just-in-Time debugging.
- You must enable Just-in-Time debugging during the compiling and linking of your application.
- The debug version of your application must be on the target system.
- The debugging environment must be loaded onto the target system.
- All source code used to create the application must be available to the debugger. ▓

ISAPI Benefits

With the introduction of IIS, Microsoft has embarked on a new direction for extending the capabilities of Web servers and Web sites. This is an API specifically for the Internet server called ISAPI.

N O T E In traditional Microsoft fashion, ISAPI is positioned as an open specification. Any vendor's Web server software can be compatible with applications that use ISAPI. ▓

ISAPI enables Web developers to tailor their Web sites through the use of ISAPI extensions and ISAPI filters. Extensions offer capabilities like those of CGI applications. Filters allow preprocessing and post-processing of HTTP requests for services such as authentication, custom logging, and security.

ISAPI is part of a common trend initiated by Microsoft to blend ancillary programming interfaces into the operating system. One look at the Win32 API reveals this trend.

ISAPI is the first step toward a standard Internet interface to the Win32 development platform. IIS is included as a standard part of the Windows NT server operating system.

In addition, IIS Peer Web Services, which works with ISAPI, is included with Windows NT Workstation. The result is one-stop shopping developers of Internet applications.

If you buy Windows NT you get a Web server and a standard programming interface with the server. This makes the life of a system administrator and also a developer much easier.

Its tight integration with Windows NT enables IIS to take advantage of the benefits of the operating system.

Page Generation Speed

When a client issues a request to your Web server, you would like your response to be returned as fast as possible. HTML pages are generated much faster by ISAPI extensions by comparison to CGI applications.

ISAPI extensions are used as DLLs, which means that the extension is loaded into the address space of the server. When a client requests information from an ISAPI extension, the server looks to see if the extension is loaded into memory.

If the extension is already loaded into memory, the server calls the entry point into the extension to pass any search criteria and to get the generated page response. If the extension is not loaded into memory, the extension is loaded from disk and the entry-point function is called.

Loading a DLL and calling a function are much faster than starting a CGI application and waiting for the response. In a recent study done comparing the throughput of an ISAPI extension versus a CGI application using IIS, ISAPI extensions outperformed CGI by a factor of 5.

Figure 4.2 shows the results of this test.

N O T E The study was done by Microsoft Business Systems Division in March 1996. Two Web server performance benchmark tools were used in the study—National Software Testing Laboratories, Inc. (NSTL) Web benchmark tests and WebStone version 1.1 from Silicon Graphics.

The NSTL tests were done by the NSTL at its corporate offices. The WebStone tests were done by Shiloh Consulting and Haynes & Company at the offices of Shiloh Consulting.

More information on these tests can be found on the Microsoft Web site at **http://www.microsoft.com/infoserv/**. The test platforms were Pentium 133-Mhz machines with 32M of RAM. ▨

FIG. 4.2
Comparison of ISAPI and CGI throughput.

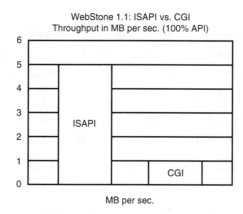

The test comparing ISAPI and CGI throughput was configured to return only pages generated by CGI or ISAPI applications. No static HTML pages were used. The results were run with 64 clients.

Reduced Server Load

One advantage of a CGI application that runs as a separate process from the Web server is also one of its biggest drawbacks. Each client request to a CGI application causes a separate instance of the application to be started. As a result:

- ▨ More resources are consumed on the server for each instance of the CGI application started.

- ▨ Response time is increased because of the overhead to start an instance of the CGI application.

As you can see, if your server is extremely busy and handles hundreds, even thousands, of simultaneous requests, starting a CGI application for each request quickly reduces the throughput of the server.

ISAPI extensions overcome these problems with CGI applications because ISAPI extensions are used as DLLs. As DLLs, the ISAPI extensions are loaded into the address space of the Web server when the first request for the extension is issued.

Part
II

Ch
4

The DLL doesn't need to be reloaded for subsequent calls to the ISAPI extension, resulting in increased speed and decreased use of resources. Task switching by the operating system is also reduced since the extension is treated as part of the Web server.

For each client connection to the Web server that uses an ISAPI extension, the Web server starts a separate thread of execution to call and process the ISAPI extension. The ISAPI extension executes within the confines of the newly created thread on the Web server.

For this invocation of a new thread, ISAPI extensions use thread-safe synchronization to protect shared resources in the extension from simultaneous access.

Chapter 18, "Making Your Extensions Thread-Safe," tells you how to create thread-safe ISAPI extensions.

In a test comparing the number of connections per second that could be handled by ISAPI extensions and CGI applications, ISAPI was approximately five times faster then CGI. Figure 4.3 illustrates this point.

FIG. 4.3

Comparison of number of connections handled per second by ISAPI and CGI.

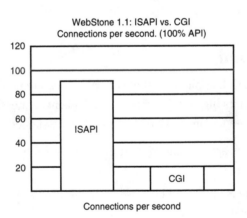

WebStone 1.1: ISAPI vs. CGI
Connections per second. (100% API)

Connections per second

This test shows that clients at a Web site using ISAPI extensions have less waiting than at a Web site using CGI applications.

Finer-Grained Control

ISAPI gives the Web site more control than CGI. ISAPI filters allow both preprocessing and postprocessing of HTTP requests sent to the Web server. This means that you can administer custom handling of all events *before* the request is passed to an ISAPI extension or other handler.

You can use ISAPI filters for user authentication and security checks. Failed security credentials are returned before they reach the ISAPI extension.

You can use filters for custom logging and auditing of Web server usage. With filters, all HTTP requests are sent back to the client from an ISAPI extension to be processed if necessary.

ISAPI filters, like ISAPI extensions, are used as DLLs. ISAPI filters are loaded by the server at startup, not on demand like extensions.

When a filter is loaded it registers with the Web server for each event it is supposed to get. When the event is received by the server, it is routed through the filter before it reaches its target destination.

The filter can process and forward the request. Or it can reject the request without forwarding it to the destination.

Chapter 12, "Using ISAPI Filters," and Chapter 13, "Understanding ISAPI Filters," analyze how ISAPI filters can be used by a Web site.

Part
II

Ch

4

URL Mapping

When a client request is issued to an ISAPI extension, the extension can map the request to another URL. This is useful if information is moved from one URL to another. The original URL can stay in place and, when the request arrives, can be routed to the right location.

URL mapping is done by the API `ServerSupportFunction`, which redirects and maps URL requests.

Chapter 8, "Using Extension Capabilities," tells you how to use URL mapping in an ISAPI extension.

Security

Security is always a concern of system administrators. ISAPI gives developers techniques to supply extra layers of security for users of the system.

One of these techniques is to use an ISAPI filter for custom authentication on the server. This allows you to do your own security checks on the server.

If the server is on a corporate intranet, you can use the Win32 API by calling the Windows NT security features to limit the access of the client. You do this with the `ImpersonateClient` function, which changes the current permission level of the application to that of the client. When the request is finished processing, the default security level is returned.

Since ISAPI implements its functions inside DLLs, it is harder to intercept and replace by hackers because custom handshaking can be designed between the filters and the extensions. With a CGI application, if the application can be replaced by a hacker, your system can become very vulnerable.

Recommendations

Your choice between ISAPI and CGI to create Web sites depends on several factors. Two important ones are the target platform and whether existing CGI applications remain at your Web sites.

If your target platform is Windows NT and IIS, ISAPI offers the best performance, capabilities, and integration possibilities. If many CGI applications remain at the sites, you might choose to maintain these applications rather than port them to ISAPI. However, ISAPI will give you the best results.

Use an API Like ISAPI

ISAPI is a standard interface for developing Internet applications on the Windows NT, IIS platform. As we saw earlier in this chapter, independent tests prove that ISAPI provides better throughput and connection handling than CGI applications.

IIS works with CGI. But for the best performance use this combination only if existing CGI applications remain at your site.

ISAPI also supplies much more functionality than CGI: ISAPI extensions offer the same benefits as CGI with less overhead and more speed. ISAPI filters supply custom authentication and security, which are unavailable from CGI.

To help you develop ISAPI applications, languages such as Visual C++ include an Application Wizard that can be used to build a template for developing ISAPI extensions.

Create a Separate Process Using IPC

Sometimes the server has to rely on separate processes for retrieving information. In these cases, you won't want to put all the logic and handling of information in an ISAPI extension.

An example of this is a process gathering environment-control information from a network of sensors in a factory. The sensors must be polled in real time for information.

If any sensor, such as a smoke detector, reports trouble, you may have to enable an output control point such as a fire alarm. A critical process like this must be running constantly.

For a facilities manager, it would be nice to have an intranet application report the status of all of the factory sensors and control points. An ISAPI extension would work best for such an application.

The ISAPI extension would query the environment control process for the current status and return the information to the client requesting the data. The ISAPI extension could use interprocess communication (IPC), such as named pipes, sockets, or remote procedure calls (RPCs), to communicate the request to and receive the information back from the extension.

Figure 4.4 illustrates the data flow of this system.

In this situation, it would not be practical for the ISAPI extension to hold the logic for interfacing to the control sensors. The extension would not be online 24 hours a day as needed, because it would only be loaded on client request. A CGI application would not be practical for the same reasons.

Part
II

Ch
4

FIG. 4.4
Data flow of an ISAPI
extension using a
Win32 IPC to request
information from an
external program.

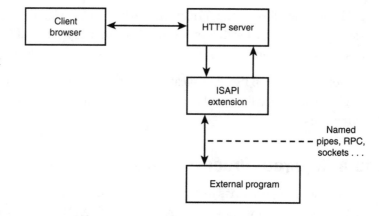

Use the Language Your Team Knows Best

Developing ISAPI extensions is straightforward. An ISAPI extension is used as a
DLL and a variety of development tools are available for developing DLLs.

You can create ISAPI extensions in any development environment that enables
developing Win32 DLLs. When you use the language your development team is
proficient in, you get the highest productivity.

From Here...

In this chapter we looked at the benefits of and drawbacks to both CGI and ISAPI.
CGI applications appear to be easier to develop and debug. But if your target plat-
form is Windows NT and your Web server is an ISAPI-compliant server such as
IIS, ISAPI offers the best results.

- Chapter 6, "Understanding ISAPI Extensions," gives you an in-depth look at
  ISAPI extensions and how they are used.

- Chapter 8, "Using Extension Capabilities," tells you how to use the extended
  capabilities of ISAPI extensions. This chapter covers the features of ISAPI
  extensions that are not compatible with CGI applications.

ISAPI Extensions

CHAPTER 5

Using ISAPI Extensions

What ISAPI extensions are

One of the uses of ISAPI extensions is to provide a new architecture for a CGI-type interface.

How ISAPI extensions can be used to add dynamic capabilities to your Web site

You can add ISAPI extensions that help you create an interactive Web site.

Why ISAPI extensions are effective replacements for CGI applications

ISAPI extensions provide a CGI-type interface with enhanced performance.

How to install and use the "Hello, World!" extension

Hello, World! is a simple ISAPI extension that we develop in this chapter.

For years, client/server computing has relied on custom applications for solving business and computing problems. These solutions have often been written in a high-level language such as Visual C++ or rapid development tools such as Visual Basic or Delphi.

One of the reasons for designing custom applications was to create a unique and different approach to solving the problem at hand. The solution was often to create a nifty user interface that provided easy data storage and access methods to application data.

Let's take a simple example such as a company personnel database. It would be easy, and in some cases practical, to use a tool such as Microsoft Access to attach to the given database tables and display a grid of all personnel and their associated information.

The user could enter SQL statements to do searches and to display the information wanted. Although this approach certainly solves the generic problem of viewing database records, it is neither an easy-to-use nor an effective method.

To solve this problem, we could design a custom application to retrieve the information efficiently and with a user-friendly interface. A custom application would also deal with different data types such as binary large objects (BLOBs) for storing, retrieving, and presenting photo or signature information.

Developing Web sites presents some of the same challenges as developing client/server applications. How can I customize my site to provide the extended function needed for the information that I want to give Web users?

Microsoft released the Internet Information Server (IIS) with the understanding that although HTML is the language of choice for publishing browser content, we would need ways to access information not in HTML format. Microsoft also realized that Web site developers would want to provide custom additions to their sites to build new and exciting Web pages.

Such Web pages would provide information from diverse data sources not readable by browser applications. The task would be to convert this information to HTML format for browser viewing. You would also need to be able to create custom functions such as user authentication and usage logs.

IIS was released with an application program interface (API), called the Internet Server API (ISAPI), that could be used to build additional capabilities into the server. These capabilities could be added through ISAPI extensions (also called *server applications*).

N O T E ISAPI is an open specification for communication between Web browsers (clients) and Web servers. It is not a proprietary Microsoft specification. Any Web vendors can use the ISAPI interface in their Web server.

Although ISAPI is predominately used for enhancing client/server interactions, ISAPI is an open specification originally developed by Process Software in collaboration with Microsoft, and specifies how DLLs can extend the function of the server. ■

What Are ISAPI Extensions?

ISAPI extensions give you the power to add dynamic interactivity to any Web site. In a traditional Web site, a browser accesses Web pages that consist of HTML data, which is predominately static. An example of HTML static data is the title of a Web page.

Static data in HTML format has its uses. It can supply, for example, product or company information, news bulletins, or product releases. But we may want to build applications for Web sites that provide more timely information and also provide other media such as audio and digital video.

To build dynamic and interactive applications, we need a vehicle that can respond to browser queries regardless of what kind of information is needed or where it is stored. This vehicle is an ISAPI extension.

ISAPI extensions are separate applications that can be queried for specific information by the browser. ISAPI extensions are implemented as DLLs that are loaded by the server on request.

Input parameters such as request information can be passed into the extension. The extension can then access the information needed, from a database, for example, and return it to the browser in the form of an HTML page.

Uses of ISAPI extensions include searching a database for information, accessing files located on a company intranet, or accessing other applications using interprocess communication techniques.

Part
III

Ch
5

Kinds of ISAPI Extensions

ISAPI was designed as a programming interface that developers could use to extend the capabilities of a Hypertext Transport Protocol (HTTP) server. ISAPI does this through extensions. You can use ISAPI to develop different kinds of extensions. For example:

- An extension that enables you to design interactive Web sites.
- Filters that allow preprocessing of client requests. ISAPI filters are covered in depth in Part IV, "ISAPI Filters."

The goal of an ISAPI extension is custom development capabilities for any Web site. ISAPI, with IIS, provides a structured approach for extending the capabilities of a Web site.

Processing Forms

How are ISAPI extensions accessed? The most common method is for the Web site to supply a fill-in form, like a dialog box in conventional programs, for users to enter criteria about the information they want to access.

Server extensions can also be accessed through other means such as HTTP GETs. Figure 5.1 is a sample fill-in form used by a Web search engine for retrieving information from the Internet.

FIG. 5.1
Fill-in form used by
the Yahoo search
engine.

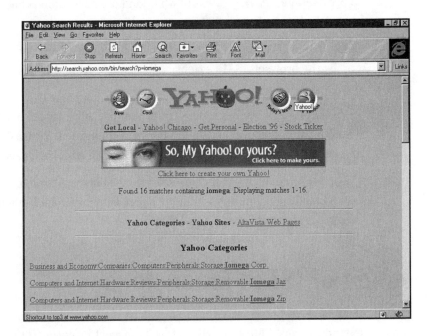

Responding to User Requests

The user fills in the form and presses a button. This causes the form to invoke the server extension. The form sends an HTTP request to the extension in the following format.

```
http://www.xyz.com/scripts/extension.dll?Foo=bar
```

As you can see, the fill-in form is programmed to invoke a specific server extension on a Web site. The information entered into the fill-in form is passed to the extension as parameters. This is like accessing a CGI application except that the extension on a CGI application would be .EXE.

Page Generation

Once the request is made to the ISAPI extension, the server loads the extension into memory (if it is not already loaded) and passes the input parameters to the extension. The input parameters are analogous to the input parameters passed into a CGI application through standard input (`stdin`).

The extension takes the input parameters and does the operations to comply with the client request. This could mean opening a connection to a database such as a SQL server and doing a database search. It could also mean opening a file on a company intranet and returning the contents for the browser to display.

After the extension finishes processing the client request, it must return a result to the client. Results are typically returned to the client as HTML pages. The job of the extension is to convert the data obtained during a client request into a form that can be interpreted by the client.

For example, if an extension is retrieving records from a database during a client request, the client can't directly process the raw database records. The extension must interpret the database results and translate the results into HTML, which is sent to the client. The client displays the HTML page to the user.

N O T E Although HTML is the most common data format used for exchanging information between the browser and Web server, your extensions are not limited to HTML. If the browser and the server can agree on another data format, you can use it. However, using nonstandard data formats may limit the accessibility of your Web sites. ▨

Part
III

Ch
5

Reasons for Using ISAPI Extensions

There are many compelling reasons for using ISAPI extensions. One reason is because they supply fast interactive capabilities to a Web site. ISAPI extensions also offer some advantages over traditional techniques such as CGI applications.

Greater Compatibility

Because of ISAPI's similarity to CGI applications, most of the Web servers that work with ISAPI also work with ISAPI extensions. This may not be the case with ISAPI filters.

ISAPI filters are a specific mechanism used for applying intelligent message-filtering to all HTTP requests. Filters are used for protections such as custom authentication schemes, compression, encryption, logging, and traffic analysis.

There is no CGI type equivalent to ISAPI filters. As a result, many Web servers may not work with ISAPI filters.

Lower Overhead

ISAPI extensions have much lower overhead than ISAPI filters. An ISAPI filter is a replaceable, dynamic link library (DLL) the server calls for every HTTP request.

When the filter is loaded, it tells the server what kinds of notifications it accepts. After that, whenever a selected event occurs, the filter is called to process the event.

In contrast, ISAPI extensions are only loaded into memory and called when a request is received specifically for the extension.

Extensions Are More Convenient

ISAPI filters register to receive incoming events. All events in the HTTP server that the filter is registered for are sent to the filter.

These events are typically the result of a client request. A filter is a mechanism for intercepting all client requests before the HTTP server processes the request.

Depending on the options chosen by the filter, it can act on several server functions.

These include reading raw data from the client, processing the headers, and communicating over a secure port—for example, using private communication technology (PCT) and the Secure Socket Layer (SSL), or at several other stages in processing the HTTP request.

ISAPI filters are like Windows hook functions for the events that they process. ISAPI filters get the first opportunity to process events sent to a server. The filters can process the events, throw them away, or pass them on to the HTTP server for processing.

An ISAPI extension and an ISAPI filter have different goals. The extension's goal is to retrieve information requested by the client and return the results to the client when a client issues a specific request to the extension. Filters, by contrast, intercede with these requests without the client's knowledge.

This difference makes it harder for filters to return client-specific information to the client on a given request.

Extensions Are More Like CGI

Part
III

Ch
5

For the experienced Web developer, a notable feature of ISAPI extensions is their similarity to CGI applications. This similarity allows programmers with CGI experience to quickly and easily convert existing CGI scripts to ISAPI extensions.

The following outlines the basic steps for converting CGI applications to ISAPI server applications:

- ISAPI extensions are used as DLLs. Make the DLL thread-safe and make sure that Win32 synchronization techniques are used when global data in the application is accessed. Chapter 18, "Making Your Extensions Thread-Safe," has more detailed information on creating thread-safe extensions.

- An ISAPI extension gets all its data from the client through the use of an extension control block (ECB) instead of reading it from `stdin`. The extension gets additional data through the `ReadClient` callback function.

- Common CGI variables are passed into the ISAPI extension through the ECB instead of calling getenv to retrieve the variables from the environment table. Variables not passed in through the ECB can be obtained through the GetServerVariable function.

- Results are sent back to the client through the WriteClient function instead of writing to standard output (stdout).

- CGI applications specify an HTTP return status code by sending a string such as "Status: NNN xxxx...." to stdout. ISAPI server extensions return a status either by sending the header directly to the client using WriteClient or by calling the ServerSupportFunction, with the request option HSE_REQ_SEND_RESPONSE_HEADER.

- When a request needs to be redirected with the header Location: or URL:, use the ServerSupportFunction with the request option HSE_REQ_SEND_URL if the URL is local or with the request option HSE_REQ_SEND_URL_REDIRECT_RESP if the URL is remote or unknown. CGI applications write the header to stdout.

Tutorial 1: Using "Hello, World!"

There is no better way to be introduced to ISAPI extensions than to build, install, and request one. As with your first C program, we use the traditional "Hello, World!" model to develop the first ISAPI extension.

The "Hello, World!" extension is a basic ISAPI extension that, when requested, returns an HTML page with the string "Hello, World!" on it. Larger extensions are developed in later chapters.

NOTE The "Hello, World!" extension was developed using Visual C++ 4.2. All the project files are on the CD-ROM in this book.

"Hello, World!": A Simple ISAPI Extension

The "Hello, World!" ISAPI extension provides a framework for building larger extensions. When a request is issued to the "Hello, World!" extension, the extension creates a new HTML page and inserts the "Hello, World!" text into the page.

The source code for this example is shown in Listing 5.1.

Listing 5.1 "Hello, World!" Source Code

```
/*++
Module Name:
    hello.c

Abstract:
    This module is an example of the Hello World ISAPI Application.

Revision History:
--*/


#include <windows.h>
#include "hello.h"

/*++


Routine Description:
    This function DllLibMain() is the main initialization function for
    this DLL. It initializes local variables and prepares it to be invoked
    subsequently.

Arguments:
    hinstDll            Instance Handle of the DLL
    fdwReason           Reason why NT called this DLL
    lpvReserved         Reserved parameter for future use.

Return Value:
    Returns TRUE is successful; otherwise FALSE is returned.
--*/

BOOL WINAPI DllMain(IN HINSTANCE hinstDll, IN DWORD fdwReason,
➥IN LPVOID lpvContext OPTIONAL )
{
    BOOL        fReturn = TRUE;

    switch (fdwReason )
    {
        //
        //  Initialize various data and modules.
        //
        case DLL_PROCESS_ATTACH:
        break;
```

Part

III

Ch

5

continues

Listing 5.1 Continued

```
        case DLL_PROCESS_DETACH:
                break;

        default:
                    break;
    }   /* switch */
    return ( fReturn);
}   /* DllLibMain() */

/*++
Routine Description:
    This is the first function that is called when this ISAPI DLL
    ➥is loaded.
    We should fill in the version information in the structure
    ➥passed in.

Arguments:
    pVer - pointer to Server Extension Version Information
    ➥structure.

Returns:
    TRUE for success and FALSE for failure.
    On success the valid version information is stored in *pVer.
--*/

BOOL WINAPI GetExtensionVersion (HSE_VERSION_INFO * pver )
{
    pver->dwExtensionVersion = MAKELONG( HSE_VERSION_MINOR,
    ➥HSE_VERSION_MAJOR );
    strcpy( pver->lpszExtensionDesc,
            "Hello World ISAPI Server Application." );
    return TRUE;
}

/*++
Routine Description:
    This is the main function that is called for this ISAPI
    ➥Extension.
    This function processes the request and sends out appropriate
    ➥response.

Arguments:
    pecb  - pointer to EXTENSION_CONTROL_BLOCK, which contains
    ➥most of the
            required variables for the extension called. In
            ➥addition,
    it contains the various callbacks as appropriate.
```

```
Returns:
    HSE_STATUS code indicating the success/failure of this call.
--*/

DWORD WINAPI HttpExtensionProc( EXTENSION_CONTROL_BLOCK * pecb )
{
    // Create a basic HTML page
    HtmlCreatePage (pecb, TEXT("Hello World Reply"));
    WriteString (pecb, TEXT("Hello, World!"));
    WriteString (pecb, TEXT("\r\n"));
    HtmlEndPage (pecb);
    return HSE_STATUS_SUCCESS;
}

//
// WriteString writes an ASCII string to the web browser
//
void WriteString (EXTENSION_CONTROL_BLOCK *pECB, LPCTSTR lpsz)
{
    DWORD dwBytesWritten;
    dwBytesWritten = lstrlen (lpsz);
    pECB->WriteClient (pECB->ConnID, (PVOID) lpsz, &dwBytesWritten, 0);
}

//
// HtmlCreatePage adds <HTML> and a title
//
void HtmlCreatePage (EXTENSION_CONTROL_BLOCK *pECB, LPCTSTR lpszTitle)
{
    // IIS does this for us
    //WriteString (pECB, TEXT("Content-Type: text/html\r\n"));
    WriteString (pECB, TEXT("<HTML>\r\n\r\n"));

    if (lpszTitle)
    {
        WriteString (pECB, TEXT("<HEAD><TITLE>"));
        WriteString (pECB, lpszTitle);
        WriteString (pECB, TEXT("</TITLE></HEAD>\r\n\r\n"));
    }
    WriteString (pECB, TEXT("<BODY>\r\n\r\n"));
}

void HtmlEndPage (EXTENSION_CONTROL_BLOCK *pECB)
{
    WriteString (pECB, TEXT("</BODY>\r\n\r\n"));
    WriteString (pECB, TEXT("</HTML>\r\n"));
}
```

Part

III

Ch

5

This example includes two functions that are needed for any ISAPI extension: GetExtensionVersion and HttpExtensionProc.

GetExtensionVersion returns a string to the server. The string contains the ISAPI version that the extension conforms to and a short description of the extension.

HttpExtensionProc is the main processing body of the extension. The "Hello, World!" example offers simple function and writes HTML text back to the client through the use of some helper functions in the extension.

Three helper functions are included in the extension: HtmlCreatePage, HtmlEndPage, and WriteString. All of these functions use the ISAPI WriteClient function to send information back to the client that called the extension.

Putting *hello.dll* in the /scripts Directory

As with all CGI applications, ISAPI extensions must reside in a directory that browsers can access and for which browsers have execute permission within that directory. Server directories can be set up through IIS Service Manager.

When IIS is first installed, the default execute directory for all CGI applications and ISAPI extensions is the /scripts directory located off of the home page directory.

For the "Hello, World!" extension to be accessed and executed, it must reside in a directory with execute permission. Put the hello.dll file in the /scripts directory or in another directory for which the browser has execute permission.

Requesting */scripts/hello.dll*

Once the server application is in a directory with execute permission, the next step is to request the extension. Since there is no fill-in form to process a client request and call the server application, we call the extension directly.

The server application can be directly accessed by using any Web browser at your disposal. To access the "Hello, World!" extension, type in the following HTTP request:

HTTP://server/scripts/hello.dll

in which the server is the URL to your Web site holding the ISAPI server, and scripts is the directory holding the "Hello, World!" extension.

Getting the "Hello, World!" Page in Response

When it gets the HTTP request for the "Hello, World!" extension, the ISAPI server loads the extension into memory and returns an HTML page with the "Hello, World!" string inserted on it. Figure 5.2 shows a successful call to the "Hello, World!" extension.

FIG. 5.2
A successful call to the "Hello, World!" ISAPI extension.

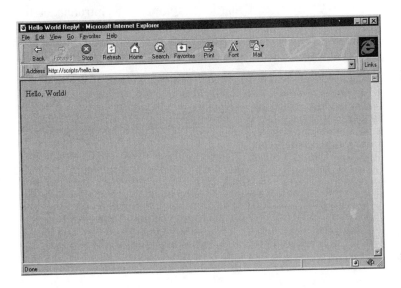

Congratulations! You have just built, installed, and requested your first ISAPI server application!

From Here...

This chapter introduced you to the world of ISAPI extensions. You learned what ISAPI extensions are and how they can add dynamic capabilities to your Web site.

Part
III

Ch
5

You also saw why ISAPI extensions are effective replacements for CGI applications. The "Hello, World!" extension showed you how extensions are built, installed, and called.

- For an in-depth look at ISAPI extensions, turn to Chapter 6, "Understanding ISAPI Extensions." This chapter shows you how ISAPI extensions work under the hood.
- For some of the more complex operations you can do with ISAPI extensions, such as redirection, see Chapter 8, "Using Extension Capabilities."
- Chapter 12, "Using ISAPI Filters," is an introduction to using ISAPI filters.

Understanding ISAPI Extensions

The Internet Server Application Programming Interface (ISAPI) can be used to create extensions, often called *server applications*, to Microsoft's Internet Information Server (IIS) or any Hypertext Transport Protocol (HTTP) server compatible with the ISAPI interface.

ISAPI extensions give Web developers an alternative to the Common Gateway Interface (CGI) for creating interactive Web sites.

Unlike CGI applications, which are stand-alone executables, ISAPI extensions are used as Win32 DLLs that are dynamically loaded by IIS on request. Using ISAPI extensions offers increased performance and resource use compared to CGI applications.

How ISAPI extensions are used by IIS

Extensions can be used to replace existing CGI applications and add functions such as HTTP GETs.

The similarities and differences between the CGI and ISAPI extension architectures

CGI and ISAPI extensions both provide gateways to non-HTML data sources, though the mechanisms for doing this are different.

What the standard entry points into ISAPI extensions are

ISAPI extensions are dynamic link libraries (DLLs) with defined entry points that are called by servers.

How interaction between an ISAPI extension interacts with a server

Servers create separate threads of execution for calling ISAPI extensions.

The flow of events in an ISAPI extension

Programming structures are used to send data into the extension. Callback functions return data to the client.

Developing a CGI application is straightforward because CGI applications are independent of the server using the application. CGI applications process client requests by retrieving the input arguments from the application's standard input (`stdin`) when it is started.

All output from a CGI application is returned through the application's standard output (`stdout`). CGI developers can develop and debug their applications without regard to the interaction of other processes, such as an HTTP server.

Since ISAPI extensions are used as DLLs, the extensions are dependent on the interaction with the applications using them. To get the maximum benefits from ISAPI extensions, the developer should have a thorough understanding of how extensions work and how extensions are used by HTTP servers. ■

How ISAPI Extensions Work

ISAPI extensions are a new approach for customizing the interactive capabilities of your Web site. An ISAPI extension is a specification which improves on the CGI that Web servers have used for years. ISAPI extensions also provide an entirely new capability for Web servers.

What does an ISAPI extension do? An ISAPI extension (and a CGI application) is a standardized way to pass data that users enter in their Web browsers to back-end programs that you provide on your Web server. This is typically done through Web fill-in forms but can be used for other communication mechanisms, including HTTP GETs.

A common example that illustrates this concept is when you do a search for information on the Internet. The information you are searching for is collected and passed into a back-end program, which then returns the results. The back-end program is typically a CGI script or an ISAPI extension.

Figure 6.1 shows a search form from the AltaVista search engine.

An ISAPI extension is a more than capable replacement for CGI applications. ISAPI extensions can provide all of the capabilities of a CGI application, plus the additional customization hooks that CGI applications cannot provide.

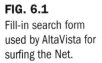

FIG. 6.1
Fill-in search form
used by AltaVista for
surfing the Net.

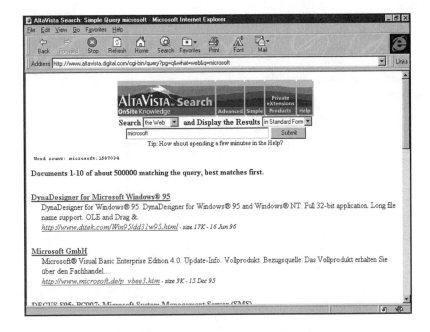

Before looking inside ISAPI extensions, we look briefly at the flow of a CGI
application to provide a meaningful comparison.

Examining the Flow of a CGI Application

CGI is an interface for running external programs (called *gateways*) on a Web
server. Only HTTP Web servers are compatible.

The external programs are called gateways because they allow browser applications access to information that is not readable by the client. In other words, the
gateways do the following:

- Accept information requests from a client.
- Access the results stored in a format not readable by the client, such as
  graphics, spreadsheets, or databases.
- Translate the information into a readable format: Hypertext Markup
  Language (HTML).

Figure 6.2 illustrates this concept.

Part
III

Ch
6

FIG. 6.2
A CGI application acts as an information translator for the client browser and Web server.

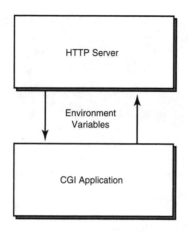

A Web server responds to a CGI execution request from a client browser by creating a new process and then passing the data received from the browser through environment variables and stdin. Results gathered by the CGI application are expected on the stdout of the newly created process. The Web server creates as many processes as the number of requests received.

To recap the flow of a CGI application, the four steps are as follows:

1. Collect all user input. This is typically done through Web fill-in forms.

2. Pass the user input from the Web fill-in form as variables into the CGI application.

3. Do the operations necessary on the input variables and collect the results.

4. Pass the results back to the user in a format compatible with the user's Web browser. This is typically in HTML format.

N O T E   For more information on the CGI specification, see **http://hoohoo.ncsa.uiuc. edu/cgi/**. ▨

Drawbacks to the CGI Architecture

A glaring shortcoming of the CGI architecture is that a separate process must be invoked whenever a request is received for the gateway. Starting separate processes can be time-consuming and need large amounts of memory.

N O T E   If your Web site gets many requests for the gateway, starting an instance of the
CGI application for each request can quickly consume memory. This could
lead to heavy disk I/O if there is not enough memory for the number of processes the
server creates.

Although the CGI interface is workable, you can imagine the bottlenecks for
heavily traveled Web servers. *PC Week* recently documented that the Microsoft
Web site was processing over 40 million requests daily!

ISAPI extensions were introduced to provide CGI functionality while reducing the
resources for filling browser requests.

An important difference between ISAPI extensions and CGI applications is that an
ISAPI extension is *not* a separate executable. An ISAPI extension is a DLL that is
loaded into memory by the server and accessed through a defined set of entry
points.

Dynamic linking provides a way for a process, in this case IIS, to call a function
that is not part of its executable code. The code in a DLL is compiled and linked
separately from the executable that uses its code. When a DLL is called, the code
in the library is shared among all processes that are using the DLL.

An example of a DLL is the Win32 API, which is used as a number of DLLs. All
32-bit applications running under Windows NT or Windows 95 use one set of
Win32 API code.

CAUTION

Since multiple applications can simultaneously use the code in a DLL, you must make sure
that the DLL is *thread-safe*. Thread-safe means that any data or resources accessed from
within the DLL must be protected from simultaneous calls from another thread or even
another executable.

Chapter 18, "Making Your Extensions Thread-Safe," covers techniques for building thread-safe
DLLs.

Part
III

Ch
6

The two methods for calling a function in a DLL are as follows:

- Load-time dynamic linking. This occurs when an application's code makes an explicit call to a DLL function. This type of linking needs the executable module of the application to be built by linking with the DLL's import library. IIS does not use this method of linking to extensions.

  The DLL import library holds information necessary to locate the DLL function when the application starts. In contrast, a static library holds code that is included as part of the application.

- Runtime dynamic linking. This occurs when a program such as IIS uses the LoadLibrary function to load the DLL into memory and the GetProcAddress function to retrieve the address of a DLL function. This kind of linking eliminates the need to link with an import library.

NOTE Runtime linking is possible because ISAPI defines known entry points that must be present in every ISAPI extension. The presence of these defined entry points allows the server to load and execute the code in any extension. ISAPI extensions would not be possible if every extension DLL consisted of different user-defined entry points.

Similarities to a CGI Executable

The following sequence explains how an ISAPI extension DLL interacts with an HTTP server. As with a CGI application, there are four steps for a browser to use an ISAPI extension. These steps are as follows:

1. Collect all user input. This is typically done through Web fill-in forms.

2. Pass the user input from the Web fill-in form as variables to the ISAPI extension.

3. Input variables and collect the results. This is done by the ISAPI extension.

4. Pass the results back to the user in a format compatible with the user's Web browser. This format is typically HTML.

Getting Program Control

When an extension is called by the server, program control for the calling thread is transferred to the extension. Even though the extension is dynamically loaded into the server's memory, the HTTP requests are processed as though the extension is a part of the server.

Since a server can process several client requests simultaneously, be sure that internal resources used by the extension are protected from access by multiple threads of execution.

Once control is transferred to the extension, control does not return to the server until a response is prepared and returned by the extension to the server.

ISAPI extensions are used as DLLs. Control is transferred from the server to the extension—that is, the extensions execute in the same process as the server. For this reason, it is important to thoroughly test and debug extensions before using them at a Web site.

An access violation by the extension can cause the server to crash, keeping the Web site from further use until the server is restarted.

ISAPI extensions can also corrupt the server's memory space or cause memory leaks if the extensions fail to clean up properly after themselves.

N O T E Many server developers protect against access violations inside ISAPI extensions by wrapping the extension entry points within try/except blocks. This way, access violations or other exceptions in the extension cannot cripple the server. The extension, however, must still be thoroughly tested and debugged. ▣

Examining the Environment

Once the ISAPI extension is loaded into memory, the extension examines its environment. Whereas a CGI application retrieves information about the environment from environment variables and stdin, an extension retrieves its information from a data structure called an extension control block (ECB). Figure 6.3 illustrates the interaction between a server and an extension.

FIG. 6.3
ECBs are used to
transfer information
between servers and
ISAPI extensions.

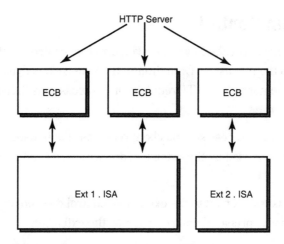

The ECB holds information used by the extension, including the client query string, path information, method name, and translated path.

ECBs, and the interaction between a server and extension, are explained in further detail later in this chapter under "Passing Control to the Extension."

Returning Custom-Generated Content

After the client request is processed by the extension, the results are sent back to the client. In a CGI application, the results are written to stdout. In an ISAPI extension, the results can be written back to a client in two ways.

The first is like writing to stdout. This is done by calling WriteClient, a callback function to the server in which the server passes a preallocated buffer. The extension uses the buffer to return the response.

If a completion status needs to be returned with the response, the client can call the ServerSupportFunction.

An explanation of how results are returned from an extension can be found later in this chapter under "Passing Control to the Extension."

Loading on First Request

Since an ISAPI extension is used as a DLL, the extension is dynamically loaded into the server's process space when the first request for the extension is received.

As additional requests for the extension are received, the overhead for calling the extension becomes minimal since the extension is already loaded into memory. This is in direct contrast to CGI applications, which start another instance of the application for each client request.

The ISAPI architecture allows for multiple extensions to coexist in the server. Typically, extensions are kept in memory until the server shuts down.

N O T E   Since the server knows what extensions are loaded into memory, the server can unload extensions that have not been used for a specified amount of time.

Naming Explicitly

When an extension is to be used by a client, the client must explicitly call for the extension. A sample HTTP request would look like this:

```
http://www.test.com/scripts/foo.dll?Parm1+Parm2
```

In this sample, the client is requesting the extension entitled foo.dll, with the parameters PARM1 and PARM2 to be passed to the extension.

When the HTTP request is made by the client, the server recognizes that foo.dll is an application extension and loads the extension into memory (if the extension is not already loaded).

Once the extension is loaded, the input parameters are passed into the extension for processing. The output response is then returned to the client.

Part

III

Ch

6

Flow of an ISAPI Extension

To understand how to use and develop ISAPI extensions, you need to know how an ISAPI extension works and is used by a server. Specifically, you need to understand the flow of information, starting with the client request and ending with the page returned to the client.

If you compare the flow of an ISAPI extension with the flow of a CGI application, you see that they are similar in nature. However, each achieves its results differently.

▶ **See** "Examining the Flow of a CGI Application," **p. 117**

The Browser Requests ISAPI Processing

The use of an ISAPI extension begins with a client request to use the extension. The client issues an HTTP request such as

```
http://www.xyz.com/scripts/test.isa?PARM1+PARM2
```

The server recognizes the .ISA extension as an ISAPI extension and starts the sequence of events for using extensions. Notice that as in CGI applications, input parameters can be passed into an extension for processing.

Loading the ISAPI Extension

ISAPI extensions are linked dynamically at runtime by the server through the Win32 API LoadLibrary. Every ISAPI extension *must* have two defined entry points: GetExtensionVersion and HttpExtensionProc. The function pointers for the entry points are retrieved by the server through the GetProcAddress API.

Unlike CGI applications, ISAPI extensions are loaded in the same address space as the server. This means all the resources that are made available by the server process are also available to the ISAPI extensions. Minimal overhead is needed to execute the extensions because there is no additional overhead for each request.

Loading an ISAPI extension is typically faster than starting a separate executable. Context and task switching are reduced to a minimum since the extension is loaded in the memory space of the server. Also, the same extension can serve multiple requests, making ISAPI extensions a more scalable solution for active Web sites.

Since a server knows the ISAPI extension DLLs that are already in memory, the server can unload the ISAPI extension DLLs that have not been accessed for a specified amount of time. This is a configurable parameter for the extension.

A server can even speed up the first request to the ISAPI extension by preloading an ISAPI extension DLL. Also, unloading ISAPI extension DLLs that have not been used for some time frees system resources.

Passing Control to the Extension

When the server loads the extension, it calls the entry point GetExtensionVersion to retrieve the version number of the specification on which the extension is based. GetExtensionVersion also provides a short text description of the extension, which is useful for server administrators.

The prototype for GetExtensionVersion is shown below.

```
BOOL WINAPI GetExtensionVersion( HSE_VERSION_INFO  *pVer )

typedef struct   _HSE_VERSION_INFO {

    DWORD  dwExtensionVersion;
    CHAR   lpszExtensionDesc[HSE_MAX_EXT_DLL_NAME_LEN];

} HSE_VERSION_INFO, *LPHSE_VERSION_INFO;

#define   HSE_VERSION_MAJOR          2      // major version of this
                                           // spec
#define   HSE_VERSION_MINOR          0      // minor version of this
                                           // spec
#define   HSE_MAX_EXT_DLL_NAME_LEN  256
```

Part
III

Ch
6

GetExtensionVersion takes one input parameter, a pointer to an HSE_VERSION_INFO structure. This structure has two member variables: dwExtensionVersion, which holds the version of ISAPI being used, and lpszExtensionDesc, which holds a description of the extension's function. The recommended use of this function is shown in Listing 6.1.

Listing 6.1 Typical Use of *GetExtensionVersion*

```
BOOL WINAPI GetExtensionVersion( HSE_VERSION_INFO  *pVer )
{
    pVer->dwExtensionVersion = MAKELONG( HSE_VERSION_MINOR,
                                         HSE_VERSION_MAJOR );
    lstrcpyn( pVer->lpszExtensionDesc,
              "This is a sample Web Server Application",
              HSE_MAX_EXT_DLL_NAME_LEN );
    return TRUE;
}
```

IIS Returns a Page to the Browser

Interaction between a server and an ISAPI extension DLL is through an ECB, as discussed earlier in this chapter under "Examining the Environment."

A client uses an ISAPI extension just as its CGI counterpart does, except that instead of referencing

```
http://www.xyz.com/scripts/foo.exe?Param1+Param2
```

in the CGI instance, it uses the form

```
http://www.xyz.com/scripts/foo.isa?Param1+Param2
```

This means that in addition to identifying the files with the extensions .EXE and .BAT as CGI executable files, the server also identifies a file with an .ISA extension as a script to execute.

All client requests are serviced through the entry point, `HttpExtensionProc`. Information needed by the extension is passed to the extension by an ECB.

A pointer to an ECB is passed as an input parameter to the `HttpExtensionProc` function. The extension gets commonly needed information such as the query string, path information, method name, and the translated path.

```
DWORD  HttpExtensionProc( LPEXTENSION_CONTROL_BLOCK  *lpEcb );
```

The ECB is represented through a data structure called the `EXTENSION_CONTROL_BLOCK` shown as follows:

```
typedef struct _EXTENSION_CONTROL_BLOCK {
    DWORD    cbSize;             // Size of this struct.
    DWORD    dwVersion;          // Version info of this spec
```

```
      HCONN      ConnID;                    // Context number not to be
                                            // modified!
      DWORD      dwHttpStatusCode;          // HTTP Status code
      CHAR       lpszLogData[HSE_LOG_BUFFER_LEN];/
/ null terminated log info specific to this Extension DLL
      LPSTR      lpszMethod;                // REQUEST_METHOD
      LPSTR      lpszQueryString;           // QUERY_STRING
      LPSTR      lpszPathInfo;              // PATH_INFO
      LPSTR      lpszPathTranslated;        // PATH_TRANSLATED
      DWORD      cbTotalBytes;              // Total bytes indicated from
                                            // client
      DWORD      cbAvailable;               // Available number of bytes
      LPBYTE     lpbData;                   // Pointer to cbAvailable
                                            // bytes
      LPSTR      lpszContentType;           // Content type of client data
      BOOL (WINAPI * GetServerVariable) ( HCONN        hConn,
                                          LPSTR
                                          ➥lpszVariableName,
                                          LPVOID       lpvBuffer,
                                          LPDWORD
                                          ➥lpdwSizeofBuffer );
      BOOL (WINAPI * WriteClient) ( HCONN      ConnID,
                                    LPVOID     Buffer,
                                    LPDWORD    lpdwBytes,
                                    DWORD      dwReserved );
      BOOL (WINAPI * ReadClient) ( HCONN      ConnID,
                                   LPVOID     lpvBuffer,
                                   LPDWORD    lpdwSize );
      BOOL (WINAPI * ServerSupportFunction)( HCONN     hConn,
                                    DWORD      dwHSERRequest,
                                    LPVOID     lpvBuffer,
                                    LPDWORD    lpdwSize,
                                    LPDWORD
                                    ➥lpdwDataType );
}
```

The ECB has the following fields:

Field (Parameter Direction)	Description
cbSize (IN)	The size of this structure.
dwVersion (IN)	The ISAPI version that the server is using. The HIWORD has the major version number and the LOWORD has the minor version number.
connID (IN)	A unique connection number assigned by the server, which should not be changed.

continues

continued

Field (Parameter Direction)	Description
dwHttpStatusCode (OUT)	The status of the current transaction when the request is completed.
lpszLogData (OUT)	A buffer of the HSE_LOG_BUFFER_LEN size. The buffer holds a null-terminated, log information string of the current transaction. This log information, which is specific to the ISAPI extension, will be entered in the server log. Maintaining a single log file with both server and ISAPI extensions transactions is useful for administration.
lpszMethod (IN)	The method with which the request was made. This is equivalent to the CGI variable REQUEST_METHOD.
lpszQueryString (IN)	A null-terminated string holding the query information. This is equivalent to the CGI variable QUERY_STRING.
lpszPathInfo (IN)	A null-terminated string holding extra path information given by the client. This is equivalent to the CGI variable PATH_INFO.
lpszPathTranslated (IN)	A null-terminated string holding the translated path. This is equivalent to the CGI variable PATH_TRANSLATED.
cbTotalBytes (IN)	The total number of bytes to be received from the client. This is equivalent to the CGI variable CONTENT_LENGTH. If this value is 0xffffffff, there are 4 gigabytes or more of available data. In this case, ReadClient should be called until no more data is returned.

Field (Parameter Direction)	Description
cbAvailable (IN)	The available number of bytes (out of a total of cbTotalBytes) in the buffer pointed to by lpbData. If cbTotalBytes is the same as cbAvailable, the lpbData variable points to a buffer that holds all the data as sent by the client.
	Otherwise, cbTotalBytes holds the total number of bytes of data received. The ISAPI extension uses the ReadClient call back function to read the rest of the data (beginning from an offset of cbAvailable).
lpbData (IN)	This points to a buffer of the cbAvailable size that holds the data sent by the client. The extension receives the first 48K of data.
lpszContentType (IN)	A null-terminated string holding the content type of the data sent by the client. This is equivalent to the CGI variable CONTENT_TYPE.
BOOL (WINAPI * Get ServerVariable)	These are pointers to callback functions used by the server. GetServerVariable and ReadClient are functions used to retrieve information from the server.
BOOL (WINAPI * ReadClient)	WriteClient and ServerSupportFunction are used to send a properly formatted response to the server.
BOOL (WINAPI * WriteClient)	
BOOL (WINAPI * ServerSupportFunction)	

Part

III

Ch

6

The HttpExtensionProc function is analogous to main for a CGI application. In other words, HttpExtensionProc is the main processing body for an ISAPI extension. After the processing of the client request is finished, HttpExtensionProc can have the following return values.

Return Value	Description
HSE_STATUS_SUCCESS	The extension has finished processing. The server can disconnect and free allocated resources.
HSE_STATUS_SUCCESS_ AND_KEEP_CONN	The extension has finished processing and the server should wait for the next HTTP request if the client uses persistent connections.
	The extension should return this only if it was able to send the right content-length header to the client. The server does not have to keep the session open.
	The extension should return this value only if it has sent a connection: a keep-alive header to the client.
HSE_STATUS_PENDING	The extension has queued the request for processing and will notify the server when it has finished.
HSE_STATUS_ERROR	The extension has found an error while processing the request. The server can discon nect and free allocated resources.

The GetServerVariable function copies information into a buffer supplied by the client. The information includes CGI variables relating to an HTTP connection or to the server itself.

The information requested is passed as a string through the lpzVariableNames parameter. Possible values include the following:

AUTH_TYPE—The type of authentication used. For example, if basic authentication is used, the string is "basic." For NT challenge-response, it is "NTLM."

Other authentication schemes have other strings. Since new authentication types can be added to the server, we can't list all the string possibilities. If the string is empty, no authentication is used.

CONTENT_LENGTH—The number of bytes that the script can expect to receive from the client.

CONTENT_TYPE—The content type of the information supplied in the body of a POST request.

PATH_INFO—Additional path information, as given by the client. This consists of the trailing part of the URL, after the script name but before the query string, if any.

PATH_TRANSLATED—The value of PATH_INFO, but with any virtual path name expanded into a directory specification.

QUERY_STRING—The information that follows the "?" in the URL that referenced this script.

REMOTE_ADDR—The IP address of the client or agent of the client—for example, the gateway that sent the request.

REMOTE_HOST—The host name of the client or agent of the client—for example, the gateway that sent the request.

REMOTE_USER—The user name supplied by the client and authenticated by the server. This comes back as an empty string when the user is anonymous (but authenticated).

UNMAPPED_REMOTE_USER—The user name before any ISAPI extensionPI filter mapped the user, making the request to an NT user account. (The NT user account appears as REMOTE_USER.)

REQUEST_METHOD—The HTTP request method.

SCRIPT_NAME—The name of the script program being executed.

SERVER_NAME—Server's host name or IP address, as it should appear in self-referencing URLs.

SERVER_PORT—TCP/IP port on which the request was received.

SERVER_PORT_SECURE—A string of either 0 or 1. If the request is being handled on the secure port, this is 1. Otherwise, it is 0.

Part
III

Ch
6

SERVER_PROTOCOL—The name and version of the information retrieval protocol relating to this request. This is normally HTTP/1.0.

SERVER_SOFTWARE—The name and version of the Web server under which the ISAPI extensionPI DLL program is running.

ALL_HTTP—All HTTP headers that were not already parsed into one of the previous variables. These variables are of the form HTTP_<header field name>. The headers consist of a null-terminated string with the individual headers separated by line feeds.

HTTP_ACCEPT—A special-case HTTP header. Values of the Accept: fields are concatenated and separated by a comma (","). For example, if the following lines are part of the HTTP header

```
accept: */*; q=0.1

accept: text/html

accept: image/jpeg
```

the HTTP_ACCEPT variable has a value of:

```
*/*; q=0.1, text/html, image/jpeg
```

URL—This gives the base portion of the URL.

> **N O T E** With respect to Auth_Type, if the string is not empty, it does not mean the user was authenticated if the authentication scheme is not "basic" or "NTLM." The server allows authentication schemes it does not understand because an ISAPI extensionPI filter may be able to handle that scheme. ▪

The ReadClient function reads information from the body of the Web client's request into the buffer supplied by the caller. This allows the call to be used to read data from an HTML form that uses the POST method.

If more than lpdwSize bytes are immediately available to be read, ReadClient returns after transferring that amount of data into the buffer. Otherwise, it blocks and waits for data to become available.

N O T E When a call to ReadClient is made and the socket on which the server is listening to the client is closed, ReadClient returns TRUE but with 0 bytes read. ■

The WriteClient function is used to send a formatted response to the HTTP client from the buffer supplied by the client. This function is also used to send binary data because it does not assume a zero-terminated string. The WriteClient function, unlike the ServerSupportFunction, handles binary data.

The ServerSupportFunction provides the ISAPI extensions with general-purpose functions, as well as functions specific to the server.

Removing the Extension from Memory

ISAPI 2.0 provides extensions with an optional function that extensions can use for control in properly shutting down and unloading the extension from memory. This function is called TerminateExtension (like GetExtensionVersion) and is called just before the server unloads the application.

This is a safe way to clean up threads and complete other shutdown type activities. The prototype is

```
BOOL  WINAPI   TerminateExtension( DWORD dwFlags );
#define HSE_TERM_ADVISORY_UNLOAD                 0x00000001
#define HSE_TERM_MUST_UNLOAD                     0x00000002
```

The dwFlags parameter is a bit field consisting of the following values:

HSE_TERM_ADVISORY_UNLOAD—The server wants to unload the extension. The extension can return TRUE if OK or FALSE if the server should not unload the extension.

HSE_TERM_MUST_UNLOAD—The server is indicating that the extension is about to be unloaded; the extension can't refuse.

Part

III

Ch

6

ISAPI Extension Rules

ISAPI extensions are easy to create and can enhance the capabilities of any Web site. Following a few simple rules ensures that your extension works properly once deployed at the Web site. These rules are as follows:

- All extensions must reside in a directory marked as executable at the Web site.
- Use ISAPI extensions as 32-bit DLLs.
- Use CGI instead of ISAPI extensions when the implementation is in the form of a console application.
- Make sure that your extension does not use any 16-bit DLLs.
- Have the mandatory entry points, `GetExtensionVersion` and `HttpExtensionProc`, exported by the extension. This is necessary for the server to use the extension.
- Design all extensions to be thread-safe to guard against simultaneous resource access from multiple threads.

Flagging a Directory as Executable

ISAPI extensions are DLLs that are loaded dynamically by a server. For the extension to be loaded by a client application, the extension must reside in a virtual directory that has execute permissions assigned. If the directory does not have execute permissions, the extension cannot be loaded by the client application.

N O T E   If your extension starts other processes or uses other files to do its work, you must make sure that the extension is using an account with adequate permissions.

For example, if your extension uses other files, the account assigned to your program must have the correct permissions to use those files. The default account for extensions is the IUSR_computername account. ■

Using Extensions as 32-Bit DLLs

ISAPI is a 32-bit interface (DLL), and the servers that work with ISAPI are also 32-bit. Since the extensions are loaded dynamically through defined entry points to the DLL, extensions must be used as 32-bit DLLs.

Avoiding 16-Bit DLLs in Extensions

Avoid 16-bit DLLs in extensions. ISAPI extensions are 32-bit DLLs and should not call, link, or use any 16-bit code or DLLs to do their functions.

Windows NT is a 32-bit operating system, and servers that use ISAPI extensions are 32-bit processes. Use only 32-bit code or DLLs in your extensions.

Even if 16-bit DLLs could be called, the DLLs would impede system performance, they would need special code to map a 32-bit address space to a 16-bit address space, and they would not allow the Win32 synchronization objects to protect against multiple threads accessing the 16-bit code.

In short, *do not use any 16-bit DLLs* for your ISAPI extensions.

Exposing Mandatory Entry Points

As explained earlier in this chapter, ISAPI extensions are used as DLLs. The extensions are also loaded by the server at runtime rather than at link time. The only way a DLL can be loaded at runtime by an executable is for the DLL to export or expose specified functions that the executable can get the address to call.

If the ISAPI extensions allowed users to specify their own functions to expose, the server could not accommodate many (if any) users. For this reason, the ISAPI design specifies mandatory functions that the extension *must* use and accept so the server can use the extension. These mandatory functions are `GetExtensionVersion` and `HttpExtensionProc`.

> **CAUTION**
>
> A common mistake made when creating an ISAPI extension is not to expose the DLL entry points. Not exposing the entry points allows the functions to be called only from functions in the extension. The functions can be exported by either
>
> - Specifying that the entry point functions are exportable in the DLL definition file (*.DEF).
> - Specifying that the function is exportable within the function prototype.

Extensions Must Be Thread-Safe

Since Windows NT is a multitasking operating system, the multiple events, such as page requests from an ISAPI extension, can occur at the same time. As a result, you must protect shared resources in the extension from simultaneous access.

For example, if your extension accesses databases as part of its function, you may need to protect it against simultaneous database access by multiple threads.

Windows NT offers a variety of thread synchronization objects that can be used by your extensions. The most common object is the critical section. A critical section serializes resource access between multiple threads in a process. The critical section object lends itself to the extension architecture because the critical section is designed for synchronizing multiple threads in a single process.

A number of other thread synchronization objects are provided by the Win32 environment. These include mutexes, semaphores, and events.

You have to make your extensions thread-safe because you cannot count on the server that is using your extension. The server may process each request from a client in a separate thread.

Without proper thread synchronization, this kind of server use could crash your extension or return erroneous results to the client.

From Here...

In this chapter, you learned how ISAPI extensions work. You learned how ISAPI extensions compare with CGI applications and why ISAPI extensions are a good alternative to CGI applications.

You also saw how an ISAPI extension is called and used by servers and learned the rules for building durable extensions.

- For more information on using threads and making your extensions thread-safe, please see Chapter 18, "Making Your Extensions Thread-Safe."

■ Step-by-step instructions for building ISAPI extensions can be found in Chapter 7, "Creating ISAPI Extensions."

■ You can also extend the capability of servers through the use of ISAPI filters. ISAPI filters add a new dimension to servers. For more information on ISAPI filters, see Chapter 12, "Using ISAPI Filters."

Part
III

Ch
6

Creating ISAPI Extensions

Now we're ready to create ISAPI extensions. You already know that a 32-bit dynamic link library (DLL) is the base for an ISAPI extension. So we'll create a 32-bit DLL project workspace in Visual C++ 4.x, define our export points, and show how extensions work.

Later, in Chapter 9, "Building Extensions with MFC," you'll learn to create ISAPI extensions using the MFC wrapper provided with Visual C++ version 4.1 and above.

You'll use the information you gain here as a basis for all the ISAPI extensions you create in C++. ■

How to create a 32-Bit DLL project workspace using Visual C++

A 32-bit DLL project workspace is the starting point for creating your ISAPI extension.

How to define and use the *GetExtensionVersion* entry point

The GetExtensionVersion entry point is a mandatory function that sets the version and description for your ISAPI extension.

How to define and use the *HTTPExtensionProc* entry point

The HTTPExtensionProc entry point is a mandatory function that your ISAPI server executes. It is like the main() function in ordinary executables.

How to build the Hello, World! ISAPI Extension

"Hello, World!" is your first working ISAPI extension that will return dynamic data to the Web client.

Step 1: Create a 32-Bit DLL

The 32-bit DLL project workspace holds a .CPP file, where your C++ code is stored, and a .DEF file, where your external declarations are defined. Visual C++ provides the make-file information for the DLL.

Visual C++ 4.x: Create a 32-Bit DLL Workspace

To create a 32-bit project workspace in Visual C++ 4.x (see Figure 7.1), follow these steps:

FIG. 7.1
Creating a project workspace.

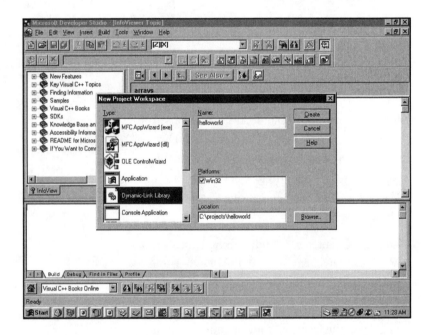

1. Open the Microsoft Developer Studio from the program manager or Start menu in Windows 95 or NT 4.0.

2. Choose File, New, and the select Project Workspace from the New dialog box and choose OK.

3. When the New Project Workspace dialog box appears, enter the name of your project in the Name text field.

4. Select Dynamic Link Library from the Type list and then select Create.

5. Choose Insert, File into Project and type the name of the .CPP file that you are creating for your extension. Since the file does not exist, Visual C++ asks you if you want to insert it anyway. Answer Yes.

6. Choose Insert, File into Project, and type the name of the .DEF file that you are creating for your extension (usually the same name as your CPP file only with a .DEF extension). Once again, the file does not exist. Answer Yes to the dialog box asking if you want to insert it anyway.

7. As a final step, open your CPP file by first double-clicking the Project Workspace folder and then double-clicking the file name (see Figure 7.2). Visual C++ prompts you to create the file. Answer Yes.

FIG. 7.2

Opening the .CPP file.

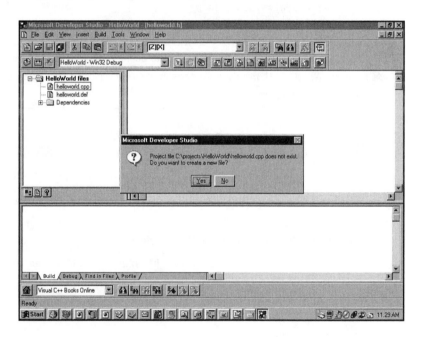

N O T E Don't forget to define your entry points. You do this in the .DEF file. Open your .DEF file by opening the Project Workspace folder and double-clicking the file name. Visual C++ prompts you to create the file. You need to answer Yes. Here, you enter your entry-point information.

```
LIBRARY HelloWorld
EXPORTS GetExtensionVersion
HttpExtensionProc
DllMain
```

Part

III

Ch

7

continues

continued

In version 2.0 of ISAPI, you can expose an optional export function called `TerminateExtension`.

>   BOOL WINAPI `TerminateExtension`(DWORD dwFlags);

This provides a safe way to clean up any memory or free any resources you may have allocated. ▨

Besides including WINDOWS.H in your extension, you also need to include httpext.h, which is part of the Win32 Software Development Kit (SDK) or available in any version of Visual C++ after 4.0 (.1 or 4.2).

```
#include <windows.h>
#include <httpext.h>
```

 TIP   To save some compile time, you may want to define `WIN32_LEAN_AND_MEAN` before you include WINDOWS.H. This exempts parts of the windows.h file, like sound and video support, and gives you a faster compile.

Add *DllMain()* for Startup/Shutdown Processing

The first function we'll look at is `DllMain`. With simple ISAPI extensions, `DllMain` does not need to be more complicated than the example in Listing 7.1.

Listing 7.1   DLLMAIN.CPP—*DllMain*

```
BOOL WINAPI DllMain (HINSTANCE hinstDLL, DWORD dwReason, LPVOID lpv)
{
        return TRUE;
}
```

STEP 2: Define *GetExtensionVersion()*

ISAPI servers need to know what version of the ISAPI specification your extension complies with. You get this information with the first call after `DllMain` made to your extension: the GetExtensionVersion entry point. Let's look at what happens in GetExtensionVersion.

The *GetExtensionVersion* Function Prototype

You know from the previous chapter that all ISAPI extensions need two standard entry points. The first is the GetExtensionVersion entry point.

```
BOOL WINAPI GetExtensionVersion (HSE_VERSION_INFO *pVersion)
```

You use this mandatory entry point to allow your ISAPI extension to load on the Web server. The GetExtensionVersion entry point passes a pointer to the HSE_VERSION_INFO structure.

```
typedef struct   _HSE_VERSION_INFO {

    DWORD  dwExtensionVersion;
    CHAR   lpszExtensionDesc[HSE_MAX_EXT_DLL_NAME_LEN];

} HSE_VERSION_INFO, *LPHSE_VERSION_INFO;
```

 If you are using global variables, they should be initialized in the GetExtensionVersion function. If you need to allocate or reserve any system resources or read registry settings, GetExtensionVersion may be the best place to do this.

Set the ISAPI Version Number

The first task in the GetExtensionVersion entry point is to set the ISAPI version number. HTTPEXT.H defines the ISAPI version number. The dwExtensionVersion member of HSE_VERSION_INFO needs to be set to it. You set this value with the following line of code:

```
pVersion->dwExtensionVersion = MAKELONG(HSE_VERSION_MINOR,
➥HSE_VERSION_MAJOR);
```

When the server first loads your ISAPI extension, it executes the GetExtensionVersion entry point and evaluates the return of the HSE_VERSION_INFO structure. The ISAPI version you set here tells the server what type of functionality to expect.

Part

III

Ch

7

This information tells the server what to send to the extension as server parameters and extended browser information. In the future, ISAPI could offer extended information that the current version of ISAPI does not allow.

It is always important for the ISAPI server to know what to send to the extension and what to hide from the extension.

Set the ISAPI Extension Description

The next information for the server is a description of your ISAPI extension.

The lpszExtensionDesc member of HSE_VERSION_INFO points to the description string for your ISAPI extension. By using the lstrcpyn function to set your description, you won't exceed the maximum length allowed. HSE_MAX_EXT_DLL_NAME_LEN holds the maximum length of the DLL description.

```
lstrcpyn(pVersion->lpszExtensionDesc, "Hello, World", HSE_MAX_
➥EXT_DLL_NAME_LEN);
```

TIP Keep your extension description descriptive. Use the full name of your program, with spaces, in the description. Remember, the server may provide this information in its administration tools.

Once this description has been set, the server's administrative tools may display it. This enables the server administrator to see what ISAPI extensions are running or have been run.

You can also do additional DLL initialization in GetExtensionVersion. You are guaranteed that this entry point is called only once.

N O T E GetExtensionVersion is called with the system-user context, allowing you to read from the system registry without impersonating another user. If you need to read registry settings from within HTTPExtensionProc, you'll need to impersonate a user with the proper access, using ImpersonateLoggedOnUser. ▒

Return *TRUE* If Succeeded, *FALSE* If Failed

The final step to GetExtensionVersion is to return a value. If you have initialized something that your DLL needs and the initialization failed, you can return FALSE. This tells the server not to proceed with calling HttpExtensionProc. Typically, you should be returning a value of TRUE.

A bare-bones GetExtensionVersion function is shown in Listing 7.2.

Listing 7.2   GetExtensionVersion.CPP—*GetExtensionVersion*

```
BOOL WINAPI GetExtensionVersion(HSE_VERSION_INFO *pVersion)
{
        pVersion->dwExtensionVersion = MAKELONG(HSE_VERSION_MINOR,
        HSE_VERSION_MAJOR);

        lstrcpyn(pVersion->lpszExtensionDesc,
                                        "Hello World Extension 1.1",
                                        HSE_MAX_EXT_DLL_NAME_LEN);

        return TRUE;
}
```

Step 3: Define *HttpExtensionProc()*

HttpExtensionProc can be considered the "main" function of the program. This is where the heart of the extension is and where you handle all the requests that come to your extension.

Use the Mandatory Function Prototype

HttpExtensionProc is the second mandatory entry point. You need to use the mandatory function prototype for it.

```
DWORD WINAPI HttpExtensionProc(EXTENSION_CONTROL_BLOCK *pECB)
```

Part

III

Ch

7

HttpExtensionProc is passed in a pointer to the Extension Control Block (ECB) structure. The ECB gives you all the information you need to process a request.

You'll use the ECB to execute functionality exposed by the server, to get information from the Web client, and to post information back to it. Many of the variables in the structure are like variables defined in the environment of a CGI application (see Table 7.1).

Table 7.1   The ECB Member Variables

Member	Type	CGI Equivalent	Description
cbSize	DWORD	none	This member contains the size of the ECB structure.
dwVersion	DWORD	none	This contains the version of the ISAPI specification.
ConnID	HCONN	none	This is a handle to the connection ID. The connection ID is assigned by the server and certain functions, like WriteClient, that need it passed to understand which connection to send data to. This number should not be changed.
dwHttpStatusCode	DWORD	none	This is the status of the current transaction when the request is completed.
lpszLogData	CHAR	none	This is a null-terminated string. This string contains extended log information for the server log file. What you put here will show up in the server log file and should offer a description of what the user did in your extension or any error conditions.

Member	Type	CGI Equivalent	Description
lpszMethod	LPSTR	Request_Method	This contains the method with which the HTTP request was made. This usually contains POST or GET.
lpszQueryString	LPSTR	Query_String	This is a null-terminated string containing the encoded query information from the client.
lpszPathInfo	LPSTR	Path_Info	PathInfo contains extra path information.
lpszPathTranslated	LPSTR	Path_Translated	PathTranslated contains the physical path of the ISAPI DLL.
cbTotalBytes	DWORD	Content_Length	TotalBytes contains the total number of bytes returned by the client. This information is used when receiving data from the client from a POST request. If the value is *0xffffffff* then there are 4G available and it should be read using ReadClient until no additional data is returned.
cbAvailable	DWORD	none	This contains the total available bytes already read into the lpbData buffer. The difference between cbAVailable and cbTotalBytes needs to be read in using the ReadClient member function.
lpbData	LPBYTE	none	This contains some or all of the data sent by the client. It is a buffer the size of cbAvailable. If there is more information from the client,

Part
III

Ch
7

continues

Table 7.1 Continued

Member	Type	CGI Equivalent	Description
			cbTotalBytes will contain the total size of the data block being posted back to the server by the client, and you must use ReadClient to retrieve it.
lpszContentType	LPSTR	Content_Type	This contains the content type of data sent from the client. This could be any legal MIME type.

Using the *ServerSupportFunction* and *WriteClient* to Return a Page to the Client

Before you can send any information to the client, you should send a hypertext transport protocol (HTTP) response header. In this header, you can send special commands to the Web browser, like the redirect command, or you can send information about the type of content you want to return. In most cases you are informing the browser what content you will be sending.

The content information the browser gets in the header must be in a strict format. Always start with Content-type: and follow with a mail Internet extension (MIME) type of what type of data you will be sending.

In the tutorial at the end of this chapter, we create a function that simplifies writing the header. To write a header, you need to use ServerSupportFunction, a member of the ECB structure.

```
BOOL WINAPI ServerSupportFunction(HCONN hConn., DWORD
➥dwHSERRequest, LPVOID lpvBuffer, LPDWORD lpdwSize, LPDWORD
➥lpdwDataType);
```

The MIME type we need to use for any Hypertext Markup Language (HTML) we are returning is text/html. So our first step in returning data in our HttpExtensionProc is to send the HTTP header.

The header you are returning here is very precise. Case sensitivity matters in most instances and the end of the response header is critical. You *must* return an \r\n at the end of the header or the client will not know what to do.

```
Content-type: text/html \ r \ n
        DWORD dwWritten;
        LPTSTR header = new TCHAR[200];

        lstrcpy(header,"Content-type: text/html\r\n");

        dwWritten = sizeof(header);

        pECB->ServerSupportFunction(pECB->ConnID,
                                    HSE_REQ_SEND_RESPONSE_HEADER,
                                    NULL,
                                    &dwWritten,
                                    (LPDWORD) header);
```

Once we have told the client what we are about to send, we can send the actual content.

To send information to the client, you use the `WriteClient` function, a member of the ECB. The `WriteClient` function updates a buffer that the server will be sending to the client.

```
BOOL WINAPI WriteClient (HCONN ConnID, LLPVOID Buffer, LPDWORD
➥lpdwBytes, DWORD dwReserved)
```

As with `ServerSupportFunction`, we need to pass a connection ID to the `WriteClient` function. The connection ID is a member of ECB. If you combine the following code with the previous example of `ServerSupportFunction`, you will write "Hello, World..." to the browser.

```
strcpy(outputstring,"Hello, World...");
dwBytesWritten=lstrlen(outputstring);
pECB->WriteClient(pECB->ConnID, (PVOID) outputstring,
➥&dwBytesdWritten,0);
```

You can also use `WriteClient` to write binary data, such as images, to the client.

Once you have completed the tasks in `HttpExtensionProc`, you need to return the status of your command to the server.

Part

III

Ch

7

Return the Appropriate Status Code

HSE_STATUS_SUCCESS is returned when your application has finished processing. When this is returned, the server disconnects from the client and frees allocated resources.

You can return a total of four different status codes to the client. These status codes are listed in Table 7.2.

Table 7.2 Status Codes

Status Code	Description
HSE_STATUS_SUCCESS	Your extension has successfully completed and the server can continue with the disconnection of the client.
HSE_STATUS_SUCCESS_AND_KEEP_CONN	Your extension has completed and instructs the server to wait for the next request for the client if the client supports persistent connections. The server does not have to keep the communication open.
HSE_STATUS_PENDING	Your extension has not completed and will notify the server when it is finished.
HSE_STATUS_ERROR	Your extension has not completed properly. The server is instructed to disconnect the client.

Tutorial 2: Building "Hello, World!"

Earlier, we built a simple "Hello, World!" ISAPI extension. Now we build another ISAPI extension, based on the previous instructions, and customize it.

First create a 32-bit project workspace, as instructed earlier in this chapter. Then add the DllMain function and the mandatory prototypes HttpExtensionProc and GetExtensionVersion.

We will use two functions to simplify our extension. These are WriteHTML and WriteHTMLHeader (see Listing 7.3). We can use these to make calling do the WriteClient and ServerSupportFunction functions a little easier.

Listing 7.3   WriteFunctions.CPP—WriteHTML and WriteHTMLHeader

```
BOOL WriteHTML(EXTENSION_CONTROL_BLOCK *pECB,
           TCHAR &OutputString)
{
     DWORD dwBytes;
     dwBytes = lstrlen(OutputString);
     return pECB->WriteClient(pECB->ConnID,
                         (PVOID) OutputString,
                         &dwBytes,
                         0);
}


BOOL WriteHTMLHeader(EXTENSION_CONTROL_BLOCK *pECB)
{
     DWORD dwSize;
     TCHAR str[] = TEXT("Content-type: text/html\r\n");
     dwSzie = sizeof(str);
     return pECB->ServerSupportFunction(pECB->ConnID,
                             HSE_REQ_SEND_RESPONSE_HEADER,
                             NULL,
                             &dwSize,
                             (LPDWORD) str);
}
```

Examining *GetExtensionVersion*

The "Hello, World!" GetExtensionVersion is as simple as the one at the beginning of this chapter. We set the ISAPI version, copy the description into the description variable, and return a value of TRUE for success.

Part
III

Ch

7

Examining *HttpExtensionProc*

Now that we have written the two utility functions WriteHTML and WriteHTMLHeader, our HttpExtensionProc is pretty bare-bones. Our first step is to send the Content-type header back to the client using the function we wrote, WriteHTMLHeader.

WriteHTMLHeader does a ServerSupportFunction that sends a response header of Content-type: text/html\r\n, which lets the client know we are sending HTML. The function gets a pointer to the ECB, which it uses to make its calls.

WriteHTML simplifies the WriteClient function by determining the size of the string we are sending and passing it to the WriteClient function. This works well for sending text strings.

You can use WriteClient and ServerSupportFunction to send any kind of data back to the client that the client understands. You may want to dynamically generate a chart in a gif image and send it back to the client.

You then have to set the Content-type header to image/gif and send the gif binary data with the WriteClient function.

Once "Hello, World!" has written out its information to the client, the final step is to tell the server it has completed its task by returning a HSE_STATUS_SUCCESS.

An easy way for you to test your extension without having to load it into the server is by using EyeSAPI. EyeSAPI loads and logs your DLL, executes it, and lets you view the results in any browser.

When writing the "Hello, World!" extension, I used EyeSAPI rather than my server to do most of the testing. EyeSAPI is available on the companion CD to this book and from **http://rampages.onramp.net/~steveg/eyesapi1.zip**.

Adding Dynamic Data

Let's give the "Hello, World!" extension some life. We use the GetLocalTime API call to retrieve the current date and time, and send it to the client. We can also enhance the "Hello, World!" extension with some HTML.

Change `HttpExtensionProc` to look like the following:

```
TCHAR temp[200];
SYSTEMTIME CurrentTime;
WriteHTMLHeader(pECB);
WriteHTML(pECB,"<html><head><title>");
WriteHTML(pECB,"Hello, World");
WriteHTML(pECB,"</title></head><body bgcolor=#ffffff>");
WriteHTML(pECB,"<p align=center>");
GetLocalTime(&CurrentTime);
sprintf(temp,"Hello, World. It is currently %02d:%02d on
➥%02d/%02d/%02d.",
                CurrentTime.wHour,
                CurrentTime.wMinute,
                CurrentTime.wMonth,
                CurrentTime.wDay,
                CurrentTime.wYear);
WriteHTML(pECB,temp);
WriteHTML(pECB,"</p></body></html>");
```

Now rebuild the DLL and execute it in your browser. The results are shown in Figure 7.3.

FIG. 7.3
Results of "Hello, World!"

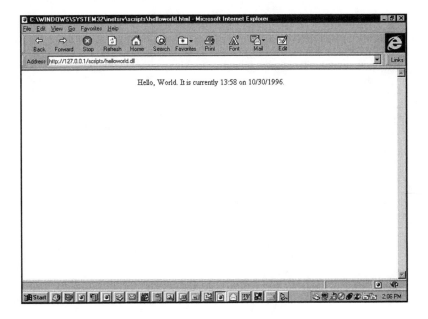

Part
III

Ch

7

From Here...

In this chapter, we look at how to build a simple ISAPI extension. We discuss the mandatory entry points for ISAPI extension DLLs—GetExtensionVersion and HttpExtensionProc.

In the next chapters, we look at building more complex extensions and how to use the MFC. Finally, we build some extensions you can use, with or without change to your server.

- Chapter 8, "Using Extension Capabilities," looks at handling parameters and data sent from the client and responding to them.

- Chapter 9, "Building Extensions with MFC," looks at using the MFC wrapper for ISAPI extensions.

- In Chapter 10, "Extending Your Web Server with Extensions," we work on some ISAPI extensions you can use for your server.

Using Extension Capabilities

The two examples in this chapter should give you a feel for the capabilities of an Internet server application programming interface (ISAPI) extension. The first example introduces you to a comment entry form and shows you how to parse data sent by the client to the extension.

The second example prints out information on how you called the extension. This shows you how the extension has affected Microsoft's Internet Information Server (IIS) variables. ▪

How data is received from a client

Learn how data is sent to the extension from the client.

How to parse data from the client

Learn how you decode data you have just read from the client so you can use it.

Information for free

Learn where you can find extra information about the connected client.

Redirection

Learn how to automatically switch the connected client to another page.

Handling *GET* Parameters

When a form uses the GET method to pass information to the extension, it is called like this:

http://www.fred.com/extension.dll?param1=value1&param2=value2

When the extension is executed, it reads the information either by reading the QUERY_STRING server variable or by looking at pECB->lpszQueryString. Working with pECB->lpszQueryString is the preferred way of reading the data because you don't have to call any functions to receive the data.

The snippet of code in Listing 8.1 shows how you can tell that GET is the request method used.

Listing 8.1   IISEMAIL.CPP—How to Determine a *GET* Request Method

```
DWORD
HttpExtensionProc( EXTENSION_CONTROL_BLOCK *pECB )
{
      CHAR    *lpszQuery = NULL;

      // get the data from the form
      if( 0 == stricmp(pECB->lpszMethod, "get") )
            lpszQuery = pECB->lpszQueryString;

      . . . . . . . . . . . . . . . . . .

}
```

But you still have some work to do before you can use the query string.

Contents of *lpszQueryString*

lpszQueryString is the equivalent of the QUERY_STRING server variable (explained later in this chapter). Like the server variable, lpszQueryString is encoded into name/value pairs.

Figure 8.1 shows you the HTML form for a comment entry page.

FIG. 8.1
Comment entry page.

If you take the HTML form shown in Figure 8.1 as an example, you end up with a query string like this

```
FirstName=Martin&LastName=Norman&WebUse=
➥Web+Surfer&FromEMail=&HomePage=http%3A%2F%2Fstaff.
➥ndl.co.uk%2Fmartin&text=
```

in which `FirstName=Martin` is a name/value pair.

Parsing URL-Encoded Parameters into Name/Value Pairs

Now that you have the query string, you have to parse it to turn it into something meaningful.

In this example, we first extract the names in the form. These are:

- FirstName
- LastName
- WebUse
- FromEMail
- HomePage
- text

The name is separated from the value by the '=' character: for example, FirstName=Martin. So first you scan the query string for an occurrence of FirstName. If you take the '=' character into account, you have the start of the value.

The end of the value is either the & character or the end of the buffer. The function shown in Listing 8.2 returns the value part of the name/value pair.

Listing 8.2   PARSE.CPP—Getting One Name/Value Pair Out of the Query String

```cpp
CHAR * CIissmtpExtension::
GetParamValue(CHAR *lpszQuery, CHAR *lpszParam)
{
    CHAR *pValueStart = NULL;
    CHAR *pValueEnd   = NULL;
    CHAR *lpszValue   = NULL;
    CHAR *szTemp1     = NULL;
    ULONG cbValue;

    pValueStart = strstr( lpszQuery, lpszParam );
    if( !pValueStart )                   // parameter doesn't exist
            return NULL;

    pValueStart += strlen( lpszParam ) + 1;

    // Now determine the length of the value string.
    pValueEnd = strchr(pValueStart, '&');

    if(pValueEnd)
  cbValue = pValueEnd - pValueStart;
    else
        // this was the last param in the list
        cbValue = strlen(pValueStart);

    // Return NULL if we  have zero length string.
    if( !cbValue )
        return NULL;

    if( !(lpszValue = (CHAR *)LocalAlloc(LPTR, cbValue + 1) ) )
        return NULL;

    strncat(lpszValue, pValueStart, cbValue);

    szTemp1 = lpszValue;
    while( * szTemp1 )
    {
```

```
        if( *szTemp1 ==  '+' )
            *szTemp1 = ' ';

        szTemp1++;
    }

    EscapeToAscii(lpszValue);

    return lpszValue;
} // GetParamValue
```

In the query string example above, notice that the HomePage parameter has a lot of odd characters in it:

```
HomePage=http%3A%2F%2Fstaff.ndl.co.uk%2Fmartin
```

Some characters are reserved and can't be used. So the client converts them to hex values, denoted by the % character. All spaces are converted to the + character.

In Listing 8.2, you saw a reference to a function called `EscapeToAscii`. This function does the conversion from hex values to ASCII characters for you (see Listing 8.3).

Listing 8.3   PARSE.CPP—Converting a Hex Value into a Character

```
void   CIissmtpExtension::
EscapeToAscii(CHAR *lpEscape)
{
    int i, j;

    for( i = 0, j = 0; lpEscape[j] ; ++i, ++j )
    {
        if( (lpEscape[i] = lpEscape[j]) == '%' )
        {
            lpEscape[i] = HexToAscii( &lpEscape[j+1] );
            j+=2;
        }
    }

    lpEscape[i] = '\0';
}

//----------------------------------------------------------------
----
```

continues

Listing 8.3 Continued

```
CHAR  CIissmtpExtension::
HexToAscii(CHAR *lpString)
{
    CHAR CH;

    CH =  (lpString[0] >= 'A' ? ( (lpString[0] & 0xDF) - 'A' ) + 10
    ➥: (lpString[0] - '0') );
    CH *= 16;
    CH += (lpString[1] >= 'A' ? ( (lpString[1] & 0xDF) - 'A' ) + 10
    ➥: (lpString[1] - '0') );

    return CH;
}
```

Now you have converted your query string into something you can use.

Handling *POST* Parameters

Reading data that was sent using the POST request method is slightly more complex than reading data that was sent using the GET method. But it's worth it. You can read considerably more data from the client using the POST method and that data can be binary (see Listing 8.4).

Listing 8.4 IISEMAIL.CPP—How to Determine a *Post* Method

```
DWORD
HttpExtensionProc( EXTENSION_CONTROL_BLOCK *pECB )
{
     CHAR    *lpszQuery = NULL;

     // get the data from the form
     if( 0 == stricmp(pECB->lpszMethod, "post") )
{
// extract post data here
     ..................
     ..................
     ..................
     ..................

}
     ..................
     ..................
```

```
        . . . . . . . . . . . . . . . . . . .
        . . . . . . . . . . . . . . . . . . .
  }
```

The first 48K of data (if you have that much) from the POST request are pointed to by the EXTENSION_CONTROL_BLOCK pointer lpbData, with the total amount of data available shown by cbTotalBytes.

N O T E This 48K is a limitation of Microsoft's IIS. Different servers may have a different value.

In version 3.0 of Microsoft's IIS, the value is configurable. The default is still 48K. To change the default, you have to change the registry value under HKEY_LOCAL_MACHINE\SYSTEM\CurrentControlSet\Services\w3svc\ parameters\UploadReadAhead.

The value range for this parameter is 0 - 0x80000000. ▪

The maximum amount of data you can send using this request method is 4G. Sending the full amount of data is covered later in this chapter.

N O T E There is no end-of-file (EOF) at the end of the lpbData buffer. ▪

If the data is not binary, it is URL-encoded just like the GET method. So you have to parse the data. Then you can decode the data.

Difference Between *cbTotalBytes* and *cbAvailable*

The content of cbTotalBytes is the equivalent of the server variable CONTENT_LENGTH (explained later in this chapter). If its value is 0xffffffff, then the connecting client has just sent the over 4G of data to the extension.

The contents of cbAvailable are the number of bytes immediately available (out of a total of cbTotalBytes). To read the remaining data, you use the ReadClient function, which is covered in the next section.

Both of these values refer to the content of the lpbData buffer. The maximum amount of data this can hold depends on the implementation of the ISAPI interface you are using. In Microsoft's IIS, the default value is 48K. But this value can be changed using the registry.

Getting the Full *POST* Buffer

To get the full POST buffer, read the data to check if cbAvailable is equal to
cbTotalBytes. If it is, make a copy of the contents of lpbData. If cbAvailable is less
than cbTotalBytes, use ReadClient() until all the data has been read. Listing 8.5
shows you how to do this.

Listing 8.5   IISEMAIL.CPP—How to Get the Whole *POST* Buffer

```
// Start processing of input information here.
        lpszTemp = (CHAR *)LocalAlloc( LPTR,
        ➥pECB->cbTotalBytes);
        if( NULL == lpszTemp )
            return HSE_STATUS_ERROR;

        // do not always trust the compiler to zero the memory
        memset(lpszTemp, '\0', pECB->cbTotalBytes);
        strncpy(lpszTemp, (CHAR *)pECB->lpbData,
        ➥pECB->cbAvailable );
        cbQuery = pECB->cbTotalBytes - pECB->cbAvailable;

        if( cbQuery > 0 )
        {
            pECB->ReadClient(pECB->ConnID,
                            (LPVOID)(lpszTemp +
                                            ÂpECB->cbAvailable),
                            &cbQuery);
        }
            lpszQuery = lpszTemp;
```

Using *lpszContentType*

The content type entry shows the type of data sent by the client. It is only used
when the request method is the POST.

lpszContentType is the equivalent of the server variable CONTENT_TYPE.

When you use Internet Explorer (IE) 3.0 to send a POST request, lpszContentType
is typically set to application/x-www-form-urlencoded.

Normally, the client browser sets the content type to ASCII. But it could be
changed at the client side if you had to send binary data, for example.

Getting Server Variables

To get a server variable, you use the GetServerVariable, which is one of the functions in the EXTENSION_CONTROL_BLOCK. GetServerVariable is the equivalent to the getenv CGI function.

It is worth noting that the EXTENSION_CONTROL_BLOCK includes some server variables, as shown in Table 8.1.

Table 8.1   Compatible Entries

Control Block	Server Variable
lpszMethod	REQUEST_METHOD
lpszQueryString	QUERY_STRING
lpszPathInfo	PATH_INFO
lpszPathTranslated	PATH_TRANSLATED
cbTotalBytes	CONTENT_LENGTH

It is far more efficient to look at these variables using the EXTENSION_CONTROL_BLOCK because it does not include any function calls. To use GetServerVariable(), you pass it the current connection ID, the variable name you want, a buffer address to receive the contents of the variable, and the size of the buffer you are using.

You must use a pointer to a DWORD for the size of the buffer. This is because when it is completed, the DWORD is set to the amount of transferred data, including a null terminating byte. Listing 8.6 shows you how to get server variables.

Listing 8.6   VARIABLES.CPP—How to Get a Server Variable

```
DWORD    cbdwbuff2;
CHAR     ServerPort[20] = { 0 };

cbdwbuff2 = 10;
if( FALSE == pECB->GetServerVariable(pECB->ConnID,
➥"SERVER_PORT", &ServerPort, &cbdwbuff2) )
{
   DisplayError( GetLastError() );
}
```

If the call fails, `GetServerVariable` returns a value of FALSE. You can find the reason for the error by calling `GetLastError` (see Table 8.2).

Table 8.2   Possible Error Returns from *GetServerVariable*

Value	Meaning
`ERROR_INVALID_PARAMETER`	Bad connection handle
`ERROR INVLAID_INDEX`	Bad or incompatible variable identifier
`ERROR_INSUFFICIENT_BUFFER`	Buffer too small, needed size returned in *lpdwSize
`ERROR_MORE_DATA`	Buffer too small, only part of data returned. The total size of the data is not returned.
`ERROR_NO_DATA`	The data request is not available.

What Are Server Variables?

You can use server variables to supply information about the currently connected client and about the server itself. For example, you can learn the Internet protocol (IP) address of the client that has just called your extension or the type of browser used.

Listed below are the server variables, and a simple extension that shows you how `POST` and `GET` request methods affect server variables.

N O T E   An overview of most server variables can be found in the CGI specification. This is maintained by the NCSA Software Development Group at **http://hoohoo.ncsa.uiuc.edu/cgi/env.html**. ▓

Information from the Browser on Every Request

Server variables supply information about where and what the browser is. The variables with this information usually start with `REMOTE_<type>`—for example, `REMOTE_ADDR` or `REMOTE_USER`.

Other variables also supply client information such as HTTP_USER_AGENT, as explained later in this chapter.

Some Server-Specific Variables

Some variables provide information about the server that the extension is running on.

For example, you might be writing a secure extension that has to run on only one server machine. For this, you could use the SERVER_NAME variable to check the machine name.

Or your extension might need a certain version of IIS to be running. For this, you would check the SERVER_SOFTWARE variable.

Useful for Configuring Custom Results

Different browsers have different capabilities. For example, Internet Explorer 1.x does not allow frames or tables, and Netscape 2.x does not allow scripts as Visual Basic does. So when you run an extension, you want to give that browser the best output possible.

The extension can detect the type of browser connected by looking at the HTTP_USER_AGENT server variable, as shown in Table 8.3.

Table 8.3 Examples of Browser Type and Variable Setting

Browser	HTTP_USER_AGENT
IE 2.0	MSIE 2.0/Mozilla-Spoofer Mozilla/1.22 (compatible; MSIE 2.0; Windows 95)
IE 3.0	Mozilla/2.0 (compatible; MSIE 3.0; Windows NT)
Netscape 3.0	Mozilla/3.0 (WinNT; I)
Netscape 2.02	Mozilla/2.02 (Win16; I)
Information collector for excite	ArchitextSpider

N O T E   Not everything that connects is a browser. There are a lot of spiders and robots
out there.

Spiders and robots are programs that automatically search the Web by following
hypertext links that retrieve all documents referenced.

A list of robots and spiders is at **http://info.webcrawler.com/mak/projects/robots/
robots.html**. ■

Server Variables

Listing 8.7 is the code that shows the contents of the server variables, and how
POST and GET can influence them. The listing includes all the server variables mentioned in this chapter. Use the Hypertext Markup Language (HTML) form in Listing 8.8 to try the extension with both request methods.

Listing 8.7   VARIABLES.CPP—Function That Displays Server Variables

```
//------------------------------------------------------------------
----------
BOOL
DisplayVariable(char *lpszQuery, EXTENSION_CONTROL_BLOCK *pECB )
{
    DWORD    dwErr = 0;
    DWORD    cbdwbuff2;
    DWORD    dwLen = 0;
    CHAR     tmpbuf[4000]  = { 0 };
    CHAR     ServerSoftware[200] = { 0 };
    CHAR     ServerProtocol[200] = { 0 };
    CHAR     RemoteAddress[200] = { 0 };
    CHAR     RemoteHost[200] = { 0 };
    CHAR     RemoteUser[200] = { 0 };
    CHAR     HttpAccept[200] = { 0 };
    CHAR     HttpUserAgent[356] = { 0 };
    CHAR     AuthType[200] = { 0 };
    CHAR     ContentLength[200] = { 0 };
    CHAR     ContentType[200] = { 0 };
    CHAR     GatewayInterface[200] = { 0 };
    CHAR     PathInfo[200] = { 0 };
    CHAR     PathTranslated[200] = { 0 };
    CHAR     QueryString[200] = { 0 };
    CHAR     RequestMethod[200] = { 0 };
    CHAR     ScriptName[200] = { 0 };
    CHAR     ServerName[200] = { 0 };
    CHAR     ServerPort[200] = { 0 };
```

```
CHAR      AuthPass[200] = { 0 };
CHAR      AllHttp[200] = { 0 };

cbdwbuff2 = 200;
pECB->GetServerVariable(pECB->ConnID, "AUTH_TYPE", &AuthType,
➥&cbdwbuff2);

cbdwbuff2 = 200;
pECB->GetServerVariable(pECB->ConnID, "CONTENT_LENGTH",
➥&ContentLength, &cbdwbuff2);

cbdwbuff2 = 200;
pECB->GetServerVariable(pECB->ConnID, "CONTENT_TYPE",
➥&ContentType, &cbdwbuff2);

cbdwbuff2 = 200;
pECB->GetServerVariable(pECB->ConnID, "GATEWAY_INTERFACE",
➥&GatewayInterface, &cbdwbuff2);

cbdwbuff2 = 200;
pECB->GetServerVariable(pECB->ConnID, "PATH_INFO", &PathInfo,
➥&cbdwbuff2);

cbdwbuff2 = 200;
pECB->GetServerVariable(pECB->ConnID, "PATH_TRANSLATED",
➥&PathTranslated, &cbdwbuff2);

cbdwbuff2 = 200;
pECB->GetServerVariable(pECB->ConnID, "QUERY_STRING",
➥&QueryString, &cbdwbuff2);

cbdwbuff2 = 200;
pECB->GetServerVariable(pECB->ConnID, "REQUEST_METHOD",
➥&RequestMethod, &cbdwbuff2);

cbdwbuff2 = 200;
pECB->GetServerVariable(pECB->ConnID, "SCRIPT_NAME",
➥&ScriptName, &cbdwbuff2);

cbdwbuff2 = 200;
pECB->GetServerVariable(pECB->ConnID, "SERVER_NAME",
➥&ServerName, &cbdwbuff2);

cbdwbuff2 = 200;
pECB->GetServerVariable(pECB->ConnID, "SERVER_PORT",
➥&ServerPort, &cbdwbuff2);

cbdwbuff2 = 200;
pECB->GetServerVariable(pECB->ConnID, "AUTH_PASS",
➥&AuthPass, &cbdwbuff2);
```

continues

Listing 8.7 Continued

```
cbdwbuff2 = 200;
pECB->GetServerVariable(pECB->ConnID, "ALL_HTTP", &AllHttp,
➥&cbdwbuff2);

cbdwbuff2 = 200;
pECB->GetServerVariable(pECB->ConnID, "SERVER_PROTOCOL",
➥&ServerProtocol, &cbdwbuff2);

cbdwbuff2 = 200;
pECB->GetServerVariable(pECB->ConnID, "SERVER_SOFTWARE",
➥&ServerSoftware, &cbdwbuff2);

cbdwbuff2 = 200;
pECB->GetServerVariable(pECB->ConnID, "REMOTE_ADDR",
➥&RemoteAddress, &cbdwbuff2);

cbdwbuff2 = 200;
pECB->GetServerVariable(pECB->ConnID, "REMOTE_HOST",
➥&RemoteHost, &cbdwbuff2);

cbdwbuff2 = 200;
pECB->GetServerVariable(pECB->ConnID, "REMOTE_USER",
➥&RemoteUser, &cbdwbuff2);

cbdwbuff2 = 200;
pECB->GetServerVariable(pECB->ConnID, "HTTP_ACCEPT",
➥&HttpAccept, &cbdwbuff2);

cbdwbuff2 = 356;
pECB->GetServerVariable(pECB->ConnID, "HTTP_USER_AGENT",
➥&HttpUserAgent, &cbdwbuff2);

//-------------------------------------------------
wsprintf(tmpbuf,"<p>\n"
                "Auth Type         = %s<br>\n"
                "Content Length    = %s<br>\n"
                "Content Type      = %s<br>\n"
                "Gateway Interface = %s<br>\n"
                "Path Info         = %s<br>\n"
                "Path Translated   = %s<br>\n"
                "Query String      = %s<br>\n"
                "Remote Address    = %s<br>\n"
                "Remote Host       = %s<br>\n"
                "Remote User       = %s<br>\n"
                "Request Method    = %s<br>\n"
                "Script Name       = %s<br>\n"
                "Server Name       = %s<br>\n"
                "Server Port       = %s<br>\n"
                "Server Protocol   = %s<br>\n"
```

```
                    "Server Software    = %s<br>\n"
                    "Auth Pass          = %s<br>\n"
                    "All Http           = %s<br>\n"
                    "HTTP ACCEPT        = %s<br>\n"
                    "HTTP User Agent    = %s<br>\n"
                    "</p>\n",
                    AuthType,
                    ContentLength,
                    ContentType,
                    GatewayInterface,
                    PathInfo,
                    PathTranslated,
                    QueryString,
                                    RemoteAddress,
                    RemoteHost,
                                    RemoteUser,
                    RequestMethod,
                    ScriptName,
                    ServerName,
                    ServerPort,
                    ServerProtocol,
                    ServerSoftware,
                    AuthPass,
                    AllHttp,
                    HttpAccept,
                                    HttpUserAgent);

        dwLen = lstrlen( tmpbuf );
        pECB->WriteClient(pECB->ConnID, tmpbuf, &dwLen, dwLen );

        return TRUE;
}
```

Listing 8.8   VARIABLES.HTM—HTML Code for Calling the *variables.dll* Extension

```
<html>
<head>
<title>Server Variables Display</title>
</head>

<body>

<h2>Get:</h2>
<form action="/scripts/variables.dll" method=get>
<INPUT NAME="param1" VALUE="" >
<input type="submit" value="Submit get Entry">
```

continues

Listing 8.8 Continued

```
<input type="reset" value="Reset Form">
</form>

<hr>

<h2>Post:</h2>
<form action="/scripts/variables.dll" method=post>
<INPUT NAME="param1" VALUE="" >
<input type="submit" value="Submit post Entry">
<input type="reset" value="Reset Form">
</form>

</body>
</html>
```

Figure 8.2 is an example of running the form in Listing 8.8 with the GET request method.

FIG. 8.2

Results of calling the display variables extension using the GET request method.

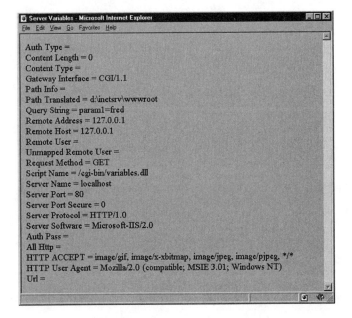

The following is a list of the server variables.

■ AUTH_TYPE. If the user name has been authenticated, this variable shows the authentication method used to validate the user. There is no set list because methods can be added to the base methods. The base methods are shown in Table 8.4.

Table 8.4   The Three Methods Supplied with IIS

Method	Variable Contents
Allow Anonymous	the variable is empty
Basic clear text	basic
Windows NT challenge/response	NTLM

- CONTENT_LENGTH. The total number of bytes received from the client when the request method is POST.
- CONTENT_TYPE. Used to tell the extension the type of data sent by the client when the request method is POST.

  For example, if the variable example in Figure 8.2 was called using the POST method with foo=bar as the passed data, we would get the following from this variable:

  ```
  Content Type = application/x-www-form-urlencoded
  ```

  and the CONTENT_LENGTH variable would be :

  ```
  Content Length = 22
  ```

- GATEWAY_INTERFACE. The revision of the CGI specification this server complies with. For IIS, this is CGI/1.1. The format is CGI/revision.
- PATH_INFO. A variable with extra path information as given by the client. This is the trailing part of the URL after the extension name but before the query string. If you use the variables extension again, call it like this:

  http://staff/scripts/variables.dll/martin/?foo=var.

Figure 8.3 shows the output from the extension.

NOTE   Notice that /martin/ is included between the end of the extension name and the query string. ■

FIG. 8.3

Results of the PATH_INFO example.

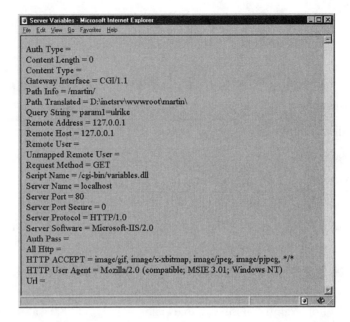

- **PATH_TRANSLATED.** This is the translated version of PATH_INFO, which is the physical path mapping.

- **QUERY_STRING.** The information following the ? in the URL that called the script. This is the request information and it should not be decoded. This variable should always be set when there is request information, regardless of command line decoding.

- **REMOTE_ADDR.** The IP address of the remote client making the request.

- **REMOTE_HOST.** Normally set to the domain name service (DNS) host name of the connected client if the server can do DNS lookups. IIS does not do DNS lookups, so it is just set equal to REMOTE_ADDR.

- **REMOTE_USER.** The user name supplied by the connected client that IIS has authenticated.

- **UNMAPPED_REMOTE_USER.** A copy of the user name before any IIS filter has changed it—for example, by mapping the user name to an NT user account name.

- **REQUEST_METHOD.** The method used by the connected client to make a request—for example, GET or POST.

- ■ SCRIPT_NAME. The name of the extension being executed.

- ■ SERVER_NAME. The server's host name, DNS alias, or IP address.

- ■ SERVER_PORT. The port number to which the request was sent. This is normally 80.

- ■ SERVER_PORT_SECURE. A Boolean value to indicate if the request is on the secure port. If the result is 1, the request is on the secure port. If the result is 0, it is not.

- ■ SERVER_PROTOCOL. The name and revision of the information retrieval protocol this request came from. For example, the server protocol from Figure 8.3 is HTTP/1.0, where the format is protocol/revision.

- ■ SERVER_SOFTWARE. The name and version of IIS that is running. The format of the variable is name/version. For example, for IIS version 3.0, which comes with NT 4.0, the name and version would be Microsoft-IIS/3.0.

- ■ AUTH_PASS. The password supplied by the user. This is only supplied to a CGI script if the first character of its name is $. To guard against scripts "stealing" user passwords, install $ scripts only from trusted sources.

N O T E Although AUTH_PASS is not used by IIS, it is possible to read the variable if AUTH_TYPE is BASIC.

You would have to query the HTTP_AUTHORIZATION header and then decode it. ■

- ■ ALL_HTTP. All HTTP headers that were not already parsed into one of the above variables. These variables are of the form HTTP_<header field name>. Following is an example of output from the variable:

  HTTP_ACCEPT:image/gif, image/x-xbitmap, image/jpeg, image/pjpeg, */*

  HTTP_CONNECTION:Keep-Alive HTTP_HOST:staff
  HTTP_REFERER:http://staff/martin/variables.htm

  HTTP_USER_AGENT:Mozilla/3.0 (WinNT; I)

- ■ HTTP_USER_AGENT. The browser the client is using to send the request. The format for this variable is software/version library/version. For a client running IE 3.0 on Windows 95, the variable would have Mozilla/2.0 (compatible; MSIE 3.0; Windows 95).

■ HTTP_ACCEPT. The mail Internet extension (MIME) type the client accepts, as given by HTTP headers. Each item in this list should be separated by commas, according to the HTTP spec, and has the format type/subtype,type/subtype. So for an IE 3.0 connection, the variable could have

```
image/gif, image/x-xbitmap, image/jpeg, image/pjpeg, */*
```

■ URL. Gives the base portion of the URL.

Writing to the Client

The two ways of writing to the client from the extension are using `WriteClient` and `ServerSupportFunction`.

`ServerSupportFunction` has limitations in that it can only send ASCII data to the client. It is used for sending completion status information and other header details to the client, as shown in Listing 8.9. An example is the content type of the data you are going to send to the client.

Listing 8.9   VARIABLES.CPP—Partial Listing from *HttpExtensionProc*

```
    DWORD    dwLen = 0;
    CHAR     szBuff[1024] = { 0 };

    wsprintf( szBuff, "Content-Type: text/html\r\n\r\n");

dwLen = lstrlen( szBuff );
pECB->ServerSupportFunction( pECB->ConnID,
            HSE_REQ_SEND_RESPONSE_HEADER, "200 OK", &dwLen,
            ➡( LPDWORD )
            szBuff );
```

`WriteClient` just sends the stated number of bytes to the client so it can send both ASCII and binary data, as shown in Listing 8.10. It can also be used for sending completion status information back to the client. But to do this, you would have to format the full header yourself.

Listing 8.10 VARIABLES.CPP—Writing Data to the Client

```
        DWORD   dwLen = 0;
        CHAR    szBuff[1024] = { 0 };

        wsprintf(szBuff, "<body>");
        dwLen = lstrlen( szBuff );
        if( FALSE == pECB->WriteClient( pECB->ConnID, szBuff, &dwLen,
        ➥dwLen) )
{
        DisplayError( GetLastError() );
        }
```

If the function returns FALSE, call GetLastError to see what the problem is.

Reading from the Client

If the request method was GET, all the data from the client can be read from the lpszQueryString buffer or from the QUERY_STRING server variable (as shown earlier in this chapter).

If the request method is POST, part or all of the data is in lpbData. If all the data is not in lpbData, you have to use ReadClient to read it. (See Listing 8.11.)

Listing 8.11 VARIABLES.CPP—Reading Data Sent by the Client

```
CHAR    *lpszTemp = NULL;
DWORD   cbQuery = 0;

cbQuery = pECB->cbTotalBytes - pECB->cbAvailable;
lpszTemp = (CHAR *)LocalAlloc( LPTR, cbQuery);

if( FALSE == pECB->ReadClient(pECB->ConnID,
                        (LPVOID)lpszTemp,
                        &cbQuery) )
{
      DisplayError( GetLastError() );
      }
```

If the buffer size that is passed to ReadClient is more than the amount of available data, the function blocks until either the client sending the data sends it or the communications socket that the server is using is closed.

If the socket is closed before all the data is sent, `ReadClient` returns TRUE but with zero bytes read. If the function returns FALSE, call `GetLastError` to see what the problem is.

TerminateExtension

If you do anything special when you start your extension that needs to be cleaned up when the extension is unloaded, the `TerminateExtension` function is for you. But it is only available in Microsoft's IIS version 3.0 or later.

`TerminateExtension` is called just before the server unloads the extension. A bit-field parameter is passed to the function by the server, indicating whether the extension has a choice about unloading (see Table 8.5).

Table 8.5   *TerminateExtension* Bit-Field Values

Value	Meaning
`HSE_TERM_ADVISORY_UNLOAD`	The server wants to unload the extension. The extension can return TRUE if that is OK, or FALSE if the extension does not want to unload.
`HSE_TERM_MUST_UNLOAD`	The server wants to unload the extension and does not give the extension a choice. At this point, the extension must clean up and be unloaded.

Using URL Redirection

You may want to redirect a connected client to another page on your server or even to another server altogether. This section introduces you to the idea of redirecting a client to another URL without the user doing the connect.

Why Redirection?

There are any number of reasons why you would want to redirect automatically from an extension. You might want a menu selection for your Web pages. Or you might want special pages for different kinds of browsers.

Listing 8.12 is for a simple Web page menu system using a list box. You select the target you want and that information is passed to an extension called `redir`.

Listing 8.12   REDIR.HTM—HTML Page with a Page Redirect Menu

```html
<html>
<head><title>Redirect URL</title></head>
<body>
<hr>
<h2>Redirect</h2>
<FORM ACTION="/scripts/redir.dll" target="_top">
    <SELECT NAME="Target">
        <OPTION SELECTED VALUE="/martin/">Default
            <OPTION VALUE = "/martin/york/">City of York
            <OPTION VALUE = "/martin/wetherby/">Wetherby
            <OPTION VALUE = "/martin/isapi.htm">IPASI
            <OPTION VALUE = "/martin/weather.htm">The Weather
            <OPTION VALUE = "/martin/films-tv.htm">Films and TV
            <OPTION VALUE = "/martin/otherbee.htm">Sites about Beer
            <OPTION VALUE = "/martin/maps.htm">Sites about Maps
    </SELECT>
    <input type="submit" value="Select page">
</FORM>
<hr>

</body>
</html>
```

Using *ServerSupportFunction()* to Redirect

The extension in Listing 8.12 uses `ServerSupportFunction` to redirect to the target page. The target page is passed into the extension as a query. The query is parsed and passed to the `ServerSupportFunction` with the `dwHSERequest` type set to `HSE_REQ_SEND`.

Listing 8.13 shows how the target was parsed and then used.

Part
III

Ch
8

Listing 8.13   REDIR.CPP—Partial Listing for the *HttpExtensionProc()*

```
//----------------------------------------------------------------
----------
DWORD CRedirExtension::
HttpExtensionProc( EXTENSION_CONTROL_BLOCK *pECB )
{
    CHAR    *lpszQuery = NULL;
    CHAR    szNewUrl[1024] = { 0 };
    DWORD   dwLen = 0;

    if( !stricmp(pECB->lpszMethod, "get") )
      // GET
      lpszQuery = pECB->lpszQueryString;
    else
    {

      // POST
      return HSE_STATUS_ERROR;
    }

    //------------------------------------------------
    if( NULL != GetParamValue(lpszQuery, "Target") )
        lstrcpy(szNewUrl, GetParamValue(lpszQuery, "Target") );

    //------------------------------------------------
    dwLen = lstrlen( szNewUrl );
    pECB->ServerSupportFunction( pECB->ConnID,
                        HSE_REQ_SEND_URL, szNewUrl, &dwLen,
                        ➥(LPDWORD)NULL );

        return HSE_STATUS_SUCCESS;
}
```

The redirection does not involve the client at all: The work is done by the server. This kind of redirect only works for the current server. You can't redirect to another server.

To do this you would have to use the HSE_REQ_SEND_URL_REDIRECT_RESP request type, which sends a 302 (URL redirection) message back to the client. The client automatically connects to the new URL, which was also passed back by the extension.

If we convert our menu example to this new method, the new HTML code is in Listing 8.14 and the HttpExtensionProc is in Listing 8.15.

Listing 8.14   URLREDIR.HTM—HTML Code from a Web Page Menu

```html
<html>
<head><title>Redirect URL</title></head>
<body>
<hr>
<h2>Redirect</h2>
<FORM ACTION="/scripts/urlredir.dll" target="_top">
    <SELECT NAME="Target">
        <OPTION SELECTED VALUE="http://staff/martin/">Default
            <OPTION VALUE = "http://staff/martin/york/">City of York
            <OPTION VALUE = "http://staff/martin/wetherby/">Wetherby
            <OPTION VALUE = "http://staff/martin/isapi.htm">IPASI
            <OPTION VALUE = "http://staff/martin/weather.htm">The
            ➥Weather
            <OPTION VALUE = "http://staff/martin/films-tv.htm">Films
            ➥and TV
            <OPTION VALUE = "http://staff/martin/otherbee.htm">Sites
            ➥about Beer
            <OPTION VALUE = "http://staff/martin/maps.htm">Sites
            ➥about Maps
            <OPTION VALUE = "http://www.ndl.co.uk/">Network Designers
            <OPTION VALUE = "http://www.exponet.co.uk">Exponet
    </SELECT>
    <input type="submit" value="Select page">
</FORM>
<hr>
</body>
</html>
```

Notice that unlike the HTML code in Listing 8.12, in Listing 8.14 you have to put in the full new URL that we want to redirect to. You have to add the http:// for the redirection to work.

Listing 8.15   URLREDIR.CPP—*HttpExtensionProc*

```cpp
//-------------------------------------------------------------------
----------
DWORD CUrlredirExtension::
HttpExtensionProc( EXTENSION_CONTROL_BLOCK *pECB )
{
    CHAR    *lpszQuery = NULL;
    CHAR    szNewUrl[1024] = { 0 };
    DWORD   dwLen = 0;

    if( !stricmp(pECB->lpszMethod, "get") )
      // GET
```

continues

Listing 8.15   Continued

```
        lpszQuery = pECB->lpszQueryString;
    else
    {

        // POST
        return HSE_STATUS_ERROR;
    }

    //--------------------------------------------------
    if( NULL != GetParamValue(lpszQuery, "Target") )
        lstrcpy(szNewUrl, GetParamValue(lpszQuery, "Target") );

    //--------------------------------------------------
    dwLen = lstrlen( szNewUrl );
    pECB->ServerSupportFunction( pECB->ConnID,
                        HSE_REQ_SEND_URL_REDIRECT_RESP, szNewUrl,
                        ➥&dwLen, (LPDWORD)NULL );

    return HSE_STATUS_SUCCESS;
}
```

From Here...

This chapter introduced you to the capabilities you can use to write ISAPI extensions, including:

- Getting information from a client
- Parsing the information from the client
- Replying to the client that sent the data
- Redirecting the client to another server or page when necessary

The following chapters give you more information on how to expand the capabilities of your extensions.

- In Chapter 9, "Building Extensions with MFC," you'll learn how the latest VC++ version can give you a head start in writing your extension.
- In Chapter 10, "Extending Your Web Server with Extensions," you'll learn how to use tokens and talk to databases with open database connectivity (ODBC).

Building Extensions with MFC

Version 4.1+ of the Microsoft Foundation Classes (MFC) comes with extensive support for Internet Server Application Programming Interface (ISAPI) extensions. The ISAPI Extension Wizard creates the MFC framework on which your Web server application is built.

Processing a form is the mainstay of Internet-based interactive applications and a key to unlocking the power of the Web. In this chapter, you learn how to use the framework supplied by the wizard to create an ISAPI extension that processes a Hypertext Markup Language (HTML) form. ■

The foundation

You'll learn about the framework supplied by the Extension Wizard.

From there to here

You'll learn how requests are mapped to functions.

Getting a project up and running

You'll create a new project and look at some output.

Going from *GET* to *POST*

You'll set up your form processor to accept input only from POST requests.

Adding some form elements

You'll see everything come together.

The Foundation

You have some work to do before you build. In Microsoft Developer Studio, create a new Project Workspace. For the name, enter **My** and choose ISAPI Extension Wizard as the type. Press Create.

Leave the Extension Class Name as `CMyExtension`, press Finish, and press OK. Now open the FileView of your project. AppWizard, as you can see, has inserted seven files (see Table 9.1).

Table 9.1   My Project Files

File Name	Description
MY.H	`CMyExtension`'s declaration
MY.CPP	`CMyExtension`'s implementation
MY.RC	My's resource file
MY.DEF	My's exports definition file
STDAFX.H	Application framework header
STDAFX.CPP	Includes STDAFX.H
MY.PCH	My's precompiled header

Open the MY.H file and you should see the code shown in Listing 9.1.

Listing 9.1   MY.H—CMyExtension's Class Declaration

```
// MY.H - Header file for your Internet Server
//    My Extension

#include "resource.h"

class CMyExtension : public CHttpServer
{
public:
     CMyExtension();
     ~CMyExtension();

// Overrides
     // ClassWizard generated virtual function overrides
          // NOTE - the ClassWizard will add and remove member
     // functions here.
```

```
                    //      DO NOT EDIT what you see in these blocks of
                    //      generated code !
            //{{AFX_VIRTUAL(CMyExtension)
            public:
            virtual BOOL GetExtensionVersion(HSE_VERSION_INFO* pVer);
            //}}AFX_VIRTUAL

            // TODO: Add handlers for your commands here.
            // For example:

            void Default(CHttpServerContext* pCtxt);

            DECLARE_PARSE_MAP()

            //{{AFX_MSG(CMyExtension)
            //}}AFX_MSG
        };
```

As mentioned earlier, this file holds your CHttpServer- derived class declaration. If you've never used MFC before, this code probably looks like most other class declarations you've created.

A closer look reveals some lines that may seem strange. These are the ClassWizard's override declaration section shown in Listing 9.2.

Listing 9.2   MY.H—ClassWizard Override Declarations

```
1       //{{AFX_VIRTUAL(CMyExtension)
2       public:
3       virtual BOOL GetExtensionVersion(HSE_VERSION_INFO* pVer);
4       //}}AFX_VIRTUAL
```

Lines 1 and 4 are the comment delimited lines that help ClassWizard find the beginning and end of virtual function overrides. When AppWizard creates the extension's skeleton code, there is only one overridden function. As you override and remove CHttpServer virtual functions with ClassWizard, their declarations are automatically added and deleted from the AFX_VIRTUAL section in Listing 9.1.

Near the end of MY.H, you see the code in Listing 9.3.

Part

III

Ch

9

Listing 9.3   MY.H—*CMy's* Parse Map Declaration

```
1      DECLARE_PARSE_MAP()
```

Depending on when your extension links to MFC, the DECLARE_PARSE_MAP() macro adds one private member and up to four public members to your CHttpServer-derived class. The definition of DECLARE_PARSE_MAP() is in AFXISAPI.H.

When I first started Windows 3.x programming, I read somewhere that WINDOWS.H was the ultimate reference for Windows developers. By the same token, the ultimate encyclopedia for MFC developers is the MFC source code provided by Microsoft on your Visual C++ CD-ROM. Although it's substantially larger than WINDOWS.H, it's also where many questions can be answered.

Listing 9.4 shows the implementation file for your extension.

Listing 9.4   MY.CPP—*CMy's* Implementation File

```
// MY.CPP - Implementation file for your Internet Server
//     My Extension

#include "stdafx.h"
#include "My.h"

///////////////////////////////////////////////////////////////////
///
// The one and only CWinApp object
// NOTE: You may remove this object if you alter your project to no
// longer use MFC in a DLL.

CWinApp theApp;

///////////////////////////////////////////////////////////////////
///
// command-parsing map

BEGIN_PARSE_MAP(CMyExtension, CHttpServer)
        // TODO: insert your ON_PARSE_COMMAND() and
        // ON_PARSE_COMMAND_PARAMS() here to hook up your commands.
        // For example:

        ON_PARSE_COMMAND(Default, CMyExtension, ITS_EMPTY)
        DEFAULT_PARSE_COMMAND(Default, CMyExtension)
END_PARSE_MAP(CMyExtension)
```

```cpp
/////////////////////////////////////////////////////////////////
///
// The one and only CMyExtension object

CMyExtension theExtension;


/////////////////////////////////////////////////////////////////
///
// CMyExtension implementation

CMyExtension::CMyExtension()
{
}

CMyExtension::~CMyExtension()
{
}

BOOL CMyExtension::GetExtensionVersion(HSE_VERSION_INFO* pVer)
{
     // Call default implementation for initialization
     CHttpServer::GetExtensionVersion(pVer);

     // Load description string
     TCHAR sz[HSE_MAX_EXT_DLL_NAME_LEN+1];
     ISAPIVERIFY(::LoadString(AfxGetResourceHandle(),
                 IDS_SERVER, sz, HSE_MAX_EXT_DLL_NAME_LEN));
     _tcscpy(pVer->lpszExtensionDesc, sz);
     return TRUE;
}

/////////////////////////////////////////////////////////////////
///
// CMyExtension command handlers

void CMyExtension::Default(CHttpServerContext* pCtxt)
{
     StartContent(pCtxt);
     WriteTitle(pCtxt);

     *pCtxt << _T("This default message was produced by the
     ➥Internet");
     *pCtxt << _T(" Server DLL Wizard. Edit your
     ➥CMyExtension::Default()");
     *pCtxt << _T(" implementation to change it.\r\n");

     EndContent(pCtxt);
}
```

continues

Listing 9.4 Continued

```
// Do not edit the following lines, which are needed by ClassWizard.
#if 0
BEGIN_MESSAGE_MAP(CMyExtension, CHttpServer)
        //{{AFX_MSG_MAP(CMyExtension)
        //}}AFX_MSG_MAP
END_MESSAGE_MAP()
#endif   // 0



/////////////////////////////////////////////////////////////////////////
///
// If your extension will not use MFC, you'll need this code to make
// sure the extension objects can find the resource handle for the
// module.  If you convert your extension to not be dependent on
// MFC, remove the comments around the following AfxGetResourceHandle()
// and DllMain() functions, as well as the g_hInstance global.

/****

static HINSTANCE g_hInstance;

HINSTANCE AFXISAPI AfxGetResourceHandle()
{
        return g_hInstance;
}

BOOL WINAPI DllMain(HINSTANCE hInst, ULONG ulReason,
                                    LPVOID lpReserved)
{
        if (ulReason == DLL_PROCESS_ATTACH)
        {
                g_hInstance = hInst;
        }

        return TRUE;
}

****/
```

Now that you've browsed MY.CPP, let's break it down piece by piece.

When you looked at the code in Listing 9.5, you probably did a double take. Don't worry, you're not seeing things. A `CWinApp` object is needed by all MFC programs. As long as your extension uses MFC, you'll need this object.

Listing 9.5 MY.CPP—CWinApp Declaration

```
///////////////////////////////////////////////////////////////////////
///
// The one and only CWinApp object
// NOTE: You may remove this object if you alter your project to no
// longer use MFC in a DLL.

CWinApp theApp;
```

Listing 9.6 shows `CMyExtension`'s parse map.

Listing 9.6 MY.CPP—*CMyExtension*'s Parse Map

```
///////////////////////////////////////////////////////////////////////
///
// command-parsing map

1   BEGIN_PARSE_MAP(CMyExtension, CHttpServer)
2       // TODO: insert your ON_PARSE_COMMAND() and
3       // ON_PARSE_COMMAND_PARAMS() here to hook up your commands.
4       // For example:

5       ON_PARSE_COMMAND(Default, CMyExtension, ITS_EMPTY)
6       DEFAULT_PARSE_COMMAND(Default, CMyExtension)
7   END_PARSE_MAP(CMyExtension)
```

By default, AppWizard creates a parse map for each MFC-based ISAPI extension. ISAPI parse maps are the way MFC ISAPI developers commonly chart requests from Web clients to specific functions in their extension DLL. Line 1,

```
BEGIN_PARSE_MAP(CMyExtension, CHttpServer)
```

is self-explanatory. This is where your parse map's definition begins. The first parameter, `CMyExtension`, specifies the owner of this parse map. The second must be `CHttpServer`, which is the base class. Now, move down to line 5.

```
ON_PARSE_COMMAND(Default, CMyExtension, ITS_EMPTY)
```

This is where the command-to-function mapping takes place. The first parameter, which in this case is Default, identifies the command name and member function it corresponds with. When using a parse map in ISAPI, each command must have a comparable handler function of the same name.

The second parameter, CMyExtension, represents the class the function is mapped to. The third parameter, ITS_EMPTY, specifies the number and types of arguments the function accepts, which in this case is none.

Line 6 is where we define the command to be used when one is not specified.

```
DEFAULT_PARSE_COMMAND(Default, CMyExtension)
```

The parameters this macro accepts are almost identical to ON_PARSE_COMMAND. In fact, the only difference is that you don't have to specify the number and type of the arguments.

The last line in Listing 9.6 is line 7.

```
END_PARSE_MAP(CMyExtension)
```

BEGIN_PARSE_MAP starts the definition of the parse map and END_PARSE_MAP ends the definition. The only parameter this macro takes is the name of the class that owns this parse map.

Although we've covered each of the entries in Listing 9.6, there's one parse map macro not represented: ON_PARSE_COMMAND_PARAMS. This macro is not part of the parse map created when a new ISAPI extension is started because the only command handler, Default, takes no parameters.

To illustrate this macro, we rewrite our parse map, as follows:

```
  BEGIN_PARSE_MAP(CMyExtension, CHttpServer)
        // TODO: insert your ON_PARSE_COMMAND() and
        // ON_PARSE_COMMAND_PARAMS() here to hook up your commands.
        // For example:

5       ON_PARSE_COMMAND(Default, CMyExtension, ITS_PSTR)
6       ON_PARSE_COMMAND_PARAMS("Name")
        DEFAULT_PARSE_COMMAND(Default, CMyExtension)
  END_PARSE_MAP(CMyExtension)
```

The only lines you should be concerned with are 5 and 6. Notice how, when I add ON_PARSE_COMMAND_PARAMS, I also change ON_PARSE_COMMAND. Earlier, I said that ON_PARSE_COMMAND's third parameter specifies the number and types of arguments the function accepts.

But because we added an argument to ON_PARSE_COMMAND_PARAMS, our command handler is no longer empty. The ITS_PSTR entry means the parameter is a pointer to a string. In MSVC 4.2, ON_PARSE_COMMAND recognizes six different constants as representing data types, as shown in Table 9.2.

Table 9.2 *ON_PARSE_COMMAND* Data Types

Constant	Type
ITS_EMPTY	N/A
ITS_PSTR	string pointer
ITS_I2	short
ITS_I4	long
ITS_R4	float
ITS_R8	double

ON_PARSE_COMMAND_PARAMS is where the parameters accepted in ON_PARSE_COMMAND are specified by the name of the HTML form's input element. These two macros work hand-in-hand. In fact, the only time you shouldn't have the ON_PARSE_COMMAND_PARAMS macro after ON_PARSE_COMMAND, is when the argument parameter of ON_PARSE_COMMAND has a value of ITS_EMPTY.

Here are some simple rules for using these two macros when ON_PARSE_COMMAND does not have an argument value of ITS_EMTPY:

- ON_PARSE_COMMAND_PARAMS must immediately follow the matching ON_PARSE_COMMAND macro.
- For each entry in ON_PARSE_COMMAND, you should have exactly one entry in ON_PARSE_COMMAND_PARAMS.
- Multiple entries in the argument parameter of ON_PARSE_COMMAND and ON_PARSE_COMMAND_PARAMS are separated with a single space, even if they span multiple lines.
- The order in which the data types are declared in ON_PARSE_COMMAND applies to the order in which the names are declared in ON_PARSE_COMMAND_PARAMS.

The last entry in the preceding list may be confusing, so let's look at some examples. For clarity, BEGIN_PARSE_MAP, END_PARSE_MAP, and DEFAULT_PARSE_COMMAND are not present.

```
ON_PARSE_COMMAND(WriteToFile, CSampleExtension, ITS_PSTR ITS_PSTR)
ON_PARSE_COMMAND_PARAMS("Name Country")
```

By now you should be able to recognize immediately what this code does. WriteToFile represents the function and CSampleExtension is the class. WriteToFile takes two string pointers: Name and Country.

This is simple. And since each parameter has the same data type, the order is irrelevant. Now, let's add another parameter:

```
ON_PARSE_COMMAND(WriteToFile, CSampleExtension, ITS_PSTR ITS_PSTR
➥ITS_I2)
ON_PARSE_COMMAND_PARAMS("Age Name Country")
```

A browser sends a command:

```
/scripts/sample.dll?WriteToFile&Age=21&Name=Joe&Country=US
```

Instead of assigning Age the integer 21, this example assigns it the string value of 21. Also, Country is not assigned the string value of US but the integer value of 0.

To fix this problem, we change the order of the variable names in ON_PARSE_COMMAND_PARAMS to match their respective data types declared in ON_PARSE_COMMAND:

```
ON_PARSE_COMMAND(WriteToFile, CSampleExtension, ITS_PSTR ITS_PSTR
➥ITS_I2)
ON_PARSE_COMMAND_PARAMS("Name Country Age")
```

Now the same command yields the anticipated results:

```
Name=Joe
Country=US
Age=21
```

This ends our overview of the parse map. We'll return to it once we reach the actual command handler. For now, let's keep inching our way down the source file.

Listing 9.7 is where your extension object comes to life. As in other object-oriented programs you may have written, before you can access the methods in a class, you must have an object created from that class.

Listing 9.7 MY.CPP—*CMyExtension* Declaration

```
///////////////////////////////////////////////////////////////////////
///
// The one and only CMyExtension object

CMyExtension theExtension;
```

Listing 9.8 begins simply enough. Lines 1 through 3 are the constructor for
CMyExtension. Lines 4 through 6 are the destructor. As in other C++ programs, you
can use these components to initialize and destroy any elements your class uses.

Unless you're already familiar with programming in a multithreaded environment,
you should understand what's involved before using constructors and destructors
in an ISAPI DLL. This is covered in Chapter 18, "Making Your Extensions Thread-
Safe." For now, though, the classes we create don't use their constructors and
destructors, as shown in Listing 9.8.

Listing 9.8 MY.CPP—*CMyExtension's* Startup

```
///////////////////////////////////////////////////////////////////////
///
// CMyExtension implementation

1   CMyExtension::CMyExtension()
2   {
3   }

4   CMyExtension::~CMyExtension()
5   {
6   }

7   BOOL CMyExtension::GetExtensionVersion(HSE_VERSION_INFO* pVer)
8   {
9       // Call default implementation for initialization
10      CHttpServer::GetExtensionVersion(pVer);

11      // Load description string
12      TCHAR sz[HSE_MAX_EXT_DLL_NAME_LEN+1];
13      ISAPIVERIFY(::LoadString(AfxGetResourceHandle(),
                     IDS_SERVER, sz, HSE_MAX_EXT_DLL_NAME_LEN));
14      _tcscpy(pVer->lpszExtensionDesc, sz);
15      return TRUE;
16  }
```

Part
III

Ch
9

Lines 7 through 16 show the GetExtensionVersion()function. This is one of two functions that all ISAPI extensions, MFC and non-MFC, must export. The other, HttpExtensionProc(), is a virtual function that AppWizard does not automatically override.

GetExtensionVersion() is called by your server once when your extension is loaded and does two tasks. The first is to check the extension's ISAPI specification version number and compare it to the server's. The second is to give the server a short text description of the extension.

The default HttpExtensionProc() is shown in Listing 9.9.

Listing 9.9   ISAPI.CPP—*HttpExtensionProc*

```
DWORD CHttpServer::HttpExtensionProc(EXTENSION_CONTROL_BLOCK *pECB)
{
        DWORD dwRet = HSE_STATUS_SUCCESS;
        BOOL bDefault = FALSE;
        LPTSTR pszPostBuffer = NULL;
        LPTSTR pszQuery;
        LPTSTR pszCommand = NULL;
        int nMethodRet;
        LPTSTR pstrLastChar;
        DWORD cbStream = 0;
        BYTE* pbStream = NULL;
        CHttpServerContext ctxtCall(pECB);

        pECB->dwHttpStatusCode = 0;

        ISAPIASSERT(NULL != pServer);
        if (pServer == NULL)
        {
                dwRet = HSE_STATUS_ERROR;
                goto CleanUp;
        }

        // get the query

        if (_tcsicmp(pECB->lpszMethod, szGet) == 0)
        {
                pszQuery = pECB->lpszQueryString;
        }
        else if (_tcsicmp(pECB->lpszMethod, szPost) == 0)
        {
                pszCommand = pECB->lpszQueryString;
                pszPostBuffer = new TCHAR[pECB->cbAvailable + 1];
                pszQuery = GetQuery(&ctxtCall, pszPostBuffer,
                ➥pECB->cbAvailable);
```

```
}
else
{
        ISAPITRACE1("Error: Unrecognized method: %s\n",
        ➥pECB->lpszMethod);
        dwRet = HSE_STATUS_ERROR;
        goto CleanUp;
}

// trim junk that some browsers put at the very end

pstrLastChar = pszQuery + _tcslen(pszQuery) -1;
while ((*pstrLastChar == ' ' || *pstrLastChar == '\n' ||
        *pstrLastChar == '\r') && pstrLastChar > pszQuery)
{
        *pstrLastChar-- = '\0';
}

// do something about it

if (!pServer->InitInstance(&ctxtCall))
        dwRet = HSE_STATUS_ERROR;
else
{
        pECB->dwHttpStatusCode = HTTP_STATUS_OK;
        try {
                nMethodRet = pServer->CallFunction(&ctxtCall,
                ➥pszQuery, pszCommand);
        }
        catch (...)
        {
                ISAPITRACE1("Error: command %s caused an unhandled
                ➥exception!\n",
                        pszQuery);
                nMethodRet = callNoStackSpace;
        }

        // was an error caused by trying to dispatch?

        if (nMethodRet != callOK && pECB->dwHttpStatusCode ==
        ➥HTTP_STATUS_OK)
        {
                dwRet = HSE_STATUS_ERROR;
                switch (nMethodRet)
                {
                case callNoStream:
                        pECB->dwHttpStatusCode =
                        ➥HTTP_STATUS_NO_CONTENT;
                        break;
```

continues

Listing 9.9 Continued

```
                    case callParamRequired:
                    case callBadParamCount:
                    case callBadParam:
                            pECB->dwHttpStatusCode =
                            ➥HTTP_STATUS_BAD_REQUEST;
                            break;

                    case callBadCommand:
                            pECB->dwHttpStatusCode =
                            ➥HTTP_STATUS_NOT_IMPLEMENTED;
                            break;

                    case callNoStackSpace:
                    default:
                            pECB->dwHttpStatusCode =
                            ➥HTTP_STATUS_SERVER_ERROR;
                            break;
                }
        }

        // if there was no error or the user said they handled
        // the error, prepare to spit out the generated HTML

        if (nMethodRet == callOK ||
                OnParseError(&ctxtCall, nMethodRet) == TRUE)
        {
                cbStream = ctxtCall.m_pStream->GetStreamSize();
                pbStream = ctxtCall.m_pStream->Detach();
        }
    }

CleanUp:
        // if there was an error, return an appropriate status
        TCHAR szResponse[64];
        BuildStatusCode(szResponse, pECB->dwHttpStatusCode);

        DWORD dwSize = cbStream - ctxtCall.m_dwEndOfHeaders;
        BYTE* pbContent = NULL;
        BYTE cSaved;

        if (pbStream != NULL)
        {
                cSaved = pbStream[ctxtCall.m_dwEndOfHeaders];
                pbStream[ctxtCall.m_dwEndOfHeaders] = '\0';
                pbContent = &pbStream[ctxtCall.m_dwEndOfHeaders];
        }

        if (!ctxtCall.ServerSupportFunction(
                HSE_REQ_SEND_RESPONSE_HEADER, szResponse, 0, (LPDWORD)
                ➥pbStream) &&
```

```
                    ::GetLastError() != 10054)    // WSAECONNRESET
      {
                pECB->dwHttpStatusCode = HTTP_STATUS_SERVER_ERROR;
                dwRet = HSE_STATUS_ERROR;
#ifdef _DEBUG
                DWORD dwCause = ::GetLastError();
                ISAPITRACE1("Error: Unable to write headers: %8.8X!\n",
                ➡dwCause);
#endif
      }
      else
      {
                if (pbContent != NULL)
                {
                        // write a newline to separate content from headers

                        *pbContent = cSaved;
                        DWORD dwNewLineSize = 2;
                        if (!ctxtCall.WriteClient(_T("\r\n"),
                        ➡&dwNewLineSize, 0) ¦¦
                                !ctxtCall.WriteClient(pbContent, &dwSize, 0))
                        {
                                dwRet = HSE_STATUS_ERROR;
                                pECB->dwHttpStatusCode = HTTP_STATUS_SERVER_
                                ➡ERROR;
                                ISAPITRACE("Error: Unable to write content
                                ➡body!\n");
                        }
                }
                else
                        ISAPITRACE("Error: No body content!\n");
      }

      if (pbStream != NULL)
            ctxtCall.m_pStream->Free(pbStream);

      if (dwRet == HSE_STATUS_SUCCESS)
            pECB->dwHttpStatusCode = HTTP_STATUS_OK;

      if (pszPostBuffer != NULL)
            delete [] pszPostBuffer;

      return dwRet;
}
```

HttpExtensionProc() is the second function that all ISAPI extensions export. Unlike GetExtensionVersion(), which is only called once, HttpExtensionProc() is called by the server each time a client makes a request to your DLL.

The server gives your DLL the necessary connection information through the
EXTENSION_CONTROL_BLOCK (ECB) structure. This structure is shown in Listing 9.10.

**Listing 9.10   HTTPEXT.H—ISAPI *EXTENSION_CONTROL_BLOCK*
Structure**

```
typedef struct _EXTENSION_CONTROL_BLOCK {

    DWORD     cbSize;                      // size of this struct.
    DWORD     dwVersion;                   // version info of this spec
    HCONN     ConnID;                      // Context number not to be
                                           // modified!
    DWORD     dwHttpStatusCode;            // HTTP Status code
    CHAR      lpszLogData[HSE_LOG_BUFFER_LEN];// null terminated
                                           // log info specific to
                                           // this Extension DLL

    LPSTR     lpszMethod;                  // REQUEST_METHOD
    LPSTR     lpszQueryString;             // QUERY_STRING
    LPSTR     lpszPathInfo;                // PATH_INFO
    LPSTR     lpszPathTranslated;          // PATH_TRANSLATED

    DWORD     cbTotalBytes;                // Total bytes indicated from
                                           // client
    DWORD     cbAvailable;                 // Available number of bytes
    LPBYTE    lpbData;                     // pointer to cbAvailable
                                           // bytes

    LPSTR     lpszContentType;             // Content type of client data

    BOOL (WINAPI * GetServerVariable) ( HCONN      hConn,
                                        LPSTR
                                        ➥lpszVariableName,
                                        LPVOID     lpvBuffer,
                                        LPDWORD    lpdwSize );

    BOOL (WINAPI * WriteClient)    ( HCONN      ConnID,
                                     LPVOID     Buffer,
                                     LPDWORD    lpdwBytes,
                                     DWORD      dwReserved );

    BOOL (WINAPI * ReadClient)     ( HCONN      ConnID,
                                     LPVOID     lpvBuffer,
                                     LPDWORD    lpdwSize );

    BOOL (WINAPI * ServerSupportFunction)( HCONN      hConn,
                                           DWORD      dwHSERRequest,
                                           LPVOID     lpvBuffer,
                                           LPDWORD    lpdwSize,
```

```
                              LPDWORD
                              ➥pdwDataType );

} EXTENSION_CONTROL_BLOCK, *LPEXTENSION_CONTROL_BLOCK;
```

Just as all ISAPI extension DLLs must export `GetExtensionVersion()` and `HttpExtensionProc()`, the ECB is a common thread between MFC and non-MFC ISAPI extensions. The ECB is how the server and extension communicate— if your access to the ECB is the `CHttpServerContext` object created in `HttpExtensionProc()`:

```
CHttpServerContext ctxtCall(pECB);
```

Each command handler you create takes a pointer to the `CHttpServerContext` object created in `HttpExtensionProc()`. This pointer gives your functions easy access to the connection-specific information in the ECB and more.

Line 2 in Listing 9.11 shows the bond between your parse map and command handlers.

Listing 9.11 ISAPI.CPP—The Default *HttpExtensionProc()*

```
1        try {
2                nMethodRet = pServer->CallFunction(&ctxtCall,
                 ➥pszQuery, pszCommand);
3        }
4        catch (...)
5        {
6                ISAPITRACE1("Error: command %s caused an unhandled
                 ➥exception!\n",
7                        pszQuery);
8                nMethodRet = callNoStackSpace;
9        }
```

`CHttpServer::CallFunction()` is what the framework uses to find and execute command handlers. Since `CallFunction()` is a virtual function, you can override it and customize how the query string is parsed.

From There to Here

We now know how to use the parse map macros and how our parse map gets connected to our extension. Before we can act on the data sent by a client, however, we need to connect our parse map to our command-handling functions. We do this with the first parameter of ON_PARSE_COMMAND, the command handlers themselves.

Listing 9.12 shows CMyExtension's default command handler.

Listing 9.12   MY.CPP—*CMyExtension*'s Default Command Handler

```
///////////////////////////////////////////////////////////////////////
///
// CMyExtension command handlers

1   void CMyExtension::Default(CHttpServerContext* pCtxt)
2   {
3       StartContent(pCtxt);
4       WriteTitle(pCtxt);

5       *pCtxt << _T("This default message was produced by the Internet");
6       *pCtxt << _T(" Server DLL Wizard. Edit your
        ➥CMyExtension::Default()");
7       *pCtxt << _T(" implementation to change it.\r\n");

8       EndContent(pCtxt);
9   }
```

Recall that Default's ON_PARSE_COMMAND macro had an argument value of ITS_EMPTY when AppWizard generated the ISAPI framework for us. If the macro says it was empty, why does our function show a single parameter?

For our handlers to have access to connection-specific information, each one must take a pointer to the CHttpServerContext object created in HttpExtensionProc(). This pointer is not shown in the parse map because when our command handler is called, the MFC framework automatically passes the CHttpServerContext pointer to our function.

This object is what allows the DLL to handle multiple connections with multiple threads instead of with multiple processes. If we were to edit our parse map's arguments parameter, we would also have to edit the declaration of the command handling function.

To illustrate, let's again look at the parse map we used earlier:

```
ON_PARSE_COMMAND(WriteToFile, CSampleExtension, ITS_PSTR ITS_PSTR
➥ITS_I2)
ON_PARSE_COMMAND_PARAMS("Name Country Age")
```

Given the above macros, our WriteToFile() handler would need to take four, not three, parameters:

```
void CSampleExtension::WriteToFile(CHttpServerContext* pCtxt,
➥LPTSTR pstrName, LPTSTR pstrCountry
                                 INT iAge)
```

If we change our parse map macros to reflect only two parameters, we would also need to change our function once again.

```
ON_PARSE_COMMAND(WriteToFile, CSampleExtension, ITS_PSTR ITS_PSTR)
ON_PARSE_COMMAND_PARAMS("Name Country")

void CSampleExtension::WriteToFile(CHttpServerContext* pCtxt,
➥LPTSTR pstrName, LPTSTR pstrCountry)
```

Notice how the arguments parameter types of ON_PARSE_COMMAND correspond with the types in our command handler. Just as you need to make sure the names in ON_PARSE_COMMAND_PARAMS are in line with the arguments in ON_PARSE_COMMAND, you need to make sure the declarations following the CHttpServerContext pointer in your command handlers match the types in the arguments section of ON_PARSE_COMMAND.

In addition, because you will be manipulating the data sent from a Web browser, the function declaration must also match the order in which you expect to get them. For example, in the previous command handler, we are expecting a name as the first parameter following the CHttpServerContext pointer. If we expected a Country instead, we would have to change not only the ON_PARSE_COMMAND_PARAMS macro but also the position of the variable we expect to hold the Country value.

```
ON_PARSE_COMMAND(WriteToFile, CSampleExtension, ITS_PSTR ITS_PSTR)
ON_PARSE_COMMAND_PARAMS("Country Name")
void CSampleExtension::WriteToFile(CHttpServerContext* pCtxt,
➥LPTSTR pstrCountry, LPTSTR pstrName)
```

Although this method is tedious and needs attention to detail, it keeps you from having to write your own parsing algorithm. MFC does not require you to use parse maps in your ISAPI extension. Instead, the parse maps are supplied as generic tools to speed the development cycle. For more information on parse maps, see Microsoft Visual C++ *Books Online*.

Part
III

Ch
9

Now that you understand a little more about MFC's ISAPI implementation, you're ready to create your form processor. I'll point out common errors and solutions as we go.

The form you'll process is shown in Figure 9.1.

FIG. 9.1
The target HTML form.

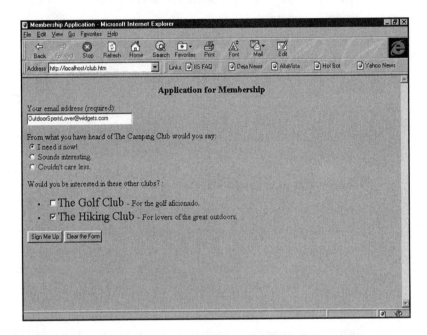

Once again, create a new Project Workspace in Developer Studio. From the New Project Workspace dialog box, select the ISAPI Extension Wizard type and enter **MembrApp** as the project name, as shown in Figure 9.2. Click Create.

The one-step ISAPI Extension Wizard appears. The default settings are just right for our purposes.

We want an extension object and not a filter object so the class name of `CMembrAppExtension` is fine. We'll use the MFC library as a shared DLL to make our extension compact (see Figure 9.3).

Click Finish. The wizard brings up a confirmation dialog box. Pressing OK allows the wizard to create the extension's skeleton code.

FIG. 9.2
The New Project
Workspace dialog
box.

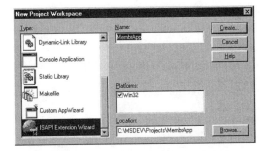

FIG. 9.3
One-step Extension
Wizard.

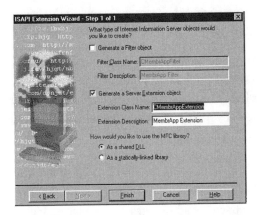

Just as we saw earlier in this chapter, the wizard takes care of many details. It creates a CWinApp object to cover the DllMain startup/shutdown processing. It also creates an exported GetExtensionVersion() and HttpExtensionProc(), which you are familiar with by now.

The wizard creates a derived CHttpServer object, in this example called CMembrAppExtension, shown in Listing 9.13. This object has a parse map, a GetExtensionVersion member function, and a Default function, which does very little at the moment.

Listing 9.13 *CMembrAppExtension*—A CHttpServer Object

```
void CMembrAppExtension::Default(CHttpServerContext* pCtxt)
{
        StartContent(pCtxt);
        WriteTitle(pCtxt);
```

continues

Listing 9.13 Continued

```
        *pCtxt << _T("This default message was produced by the
        ➥Internet");
        *pCtxt << _T(" Server DLL Wizard. Edit your
        ➥CMembrAppExtension::Default()");
        *pCtxt << _T(" implementation to change it.\r\n");

        EndContent(pCtxt);
    }
```

Now that we have constructed the framework using the wizard, we'll build the extension itself. Before we can do this, though, we need to iron out a couple of wrinkles.

First, a DLL needs a host application to run with. Second, because we're using Microsoft Internet Information Server (IIS), our host application is configured to run only as a service. If you are using a different ISAPI Web server, you may need to ask your vendor for instructions.

You need to set up your ISAPI extension to run with IIS and Visual C++ in debug mode in this sequence:

1. Make sure you have set administrative privileges, including the "Act as part of the operating system" and "Log on as a service" for your account.

   To do this, go to the User Manager, Policies/User-Rights, and select the Show Advanced User Rights check box. Select each of the privileges and add your logon to the list of groups and users granted these rights.

2. Go to the Control Panel Services icon, scroll down to the World Wide Web Publishing Service, and stop the service. Only one copy of IIS can successfully run at one time and we'll be running IIS from our debugger.

3. Back at the CMembrAppExtension extension, select Build/Settings and select the Link tab.

4. Type in the full path name of the DLL in the Output File Name text box. Select and copy this path name to the Clipboard.

5. Select the Debug tab and go to the Additional DLLs category. Under Modules, paste the full path name into the first entry for Local Name. This ensures that the symbol table for the DLL is preloaded for debugging.

6. While in the Debug tab dialog box, go to the General category.

7. In the Executable for debug session text box, type in **c:\inetsrv\server\ INetInfo.Exe** or the path for IIS if you installed it in a different directory.

8. In Program Arguments, type in **-e W3Svc**. This allows IIS to start as an application.

9. Save your work. Compile and run the CMembrAppExtension. Wait a few moments for IIS to initialize.

The next steps enable you to run your extension with IIS. If you are using a different ISAPI Web server, you may need to ask your vendor for instructions.

1. Go to the Internet Service Manager and notice that the State for your computer's WWW service says Stopped. Even though IIS is running under the debugger, this is what it says.

2. Double-click the Services computer name to see its properties. When you see the Properties dialog box, you know that IIS is running in debug mode with your extension.

3. Add a virtual directory that points to your debug directory. Select an alias of /MembrApp and be sure to select the Execute check box in the Access group (see Figure 9.4). Turn Read permissions off by making sure the READ check box is not on.

4. Now bring up your favorite browser and enter the URL of the directory you entered above. For example, enter **http://127.0.0.1/MembrApp/ MembrApp.Dll**.

5. At last! You see the output of your extension DLL as follows:

```
This default message was produced by the
Internet Server DLL Wizard. Edit your
CMembrAppExtension::Default()implementation
to change it.
```

FIG. 9.4
Directory properties
for the MembrApp
debug session.

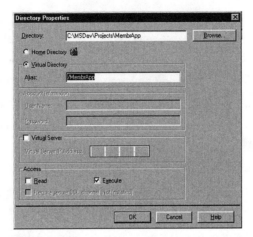

From *GET* to *POST*

In this section, you'll change the Default function to handle GET and POST requests separately. A GET request directs the user to an HTML file holding a basic form. A POST request acknowledges receipt.

You'll also create an HTML file holding the form. Creating a separate HTML file rather than coding HTML into the source code is often preferable. It is certainly more readable for our purposes.

So far, we have taken the supplied CHttpServer member functions StartContent, WriteTitle, and EndContent at face value. They are simple functions that hold the basic elements of an HTML page. To distinguish between a GET and a POST command, we must look at contents of CHttpServerContext, which we discussed earlier.

Change the Default function above as follows:

```
void CMembrAppExtension::Default(CHttpServerContext* pCtxt)
{
    StartContent(pCtxt);
    WriteTitle(pCtxt);
    CString method = pCtxt->m_pECB->lpszMethod;
    if (0 == method.CompareNoCase("POST"))
            *pCtxt << _T("Thanks for the POST!\r\n");
    else
            *pCtxt << _T("<A HREF=\"/club.htm\">Click here to
            ➥continue.</A>\r\n");
    EndContent(pCtxt);
}
```

The CHttpServer-derived class, which in this case is CMembrAppExtension, is instantiated at DLL startup. Each time a request to the DLL is processed by the Web server, the CHttpServer command handler is called with a request context as a parameter. Using stack-based data this way is standard for passing data so that it is thread-safe.

The request context is an instance of the CHttpServerContext class, which holds useful functions and data that are used when processing a request.

In our latest version of the Default function, we access the lpszMethod method string of CHttpServerContext's EXTENSION_CONTROL_BLOCK. We could have called the GetServerVariable function with the REQUEST_METHOD argument.

Both requests yield the same result, whether the request was a GET, as when we typed in the **http://127.0.0.1/MembrApp/ MembrApp.dll? URL**, or whether the request was a POST, as when we submit the club.htm HTML form shown in Listing 9.14.

Listing 9.14   Code for HTML Form

```
<HTML>
<HEAD>
    <TITLE>Membership Application</TITLE>
</HEAD>
<BODY>

<CENTER>
<H3>Application for Membership </H3>
</CENTER>

<FORM action="MembrApp.dll?" method="post">

<P><INPUT type=submit value="Access-Member-Area">
<INPUT type=reset value="Clear Form"></P>

</BODY>
</HTML>
```

You may have noticed that this form POSTs precisely nothing. Now that you have come this far, it is time to start processing some real data.

Adding Some Form Elements

In this section, you'll create a new function to handle the form's submission. To do this, you use the ON_PARSE_COMMAND family of macros covered earlier.

Recall that DEFAULT_PARSE_COMMAND sends a request without a command to the function in its first argument. Requests without a command have nothing following the question mark in their URL.

The wizard sets up a default DEFAULT_PARSE_COMMAND to pass control to the Default function we previously changed. The ON_PARSE_COMMAND and ON_PARSE_COMMAND_PARAMS work together to process non-Default commands.

Remember that ON_PARSE_COMMAND takes three parameters. The first is the name of the function to be called. The second is the CHttpServer class (here CMembrAppExtension). The third defines the number and type of the arguments to the function.

This third parameter can cause some confusion. It can have the ITS_EMPTY argument. Or it can have a combination of the ITS_PSTR (a string) and ITS_I4 (a long integer) arguments, among others.

The confusion arises because this parameter must have at least one argument and can have several. But if this parameter has several arguments, these arguments *must not* be separated by commas or compile errors will result. The ITS_EMPTY parameter shows that there are *no* arguments.

At runtime, this parameter provides crucial information for a special assembler function, _AfxParseCall, borrowed from the low-level OLE Idispatch implementation. This function pushes the right number of arguments onto the stack just before calling your handler function. It is coded differently for each NT-compatible processor type.

The ON_PARSE_COMMAND macros process both the URL query arguments (following the second question mark) and the posted contents of a form.

ON_PARSE_COMMAND_PARAMS gives the names and possible defaults for the arguments.

If you mismatch the number of parameters declared in ON_PARSE_COMMAND, you either get a stack leak from _AfxParseCall or the dreaded Document contains no data error message. So be careful to build your HTML forms, create the parameter maps, and declare the handler functions together so that all the parameters match up.

Change the Form

In your `club.htm` form, add the following lines right before the input-type-submit button directive:

```
Your email address (required):<BR>
<INPUT name="Email" size=40>
<P>
```

This permits the user to enter an e-mail address of up to 40 characters.

Change the Parse Map

Add the following lines to the parse map:

```
ON_PARSE_COMMAND(HandleApp, CMembrAppExtension, ITS_PSTR)
ON_PARSE_COMMAND_PARAMS("Email=unknown")
```

This pair of commands shows that the CMembrAppExtension:: HandleApp function handles one parameter of the string type, the parameter's HTML name is Email, and its default value is Unknown.

Note that although we declare a default value for Email, defaults generally apply only to URL queries. This is because POSTing a form with an empty Email text field overrides any default.

For example, if the user submits the above form without filling out any fields, the value for Email is an empty string and not Unknown.

Declare and Use the Handler Function

Add the function in Listing 9.15 to your CMembrAppExtension class:

Listing 9.15   The Handler Function

```
void CMembrAppExtension::HandleApp(CHttpServerContext* pCtxt,
➥LPCTSTR pstr)
{
     StartContent(pCtxt);
     WriteTitle(pCtxt);
```

continues

Listing 9.15 Continued

```
        CString method = pCtxt->m_pECB->lpszMethod;
        if (0 == method.CompareNoCase("POST"))
                {
                *pCtxt << _T("Thanks for the POST, ");
                CString email = pstr;
                *pCtxt << _T(email);
                *pCtxt << _T("!\r\n");
                }
        else
                *pCtxt << _T("This forms processor expects to be Posted
                ➥to!\r\n");

        EndContent(pCtxt);
}
```

In Listing 9.15, you collect the form data into a convenient string and output a message to the user.

Now you are ready to compile and run the extension again. Be sure that the `club.htm` file resides in your /wwwroot (root HTML) directory. Start your browser, request the URL of **http://localhost/club.htm**, and fill in the form. If all goes well, when you enter your email address of email@net.com, the extension replies

`Thanks for the POST, email@net.com!`

Congratulations!

Add a Radio Button

In this section, we add another input element, the radio button. We learn about error messages that commonly occur during development of an HTML file and its MFC ISAPI forms handler. This leads us to the conclusion that HTML files and their MFC ISAPI forms handlers should be carefully designed and planned in advance.

Change the Form

In your `club.htm` form, add the following lines right before the input-type-submit button directive:

```
<P>
<INPUT type="radio" name="need" value="Need_now">I need it now! <BR>
<INPUT type="radio" name="need" value="sounds_interesting">Sounds
➥interesting. <BR>
<INPUT type="radio" name="need" value="dont_care">Couldn't care
➥less. <BR>
<P>
```

Save the changed form and reload the form in your browser.

Without making any changes to MembrApp (it should still be running), type in your e-mail address again and select the Sounds Interesting radio button.

Submit the form and observe (if you are using Netscape) the Document contains no data browser error message. Other browsers, such as Microsoft Internet Explorer (IE), might reply Unable to open file. Sometimes the browser just produces a blank screen.

Needless to say, this could cause some confusion on the part of the person visiting your Web site. It is not particularly helpful for the developer either when you are trying to track down the cause of an ISAPI problem.

For example, your production Webmaster may innocently decide to add a couple of fields to a form for which you have supplied an MFC forms handler. The Webmaster's problem report might be that nothing significant had been changed but that now "nothing works." Be aware that changing the elements of a form *is* a significant event in the life of an ISAPI MFC DLL.

What Went Wrong?

After CHttpServer::HttpExtensionProc is called and CHttpServer::CallFunction collects its data in pszMethod (HandleApp) and pszParams (Email=email@net.com& need=sounds_interesting), CHttpServer::Lookup finds the parse map entry you entered between BEGIN_PARSE_MAP and END_PARSE_MAP.

Then CHttpServer::PushDefaultStackArgs looks at the arguments supplied, pushing them onto the stack in preparation for the processor-dependent _AfxParseCall. But it finds that the number of arguments does not match the parse map definition. So CallMemberFunc (and CallFunction, in turn) returns callBadParamCount.

A 400 Bad Request response is generated. And because CallMemberFunc encountered an error, it creates no HTML content to be returned.

Part
III

Ch
9

The difficulties are compounded because `CHttpServer::OnParseError` fails to load a string from the resource table and just outputs a TRACE debug message. So Listing 9.16 is a quick override of that function, which at least will give some indication of what is going on:

Listing 9.16   MembrApp.CPP—*OnParseError* Override

```
BOOL CMembrAppExtension::OnParseError(CHttpServerContext* pCtxt,
➥int nMethodRet)
{
      UNUSED(nMethodRet);
      CString errString;

      if (pCtxt->m_pStream != NULL)
      {
            LPCTSTR pszObject = NULL;

            switch (pCtxt->m_pECB->dwHttpStatusCode)
            {
            case HTTP_STATUS_BAD_REQUEST:
                  errString = "HTTP_BAD_REQUEST";
                  if (pCtxt->m_pECB->lpszQueryString)
                        pszObject = pCtxt->m_pECB->lpszQueryString;
                  else
                        pszObject = pCtxt->m_pECB->lpszPathInfo;
                  break;

            case HTTP_STATUS_AUTH_REQUIRED:
                  errString = "HTTP_AUTH_REQUIRED";      break;

            case HTTP_STATUS_FORBIDDEN:
                  errString = "HTTP_FORBIDDEN";      break;

            case HTTP_STATUS_NOT_FOUND:
                  errString = "HTTP_NOT_FOUND";      break;

            case HTTP_STATUS_SERVER_ERROR:
                  errString = "HTTP_SERVER_ERROR";      break;

            case HTTP_STATUS_NOT_IMPLEMENTED:
                  errString = "HTTP_NOT_IMPLEMENTED";
                  pszObject = pCtxt->m_pECB->lpszQueryString;
                  break;

            default:
                  errString = "HTTP_NO_TEXT";
```

```
                        pszObject = (LPCTSTR)
                        ➥pCtxt->m_pECB->dwHttpStatusCode;
                        break;
                }

                CHttpServer::StartContent(pCtxt);

                if (pszObject != NULL)
                {
                        *pCtxt << pszObject;
                        *pCtxt << "\r\n";
                        *pCtxt << errString;
                }
                else
                        *pCtxt << errString;
                CHttpServer::EndContent(pCtxt);
        }

        return TRUE;
}
```

Change the Parse Map

Now that we have learned about keeping the form and the DLL synchronized, change the parse map again to handle the new radio button.

Add another ITS_PSTR to the ON_PARSE_COMMAND macro for HandleApp, remembering to leave just a space and no comma between the arguments. Compile and run the program, and resubmit the form (see Figure 9.5).

FIG. 9.5
Assertion Failed!

CHttpServer::ParseDefaultParams found a problem. Indeed, we forgot to match up ON_PARSE_COMMAND and ON_PARSE_COMMAND_PARAMS. If we continue beyond the assertion failure, our new OnParseError routine tells the browser:

```
HandleApp HTTP_BAD_REQUEST
```

Bad request! OK, let's fix ON_PARSE_COMMAND_PARAMS by adding radioButton. Now compile, run, and reload.

Uh-oh. This time a parameter has a bad format. Of course, we forgot to change the HandleApp function to accommodate the extra parameter we defined in ON_PARSE_COMMAND_PARAMS, as shown in Listing 9.17.

Listing 9.17 MembrApp.CPP—Handle App to Handle *radioButton*

```
void CMembrAppExtension::HandleApp(CHttpServerContext* pCtxt,
➥LPCTSTR pstr, LPCTSTR radio)
{
        StartContent(pCtxt);
        WriteTitle(pCtxt);

        CString method = pCtxt->m_pECB->lpszMethod;
        if (0 == method.CompareNoCase("POST"))
                {
                *pCtxt << _T("Thanks for the POST, ");
                CString email = pstr;
                *pCtxt << _T(email);
                *pCtxt << _T("!\r\n");
                CString msg;
                msg = "You interest is ";
                msg += radio;
                msg += "\r\n";
                *pCtxt << _T(msg);
                }
        else
                *pCtxt << _T("This forms processor expects to be Posted
                ➥to!\r\n");

        EndContent(pCtxt);
}
```

Again, compile, run, reload.

```
HandleApp HTTP_BAD_REQUEST
```

Hmmm. What is it this time? Turns out that the name radioButton in ON_PARSE_COMMAND_PARAMS does not match the name of the radio button in the form. Change the radio button's name to radioButton and reload. (Changing the form rather than changing ON_PARSE_COMMAND_PARAMS means we don't have to recompile.)

Voilà!

The extension replies to the browser:

```
Thanks for the POST, email@net.com! Your interest level in the club
is sounds_interesting.
```

Granted, your usual development process doesn't include mistakes at every turn as it does here. But now we know what causes most errors and how to fix them.

I hope you agree that HTML files and their MFC ISAPI forms handlers should be carefully designed and planned in advance.

Other Form Input Elements

Now that we know the pitfalls to avoid, all that remains is to beef up your code and the HTML file so that you can handle the other elements in our example (see Figure 9.1). Since all input elements in a form are returned as strings, there is no difference in the handling of items such as check boxes and list boxes.

Change the Form

Our final version of the form `club.htm` looks like the code in Listing 9.18.

Listing 9.18   club.htm—Final HTML

```
<HTML>
<HEAD>
    <TITLE>Member Application Form</TITLE>
</HEAD>
<BODY>
<CENTER>
<H3> Application for Membership</H3>
</CENTER>

<FORM action=" MembrApp.dll?HandleApp" method="post">

Your email address (required):<BR>
<INPUT name="Email" size=40>
<P>
From what you have heard of
The Camping Club
would you say:
<br>
<INPUT type="radio" name="radioButton" value="Need_now">I need it
➥now! <BR>
```

continues

Listing 9.18   Continued

```
<INPUT type="radio" name="radioButton" value="sounds_interesting">
➥Sounds interesting. <BR>
<INPUT type="radio" name="radioButton" value="dont_care">Couldn't
➥care less. <BR>
<P>
Would you be interested in these other clubs? :
<UL>
<LI>
<INPUT NAME="TheGolfingClub"
     type=checkbox checked>
<font size = +2>
The Golf Club
</font> - For the golf aficionado.
</LI>
<LI>
<INPUT NAME="TheHikingClub"
     type=checkbox checked>
<font size = +2>
The Hiking Club
</font> - For lovers of the great outdoors.
</LI>
</UL>
<P><INPUT type=submit value="Sign Me Up">
<INPUT type=reset value="Clear the Form"></P>
</FORM>
</BODY>
</HTML>
```

Change the Parse Map

We need to add two more arguments to ON_PARSE_COMMAND and match up their names in ON_PARSE_COMMAND_PARAMS, as follows:

```
ON_PARSE_COMMAND(HandleApp, CMembrAppExtension, ITS_PSTR ITS_PSTR
➥ITS_PSTR ITS_PSTR)
ON_PARSE_COMMAND_PARAMS("Email radioButton=none_expressed
➥TheGolfClub=No TheHikingClub=No")
```

Now we have four string arguments, the last three of which have defaults.

Change the Handler Function

Along with adding the function parameters to handle the two new strings, let's clean up the code and make sure that the necessary email field is entered, as shown in Listing 9.19.

Listing 9.19   MembrApp.CPP—Final Handler

```
void CMembrAppExtension::HandleApp(CHttpServerContext* pCtxt,
➥LPCTSTR emailIn, LPCTSTR radio, LPCTSTR TheGolfClub,
LPCTSTR TheHikingClub)
{
    StartContent(pCtxt);
    WriteTitle(pCtxt);

    CString method = pCtxt->m_pECB->lpszMethod;
    if (0 == method.CompareNoCase("POST"))
            {
            CString email = emailIn;
            if (email.IsEmpty())
                    *pCtxt << _T("Email address is required!");
            else
                    {
                    CString msg;
                    msg += "Your email is ";
                    msg += emailIn;
                    msg += "<P>Your interest level is ";
                    msg += radio;
                    msg += "<P>The Golf Club: ";
                    msg += TheGolfClub;
                    msg += "<P>The Hiking Club: ";
                    msg += TheHikingClub;
                    *pCtxt << _T(msg);
                    }
            }
    else
            *pCtxt << _T("This forms processor expects to be Posted
            ➥to!\r\n");

    EndContent(pCtxt);
}
```

Now our extension can process the form in Figure 9.1.

Full source code and the form itself are on the companion CD to this book. You now have a basis for developing fully functional, interactive applications on the Web.

From Here...

In this chapter, you learned about the framework provided by the ISAPI Extension Wizard and how to build on it using MFC. You use these ISAPI classes to build an ISAPI extension that can process a form.

To learn more about MFC and extending your Web server see the following chapters.

- Chapter 10, "Extending Your Web Server with Extensions," is about extending your Web server using ISAPI extensions. You build a couple of live extensions that you can easily extend and use on your Web server.

- Chapter 15, "Building Filters with MFC ISAPI Classes," is about using MFC to create ISAPI filters. You create a filter using MFC and learn how MFC works. You also learn how to avoid the pitfalls of MFC.

- Chapter 17, "Troubleshooting and Debugging Extensions and Filters," shows you how to avoid common problems with building ISAPI DLLs.

CHAPTER 10

Extending Your Web Server with Extensions

How to build a redirection extension

We extend the server with an extension that allows you to redirect visitors based on selections they make from a drop-down list box.

How to build a Guestbook extension using ODBC

We use ODBC to build a Guestbook extension.

How ODBC works with ISAPI

You learn how to build your own ODBC-enabled ISAPI extensions—with or without MFC.

In this chapter, we increase the scope of your Web server with two ISAPI extensions. These are URLJump, which redirects Web client browsers to another page, and ISAPI Guestbook. We build these extensions from the ground up.

By now you are familiar with the Microsoft Foundation Classes (MFC) implementation of ISAPI, with Open Database Connectivity (ODBC), and with the basics of the Common Gateway Interface (CGI) and Hypertext Transport Protocol (HTTP). In this chapter, we highlight those aspects of ISAPI development as we build our ISAPI extensions. ■

URLJump

Have you ever been to a Web site and wondered how they created those nifty drop-down list boxes that send you to another URL? If you thought it was magic, you'll soon find out that it's simple.

We create these list boxes by sending the client a redirect message. The HTTP 1.1 draft defines a redirect as follows:

> "[The] class of status code indicates that further action needs to be taken by the user agent to fulfill the request."

A redirect tells the browser the page has moved. Although most popular Web browsers automatically request the new URL, some legacy browsers do not.

This means that we need to send a redirect message to the client—and we need to give a Hypertext Markup Language (HTML) body a link to the final page. If we don't send an HTML body, a visitor with an older browser will be left staring at a blank page.

Now that we know what the code does, let's write it:

1. Open Microsoft Developer Studio.
2. Create a new project workspace.
3. Specify ISAPI Extension Wizard as the type and URLJump as the name.
4. Check that a Server Extension object is selected by default.
5. Change the Extension Class Name to CURLJump, click Finish, and click OK.

AppWizard inserts seven files into your project. The files are listed in Table 10.1.

Table 10.1   Files Generated by AppWizard

File Name	Description
URLJUMP.H	Header file for CURLJump
URLJUMP.CPP	Implementation file for CURLJump
URLJUMP.DEF	Exports definition file for the extension
URLJUMP.RC	Resource file for the extension

File Name	Description
STDAFX.H	Standard Application Framework header file for MFC extensions
STDAFX.CPP	Simply #includes STDAFX.H
URLJUMP.PCH	The extension's precompiled header

Constants

URLJump uses only one constant: the virtual path of your script folder, shown in Listing 10.1. If your path is different, you need to change this value.

Part
III

Ch
10

Listing 10.1   URLJUMP.CPP—Constant Used in URLJump

```
/*
     server specific
     THIS VALUE SHOULD BE CHANGED TO REFLECT YOUR SERVER'S SETUP
*/
static const TCHAR SCRIPTPATH[]             = _T("/scripts/");
```

Parse Map

Since URLJump is an MFC ISAPI extension, we use a parse map.
In URLJUMP.CPP, edit the default parse map so it matches this one, as shown in Listing 10.2.

Listing 10.2   URLJUMP.CPP—URLJump's Parse Map

```
BEGIN_PARSE_MAP(CURLJump, CHttpServer)
     ON_PARSE_COMMAND(Test, CURLJump, ITS_EMPTY)

     ON_PARSE_COMMAND(Default, CURLJump, ITS_PSTR)
     ON_PARSE_COMMAND_PARAMS("URL=default")

     DEFAULT_PARSE_COMMAND(Default, CURLJump)
END_PARSE_MAP(CURLJump)
```

As you can see, URLJump accepts two commands, Test and Default. The first function we code is Default(), as shown in Listing 10.3.

Listing 10.3   URLJUMP.CPP—*CURLJump*'s Default Command Handler

```
void CURLJump::Default(CHttpServerContext* pCtxt, LPTSTR pURL)
{
StartContent(pCtxt);
WriteTitle(pCtxt);

DWORD   dwBuf = sizeof(pURL);

/*
      Send the redirect message
*/
if(!pCtxt->ServerSupportFunction(HSE_REQ_SEND_URL_REDIRECT_RESP, pURL, &dwBuf, NULL))
{
*pCtxt <<      "<center>Redirect message could not be sent</center>";
return;
}
/*
      this code should execute only if the user's browser doesn't
      support automatic redirection
*/
*pCtxt << "<center>Your browser does not support automatic redirection</center>";
*pCtxt << "<br>";
*pCtxt << "<center>To upgrade, click <a href=\"http://www.microsoft.com/ie/
➥ie.htm\">here</a></center>";
*pCtxt << "<br>";
*pCtxt << "<center>To go to the anticipated URL, click <a href=" << pURL <<
➥">here</a></center>";
EndContent(pCtxt);
}
```

The line statement

```
pCtxt->ServerSupportFunction(HSE_REQ_SEND_URL_REDIRECT_RESP, pURL,
➥&dwBuf, NULL)
```

sends a 302 Moved Temporarily redirect message to the client. If the client does
not accept automatic redirection, it can upgrade to Microsoft Internet Explorer
(IE) and get a link to the intended page.

TIP If you need to send a different redirect status code, such as 301 Moved Permanently or
303 See Other, you can do this by manipulating the header information before it's sent to
the client.

Now let's override `WriteTitle()` so it fits our extension, just in case we have a visitor with an older browser. To do this, open `ClassWizard` and scroll down using the Messages list box until you see `WriteTitle`.

Click `WriteTitle`, click Add Function, and click Edit Code. Edit `WriteTitle()` so it looks like the code in Listing 10.4.

Listing 10.4   URLJUMP.CPP—Overridden *WriteTitle* Function

```
void CURLJump::WriteTitle(CHttpServerContext* pCtxt) const
{
        *pCtxt      <<      "<title>SE Using ISAPI</title>";

}
```

Testing the Redirection

URLJump includes a second command handler, `Test`. This makes it easy for others to put the dynamic link library (DLL) on their server and make sure it's working properly. Open URLJUMP.CPP in your editor and add the `Test()` function after `Default()`.

Listing 10.5   URLJUMP.CPP—*CURLJump*'s Test Command Handler

```
void CURLJump::Test(CHttpServerContext* pCtxt)
{
        StartContent(pCtxt);
        WriteTitle(pCtxt);

        /*
                HTML for the test page
        */
        *pCtxt   <<      "<body bgcolor=\"#ffffff\" test=\"#000000\">\n";
        *pCtxt   <<      "<font face=Arial>\n";
        *pCtxt   <<      "<font size=+2><b>URLJump Test
                        ➥Page</b></font><br><br>\n";
        *pCtxt   <<      "<center>\n";
        *pCtxt   <<      "This page tests our URLJump ISAPI
                        ➥Extension<br>\n";
        *pCtxt   <<      "View this page's source code to see how URLJump
                        ➥is used\n<br><br><br>\n\n";
```

continues

Listing 10.5   Continued

```
     *pCtxt  <<      "<!--Your form action statement should look
                     ➥like this.  Be sure to use the POST
                     ➥method or you'll get an error-->\n";
     *pCtxt  <<      "<form action=\"" << SCRIPTPATH <<
                     ➥"urljump.dll\" method=post>\n";
     *pCtxt  <<      "<select name=\"URL\">\n\n";
     *pCtxt  <<      "<!--Notice how the URL is set as the value
                     ➥of each option-->\n";
     *pCtxt  <<      "<!--For the extension to work properly, you
                     ➥must follow this example-->\n";
     *pCtxt  <<      "<option value=\"http://rampages.onramp.net/
                     ➥~steveg/isapi.html\">The ISAPI
                     ➥Developer's Site\n";
     *pCtxt  <<      "<option value=\"http://rampages.onramp.net/
                     ➥~steveg/isapifaq.html\">ISAPI
                     ➥Frequently Asked Questions\n";
     *pCtxt  <<      "<option value=\"http://microsoft.ease.lsoft.com/
                     ➥archives/isapi.html\">ISAPI Issues
                     ➥Mailing List Archive\n";
     *pCtxt  <<      "<option value=\"http://rampages.onramp.net/
                     ➥~steveg/iis.html\">IIS Frequently
                     ➥Asked Questions\n\n";
     *pCtxt  <<      "<!--Notice how the next value is set to
                     ➥the script's URL. This let's us
                     ➥section off our drop down list box
                     ➥to avoid an error-->\n";
     *pCtxt  <<      "<option value=\"" << SCRIPTPATH <<
                     ➥"urljump.dll?Test\">===== NEWS
                     ➥LINKS =====\n\n";
     *pCtxt  <<      "<option value=\"http://www.cnn.com/
                     ➥\">CNN Online\n";
     *pCtxt  <<      "<option value=\"http://www.usatoday.com/
                     ➥\">USA Today\n";
     *pCtxt  <<      "<option value=\"http://www.cbs.com/news/
                     ➥\">CBS News\n";
     *pCtxt  <<      "</select>\n";
     *pCtxt  <<      "<br><br><br><br>\n";
     *pCtxt  <<      "<input type=submit value=\"Test It\">\n";
     *pCtxt  <<      "<input type=reset value=\"Reset\">\n";
     *pCtxt  <<      "</form>\n";
     *pCtxt  <<      "</center>\n";
     *pCtxt  <<      "</font>\n";
     *pCtxt  <<      "</body>\n";
     EndContent(pCtxt);

}
```

Test() just sends a "quicky" Web page. This allows the Webmaster to install the
script and verify that it's working. It's one less file to distribute.

N O T E For those of you who are new to CGI, some potential problems are lurking. Carefully examining the `Test()` command handler will reveal them.

Using URLJump

Because this section deals mainly with calling the DLL from a Web page, we include only the dynamically generated HTML.

The easiest way to use URLJump is to create an HTML-based form with one select element, one submit button, and one reset button. Name the select element URL because this is what `Default()` expects.

For each option on the list, specify the URL to which you want the client directed. Immediately following the `OPTION` tag, enter the characters you want displayed in the list box. Here's a simple example:

```
<form action="/scripts/urljump.dll?" method=post>
      <select name="URL">
            <option value=" http://www.mcp.com/que/">QUE Publishing
            ➡Home Page
      </select>
</form>
```

The rest is covered in CGI, HTTP, and HTML references. Some of the ones that are used are shown in Table 10.2.

Part
III

Ch
10

Table 10.2   CGI, HTTP, and HTML References

Title	Author(s)	ISBN/Location
SE Using CGI	Jeffry Dwight and Michael Erwin	0-7897-0740-3
HTML Quick Reference	Robert Mullen	0-7897-0867-1
Webmaster's Professional Ref	Loren Buhle, Mark Pesce, Vinay Kumar, et al.	1-56205-473-2
"Hyper Text Transfer Protocol"	R. Fielding, J. Gettys, J. C. Mogul, H. Frystyk, T. Berners-Lee	http://www.w3. org/pub/WWW/ Protocols/

Now on to our Guestbook.

ISAPI Guestbook

I know—just what the Web needs—yet another guestbook. In my defense, a guestbook seems like the perfect example. The meaning of a guestbook is universal. No matter what the context, a guestbook in its simplest sense is a storage facility that allows visitors to leave their mark.

Furthermore, it's easy to create and doesn't need complex queries or coding. Our guestbook only has eight fields and fits nicely into a single table.

I admit that using Microsoft Structured Query Language (SQL) Server 6.x for such a task is like using a sledge hammer on a push pin. But at this point, that's probably not such a bad idea.

Our guestbook is designed to be a simple extension that fills a real-world need. Ok, maybe not exactly a *need*, but you get the idea.

When we finish our extension, you'll have a fully functioning guestbook that visitors to your site can sign. And you'll know how to build your own ODBC-enabled ISAPI extensions, with or without MFC.

 If you decide to use this guestbook on your Web site, you may want to think about removing the code that allows others to edit and delete guestbook entries.

Before You Begin

Although you can configure the data source to work with another SQL database server, the following instructions are for Microsoft SQL Server:

1. In Microsoft SQL Enterprise Manager, create a new database named Guestbook.
2. Close Enterprise Manager and open the script in Microsoft ISQL/W.
3. Select the Guestbook database from the DB drop-down box.
4. Open the GUESTBOOK.SQL file on the companion CD to this book.
5. Execute the query to create the Guestbook table.

Before visitors to your Web site can access this data source, you'll need to designate it as a System Data Source name (DSN). To make this a DSN, do the following:

1. From Control Panel, select the ODBC32 applet and click System DSN.

2. When the System Data Sources dialog box appears, click Add.

3. Select the appropriate ODBC driver for your database server and click Setup.

4. Specify Guestbook as the Data Source Name and database.

5. Close the System Data Source dialog box and the Data Sources dialog box.

Figure 10.1 shows the System Data Sources dialog box in Windows NT Server 3.51.

FIG. 10.1

System Data Sources dialog box in Windows NT Server 3.51.

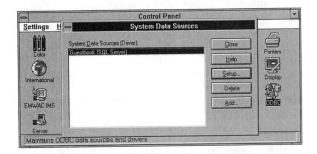

 T I P The System DSN specifies data sources that are local to a computer versus dedicated to a user. Any user with the right privileges can use a System DSN. So any ODBC ISAPI extension you create should use a System Data Source Name (DSN).

We use MFC's ISAPI `CHttpServer` and `CHttpServerContext` classes to create the ISAPI Guestbook. To use this code for the guestbook, you need Microsoft Visual (MSVC) C++ 4.2 or higher.

Although MSVC 4.1 allows you to create ISAPI extensions, the database `CDatabase` and `CRecordset` classes are not thread-safe. Therefore, you should not use them in a multithreaded environment unless you apply some form of thread synchronization.

This is usually done by putting susceptible code in a critical section. For more information on critical sections, see Chapter 18, "Making Your Extensions Thread-Safe," or see Microsoft Visual C++ *Books Online*.

As an alternative, you can code the ISAPI extension using MFC. But use the ODBC API directly instead of `CDatabase` and `CRecordset`. (Chapter 18 also covers multithreading.) In addition, I've found the references in Table 10.3 handy.

Table 10.3   References on Multithreading

Title	Author	ISBN
The Revolutionary Guide to MFC4	Mike Blasczak	1-874416-92-3
Advanced Windows	Jeffrey Richter	1-55615-677-4

Let's get started.

 TIP You can use Microsoft's data access objects (DAO) in CGI scripts built as console applications. But trying to use them in an ISAPI DLL can be fatal. The reason for this goes beyond normal thread safety. For more information, see Technical Note 67 in the *Microsoft KnowledgeBase*.

Open Developer Studio and create a new project workspace with ISAPI Extension Wizard as the type and Guestbook as the name (see Figure 10.2).

FIG. 10.2
Developer Studio's
New Project
Workspace
dialog box.

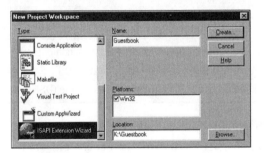

Generate a Server Extension Object should be selected by default (see Figure 10.3). Change the Extension Class Name to CGuestbook, click Finish, and click OK to have AppWizard create your ISAPI skeleton project.

Remember from Chapter 9, "Building Extensions with MFC," that you have seven files added to your project. These files are listed in Table 10.4.

Table 10.4   Files Generated by AppWizard

File Name	Description
GUESTBOOK.H	Header file for CGuestbook
GUESTBOOK.CPP	Implementation file for CGuestbook

File Name	Description
GUESTBOOK.DEF	Exports definition file for the extension
GUESTBOOK.RC	Resource file for the extension
STDAFX.H	Standard Application Framework header file for MFC extensions
STDAFX.CPP	Simply #includes STDAFX.H
GUESTBOOK.PCH	The extension's precompiled header

FIG. 10.3
Developer Studio's
ISAPI Extension
Wizard.

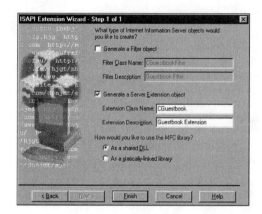

Part
III

Ch
10

AppWizard does not automatically include the header file you need for database applications when building an MFC ISAPI extension. So we have to manually enter the file name. Open STDAFX.H and add the following line to the end:

```
#include <afxdb.h>
```

Now that our extension has access to MFC's database classes, let's add the data source and the CGuestbookQuery class. CGuestbookQuery will be the interface to our database.

To add CGuestbookQuery, click View, ClassWizard. This opens the MFC ClassWizard (see Figure 10.4). Click Add Class and click New.

The Create New Class dialog box opens (see Figure 10.5). In the Name edit box, type **CGuestbookQuery**. From the drop-down box, select CRecordset, and click Create.

The Database Options dialog box appears, as shown in Figure 10.6.

FIG. 10.4
ClassWizard.

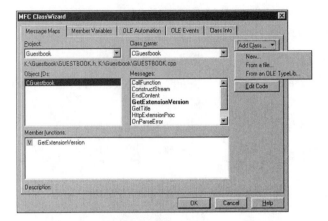

FIG. 10.5
Create New Class
dialog box.

FIG. 10.6
Database Options
dialog box.

Select Guestbook as the datasource and Dynaset as the Recordset Type.
Select Bind All Columns and click OK.

Depending on how your system is set up, you may be prompted to log into SQL
Server. If so, enter your login ID and password, if any. Click OK and select
dbo.Guestbook in the Select Database Tables dialog box (see Figure 10.7).
Click OK.

FIG. 10.7
Select Database
Tables dialog box.

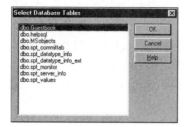

Click OK to close ClassWizard. Notice the File View in your Project Workspace
(shown in Figure 10.8).

FIG. 10.8
Project Workspace
File view.

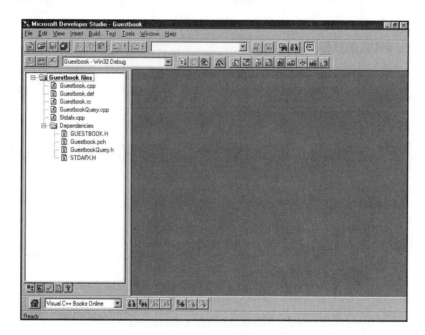

Two files were added to your project, listed in Table 10.5.

Table 10.5   Files Added by ClassWizard

File Name	Description
GUESTBOOKQUERY.H	Header file for CGuestbookQuery
GUESTBOOKQUERY.CPP	Implementation file for CGuestbookQuery

Even though ClassWizard was nice enough to add the files to your project, for your extension to have access to CGuestbookQuery, you need to add an entry to your CGuestbook implementation file. Open GUESTBOOK.CPP and add

```
#include "GuestbookQuery.h"
```

after the line following the last #include directive.

Virtually all ODBC ISAPI extensions you create will follow the steps listed in this section. Now we need to create the code for the ISAPI Guestbook extension.

Constants

We'll need several items in our extension, such as the server's Base Reference and the ISAPI scripts folder. We add these values after the last #include directive in Listing 10.6.

Listing 10.6   GUESTBOOK.CPP—Constants Used in ISAPI Guestbook

```
#define NULLSTRING                              " "
#define MAX_BUFFER                              256
/*      maximum buffer size    */

//      protocol
static const LPTSTR  HTTP_USER_AGENT  =    _T("HTTP_USER_AGENT");
static const TCHAR   HTTP_PROTOCOL[]  =    _T("http://");

//      database
static const TCHAR     CONNECTSTRING[]      =      _T("ODBC;UID=sa;
                                                   ➥PWD=;");
static const TCHAR     GUESTBOOKDB[]        =      _T("Guestbook");
                                                   ➥        //    DSN

//      helper
static const TCHAR   HTML[]                 =      _T("HTML");
```

```
//      server specific
/*      THESE VALUES SHOULD BE CHANGED TO REFLECT YOUR SERVER SETUP  */
static const TCHAR    BASEHREF[]              =
➥_T("http://test.midnite.net/");
static const TCHAR    SCRIPTPATH[]            =          _T("/scripts/");
```

The first two lines are directives to the compiler telling it to put `""` and 256 wherever NULLSTRING and MAX_BUFFER occur, respectively. NULLSTRING helps test whether or not a user entered a value in a necessary field. MAX_BUFFER is used to set the size of the buffer into which the user's browser is inserted.

The line

```
static const LPTSTR  HTTP_USER_AGENT  =  T("HTTP_USER_AGENT");
```

is used with CHttpServerContext::GetServerVariable() to detect the user's browser. Not all browsers accept this variable.

Next, the line

```
static const TCHAR   HTTP_PROTOCOL[]  =  T("http://");
```

identifies the HTTP protocol. This value is used to check whether or not a user has entered a home page in his or her guestbook entry.

This line

```
static const TCHAR   CONNECTSTRING[]    =  T("ODBC;UID=sa;PWD=;");
```

holds the text sent to SQL Server when the data source was opened and the line

```
static const TCHAR   GUESTBOOKDB[]       =  T("Guestbook");          //DSN
```

names Guestbook as the data source. The line

```
static const TCHAR   HTML[]                =  _T("HTML");
```

is used with the LoadLongResource() function to identify Web pages bound to the ISAPI DLL as custom resources.

The last two constants

```
static const TCHAR   BASEHREF[]        =  T("http://test.midnite.net/");
static const TCHAR   SCRIPTPATH[]      =  T("/scripts/");
```

are server-specific and should be changed to reflect your server's setup before you build and use ISAPI Guestbook. BASEHREF specifies the server's root folder and

SCRIPTPATH is the folder holding the Guestbook DLL. Setting these constants allows others to easily reuse this extension.

Parse Map

Recall from Chapter 9, "Building Extensions with MFC," that the MFC ISAPI extensions use parse maps. The parse map for ISAPI Guestbook is shown in Listing 10.7.

Listing 10.7   GUESTBOOK.CPP—*CGuestbook*'s Parse Map

```
BEGIN_PARSE_MAP(CGuestbook, CHttpServer)
      ON_PARSE_COMMAND(Add, CGuestbook, ITS_EMPTY)

      ON_PARSE_COMMAND(Find, CGuestbook, ITS_PSTR)
      ON_PARSE_COMMAND_PARAMS("Command=Details")

      ON_PARSE_COMMAND(Details, CGuestbook, ITS_PSTR)
      ON_PARSE_COMMAND_PARAMS("Name")

      ON_PARSE_COMMAND(Delete, CGuestbook, ITS_PSTR)
      ON_PARSE_COMMAND_PARAMS("Name=default")

      ON_PARSE_COMMAND(Edit, CGuestbook, ITS_PSTR)
      ON_PARSE_COMMAND_PARAMS("Name")

      ON_PARSE_COMMAND(WriteGuestbookEntry, CGuestbook, ITS_PSTR ITS_PSTR
                                                         ITS_PSTR ITS_PSTR
                                                         ITS_PSTR ITS_PSTR
                                                         ITS_PSTR ITS_PSTR)
      ON_PARSE_COMMAND_PARAMS("Name=default Browser=default
                              ➥Email=default "
                              "HomePage=default City=default
                              ➥State=default "
                              "Country=default Comments=default")

      ON_PARSE_COMMAND(FindGuestbookEntry, CGuestbook, ITS_PSTR ITS_PSTR
                                                       ITS_PSTR ITS_PSTR
                                                       ITS_PSTR ITS_PSTR
                                                       ITS_PSTR ITS_PSTR)
      ON_PARSE_COMMAND_PARAMS("Name=default Browser=default
                              ➥Email=default "
                              "HomePage=default City=default
                              ➥State=default "
                              "Country=default Command=default")
```

```
        ON_PARSE_COMMAND(EditGuestbookEntry, CGuestbook, ITS_PSTR ITS_PSTR
                                                          ITS_PSTR ITS_PSTR
                                                          ITS_PSTR ITS_PSTR
                                                          ITS_PSTR ITS_PSTR)

        ON_PARSE_COMMAND_PARAMS("Name=default Browser=default
                                ➥Email=default "
                                "HomePage=default City=default
                                ➥State=default "
                                "Country=default Comments=default")

        ON_PARSE_COMMAND(Default, CGuestbook, ITS_EMPTY)
        DEFAULT_PARSE_COMMAND(Default, CGuestbook)
END_PARSE_MAP(CGuestbook)
```

 When you create parse maps and SQL queries that span multiple lines, make sure you include spaces in the right places. If you don't, your extension will wander off into la-la land and when you find the bug, you might just inflict bodily harm on yourself or others.

As you can see, Guestbook accepts nine commands: Add, Delete, Find, Details, Edit, WriteGuestbookEntry, FindGuestbookEntry, EditGuestbookEntry, and Default. Open GUESTBOOK.CPP and edit your parse map so it is the same as the one in Listing 10.7.

The *Default* Function

The Default command corresponds with the Default function (see Listing 10.8).

Listing 10.8 GUESTBOOK.CPP—CGuestbook's *Default* Command Handler

```
void CGuestbook::Default(CHttpServerContext* pCtxt)
{
        StartContent(pCtxt);
        WriteTitle(pCtxt);

        Cstring         strOutput;
        Cstring         strTemp;
        Cstring         strTest;

        //      try to load the html document
        if(LoadLongResource(strTemp, IDS_HTML_MAIN))
```

continues

Listing 10.8   Continued

```
        strOutput.Format(strTemp, BASEHREF,  /*      server base
                                                  ➥url*/
                                 SCRIPTPATH, /*      script folder  */
                                 SCRIPTPATH, /*      script folder  */
                                 SCRIPTPATH, /*      script folder  */
                                 SCRIPTPATH);/*      script folder  */
    else
        strOutput.Format(IDS_ERROR, "Default",/* function */
                                    "LoadLongResource"); /*
                                    ➥operation */


    /*      send the result        */
    *pCtxt  <<      strOutput;


    EndContent(pCtxt);
}
```

As you saw in Chapter 9, "Building Extensions with MFC," all MFC ISAPI commands take a pointer to a CHttpServerContext as their first parameter. In Default(), this is the only parameter because this function just sends the main menu of the script.

Default() makes a call to the LoadLongResource() function to copy into a CString object an HTML document bound to the DLL as a resource. This function was included as part of Microsoft's WWWQuote example and is very handy (see Listing 10.9).

Listing 10.9   GUESTBOOK.CPP—*LoadLongResource* from Microsoft's WWWQuote Sample ISAPI Extension

```
/*
    LoadLongResource()
    taken from Microsoft's WWWQuote sample
*/
BOOL CGuestbook::LoadLongResource(CString& str, UINT nID)
{
    HRSRC hRes;
    HINSTANCE hInst = AfxGetResourceHandle();
    BOOL bResult = FALSE;

    hRes = FindResource(hInst, MAKEINTRESOURCE(nID), HTML);
    if (hRes == NULL)
```

```
                ISAPITRACE1("Error: Resource %d could not
                        ➥be found\r\n", nID);
        else
        {
                DWORD dwSize = SizeofResource(hInst, hRes);
                if (dwSize == 0)
                {
                        str.Empty();
                        bResult = TRUE;
                }
                else
                {
                        LPTSTR pszStorage = str.GetBufferSetLength
                        ➥(dwSize);

                        HGLOBAL hGlob = LoadResource(hInst, hRes);
                        if (hGlob != NULL)
                        {
                                LPVOID lpData = LockResource(hGlob);

                                if (lpData != NULL)
                                {
                                        memcpy(pszStorage, lpData, dwSize);
                                        bResult = TRUE;
                                }

                                FreeResource(hGlob);
                        }
                }
        }
#ifdef _DEBUG
        if (!bResult)
                str.Format(_T("<b>Could not find string %d</b>"), nID);
#endif

        return bResult;
}
```

Now you need to override the WriteTitle() function. Open ClassWizard and activate the Message Maps tab. Under the Messages list box, scroll down until you see WriteTitle.

Click WriteTitle, click Add Function, and click Edit Code. Edit WriteTitle so it looks like the code in Listing 10.10.

Listing 10.10 GUESTBOOK.CPP—*CGuestbook's WriteTitle* Function

```
/*
       WriteTitle()
       send the page title
*/
void CGuestbook::WriteTitle(CHttpServerContext* pCtxt) const
{
       CString strOutput;
       CString strTitle;

       strTitle.LoadString(IDS_TITLE);

       strOutput.Format("<title>%s</title>", strTitle);

       *pCtxt <<       strOutput;
}
```

Be sure to remove the line

```
CHttpServer::WriteTitle(CHttpServerContext* pCtxt);
```

If you don't, your title won't appear. To add the right string resource, click Insert, Resource and double-click String Resource. The identifier for your title, as you can see in Listing 10.10 above, is IDS_TITLE and it should be ISAPI Guestbook.

Adding a Guestbook Entry

The next function we enter is Add. Like Default(), the only parameter it takes is a pointer to a CHttpServerContext object. The Add function is shown in Listing 10.11.

Listing 10.11 GUESTBOOK.CPP—*CGuestbook's Add* Command Handler

```
/*
       Add()
       this command loads the form that allows the user to
       enter their information and attempts to detect their browser
*/
void CGuestbook::Add(CHttpServerContext* pCtxt)
{
       StartContent(pCtxt);
       WriteTitle(pCtxt);

       Cstring        strTemp;
       Cstring        strOutput;
```

```
Cstring          strBrowser     = GetHttpVariable(pCtxt,
➥HTTP_USER_AGENT);
/*      try to load the html document */
if(LoadLongResource(strTemp, IDS_HTML_ADD))

        strOutput.Format(strTemp, BASEHREF,    /* server root    */
                                  SCRIPTPATH,  /* script folder  */
                                  strBrowser); /* user's browser */
else
        strOutput.Format(IDS_ERROR, "Add",/* function  */
                                    "LoadLongResource");
                                    ➥/* operation */

    /* send the result    */
    *pCtxt <<      strOutput;

    EndContent(pCtxt);
}
```

Add() does a little more than Default(). It also tries to detect the user's browser by calling the GetHttpVariable() function, as shown in Listing 10.12.

Listing 10.12 GUESTBOOK.CPP—*GetHttpVariable* Tries to Retrieve a Server Variable

```
/*
    GetHttpVariable()
    attempts to retrieve a server variable
*/
CString CGuestbook::GetHttpVariable(CHttpServerContext* pCtxt,
➥LPTSTR pstrVar)
{
    LPTSTR        pstrBuf[MAX_BUFFER];
    Cstring       strVar;
    DWORD         dwSize;
    UINT          nRetCode;

    nRetCode = pCtxt->GetServerVariable(pstrVar, pstrBuf, &dwSize);

    switch(nRetCode)
    {
    case ERROR_INVALID_PARAMETER:
        return "Bad connection handle";
        break;

    case ERROR_INVALID_INDEX:
        return "Bad or unsupported variable identifier";
        break;
```

continues

Listing 10.12   Continued

```
            return "Buffer too small";
            break;

    case ERROR_MORE_DATA:
            return "Buffer too small, only part of data returned. "
                        "The total size of the data is not returned.";
            break;

    case ERROR_NO_DATA:
            return "The data requested is not available.";
            break;
    }

    strVar = (LPCTSTR)pstrBuf;

    return strVar;

}
```

GetHttpVariable() takes two parameters, a pointer to a CHttpServerContext object and a pointer to a null-terminated Windows or Unicode character string (LPTSTR). The return value is a CString object holding either the server variable or an error message.

Since Add() and GetHttpVariable() are custom functions, we need to add them to the declaration of CGuestbook. While we're here, we should also add LoadLongResource(). Open GUESTBOOK.H and add the following lines to the public: section of the class declaration:

```
//      ISAPI Commands
        void    Add(CHttpServerContext* pCtxt);

//      Helpers
        BOOL    LoadLongResource(CString &str, UINT nID);
        CString GetHttpVariable(CHttpServerContext* pCtxt, LPTSTR
        ➥pstrVar);
```

The corresponding function to Add() is WriteGuestbookEntry(), shown in Listing 10.13.

Listing 10.13   GUESTBOOK.CPP—CGuestbook's *WriteGuestbookEntry* Command Handler

```
/*
        WriteGuestbookEntry()
        writes an new entry into the guestbook
*/
void CGuestbook::WriteGuestbookEntry(CHttpServerContext* pCtxt,
                                LPTSTR pstrName,
                                /*user's name*/
                                LPTSTR pstrBrowser,
                                /*user's browser*/
                                LPTSTR pstrEmail,
                                /*user's e-mail address*/
                                LPTSTR pstrHomePage,
                                /*user's home page url */
                                LPTSTR pstrCity,
                                *user's city*/
                                LPTSTR pstrState,
                                /*user's state or province */
                                LPTSTR pstrCountry,
                                /*user's country*/
                                LPTSTR pstrComments)
                                /*user's comments*/
{
        StartContent(pCtxt);
        WriteTitle(pCtxt);

        Cstring             strQuery;
        Cstring             strOutput;
        Cstring             strHeader;
        Cdatabase     db;

        strHeader.Format(IDS_STDHEADER, BASEHREF);
        *pCtxt <<       strHeader;

        /*    make sure the required fields have values    */
        if(!strcmp(pstrName,NULLSTRING) ¦¦
        ➥!strcmp(pstrCity,NULLSTRING) ¦¦
          !strcmp(pstrState,NULLSTRING) ¦¦
          ➥!strcmp(pstrCountry,NULLSTRING))
        {
                *pCtxt <<       "<br><center>"
                        <<      "Please be certain to enter your
                                ➥Name, City,"
                        <<      " State and Country.  Thank you."
                        <<      "</center>";

                return;
        }
```

continues

Listing 10.13   Continued

```
        if(!strcmp(pstrHomePage,HTTP_PROTOCOL))
                pstrHomePage = NULLSTRING;

    /*    format the query       */
    strQuery.Format("Name = '%s'", pstrName);

    /*    try to open the database, exit if it can't be opened */
    if(!db.Open(GUESTBOOKDB,       /*lpszDSN*/
            FALSE,                 /*bExclusive*/
            FALSE,                 /*bReadOnly*/
            CONNECTSTRING,         /*lpszConnect*/
            FALSE))                /*bUseCursorLib*/
    {
        *pCtxt <<       "Could not open database";
        return;
    }

    CGuestbookQuery        rsGuestbook(&db);

    /*    assign the query to the recordset      */
    rsGuestbook.m_strFilter = strQuery;

    /*    try to open the recordset, if it can't be opened catch
          the exception and show the user        */
    try
    {
        if(rsGuestbook.Open())
        {
                /*    if the record is already on file,
                      this should return FALSE, then
                      notify the user        */
                if(!rsGuestbook.IsBOF())
                        strOutput.Format(IDS_ONFILE,
                        ➥pstrName, SCRIPTPATH);
                else
                {
                        rsGuestbook.AddNew();

                        /*    assign the values     */
                        rsGuestbook.m_Name     = pstrName;
                        /*user's name*/
                        rsGuestbook.m_Browser = pstrBrowser;
                        /*user's browser*/
                        rsGuestbook.m_Email    = pstrEmail;
                        /*user's e-mail address*/
                        rsGuestbook.m_HomePage = pstrHomePage;
                        /*user's home page*/
```

```
                                rsGuestbook.m_City      = pstrCity;
                                /* user's city*/
                                rsGuestbook.m_State     = pstrState;
                                /*user's state */
                                rsGuestbook.m_Country = pstrCountry;
                                /*user's country*/
                                rsGuestbook.m_Comments = pstrComments;
                                /*user's comments*/

                                /*      now try to add the record to
                                /* the database    */
                                if(rsGuestbook.Update())
                                        strOutput.Format(IDS_THANKYOU,
                                        ➥pstrName, SCRIPTPATH);
                                else
                                        strOutput.Format(IDS_NOUPDATE,
                                        ➥SCRIPTPATH);
                        }
                }
                else
                        /*      wonder what happened here???   */
                        strOutput.Format(IDS_UNKNOWN, SCRIPTPATH);
        }
        catch(CDBException* pEX)
        {
                TCHAR   szError[1024];

                /*    get the error message   */
                if(pEX->GetErrorMessage(szError, sizeof(szError)))
                        strOutput.Format(IDS_EXCEPTION, szError,
                        ➥SCRIPTPATH);
                else
                        strOutput.Format(IDS_UNKNOWN, SCRIPTPATH);

        }

        /*      close the recordset and database      */
        rsGuestbook.Close();
        db.Close();

        /*      send the result information to the user    */
        *pCtxt <<      strOutput;

        EndContent(pCtxt);
}
```

Part
III

Ch
10

Because WriteGuestbookEntry() is the first function we've written that manipulates our database, let's walk through it step-by-step:

```
strHeader.Format(IDS_STDHEADER, BASEHREF);
*pCtxt      <<      strHeader;
```

loads the top of our Web page from a resource string, then inserts the BASEHREF constant, which holds the server's root, into the proper location. The HTML is shown in Listing 10.14.

Listing 10.14   GUESTBOOK.RC—IDS_STDHEADER

```
<base href="%s">
<body bgcolor="#ffffff" text="#000000">
<font face=Arial>
<center>
<img src="gb.gif" width=550 height=75 units=pixels>
</center>
```

Next, we compare the necessary parameters with NULLSTRING to make sure the values have been entered. If one or more of these variables are missing, we send a message to the user and exit the function.

Notice that in this instance, the NOT (!) operator is needed to test strcmp() for a TRUE value. This is because it returns "0" if the strings are identical.

```
/*      make sure the required fields have values      */
if(!strcmp(pstrName,NULLSTRING)  || !strcmp(pstrCity,NULLSTRING) ||
   !strcmp(pstrState,NULLSTRING) || !strcmp(pstrCountry,NULLSTRING))
{
        *pCtxt   <<   "<br><center>"
                 <<   "Please be certain to enter your Name, City,"
                 <<   " State and Country.  Thank you."
                 <<   "</center>";

        return;
}
```

Now we check to see if the user entered a home page. We do this by comparing the pstrHomePage variable with the HTTP_PROTOCOL constant since the HTML form we sent in the Add() function places the http:// value in the HomePage field:

```
if(!strcmp(pstrHomePage,HTTP_PROTOCOL))
        pstrHomePage = NULLSTRING;
```

Before we add a new record, we should be sure that the new record won't try to duplicate an existing primary key. We do this with a query that filters the records.

This line formats the query; the query isn't executed until our CGuestbookQuery object is opened:

```
/*     format the query     */
strQuery.Format("Name = '%s'", pstrName);
```

Now we try to open the database. If it can't be opened, we send a message to the user and exit the function:

```
/*     try to open the database, exit if it can't be opened     */
if(!db.Open(GUESTBOOKDB,         /* lpszDSN */
             FALSE,              /* bExclusive */
             FALSE,              /* bReadOnly */
             CONNECTSTRING,      /* lpszConnect */
             FALSE))             /* bUseCursorLib */
{
        *pCtxt <<     "Could not open database";
        return;
}
```

Now for the heart of WriteGuestbookEntry(): the database code.

First, our CGuestbookQuery object is created and is passed as a pointer to our recently opened CDatabase object:

```
CGuestbookQuery         rsGuestbook(&db);
```

The CGuestbookQuery data member used for filtering records, m_strFilter, is assigned the query string we formatted earlier:

```
/*     assign the query to the recordset     */
rsGuestbook.m_strFilter = strQuery;
```

Now we try to open the CGuestbookQuery object. Notice the try and catch blocks surrounding the object's function calls. Since we're using MFC for the database code, if we don't supply exception handling, any exceptions that occur will be caught by MFC.

This will cause the extension to be terminated by the AfxTerminate function. As a result, the user will have no idea what happened because the browser will either be totally blank or it will display an error message that the user will have trouble interpreting.

So we incorporate exception handling into our database code. Then if an exception occurs, the catch block retrieves the appropriate error message (the error message associated with the exception) and displays it to the user.

As you can see, exceptions need very little extra code and can be extremely helpful for debugging not only an ISAPI extension but just about any C++ program:

```
/*      try to open the recordset, if it can't be opened catch
        the exception and show the user      */
try
{
```

When `CRecordset::Open()` is called, the query we built at the beginning of this function is executed:

```
if(rsGuestbook.Open())
{
```

Now we test for the beginning of the file using the `CRecordset::IsBOF()` function. If this function returns TRUE, the primary key resulting from adding this record is not a duplicate. So a matching record is not already on file.

Because of this, our first test is for a return value of FALSE, which would tell us the record is already on file. The Unsigned Integer (UINT) `IDS_ONFILE` value identifies the resource in our string table that the extension will display if the record is already on file. Note that if we don't do this test, an exception will result.

```
/*      if the record is already on file,
        this should return FALSE, then
        notify the user      */
if(!rsGuestbook.IsBOF())
        strOutput.Format(IDS_ONFILE, pstrName, SCRIPTPATH);
```

Because we know this is a new record, we can call the `CRecordset::AddNew()` function to prepare the table for a new record. When `CRecordset::AddNew()` is called, an empty record is created.

But our changes are not saved until we call `CRecordset::Update()`. If we were to scroll to another record between the `CRecordset::AddNew()` and `CRecordset::Update()`calls, all our changes would be lost without notification!

Because of this, make sure that any functions used between `CRecordset::AddNew()` and `CRecordset::Update()` do not change your position in the table you are working with. Failure to do so will result in a bug that's extremely difficult to track down.

```
else
{
        rsGuestbook.AddNew();
```

Now we assign values to the data members of CGuestbookQuery. The MFC framework uses a method called *record field exchange* (*RFX*). When CRecordset::AddNew() or CRecordset::Edit() are called, RFX stores the edit buffer so that it can be restored if necessary.

For CRecordset::AddNew(), the field data members are marked as empty. When Update() is called, RFX checks for changed fields, builds an SQL INSERT statement for CRecordset::AddNew() or a CRecordset::UPDATE statement for Edit().

The SQL statement built by RFX is sent to the data source. For CRecordset::AddNew(), the edit buffer is restored. If the operation was CRecordset::Edit(), the backed-up values are deleted.

```
          /*     assign the values      */
          rsGuestbook.m_Name = pstrName; /* user's name */
          rsGuestbook.m_Browser = pstrBrowser;
          ➥/* user's browser */
          rsGuestbook.m_Email   = pstrEmail;
          ➥/* user's e-mail address */
          rsGuestbook.m_HomePage = pstrHomePage;
          ➥/* user's home page */
          rsGuestbook.m_City     = pstrCity;
          ➥/*user's city */
          rsGuestbook.m_State    = pstrState;
          ➥/* user's state */
          rsGuestbook.m_Country = pstrCountry;
          ➥/* user's country */
          rsGuestbook.m_Comments
          ➥= pstrComments; /* user's comments */

          /*      now try to add the record to
          ➥the database     */
          if(rsGuestbook.Update())
                  strOutput.Format(IDS_THANKYOU,
                  ➥pstrName, SCRIPTPATH);
          else
                  strOutput.Format(IDS_NOUPDATE,
                  ➥SCRIPTPATH);
      }
  }
  else
          /*    wonder what happened here???   */
          strOutput.Format(IDS_UNKNOWN, SCRIPTPATH);
  }
  catch(CDBException* pEX)
  {
          TCHAR   szError[1024];
```

```
/*      get the error message */
if(pEX->GetErrorMessage(szError, sizeof(szError)))
        strOutput.Format(IDS_EXCEPTION, szError, SCRIPTPATH);
else
        strOutput.Format(IDS_UNKNOWN, SCRIPTPATH);

}
```

Now let's put the declaration of WriteGuestbookEntry() under the ISAPI Commands section of GUESTBOOK.H:

```
//      ISAPI Commands
        void    Add(CHttpServerContext* pCtxt);
        void    WriteGuestbookEntry(CHttpServerContext* pCtxt,
                                    LPTSTR pstrName=NULL,
                                    LPTSTR pstrBrowser=NULL,
                                    LPTSTR pstrEmail=NULL,
                                    LPTSTR pstrHomePage=NULL,
                                    LPTSTR pstrCity=NULL,
                                    LPTSTR pstrState=NULL,
                                    LPTSTR pstrCountry=NULL,
                                    LPTSTR pstrComments=NULL);
```

We complete this section with the HTML form that allows our visitors to enter their information. To import this into our project, click Insert and Resource on the Developer Studio menu bar. When the Insert Resource dialog box appears, click Import (see Figure 10.9).

FIG. 10.9

Insert Resource dialog box.

Change File of type to All Files(*.*)and change to the directory holding the HTML files. Click the ADD.HTM file and click Import. When the Custom Resource Type dialog box appears (see Figure 10.10), specify HTML as the Resource Type.

After the file is imported, change the Resource ID to IDS_HTML_ADD. The four other HTML resources you should add to your project are listed in Table 10.6.

FIG. 10.10
Custom Resource
Type dialog box.

Table 10.6   HTML Resources Used in ISAPI Guestbook

Resource ID	File Name
IDS_HTML_EDIT	EDIT.HTM
IDS_HTML_DETAILS	DETAILS.HTM
IDS_HTML_FIND	FIND.HTM
IDS_HTML_MAIN	MAIN.HTM

ISAPI Guestbook also uses several String Table resources, listed in Table 10.7.

Table 10.7   String Table Resources Used by ISAPI Guestbook

Resource ID	Caption
IDS_TITLE	ISAPI Guestbook
IDS_TABLEHEAD	`<table width=100%><tr><td align=center><b><u>Name</u></b></td><td align=center><b><u>E-Mail Address</u></b></td><td align=center><b><u>Home Page</u></b></td><td></td></tr>`
IDS_TABLEFOOT	`</table>`
IDS_TABLEROW	`<tr><td align=left>%s</td><td align=center>%s</td><td align=left>%s</td><tdalign=center><formaction="%sguestbook.dll?"method=post><input type=hidden name=MfcISAPICommand value="%s"><input type=hidden name="Name" value="%s"><input type=submit value="%s"></form></td></tr>`
IDS_MAILTO	`<a href="mailto:%s">%s</a>`

continues

Table 10.7 Continued

Resource ID	Caption
IDS_HOMEPAGE	`<a href="%s">%s</a>`
IDS_ERROR	`<body bgcolor="#ffffff" text="#000000">\n<font face=Arial>\n<center>\n<img src="gb.gif" width=550 height=75 units=pixels></center> <center><font size=+1 color="#ff0000">Error</font> The operation was aborted Function: <b> %s</b> Operation: <b>%s</b></center>`
IDS_STDHEADER	`<base href="%s">\n<body bgcolor="#ffffff" text="#000000">\n<font face=Arial>\n<center>\n<img src="gb.gif" width=550 height=75 units=pixels>\n</center>`
IDS_NOMATCH	`<center><b>No matching records were found.</b></center> <center><b><a href=%sguestbook.dll?> Return to the Main Menu</a></b></center>`
IDS_THANKYOU	`<center><b>Thank you for signing our guestbook, %s</b></center> <center><b><a href=%sguestbook.dll?> Return to the Main Menu</a></b></center>`
IDS_NOUPDATE	`<center><b>Could not update record</b>\n Data may not have changed</center> <center><b><a href=%sguestbook.dll?>Return to the Main Menu</a></b></center>`
IDS_ONFILE	`<center><b>%s is already on file</b>\n Try Edit instead of Add</center> <center><b><a href=%sguestbook.dll?>Return to the Main Menu</a></b></center>`
IDS_REMOVED	`<center><b>%s was removed from our guestbook</b></center> <center><b><ahref=%sguestbook.dll?>Return to the Main Menu</a></b></center>`
IDS_UNKNOWN	`<center><b>Query failed for an unknown reason</b></center> <center><b><ahref=%sguestbook.dll?> Return to the Main Menu</a></b></center>`
IDS_DBERROR	`<center><b>Could not open database</b></center>  <center><b><a href=%sguestbook.dll?> Return to the Main Menu</a></b></center>`

Resource ID	Caption
IDS_EXCEPTION	`<center><b>%s</b></center> <center><b><a href=%sguestbook.dll?>Return to the Main Menu</a></b></center>`

Figure 10.11 shows the custom resource properties.

FIG. 10.11
Custom resource properties.

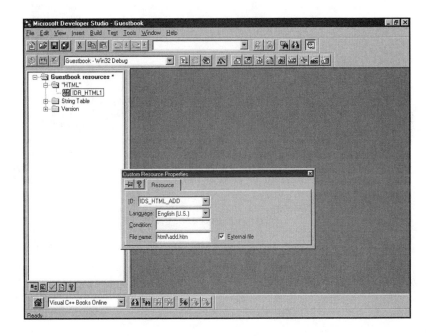

Now that our visitors can add entries to the Guestbook, we'll create the code that allows other visitors to find the entries.

Finding Guestbook Entries

The `Find()` function takes two parameters: a pointer to a `CHttpServerContext` object and an `LPTSTR` named `pstrCommand`. Much like the `Default()` and `Add()` command handlers, `Find()` sends an HTML document (see Listing 10.15). In this case, the document allows the user to enter search parameters to find entries in our Guestbook.

Listing 10.15   GUESTBOOK.CPP—*CGuestbook's Find* Command Handler

```
/*
        Find()
        sends the form that allows the user to search the guestbook
*/
void CGuestbook::Find(CHttpServerContext* pCtxt, LPTSTR pstrCommand)
{
        StartContent(pCtxt);
        WriteTitle(pCtxt);

        Cstring strTemp;
        Cstring strOutput;

        //      try to load the html document
        if(LoadLongResource(strTemp, IDS_HTML_FIND))
                strOutput.Format(strTemp, BASEHREF,
                                        /* server root */
                                        SCRIPTPATH,
                                        /* script folder */
                                        pstrCommand);
                                        /* command for find */
        else
                strOutput.Format(IDS_ERROR, "Find",  /*function*/
                                        "LoadLongResource");
                                        /*operation*/

        //      send the result
        *pCtxt <<      strOutput;

        EndContent(pCtxt);
}
```

Other functions, such as `Edit()`, `Delete()`, and `Details()`, need to find individual entries. So whenever `Find()` is called, the second parameter, `lpstrCommand`, is used to hold the resulting command. If `Find()` is called without the `lpstrCommand` specified, the `Details()` command is used.

`Details()` is covered in the next section. Supplementing `Find()` is `FindGuestBookEntry()`, shown in Listing 10.16.

Listing 10.16   GUESTBOOK.CPP—CGuestbook's FindGuestbookEntry Command Handler

```
/*
        FindGuestbookEntry()
        locates an entry in the guestbook
*/
void CGuestbook::FindGuestbookEntry(CHttpServerContext* pCtxt,
                                    LPTSTR pstrName,
                                    /* name param */
                                    LPTSTR pstrBrowser,
                                    /* browser param */
                                    LPTSTR pstrEmail,
                                    /* e-mail param */
                                    LPTSTR  pstrHomePage,
                                    /* home page param */
                                    LPTSTR pstrCity,
                                    /* city param */
                                    LPTSTR pstrState,
                                    /* state param */
                                    LPTSTR pstrCountry,
                                    /* country param */
                                    LPTSTR pstrCommand)
{
        AddHeader(pCtxt, "Pragma: no-cache\r\n");
        StartContent(pCtxt);
        WriteTitle(pCtxt);

        Cstring      strQuery;
        Cstring      strForm;
        Cstring      strOutput;
        Cdatabase    db;

        strQuery =   BuildQuery(pstrName, /* name param */
                                pstrBrowser, /*browser param */
                                pstrEmail,  /*e-mail param */
                                pstrHomePage, /*home page param */
                                pstrCity, /* city param */
                                pstrState, /* state param   */
                                pstrCountry); /* country param */

        /*     try to open the database, exit if it can't be opened */
        if(!db.Open(GUESTBOOKDB,       /*     lpszDSN           */
                    FALSE,             /*     bExclusive        */
                    FALSE,             /*     bReadOnly         */
                    CONNECTSTRING, /*     lpszConnect       */
                    FALSE))                /*     bUseCursorLib */
```

continues

Listing 10.16 Continued

```
    {
            *pCtxt <<       "Could not open database";
            return;
    }

    CGuestbookQuery         rsGuestbook(&db);

    rsGuestbook.m_strFilter = strQuery;

    strForm.Format(IDS_STDHEADER, BASEHREF);

    *pCtxt   <<      strForm;

    try
    {
            if(rsGuestbook.Open())
            {
                    if(rsGuestbook.IsBOF())
                            strOutput.Format(IDS_NOMATCH,
                            ➥SCRIPTPATH);
                    else
                    {
                            CString strRows;
                            CString strTableHead;
                            CString strTableFoot;
                            CString strTableRow;
                            CString strEntry;

                            strTableHead.LoadString(IDS_TABLEHEAD);
                            strTableFoot.LoadString(IDS_TABLEFOOT);
                            strTableRow.LoadString(IDS_TABLEROW);

                            //    create the table
                            *pCtxt <<       strTableHead;

                            /*    Load records here      */
                            while(!rsGuestbook.IsEOF())
                            {
                                    strEntry.Format(strTableRow,
                                            rsGuestbook.m_Name,
                                            rsGuestbook.m_Email,
                                        rsGuestbook.m_HomePage,
                                            SCRIPTPATH,
                                            pstrCommand,
                                            rsGuestbook.m_Name,
                                            pstrCommand);
```

```
                                      *pCtxt <<          strEntry;

                                      strEntry.Empty();

                                      rsGuestbook.MoveNext();
                            }

                            *pCtxt <<          strTableFoot;
                    }
            }
            else
                    strOutput.Format(IDS_UNKNOWN, SCRIPTPATH);
        }
        catch(CDBException* pEX)
        {
                TCHAR    szError[1024];

                if(pEX->GetErrorMessage(szError, sizeof(szError)))
                        strOutput.Format(IDS_EXCEPTION, szError,
                        ➥SCRIPTPATH);
                else
                        strOutput.Format(IDS_UNKNOWN, SCRIPTPATH);
        }

        *pCtxt <<          strOutput;

        rsGuestbook.Close();
        db.Close();

        EndContent(pCtxt);
}
```

Although `FindGuestbookEntry()` resembles `WriteGuestbookEntry()`, it's basically different. The most obvious difference is that it doesn't write a new record to our table. Instead, it finds existing entries. A more subtle difference is in the very first line:

```
AddHeader(pCtxt, "Pragma: no-cache\r\n");
```

This line instructs the browser not to cache this page. By doing this, we make sure that each time visitors look for an entry, they get the most current listing.

Another difference between `FindGuestbookEntry()` and `WriteGuestbookEntry()` is the way we build the query executed by our `CGuestbookQuery` object when `Open()` is called. In this case, our query is built by another function, `BuildQuery()`, shown in Listing 10.17.

Listing 10.17   GUESTBOOK.CPP—*BuildQuery* Formats the SQL Query for *FindGuestbookEntry*

```
/*
        BuildQuery()
        create an sql query based on the user's input
*/
CString CGuestbook::BuildQuery(LPTSTR pstrName, LPTSTR pstrBrowser,
                               LPTSTR pstrEmail, LPTSTR pstrHomePage,
                               LPTSTR pstrCity,  LPTSTR pstrState,
                               LPTSTR pstrCountry)
{
        Cstring strQuery;

        if(strcmp(pstrName, NULLSTRING))
                strQuery.Format("Name LIKE '%%%s%%'", pstrName);

        if(strcmp(pstrBrowser, NULLSTRING))
        {
                if(!strQuery.IsEmpty())
                        strQuery += " AND ";

                strQuery.Format(strQuery + "Browser LIKE
                ➥'%%%s%%'", pstrBrowser);
        }

        if(strcmp(pstrEmail, NULLSTRING))
        {
                if(!strQuery.IsEmpty())
                        strQuery += " AND ";

                strQuery.Format(strQuery + "Email LIKE
                ➥'%%%s%%'", pstrEmail);
        }

        if(strcmp(pstrHomePage, NULLSTRING))
        {
                if(!strQuery.IsEmpty())
                        strQuery += " AND ";

                strQuery.Format(strQuery + "HomePage LIKE
                ➥'%%%s%%'", pstrHomePage);
        }

        if(strcmp(pstrCity, NULLSTRING))
        {
                if(!strQuery.IsEmpty())
                        strQuery += " AND ";
```

```
            strQuery.Format(strQuery + "City LIKE
        ➥'%%s%%'", pstrCity);
    }

    if(strcmp(pstrState, NULLSTRING))
    {
            if(!strQuery.IsEmpty())
                    strQuery += " AND ";

            strQuery.Format(strQuery + "State LIKE
        ➥'%%s%%'", pstrState);
    }

    if(strcmp(pstrCountry, NULLSTRING))
    {
            if(!strQuery.IsEmpty())
                    strQuery += " AND ";

            strQuery.Format(strQuery + "Country LIKE
        ➥'%%s%%'", pstrCountry);
    }

    return strQuery;
}
```

BuildQuery() is called immediately after WriteTitle(). It takes seven LPTSTRs: pstrName, pstrBrowser, pstrEmail, pstrHomePage, pstrCity, pstrState, and pstrCountry.

BuildQuery() compares each parameter to the NULLSTRING constant. If each value is empty, so is the query. If any or all variables hold values, BuildQuery() puts them in the right locations and returns a CString object.

FindGuestbookEntry() takes our query and it becomes the m_strFilter data member of our CGuestbookQuery object.

When our record set is opened, we need to check for records matching the visitor's parameters. Since our m_strFilter member is in place, this is done when we call CRecordset::Open():

```
if(rsGuestbook.Open())
{
        if(rsGuestbook.IsBOF())
                strOutput.Format(IDS_NOMATCH, SCRIPTPATH);
```

TIP An empty m_strFilter member causes all the records in the record set to be returned. With very large record sets, you may want to check m_strFilter for an empty value. Because this is a CString object, it's easily done:

```
/*
        make sure the user entered search parameters
*/
if(m_strFilter.IsEmpty())
{
        //      send a message and don't execute the query
}
else
{
        //      execute the query
}
```

If there are matching records, we need to load the HTML that displays the list of records. We do this by breaking down an HTML table into three parts: a header, a row, and a footer:

```
else
{
    CString strTableHead;
    CString strTableFoot;
    CString strTableRow;
    CString strEntry;

    strTableHead.LoadString(IDS_TABLEHEAD);
    strTableFoot.LoadString(IDS_TABLEFOOT);
    strTableRow.LoadString(IDS_TABLEROW);
```

Our table's header is sent first, which allows each record to fall into the same HTML table:

```
//      create the table
*pCtxt <<      strTableHead;
```

This while loop scrolls through the resulting record set, record by record, sending each record to the user's browser as a row in the HTML table we created. After each record is sent, the CString strEntry object is emptied. Then we move to the next record until we reach the end of the record set:

```
/*      Load records here      */
while(!rsGuestbook.IsEOF())
                {
```

```
        strEntry.Format(strTableRow,
                        rsGuestbook.m_Name,
                        rsGuestbook.m_Email,
                        rsGuestbook.m_HomePage,
                        SCRIPTPATH,
                        pstrCommand,
                        rsGuestbook.m_Name,
                        pstrCommand);

        *pCtxt <<        strEntry;

        strEntry.Empty();

        rsGuestbook.MoveNext();
    }
```

Once each record is sent to the user, we send the table footer so our table is formatted properly:

```
        *pCtxt     <<        strTableFoot;
    }
```

Now we add our newly created functions to the CGuestbook header file. Under the ISAPI Commands section, add the declarations for Find() and FindGuestbookEntry():

```
    void     Find(CHttpServerContext* pCtxt, LPTSTR
    pstrCommand="Details");
    void     FindGuestbookEntry(CHttpServerContext* pCtxt,
                        LPTSTR pstrName=NULL,
                        LPTSTR pstrBrowser=NULL,
                        LPTSTR pstrEmail=NULL,
                        LPTSTR pstrHomePage=NULL,
                        LPTSTR pstrCity=NULL,
                        LPTSTR pstrState=NULL,
                        LPTSTR pstrCountry=NULL,
                        LPTSTR pstrCommand="Details");
```

Under the Helpers section, add BuildQuery().

```
    CString BuildQuery(LPTSTR pstrName, LPTSTR pstrBrowser,
                        LPTSTR pstrEmail, LPTSTR pstrHomePage,
                        LPTSTR pstrCity,  LPTSTR pstrState,
                        LPTSTR pstrCountry);
```

Now that we can find entries in our Guestbook, let's use the command that Find() uses by default.

Viewing Entry Details

The Details() function shows the values entered by a user (see Listing 10.18). Details() takes two parameters: a pointer to a CHttpServerContext object and an LPTSTR holding the name of the user to look up.

Listing 10.18   GUESTBOOK.CPP—CGuestbook's Details Command Handler

```
/*
        Details()
        shows a user's record
*/
void CGuestbook::Details(CHttpServerContext* pCtxt, LPTSTR pstrName)
{
        StartContent(pCtxt);
        WriteTitle(pCtxt);

        Cstring         strQuery;
        Cstring         strOutput;
        Cstring         strTemp;
        Cdatabase       db;

        strQuery.Format("Name = '%s'", pstrName);

        /*      try to open the database, exit if it can't be opened */
        if(!db.Open(GUESTBOOKDB, /* lpszDSN */
                    FALSE,       /* bExclusive */
                    FALSE,       /*  bReadOnly */
                    CONNECTSTRING, /* lpszConnect */
                    FALSE))        /* bUseCursorLib */
        {
                strOutput.Format(IDS_DBERROR, SCRIPTPATH);
                *pCtxt << strOutput;
                return;
        }

        CGuestbookQuery                 rsGuestbook(&db);

        rsGuestbook.m_strFilter = strQuery;

        try
        {
                if(rsGuestbook.Open())
                {
                        if(rsGuestbook.IsBOF())
                                strOutput.Format(IDS_NOMATCH,
                                ➡pstrName, SCRIPTPATH);
```

```
                else
                {
                        CString strEmail;
                        CString strHomePage;

                        if(!rsGuestbook.m_Email.IsEmpty())
                                strEmail.Format(IDS_MAILTO,
                                                rsGuestbook.m_Email,
                                                rsGuestbook.m_Email);
                        else
                                strEmail="Unknown";

                        if(!rsGuestbook.m_HomePage.IsEmpty())
                                strHomePage.Format(IDS_HOMEPAGE,
                                                rsGuestbook.m_HomePage,
                                                rsGuestbook.m_HomePage);
                         else
                                strHomePage="Unknown";

                        LoadLongResource(strTemp, IDS_HTML_DETAILS);
                        strOutput.Format(strTemp, BASEHREF,
                                                rsGuestbook.m_Name,
                                                rsGuestbook.m_
                                                ➥Browser,
                                                strEmail,
                                                strHomePage,
                                                rsGuestbook.m_
                                                ➥City,
                                                rsGuestbook.m_
                                                ➥State,
                                                rsGuestbook.m_
                                                ➥Country,
                                                rsGuestbook.m_
                                                ➥Comments,
                                                SCRIPTPATH);
                }
        }
        else
                strOutput.Format(IDS_UNKNOWN, SCRIPTPATH);
}
catch(CDBException* pEX)
{
        TCHAR   szError[1024];

        if(pEX->GetErrorMessage(szError, sizeof(szError)))
                strOutput.Format(IDS_EXCEPTION, szError,
                ➥SCRIPTPATH);
        else
                strOutput.Format(IDS_UNKNOWN, SCRIPTPATH);
}
```

continues

Part
III

Ch
10

Listing 10.18   Continued

```
      *pCtxt   <<       strOutput;

      rsGuestbook.Close();
      db.Close();

      EndContent(pCtxt);
}
```

By this time, the first several lines of source code should look familiar. Our SQL statement is formatted so it holds the name the CGuestbookQuery object should look for.

We open our database, create the CGuestbookQuery object, and pass a pointer to the database. Then we open the CGuestbookQuery object and check if there was a match.

Remember, we're on the Web, so let's spiff it up enough to make the user more productive. As you can see from the snippet below, our code checks both the e-mail address and the home page of the retrieved record for an empty value by using the CString::IsEmpty() function:

```
if(!rsGuestbook.m_Email.IsEmpty())
        strEmail.Format(IDS_MAILTO,
                          rsGuestbook.m_Email,
                          rsGuestbook.m_Email);
else
        strEmail="Unknown";

if(!rsGuestbook.m_HomePage.IsEmpty())
        strHomePage.Format(IDS_HOMEPAGE,
        rsGuestbook.m_HomePage,
        rsGuestbook.m_HomePage);
else
        strHomePage="Unknown";
```

The first value checked is the e-mail address. If this value is empty, we enter **Unknown**. If it holds information, we format it with a mailto: link using the IDS_MAILTO Resource ID.

The record's home page value is checked the same way. If it's not empty, it's formatted using IDS_HOMEPAGE (see Table 10.7 earlier in this chapter).

Once we've set the values of the members m_Email and m_HomePage, we load the HTML that allows us to display the record requested:

```
LoadLongResource(strTemp, IDS_HTML_DETAILS);
strOutput.Format(strTemp, BASEHREF,
                    rsGuestbook.m_Name,
                    rsGuestbook.m_Browser,
                    strEmail,
                    strHomePage,
                    rsGuestbook.m_City,
                    rsGuestbook.m_State,
                    rsGuestbook.m_Country,
                    rsGuestbook.m_Comments,
                    SCRIPTPATH);
```

Now our visitor can send e-mail or visit a home page if the values were there. If they want to find, add, edit, or delete an entry, they can return to ISAPI Guestbook's main menu.

As with previous functions, we need to add the declaration for this function to our class declaration. Put

```
void        Details(CHttpServerContext* pCtxt, LPTSTR pstrName);
```

in the ISAPI Commands section of GUESTBOOK.H.

Editing a Guestbook Entry

It's unusual for guest books to allow users to edit their entries once they've been entered. But since this guest book serves a higher purpose (or so we'd like to think), we add a couple of ISAPI command handlers that allow records to be edited. If you browse through the code in the Edit() command handler (in Listing 10.19), you'll see that it's nearly identical to the code for Add().

Listing 10.19 GUESTBOOK.CPP—*CGuestbook's Edit* Command Handler

```
/*
    Edit()
    this command loads the form that allows the user to
    enter their information
*/
```

continues

Listing 10.19 Continued

```
void CGuestbook::Edit(CHttpServerContext* pCtxt, LPTSTR pstrName)
{
        StartContent(pCtxt);
        WriteTitle(pCtxt);

        Cstring       strTemp;
        Cstring       strOutput;
        Cstring       strQuery;
        Cdatabase     db;

        /*    format the query       */
        strQuery.Format("Name = '%s'", pstrName);

        /*    try to open the database, exit if it can't be opened */
        if(!db.Open(GUESTBOOKDB,      /* lpszDSN */
                          FALSE, /* bExclusive */
                          FALSE, /* bReadOnly */
                          CONNECTSTRING, /* lpszConnect */
                          FALSE))  /* bUseCursorLib */
        {
                strOutput.Format(IDS_DBERROR, SCRIPTPATH);
                *pCtxt<<      strOutput;
                return;
        }

        CGuestbookQuery              rsGuestbook(&db);

        /*    assign the query to the recordset     */
        rsGuestbook.m_strFilter = strQuery;

        /*    try to open the recordset, if it can't be opened catch
              the exception and show the user      */
        try
        {
                if(rsGuestbook.Open())
                {
                /*    if the record is not already on file,
                      this should return FALSE, then
                      notify the user */
                if(rsGuestbook.IsBOF())
                        strOutput.Format("%s is not on file", pstrName);
                else
                {
                   LoadLongResource(strTemp, IDS_HTML_EDIT);
                     strOutput.Format(strTemp,
                           BASEHREF,
                           SCRIPTPATH,
                           rsGuestbook.m_Name,
                           rsGuestbook.m_Name,
```

```
                       rsGuestbook.m_Browser,
                       rsGuestbook.m_Email,
                       rsGuestbook.m_HomePage.IsEmpty() ? HTTP_PROTOCOL
                   ➥: rsGuestbook.m_HomePage,
                       rsGuestbook.m_City,
                       rsGuestbook.m_State,
                       rsGuestbook.m_Country,
                       rsGuestbook.m_Comments);
            }
        }
        else
            strOutput.Format(IDS_UNKNOWN, SCRIPTPATH);
    }
    catch(CDBException* pEX)
    {
            TCHAR  szError[1024];

            /*     get the error message   */
            if(pEX->GetErrorMessage(szError, sizeof(szError)))
                    strOutput = szError;
            else
                    strOutput.Format(IDS_UNKNOWN, SCRIPTPATH);
    }
    /* send the result      */
    *pCtxt <<      strOutput;

    EndContent(pCtxt);
}
```

There are two significant differences between the Add() and Edit() command handlers. First, Edit() is not called from the main menu displayed by Default(). Instead, Edit() is called from FindGuestbookEntry(), as shown in Listing 10.20.

Remember the variable Command that defaults to Details in Find() and FindGuestbookEntry()? We used that variable so we didn't have to write more than one command handler to find an entry.

The second and more noticeable difference is that Edit() retrieves the user's record from the database and allows the user to change any entry other than the name. We do this because that name is our primary key.

It would not have an adverse effect in this situation. But if our table related to records in another table not in this record set, we would risk compromising the referential integrity of the records.

Listing 10.20   GUESTBOOK.CPP—*CGuestbook*'s *EditGuestbookEntry* Command Handler

```
/*
        EditGuestbookEntry()
        writes an new entry into the guestbook
*/
void CGuestbook::EditGuestbookEntry(CHttpServerContext* pCtxt,
                                LPTSTR pstrName,
                                LPTSTR pstrBrowser,
                                LPTSTR pstrEmail,
                                LPTSTR pstrHomePage,
                                LPTSTR pstrCity,
                                LPTSTR pstrState,
                                LPTSTR pstrCountry,
                                LPTSTR pstrComments)
{
        StartContent(pCtxt);
        WriteTitle(pCtxt);

        Cstring         strQuery;
        Cstring         strHeader;
        Cstring         strOutput;
        Cdatabase       db;

        strHeader.Format(IDS_STDHEADER, BASEHREF);
        *pCtxt <<       strHeader;

        /*      make sure the required fields have values      */
        if(!strcmp(pstrName,NULLSTRING) || !strcmp(pstrCity,
        NULLSTRING) ||
          !strcmp(pstrState,NULLSTRING) || !strcmp(pstrCountry,
          NULLSTRING))
        {
                *pCtxt <<       "<br><center>"
                       <<       "Please be certain to enter your
                                Name, City,"
                       <<       " State and Country.  Thank you."
                       <<       "</center>";

                return;
        }

        if(!strcmp(pstrHomePage,HTTP_PROTOCOL))
                pstrHomePage = NULLSTRING;

        strQuery.Format("Name = '%s'", pstrName);

        /*      try to open the database, exit if it can't be opened */
```

```
if(!db.Open(GUESTBOOKDB,      /* lpszDSN */
            FALSE,            /* bExclusive */
            FALSE,            /* bReadOnly */
            CONNECTSTRING,    /* lpszConnect */
            FALSE))           /* bUseCursorLib */
{
      strOutput.Format(IDS_DBERROR, SCRIPTPATH);
      *pCtxt <<      strOutput;
      return;
}

CGuestbookQuery              rsGuestbook(&db);

rsGuestbook.m_strFilter = strQuery;

try
{
      if(rsGuestbook.Open())
      {
            if(rsGuestbook.IsBOF())
                  strOutput.Format(IDS_NOMATCH,
                  ➥pstrName, SCRIPTPATH);

            else
            {
                  rsGuestbook.Edit();

                  rsGuestbook.m_Browser = pstrBrowser;
                  rsGuestbook.m_Email   = pstrEmail;
                  rsGuestbook.m_HomePage = pstrHomePage;
                  rsGuestbook.m_City    = pstrCity;
                  rsGuestbook.m_State   = pstrState;
                  rsGuestbook.m_Country = pstrCountry;
                  rsGuestbook.m_Comments = pstrComments;

                  if(rsGuestbook.Update())
                        strOutput.Format(IDS_THANKYOU,
                        ➥pstrName, SCRIPTPATH);
                  else
                        strOutput.Format(IDS_NOUPDATE,
                        ➥SCRIPTPATH);
            }

      }
      else
            strOutput.Format(IDS_UNKNOWN, SCRIPTPATH);
}
catch(CDBException* pEX)
{
```

Part III

Ch 10

continues

Listing 10.20   Continued

```
            TCHAR   szError[1024];

            if(pEX->GetErrorMessage(szError, sizeof(szError)))
                    strOutput.Format(IDS_EXCEPTION, szError,
                    ➥SCRIPTPATH);
            else
                    strOutput.Format(IDS_UNKNOWN, SCRIPTPATH);
        }

        rsGuestbook.Close();
        db.Close();

        *pCtxt <<      strOutput;

        EndContent(pCtxt);
    }
```

`Add()` and `WriteGuestbookEntry()` work together to place a record in our database. And `Edit()` and `EditGuestbookEntry()` work together to change an existing record.

The `Name` field is stored in a hidden input object on `Edit()`'s dynamically generated page. So why do we test `pstrName` for an empty value?

```
    /*     make sure the required fields have values      */
    if(!strcmp(pstrName,NULLSTRING)  ¦¦ !strcmp(pstrCity,NULLSTRING) ¦¦
       !strcmp(pstrState,NULLSTRING) ¦¦ !strcmp(pstrCountry,NULLSTRING))
    {
            *pCtxt   <<    "<br><center>"
                     <<    "Please be certain to enter your Name, City,"
                     <<    " State and Country.  Thank you."
                     <<    "</center>";

            return;
    }
```

Because we have no guarantee that `EditGuestbookEntry()` will be called from `Edit()` only. I suppose it is possible to devise a complex method that may or may not work. But it's much simpler (and less error-prone) to make sure that a value for Name was entered.

There may be times when you want to authenticate the user who is editing the record. You'll learn how to do this in Chapter 16, "Extending Your Web Server with Filters."

Once we're sure that `pstrName` has a value, our code tries to find the record in the record set:

```
strQuery.Format("Name = '%s'", pstrName);

/*    try to open the database, exit if it can't be opened    */
if(!db.Open(GUESTBOOKDB,       /*    lpszDSN               */
            FALSE,             /*       bExclusive         */
            FALSE,             /*       bReadOnly          */
            CONNECTSTRING, /*    lpszConnect          */
            FALSE))            /*       bUseCursorLib */
{
        strOutput.Format(IDS_DBERROR, SCRIPTPATH);
        *pCtxt <<        strOutput;
        return;
}

CGuestbookQuery              rsGuestbook(&db);

rsGuestbook.m_strFilter = strQuery;

try
{
        if(rsGuestbook.Open())
```

Part III

Ch

10

We try to find the record for two reasons. First, without a current record, any call to `CRecordset::Edit()` results in an exception. Why? Because if there's no record, you can't edit it.

Second, between the `Edit()` and `EditGuestbookEntry()` calls, the record could have been deleted. Finding the record before a `CRecordset::Edit()` call is a simple way to avoid exceptions and hair loss. As with `CRecordset::AddNew()`, a call to `CRecordset::Edit()` is completed with a call to `CRecordset::Update()`:

```
if(rsGuestbook.Update())
        strOutput.Format(IDS_THANKYOU, pstrName, SCRIPTPATH);
else
        strOutput.Format(IDS_NOUPDATE, SCRIPTPATH);
```

Because we're using `CRecordset` and we're doing a `CRecordset::Edit()` function, if no fields are changed when `CRecordset::Update()` is called, it returns FALSE.

Deleting a Guestbook Entry

Unlike the other command handlers, `Delete()` does not have a supplement. `FindGuestbookEntry()` passes an `LPTSTR` specifying the name the visitor wants to delete. So we have all the information we need to proceed with the request (see Listing 10.21).

Listing 10.21   GUESTBOOK.CPP—*CGuestbook*'s *Delete* Command Handler

```
/*
      Delete()
      removes an entry from the guestbook
*/
void CGuestbook::Delete(CHttpServerContext* pCtxt, LPTSTR pstrName)
{
      StartContent(pCtxt);
      WriteTitle(pCtxt);

      Cstring       strQuery;
      Cstring       strOutput;
      Cstring       strHeader;
      Cstring       strTemp;
      Cdatabase     db;

      strQuery.Format("Name = '%s'", pstrName);

      strHeader.Format(IDS_STDHEADER, BASEHREF);
      *pCtxt <<     strHeader;

      /*    try to open the database, exit if it can't be opened */
      if(!db.Open(GUESTBOOKDB,        /* lpszDSN */
                  FALSE,              /* bExclusive */
                  FALSE,              /* bReadOnly */
                  CONNECTSTRING,/* lpszConnect */
                  FALSE))             /* bUseCursorLib */
      {
            strOutput.Format(IDS_DBERROR, SCRIPTPATH);

            *pCtxt <<     strOutput;
            return;
      }

      CGuestbookQuery             rsGuestbook(&db);

      rsGuestbook.m_strFilter = strQuery;

      try
      {
            if(rsGuestbook.Open())
            {
                  if(rsGuestbook.IsBOF())
                        strOutput.Format(IDS_NOMATCH, pstrName,
                        ➥SCRIPTPATH);
```

```
                        else
                        {
                                rsGuestbook.Delete();

                                if(rsGuestbook.IsEOF())
                                        rsGuestbook.MovePrev();
                                else
                                        rsGuestbook.MoveNext();

                                strOutput.Format(IDS_REMOVED, pstrName,
                                ➥SCRIPTPATH);

                        }
                }
                else
                        strOutput.Format(IDS_UNKNOWN, SCRIPTPATH);
        }
        catch(CDBException* pEX)
        {
                TCHAR   szError[1024];

                if(pEX->GetErrorMessage(szError, sizeof(szError)))
                        strOutput.Format(IDS_EXCEPTION, szError,
                        ➥SCRIPTPATH);
                else
                        strOutput.Format(IDS_UNKNOWN, SCRIPTPATH);
        }


        *pCtxt <<        strOutput;

        rsGuestbook.Close();
        db.Close();

        EndContent(pCtxt);
}
```

Notice that we should test to make sure the record has not been deleted between the FindGuestbookEntry() and Delete()calls, as we did in EditGuestbookEntry():

```
if(rsGuestbook.IsBOF())
        strOutput.Format(IDS_NOMATCH, pstrName, SCRIPTPATH);
```

Also, once we call CRecordset::Delete(), we should test to see if we are on either the first record or the last record, and call CRecordset::MoveNext() or CRecordset::MovePrev() accordingly.

In ISAPI Guestbook, we test for the end-of-file (EOF). If this function returns TRUE, we move to the previous record. On FALSE, we move to the next record.

Regardless of which method you use, you must move off the deleted record before your record set is considered updatable again. If we don't change to another record and subsequently try to call CRecordset::Delete(), CRecordset::AddNew(), or CRecordset::Edit(), a CDBException results.

```
else
{
        rsGuestbook.Delete();

        if(rsGuestbook.IsEOF())
                rsGuestbook.MovePrev();
        else
                rsGuestbook.MoveNext();

        strOutput.Format(IDS_REMOVED, pstrName, SCRIPTPATH);

}
```

After CRecordset::Delete() is called, the record's fields are set to NULL. If we tried another call to CRecordset::Delete() or CRecordset::Edit() before moving off the deleted record, an exception would result because there is no current record. In any event, getting into the habit of moving right after deleting a record will save you grief.

From Here...

The extensions we covered in this chapter by no means exhaust the potential of ISAPI, MFC, or CDatabase and CRecordset. By building on the basics in this chapter, you'll soon be on the edge of Internet and intranet technology.

- Chapter 13, "Understanding ISAPI Filters," shows you how ISAPI filters work. You learn about building an ISAPI filter, using the powerful features of ISAPI filters, how ISAPI filters interact with Web servers, and the rules for developing ISAPI filters.

- Chapter 15, "Building Filters with MFC ISAPI Classes," tells you about using MFC to create ISAPI filters. You create a filter using MFC and learn how MFC works. You also learn how to avoid common pitfalls with MFC.

CHAPTER 11

OLEISAPI

Object linking and embedding (OLE) has become Microsoft's interprocess communication (IPC) mechanism. It has effectively replaced dynamic data exchange (DDE) and to a lesser extent, open database connectivity (ODBC), as the semigeneric application programming interface (API)-to-everything du jour.

OLE is Microsoft's model for software component construction—the blueprint for how software works together in the Microsoft environments. Unlike its predecessors, it shows no signs of slipping into obsolescence.

It follows that OLE is the favored mechanism for extending Microsoft's Internet Information Server (IIS).

This chapter introduces you to the basics of OLE Internet Server Application Programming Interface (ISAPI), the Microsoft-supplied means to customize IIS using OLE and Visual Basic (VB) 4. ■

An introduction to OLEISAPI

Not just another unpronounceable jumble of vowels and consonants, OLEISAPI (pronounced "oh-lay-eye-sappy,") is Microsoft's answer to the UNIX world's Common Gateway Interface (CGI). This section introduces you to OLEISAPI and shows you how it works.

Tools, tricks, and requirements

If you're looking for a way to build Web server extensions with MASM 2.0 in a CP/M environment, OLEISAPI isn't it. This section names the software you need to build OLEISAPI components. Additional software you can take advantage of and a brief tour of OLEISAPI.CPP, the core OLEISAPI component, are also supplied.

How to create an OLEISAPI application and configure the runtime environment

In this section, we create simple life in our OLEISAPI test tube.

What Is OLEISAPI?

OLEISAPI supplies developers with the means to extend Microsoft's IIS. It is both a module and a mechanism that supplies hooks and entry points you can use to create custom Web server extensions using C++ or 32-bit VB4 (see Figure 11.1).

OLEISAPI is Microsoft's alternative to the common gateway interface (CGI), the tool that has facilitated interactivity on the Web. It is the server-side "smarts" that allow specific client requests to be intelligently processed by the server on a custom basis.

OLEISAPI programs live in a twilight world between "systems" and "applications" code. They act as intermediaries between an HTTP client and the resources available to the IIS HTTP server, supplying customized processing and responses via predefined hooks.

The easiest way to take advantage of these hooks is with OLEISAPI.DLL. This is a dynamic link library (DLL) thoughtfully supplied by Microsoft that enables you to write OLEISAPI components in VB4.

Without OLEISAPI.DLL, you would have to write your IIS Internet customizations in C/C++. You can also use Delphi to create ISAPI filters and extensions.

Any developer who can create OLE server DLLs (in VB4 or C/C++) can build OLEISAPI applications. Figure 11.1 is a conceptual overview of OLEISAPI.

FIG. 11.1

A conceptual
overview of OLEISAPI.

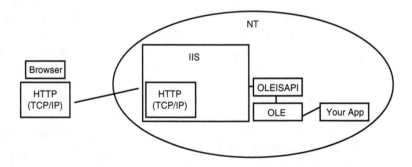

N O T E   OLEISAPI.DLL has a limitation of 4K on the output string. Some versions available on the Internet have raised this limitation to 64K. This should be large enough to handle anything. For those comfortable with C++, the source code is available on the CD so you can change it yourself. ▨

OLEISAPI 2.0: the Next Step

At this writing, a new version of OLEISAPI, OLEISAPI 2.0, is being released publicly for beta testing.

OLEISAPI 2.0 is considerably different in its implementation, but the concept is similar. OLEISAPI 2.0 is actually an OLE server. Instead of calling a method in your OLE server that expects two string parameters, OLEISAPI passes a request object, and the return page is generated by that request object's methods.

In this chapter, I include notes on how you would do this differently in OLEISAPI 2.0. You are encouraged to change the source code yourself.

Development Environment and Tools

You need several items to construct OLEISAPI programs. Note that I have chosen the latest and most stable components as my tools.

You may be able to replace something listed for something not listed. But doing this is like installing NT on a system with a peripheral device that is not on the compatibility list: *avoid if possible*. You'll save a lot of frustration and lost time.

Part
III

Ch
11

Development Operating System

We chose NT 4 as our development operating system for several reasons:

- It's durable (fully 32-bit with no Win 3.x "baggage").
- It runs IIS (in contrast to Win95, which does not).
- We can run IIS, Microsoft Internet Explorer (IE), and VB4 all on one computer.

If NT 3.51 is still available at the time of this publication, you can use it as well. You need NT 3.51 Service Pack 4 to use OLEISAPI extensions.

Because Microsoft evolves beta releases into commercial releases ever more quickly, by the time you read this you will probably only have access to NT 4.x anyway. All the better.

HTTP Programs

You will need an HTTP server (also called a *Web server*) and an HTTP client (browser). A browser object is available from Microsoft in the form of a custom control for VB4, but it is in its infancy. Better to choose a "full-grown" product than try to build a browser at this point.

As for the server, use IIS as it comes with NT4 server (or get a copy if you are using NT4 workstation). It's free, it's fully integrated with NT's security mechanisms, and it's simple to administer.

For your browser, you can use either Netscape or IE. Something to consider here is the customer you are writing your OLEISAPI application for.

If the customer already has Netscape or if you think most of the clients will be running Netscape when they run your OLEISAPI application, use Netscape as your development browser. Be aware that Netscape is not free and has somewhat intricate license requirements for commercial use.

IE Version 3 and later allow ActiveX Serve controls, which can add greatly to the presentation and use of your Web page. If you are developing OLEISAPI applications, you'll probably have the opportunity to use ActiveX as well (perhaps instead of Java). Also, IE is free.

Language Tool

Any language compiler/interpreter that can generate OLE server DLLs can be used to build OLEISAPI programs. I suppose there is a FORTRAN for NT or Lisp for '95 that you could use but stick with 32-bit VB4.

In extreme cases, you can substitute Visual C++. But you'll easily save the equivalent of the purchase price of VB4 in time when you use it as your OLEISAPI development tool.

Additional Tools

Several tools, although not absolutely necessary, are helpful to the OLEISAPI developer. These either come with VB4 or are standard issue in NT 4.x and include:

- regsvr32.exe is part of VB4. It lets you register and deregister OLE server DLLs.

- dcomcnfg.exe is part of NT 4.x. It lets you control access to all kinds of OLE servers, both local and distributed over a network.

- Oleview.exe is available from a number of sources. It lets you peek into OLE transactions.

- regedt32.exe is the registry editor. With any luck, you won't need to look up OLE class IDs in the registry (they are very long, machine-generated, magic cookies that uniquely identify every OLE server object). But if you do, this is the only tool to use.

- OLEISAPI.DLL must reside in your virtual scripts directory (usually c:\inetpub\scripts). It's the jewel that IIS calls when it is requested via an URL. OLEISAPI.DLL in turn calls your OLEISAPI program with whatever parameters were specified in the URL.

- OLEISAPI.DLL must reside in your virtual scripts directory (usually c:\inetpub\scripts) if you want to try OLEISAPI to challenge yourself. This file also has to be registered (using regsvr32.exe). For thread safety, it you can only use it on NT 4.

Part
III

Ch
11

N O T E Your VB4 application and OLEISAPI.DLL need several runtime files. The common files needed for most VB4 OLEISAPI projects are as follows:

File Name	Needed By
ven2232.olb	Setup program
olepro32.dll	Setup program
msvcrt20.dll	Setup program
msvcrt40.dll	Setup program
ctl3d32.dll	Setup program
MFC40.DLL	Average VB4 project
MSRDO32.DLL	VB4 project using RDO

OLEISAPI.CPP

The source code for OLEISAPI.DLL is supplied in the INETSDK. It is small and relatively simple with three primary functions as hooks into IIS. You should not normally have to change this code.

The three primary functions are as follows:

```
HRESULT GetClsidFromProgIdA(LPCLSID pclsid, CHAR* pszName,
➡long cbName)
```

This function gets the magic cookie class ID from the registry for a given OLE server program name.

```
BOOL CallObject(EXTENSION_CONTROL_BLOCK *pECB,
                CHAR *pszProgid,
                CHAR *pszMethod)
```

This is the heart of the OLEISAPI.DLL. It's the function that calls your OLE server.

```
void ErrorResponse(EXTENSION_CONTROL_BLOCK *pECB,
                   CHAR *pszProgid,
                   CHAR *pszMethod)
```

In the event of an error, this function tells the user (via generated HTML) that a problem occurred.

```
BOOL WINAPI GetExtensionVersion(HSE_VERSION_INFO *pVer)
```

This is a necessary exported function that returns a rudimentary version report to IIS.

```
DWORD WINAPI HttpExtensionProc(EXTENSION_CONTROL_BLOCK *pECB)
```

This exported callback function is called by IIS. It in turn invokes `CallObject`, which kicks off your OLEISAPI application.

The source code for OLEISAPI.CPP is on the companion CD to this book.

Configuring the Environment

For the following examples, we assume that IIS is installed in c:\winnt\system32\ inetsrv and that the publication directories are in c:\inetpub. The directory structure holds at least the following:

Directory	Description
c:\winnt\system32\inetsrv\server	IIS service executables, etc.
c:\inetpub\wwwroot	HTML files residing here
c:\inetpub\scripts	Executable components (such as OLEISAPI.DLL)

Components in inetpub\scripts must have execute permission. You must set this capability in IIS Manager. Make sure the files have read and execute permission for the user you set up when installing IIS (usually IUSR_XXXX) in IE as well.

Components in inetpub\wwwroot must have read permission for the IUSR_XXXX account.

N O T E If permissions are not set correctly, you'll get errors hinting that components are missing or you'll have undefined problems. The error-reporting mechanism in OLEISAPI.DLL is rather basic.

When you run SETUP for your VB4 OLE server DLL, it is put in /Program Files/ Common Files/OleSvr by default.

Creating a "Hello, World!" OLEISAPI Application

In this section, we create the ubiquitous "Hello World!" program as an OLEISAPI application.

We begin by creating a new project called testprj1.vbp. This project is composed of only two source files: testprj1.cls and modole.bas.

The Project Files

Start VB4 (32-bit edition). Remove the default Form1.frm from the project, and add one class module and one module.

From the Tools menu, select Options. Select the Project tab and amend the project name to TProject1. Select the StartMode: OLE server option and click OK (see Figure 11.2).

This is the setup for any OLEISAPI project and the basis of all samples in this chapter. The module has only a `Main` subroutine, as needed to create an OLE server (see Listing 11.1).

FIG. 11.2
The VB4.0 Project Options dialog box.

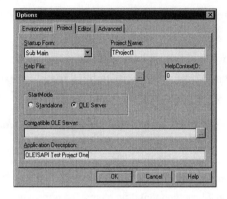

In the module, enter the code in Listing 11.1.

Listing 11.1   OLEISAPI.BAS—Test Project 1: Code Module

```
Option Explicit

Sub Main()

End Sub
```

The real meat and potatoes of our OLEISAPI application is the class module and it is very small. Enter the code in Listing 11.2.

Listing 11.2   TCLASS1.CLS—Test Project 1: Class Module

```
Option Explicit

Public Sub HelloWorld(Request As String, Response As String)
    Dim htmlHeader As String
    htmlHeader = "ContentType: Text/HTML" & vbCrLf & vbCrLf
    htmlHeader = htmlHeader & "<HTML><TITLE>Say Hello to the
    ➥World</TITLE>" & vbCrLf
    Response = htmlHeader & "<BODY>Hello World</BODY></HTML>" & vbCrLf
End Sub
```

With the code window for the class module open, right-click it and select Properties. For Instancing, select 2 - Creatable Multiuse. For Name, amend to TClass1 and set Public to True (see Figure 11.3).

This is a standard configuration for OLE server class modules to be compiled to DLLs. The module created earlier can also be named according to personal preference. The name is not critical to this example.

FIG. 11.3
The VB4.0 Class
Module Properties
dialog box.

N O T E Creatable Multiuse is for OLE server DLLs and means that all instances of the object share the same code block. If you want to make an OLE server EXE, your instancing property should be set to Creatable Singleuse.

But at this writing, NT 4.0 and IIS 3.0 were reporting an error in USER32.DLL when trying to call EXE OLE servers from IIS.

The advantage of EXE OLE servers over DLLs is that DLLs save memory by using a single code block that is shared among all instances. But this means that calls to the DLL must be serialized because VB4.0 cannot multithread an application.

OLE server EXEs do not share code because a new copy of the OLE server is loaded for each instance, so OLE server EXEs can multitask. The penalty for this is memory use of approximately 500K per instance. ▪

These settings create the core of the OLEISAPI callable OLE server, which now has a class identifier of TProject1.TClass1 and a single method of HelloWorld.

From the File menu, select Make OLE DLL File. This creates your OLE Server and puts it in the registry.

N O T E If you need to recompile your DLL and it has been accessed by IIS, you'll get an ACCESS DENIED error saying that the file is in use. To get around this, stop all IIS services (WWW, FTP, and gopher) on your computer.

This releases the DLL from use and enables you to replace the current version with the new one. Don't forget to restart the services afterwards. ▪

How It Works

As you can see from the sample `HelloWorld` function, our OLEISAPI OLE server member function has this signature:

```
HRESULT SomeMethod(request as string, response as string)
```

All OLEISAPI callable member functions must have this signature.

When your function is called from an URL, the request string holds either the HTTP query string (in the case of a `GET` request) or the data in the HTTP request (in the case of a `POST` request). The response string should be set by your OLE server object to the HTTP response you want presented to the user.

The beginning of the response string should always be Content-Type:, followed by a valid MIME type.

URLs that invoke this service from a link look like this:

> **http://machine/path/oleisapi.dll/Project.class.method?**
> **param1=foo&param2=bar**

In our case, it would be:

> **http://localhost/scripts/oleisapi.dll/TProject1.TClass1.HelloWorld**

The additional `?param1=` is not needed for this example. But if it were appended, it would be ignored. This information comes through as the request parameter in our method.

But because we do no checking on this value, it can be discarded. We'll use it in later projects.

Enter the previous URL in your preferred browser. A page is returned displaying "Hello, World!" in your default font (see Figure 11.4).

OLEISAPI.DLL also works with HTML forms that use the `POST`/`GET` methods. In this case, the parameters to the call come from the form elements rather than the URL. This is the direction for the next project.

FIG. 11.4
Output from "Hello, World!" application.

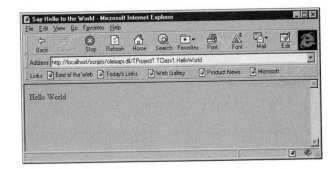

OLEISAPI 2.0 Version

To use OLEISAPI 2.0 in this project, you need to add a reference. From the Tools menu, select References. In the References dialog box, select OLEISAPI2 Type Library. Click OK.

Change the source code in the class module to the following:

```
Public Sub HelloWorld(objRequest as Request)
    objRequest.WriteResponse "<HTML><TITLE>Say Hello to the World
    ➥</TITLE>" & vbCrLf
    objRequest.WriteResponse "<BODY>Hello World</BODY></HTML>" &
    ➥vbCrLf
End Sub
```

OLEISAPI 2.0 exposes one object, called `Request`. This object has a number of methods and properties, but we use only `WriteResponse` in this project. A full list of properties and methods is in the README.TXT file that accompanies OLEISAPI2.DLL on the CD.

Change the URL to

http://localhost/scripts/oleisapi2.dll/TProject1.TClass1.HelloWorld

This highlights the differences between the OLEISAPI and OLEISAPI 2.0 implementations of a simple project, even though the basic concept is the same.

A Personalized "Hello, World!" Application

The previous example produces a static output from a static URL—hardly an exciting prospect to publish on the Web. In this example, we ask users to enter their name in an HTML form. We analyze the result and return a dynamic page based on the user input.

The Project Files

Create a new VB project as before, but set the project name to TProject2. Add one class module and one module.

In the module, add the code in Listing 11.3.

Listing 11.3   OLEISAPI.BAS—OLEISAPI Code Module

```
Option Explicit

Sub Main()

End Sub


Private Function GetField(Info As String, FieldName As String) As String
    Dim Position1 As Integer, Position2 As Integer, TempField As
    ➥String, Character As Integer
    Position1 = InStr(Info, FieldName & "=")
    If Position1 = 0 Then Exit Function
    Position1 = Position1 + Len(FieldName) + 1
    Position2 = InStr(Position1, Info, "&")
    If Position2 = 0 Then Position2 = Len(Info) + 1
    TempField = Mid(Info, Position1, Position2 - Position1)
    Position1 = InStr(TempField, "%")
    Do Until Position1 = 0
        Character = Decimal(Mid(TempField, Position1 + 1, 2))
        TempField = Left(TempField, Position1 - 1) & Chr(Character)
        ➥& Right(TempField, Len(TempField) - Position1 - 2)
        Position1 = InStr(Position1 + 1, TempField, "%")
    Loop
    Position1 = InStr(TempField, "+")
    Do Until Position1 = 0
        TempField = Left(TempField, Position1 - 1) & " " &
        ➥Right(TempField, Len(TempField) - Position1)
        Position1 = InStr(TempField, "+")
    Loop
    GetField = TempField
End Function


Private Function Decimal(sHEX As String) As Integer
    Dim iHigh As Integer, iLow As Integer
```

```
        iHigh = InStr("0123456789ABCDEF", Left(sHEX, 1)) - 1
        iLow = InStr("0123456789ABCDEF", Right(sHEX, 1)) - 1
        Decimal = iHigh * 16 + iLow
    End Function
```

In the class module, enter the code in Listing 11.4.

Listing 11.4   TCLASS2.CLS—Test Project 2: Class Module

```
Option Explicit


Public Sub SubmitNames(Request As String, Response As String)
    Dim htmlHeader As String
    htmlHeader = "ContentType: Text/HTML" & vbCrLf & vbCrLf
    htmlHeader = htmlHeader & "<HTML><TITLE>Say Hello to the World
    ➥in Person</TITLE>" & vbCrLf
    htmlHeader = htmlHeader & "<BODY>" & vbCrLf
    If GetField(Request, "FirstName") = "" Then
        Response = Response & "First Name not specified<BR>" & vbCrLf
    Else
        Response = Response & "First Name :" & GetField(Request,
        ➥"FirstName") & "<BR>" & vbCrLf
    End If
    If GetField(Request, "LastName") = "" Then
        Response = Response & "Last Name not specified<BR>" & vbCrLf
    Else
        Response = Response & "Last Name :" & GetField(Request,
        ➥"LastName") & "<BR>" & vbCrLf
    End If
    Response = htmlHeader & Response & "</BODY></HTML>"
End Sub
```

Set the properties of the new class and name it TClass2.

In this class, there is one public method, SubmitNames. The module now holds two private methods, GetField and Decimal.

The SubmitNames method is called by our HTML form. The first few lines create a standard HTML header. The line

```
    If GetField(Request, "FirstName") = "" Then
```

calls one of the private GetField functions. This function extracts fields from the request string. For example, the request parameter on the SubmitNames function

Part

III

Ch

11

might be `FirstName=Dean&LastName=Cleaver`. This is the `?param1=foo&param2 =bar` section of the URL without the "?".

The command `GetField(Request, "FirstName")` searches the request parameter for `"FirstName="`. It returns the value between that and the next "&" or the end-of-file (EOF), whichever comes first. In the previous example, it would return Dean.

The `GetField` function also looks for "%" signs and "+" signs. If our HTML form had a Name entry box and we entered Dean Cleaver!, the request string would be `Name=Dean+Cleaver%21`. The space has been changed to a "+", and the "!" has been changed to "%21".

These conversions ensure cross-platform compatibility and protect the integrity of the data. The "%" signifies HEX, 0x21 = 33 decimal, which is the ASCII code for "!".

The `Decimal` function takes a two-character HEX string ("21") and converts it to decimal (33), which can then be returned as a character. Thus `GetField` would return Dean Cleaver! correctly.

We write the `GetField` function in a generic format so it can be included in all projects of this type. Other projects in this chapter need this code, along with the `Decimal` function.

The HTML Form

For this example, we create an HTML form. In Notepad (or your preferred editor), enter the text in Listing 11.5. Take note of the exact format of the text in the listing.

Listing 11.5   TFORM2.HTM—Test Form 2: HTML

```
<HTML>
<HEAD>
<TITLE>Say Hello in Person</TITLE>

</HEAD>
<BODY>
<FORM ACTION="/scripts/oleisapi.dll/TProject2.TClass2.submitnames"
➥METHOD="GET" ENCTYPE="application/x-www-form-urlencoded">
<P>
First Name:<INPUT NAME="FirstName" VALUE="" MAXLENGTH="25" SIZE=25>
<P>
```

```
Last Name:<INPUT NAME="LastName" VALUE="" MAXLENGTH="25" SIZE=25>
<P>
<INPUT TYPE=SUBMIT VALUE="Submit" NAME="Submit">

</FORM>
</BODY>
</HTML>
```

Save this as **TForm2.htm** in your www publication directory, which is c:\inetpub\wwwroot by default in a fresh NT 4.0 install.

Open your browser and enter the URL

http://localhost/TForm2.htm

You'll see a simple HTML form, as shown in Figure 11.5.

FIG. 11.5

The TForm2.htm Web page.

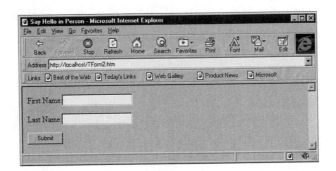

Enter your first and last name, and click Submit. The form should look like Figure 11.6.

FIG. 11.6

The output from Test Project 2.

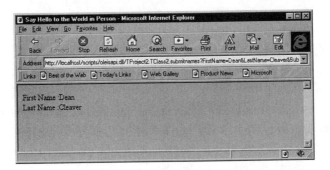

Note the URL in the browser window:

http://localhost/scripts/oleisapi.dll/TProject2.TClass2.submitnames?
FirstName=Dean&LastName=Cleaver&Submit=Submit

For OLEISAPI applications, the only difference between the GET and POST methods of form actions is the display of the parameters in the browser window. To highlight this point, edit the TForm2.htm file. Change METHOD= GET to METHOD= POST.

Save the file, refresh the form in the browser, and re-submit the information. The URL should now be displayed only as

http://localhost/scripts/oleisapi.dll/TProject2.TClass2.
submitnames

In most cases, this is preferable to displaying the full URL. However, the extra information can be useful for debugging and testing.

OLEISAPI 2.0 Version

To convert this sample to OLEISAPI 2.0, we use a new property. Instead of receiving Request as a parameter of the subroutine, we retrieve it from the objRequest.QueryString property, as follows:

```
Request = objRequest.QueryString
```

You could also convert this project to OLEISAPI 2.0 by putting this line at the top of the routine, changing the routine parameters, using the WriteResponse method, adding the reference, and changing the URL in the form. We leave this for you to do as an exercise.

A Sample Guest Book Application

In the previous sample, we analyze the input and return it to the user in a new HTML page—an interesting step but hardly useful in the real world. In this sample, we gather the information supplied by the user, store it in a guest-book database, and thank the user for the input.

The Project Files

Create a new VB project as before, but set the project name to TProject3. Add one class module and one module. The module is identical to the one in the previous example, so you may want to include that file rather than create a new one.

In the class module enter the code in Listing 11.6.

Listing 11.6 TCLASS3.CLS—Test Project 3: Class Module

```
Option Explicit


Public Sub GuestBook(Request As String, Response As String)
    Dim htmlHeader As String, htmlFooter As String, sSQL As String,
    ➥dbGuestBook As Database
    htmlHeader = "ContentType: Text/HTML" & vbCrLf & vbCrLf
    htmlHeader = htmlHeader & "<HTML><TITLE>Guestbook Application
    ➥</TITLE>" & vbCrLf
    htmlHeader = htmlHeader & "<BODY>" & vbCrLf
    htmlFooter = "</BODY></HTML>"
    sSQL = "insert into GuestBook (Title, GivenNames, Surname,
    ➥Address, Country, VB, VC, Delphi) values ("
    If GetField(Request, "Title") = "" Then
        Response = htmlHeader & "Please specify your title<BR>" &
        ➥vbCrLf & htmlFooter
        Exit Sub
    Else
        Response = htmlHeader & "Thank you for registering in my
        ➥guestbook.<BR>Your Guestbook details are as follows:<BR>" &
        ➥vbCrLf
        If GetField(Request, "Title") = "Other" Then
            Response = Response & GetField(Request, "Other") & " "
            sSQL = sSQL & "'" & GetField(Request, "Other") & "', "
        Else
            Response = Response & GetField(Request, "Title") & " "
            sSQL = sSQL & "'" & GetField(Request, "Title") & "', "
        End If
    End If
    If GetField(Request, "GivenNames") = "" Then
        Response = htmlHeader & "Please specify your given
        ➥names<BR>" & vbCrLf & htmlFooter
        Exit Sub
    Else
        Response = Response & GetField(Request, "GivenNames") & " "
        sSQL = sSQL & "'" & GetField(Request, "GivenNames") & "', "
    End If
```

Part
III

Ch
11

continues

Listing 11.6   Continued

```
    If GetField(Request, "Surname") = "" Then
        Response = htmlHeader & "Please specify your surname<BR>" &
        ➥vbCrLf & htmlFooter
        Exit Sub
    Else
        Response = Response & GetField(Request, "Surname") & "<BR>"
        ➥& vbCrLf
        sSQL = sSQL & "'" & GetField(Request, "Surname") & "', "
    End If
    If GetField(Request, "Address") = "" Then
        Response = htmlHeader & "Please specify your address<BR>" &
        ➥vbCrLf & htmlFooter
        Exit Sub
    Else
        Response = Response & GetField(Request, "Address") & "<BR>" &
        ➥vbCrLf
        sSQL = sSQL & "'" & GetField(Request, "Address") & "', "
    End If
    Response = Response & GetField(Request, "Country") & "<BR>" & vbCrLf
    sSQL = sSQL & "'" & GetField(Request, "Country") & "', "
    If GetField(Request, "PL1") = "VB" Then
        Response = Response & GetField(Request, "PL1") & "<BR>" & vbCrLf
        sSQL = sSQL & "-1, "
    Else
        sSQL = sSQL & "0, "
    End If
    If GetField(Request, "PL2") = "VC" Then
        Response = Response & GetField(Request, "PL2") & "<BR>" & vbCrLf
        sSQL = sSQL & "-1, "
    Else
        sSQL = sSQL & "0, "
    End If
    If GetField(Request, "PL3") = "Delphi" Then
        Response = Response & GetField(Request, "PL3") & "<BR>" & vbCrLf
        sSQL = sSQL & "-1)"
    Else
        sSQL = sSQL & "0)"
    End If
    Response = Response & htmlFooter
On Error Resume Next
    Set dbGuestBook = OpenDatabase("c:\data\projects\TProj3\
    ➥GuestBK.mdb")
    dbGuestBook.Execute sSQL, dbFailOnError
    If Err = 0 Then Exit Sub
    Response = htmlHeader & "I'm sorry. Your details could not be saved.
    ➥Please check them and try again later." & vbCrLf & htmlFooter
End Sub
```

The program assumes that an access database named GuestBK.mdb is in a C:\data\projects\tproj3\ directory. This can be changed to suit your needs (to a FoxPro table or ODBC data source, for example). But it's up to you to open the new database correctly.

The database has eight fields, as shown in Table 11.1.

Table 11.1 Guest-Book Table Definition

Field Name	Data Type
Title	Text
GivenNames	Text
Surname	Text
Address	Text
Country	Text
VB	Yes/No (Boolean or Integer)
VC	Yes/No
Delphi	Yes/No

This sample analyzes the returned string in much the same way as the previous example. But it returns an error to the user if one of the text entries is not filled out.

As it checks each field, this sample is also compiling a standard query language (SQL) insert statement, which is executed just before the end of the subroutine. If there is an error in saving to the database, the user is informed of an error and told to try again.

Typical errors occur when a user enters O'Rielly as a surname, for example. The SQL statement would be "..., 'O'Rielly', ..." which causes an error. But it is beyond the scope of this chapter to discuss and develop workarounds for this type of error.

The HTML Form

We need a fairly complex HTML form to test this project. In Notepad (or your preferred editor), enter the code in Listing 11.7.

Listing 11.7 TFORM3.HTM—Test Form 3: HTML

```
<HTML>
<HEAD>

<TITLE>Register in my Guest Book</TITLE>
</HEAD>
<BODY>
<FORM ACTION="/scripts/oleisapi.dll/TProject3.TClass3.GuestBook"
➥METHOD="POST" ENCTYPE="application/x-www-form-urlencoded">
<P>
Surname:<INPUT NAME="Surname" VALUE="" MAXLENGTH="25" SIZE=25>
<P>
Given Names:<INPUT NAME="GivenNames" VALUE="" MAXLENGTH="25" SIZE=25>
<P>
Title:<INPUT TYPE="RADIO" NAME="Title" VALUE="Mr">Mr <INPUT TYPE=
➥"RADIO" NAME="Title" VALUE="Mrs">Mrs
<INPUT TYPE="RADIO" NAME="Title" VALUE="Miss">Miss <INPUT TYPE=
➥"RADIO" NAME="Title" VALUE="Ms">Ms
<INPUT TYPE="RADIO" NAME="Title" VALUE="Other">Other <INPUT NAME=
➥"Other" VALUE="" MAXLENGTH="10" SIZE=10>
<P>
Address:
<TEXTAREA NAME="Address" ROWS=2 COLS=50>
</TEXTAREA>

<P>
Country:<SELECT NAME="Country"    >
<OPTION VALUE="USA">USA
<OPTION SELECTED VALUE="NZ">New Zealand
<OPTION VALUE="Other">Other</SELECT>
<P>
Programming Languages:
<P>
<INPUT TYPE="CHECKBOX" NAME="PL1" VALUE="VB">Visual Basic
<P>
<INPUT TYPE="CHECKBOX" NAME="PL2" VALUE="VC">Visual C++
<P>
<INPUT TYPE="CHECKBOX" NAME="PL3" VALUE="Delphi">Delphi
<P>
<INPUT TYPE=SUBMIT VALUE="Submit" NAME="Submit">    <INPUT TYPE=
➥RESET VALUE="Reset">
</FORM>

</BODY>
</HTML>
```

Save this file to your www publishing directory and call it **TForm3.htm**.

Enter the following URL in your browser:

http://localhost/tform3.htm

You see the HTML form shown in Figure 11.7.

FIG. 11.7
The TForm3.htm Web page.

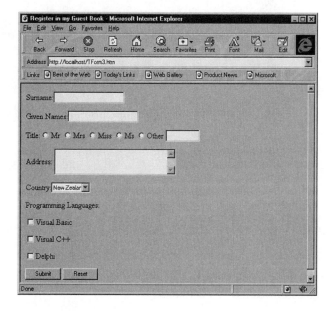

To submit this form, fill in all the text boxes (the Other box is not needed). Optionally select a Country and the languages that you program in. A sample HTML page from the project is shown in Figure 11.8.

OLEISAPI 2.0 Version

To convert the form to OLEISAPI 2.0, you would need a similar change to the project just discussed. The base methods and properties are the same.

Part

III

Ch

11

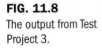

FIG. 11.8
The output from Test
Project 3.

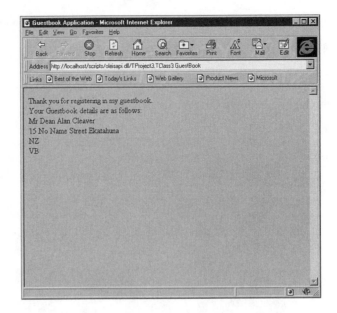

A Sample Database Query Application

This sample queries a database and returns the results to the user. In this case, the results are links to physical documents (.DOC or .XLS files) on the server in an IIS virtual directory called /Bulletins.

This sample is a shortened version of a project developed for BMW New Zealand Limited. It is reproduced in part with their kind permission.

The Project Files

Create a new VB project as before but set the project name to TProject4. Add one class module and one module. With one addition, the module is identical to the one in the previous example, so you may want to include that file rather than create a new one or make a copy of it.

Add the new code shown in Listing 11.8.

Listing 11.8   OLEISAPI.BAS—OLEISAPI Code Module

```
Private Function NoSpaces(Info As String) As String
    Dim tmpString As String, Position1 As Integer
    tmpString = Info
    Position1 = InStr(tmpString, " ")
    Do Until Position1 = 0
        tmpString = Left(tmpString, Position1 - 1) & "+" &
        ➥Right(tmpString, Len(tmpString) - Position1)
        Position1 = InStr(tmpString, " ")
    Loop
    NoSpaces = tmpString
End Function
```

In the class module, enter the code shown in Listing 11.9.

Listing 11.9   TCLASS4.CLS—Test Project 4: Class Module

```
Public Sub GetBulletins(Request As String, Response As String)
On Error Resume Next
    Dim Information As String
    Dim HTMLHeader As String
    Dim FileName    As String
    Dim FileDate As Date
    Dim FileTopic As String
    Dim Position1 As Integer
    Dim Position2 As Integer
    Dim Position3 As Integer
    Dim Result As String
    Dim Spacer As String
    Dim dbBulletins As Database
    Dim rsBulletins As Recordset
    Dim Counter As Integer
    Dim I As Integer
    Const iNumberOfBulletins = 7    ' Limits the number of lines
    ➥displayed
    Set dbBulletins = Workspaces(0).OpenDatabase("c:\data\project
    ➥\tproj4\bulletin.mdb")
    HTMLHeader = "Content-type: text/html" & vbCrLf
    If Request <> "" Then
        If InStr(UCase(Request), "TOPIC") <> 0 Then
            Result = GetField(Request, "TOPIC")
            Set rsBulletins = dbBulletins.OpenRecordset("SELECT
            ➥date,description,filename FROM Bulletin WHERE bulletin
            ➥level like '" & Result & "%' ORDER BY date DESC",
            ➥dbOpenSnapshot)
```

continues

Part

III

Ch

11

Listing 11.9 Continued

```
Response = Response & HTMLHeader & vbCrLf
Response = Response & "<TITLE>" & GetField(Request,
➥"TITLE") & "</TITLE>" & vbCrLf
Response = Response & "<BODY BGCOLOR=FFFFFF>" & vbCrLf
Response = Response & "<P>" & vbCrLf
Response = Response & "<TABLE>" & vbCrLf
Response = Response & Spacer
Result = GetField(Request, "BACK")
If InStr(UCase(Request), "START") <> 0 Then
    For Counter = 1 To Val(GetField(Request, "START"))
        rsBulletins.MoveNext
    Next
    Counter = 0
    Do Until rsBulletins.EOF
        Response = Response & "<TR><TD WIDTH=100><A
        ➥HREF=/Bulletins/" & rsBulletins!FileName & ">" &
        ➥rsBulletins!Date & "</A></TD>" & vbCrLf
        Response = Response & "<TD WIDTH=1000><A HREF=
        ➥/Bulletins/" & rsBulletins!FileName & ">" &
        ➥rsBulletins!Description & "</A></TD></TR>" & vbCrLf
        ➥& vbCrLf
        rsBulletins.MoveNext
        Counter = Counter + 1
        If Counter = iNumberOfBulletins Then
            Response = Response & "</TABLE>" & vbCrLf
            If rsBulletins.EOF Then
                If Val(GetField(Request, "START")) <=
                ➥iNumberOfBulletins Then
                    Response = Response & "<TABLE
                    ➥BORDER=0><TR><TD><FONT COLOR=#FF0000>
                    ➥<A HREF=/scripts/oleisapi.dll/
                    ➥tproject4.tclass4.getbulletins?Topic="
                    ➥& GetField(Request, "Topic") & "&Back="
                    ➥& Result & "&Title="
                    ➥& NoSpaces(GetField(Request, "TITLE"))
                    ➥& ">...Previous</A></TD>"
            Else
                Response = Response & "<TABLE
                ➥BORDER=0><TR><TD><FONT COLOR=#FF0000>
                ➥<A HREF=/scripts/oleisapi.dll/
                ➥tproject4.tclass4.getbulletins?Topic="
                ➥&GetField(Request, "Topic") & "&Back="
                ➥& Result & "&Start=" &
                ➥ Val(GetField(Request, "START")) -
                ➥iNumberOfBulletins & "&Title=" &
                ➥NoSpaces(GetField(Request, "TITLE")) &
                ➥">...Previous</A></TD>"
            End If
        Else
```

```
                    If Val(GetField(Request, "START")) <=
                    ➡️iNumberOfBulletins Then
                        Response = Response & "<TABLE
                        ➡️BORDER=0><TR><TD><FONT COLOR=#FF0000>
                        ➡️<A HREF=/scripts/oleisapi.dll/
                        ➡️tproject4.tclass4.getbulletins?Topic=
                        ➡️" & GetField(Request, "Topic") &
                        ➡️"&Back=" & Result & "&Title=" &
                        ➡️NoSpaces(GetField(Request, "TITLE")) &
                        ➡️">...Previous</A></TD>"
                    Else
                        Response = Response & "<TABLE
                        ➡️BORDER=0><TR><TD><FONT COLOR=#FF0000>
                        ➡️<A HREF=/scripts/oleisapi.dll/
                        ➡️tproject4.tclass4.getbulletins?Topic="
                        ➡️& GetField(Request, "Topic") & "&Back="
                        ➡️& Result & "&Start="
                        ➡️& Val(GetField(Request, "START")) -
                        ➡️iNumberOfBulletins & "&Title=" &
                        ➡️NoSpaces(GetField(Request, "TITLE")) &
                        ➡️"&Title=" & ">... Previous</A></TD>"
                    End If
                    Response = Response & "<TD><FONT
COLOR=#FFFFFF>XXXXXXXXXXXXXXXXXXXXXXXXXXXXXXXXXXXXX</TD>"
                    Response = Response & "<TD><FONT COLOR=
                    ➡️#FF0000><A HREF=/scripts/oleisapi.dll/
                    ➡️tproject4.tclass4.
                    ➡️getbulletins?Topic=" & GetField(Request,
                    ➡️"Topic") & "&Back=" & Result & "&Start=" &
                    ➡️Val(GetField(Request, "START")) +
                    ➡️iNumberOfBulletins & "&Title=" &
                    ➡️NoSpaces(GetField(Request, "TITLE"))
                    ➡️& ">More...</A></TD></TR></TABLE>"
                End If
                Exit Do
            End If
        Loop
        If Counter < iNumberOfBulletins Then
            For I = Counter To iNumberOfBulletins - 1
                Response = Response & "<TR><TD WIDTH=
                ➡️100>  </TD>" & vbCrLf
                Response = Response & "<TD WIDTH=
                ➡️1000></TD></TR>" & vbCrLf & vbCrLf
            Next
        Response = Response & "</TABLE>" & vbCrLf
        If Val(GetField(Request, "START")) <=
        ➡️iNumberOfBulletins Then
            Response = Response & "<TABLE BORDER=
            ➡️0><TR><TD><FONT COLOR=#FF0000><A HREF=/scripts/
```

continues

Part

III

Ch

11

Listing 11.9   Continued

```
                                    ➥oleisapi.dll/tproject4.tclass4.getbulletins?
                                    ➥Topic=" & GetField(Request, "Topic") & "&Back="
                                    ➥& Result & "&Title=" & NoSpaces
                                    ➥(GetField(Request, "TITLE")) & ">...Previous</
                                    ➥A></TD>"
                        Else
                            Response = Response & "<TABLE BORDER=
                            ➥0><TR><TD><FONT COLOR=#FF0000><A HREF=/scripts/
                            ➥oleisapi.dll/tproject4.tclass4. getbulletins?
                            ➥Topic=" & GetField(Request, "Topic") & "&Back="
                            ➥& Result & "&Start=" & Val(GetField(Request,
                            ➥"START")) - iNumberOfBulletins & "&Title=" &
                            ➥NoSpaces(GetField(Request, "TITLE")) &
                            ➥">...Previous</A></TD>"
                        End If
                    End If
                    Response = Response & "</TABLE>" & vbCrLf
                Else
                    Do Until rsBulletins.EOF
                        Response = Response & "<TR><TD WIDTH=100><A
                        ➥HREF=/Bulletins/" & rsBulletins!FileName & ">" &
                        ➥rsBulletins!Date & "</A></TD>" & vbCrLf
                        Response = Response & "<TD WIDTH=1000><A
                        ➥HREF=/Bulletins/" & rsBulletins!FileName & ">" &
                        ➥rsBulletins!Description & "</A></TD></TR>" & vbCrLf
                        ➥& vbCrLf
                        rsBulletins.MoveNext
                        Counter = Counter + 1
                        If Counter = iNumberOfBulletins Then
                            Response = Response & "</TABLE>" & vbCrLf
                            If Not rsBulletins.EOF Then
                                Response = Response & "<TABLE
                                ➥BORDER=0><TR><TD><FONT COLOR=#FFFFFF>
                                ➥...Previous</TD>"
                                Response = Response & "<TD><FONT
        COLOR=#FFFFFF>XXXXXXXXXXXXXXXXXXXXXXXXXXXXXXXXX</TD>"
                                Response = Response & "<TD><FONT
                                ➥COLOR=#FF0000><A HREF=/scripts/
                                ➥oleisapi.dll/tproject4.tclass4.
                                ➥getbulletins?Topic=" & GetField(Request,
                                ➥"Topic") & "&Back=" & Result & "&Start=" &
                                ➥Val(GetField(Request, "START")) +
                                ➥iNumberOfBulletins & "&Title=" & NoSpaces
                                ➥(GetField(Request, "TITLE")) & ">More...
                                ➥</A></TD></TR>"
                            End If
                            Exit Do
                        End If
                    Loop
```

```
            If Counter < iNumberOfBulletins Then
                For I = Counter To iNumberOfBulletins - 1
                    Response = Response & "<TR><TD WIDTH=
                    ➥100>  </TD>" & vbCrLf
                    Response = Response & "<TD WIDTH=
                    ➥1000></TD></TR>" & vbCrLf & vbCrLf
                Next
                Response = Response & "</TABLE>" & vbCrLf
                Response = Response & "<TABLE BORDER=
                ➥0><TR><TD><FONT COLOR=#FFFFFF>...Previous</TD>"
            End If
            Response = Response & "</TABLE>" & vbCrLf
        End If
    End If
  End If
  Close
End Sub
```

The sample expects a database called `Bulletin.mdb` to be in the c:\oleisapi\ samples\four\ directory. This database holds a Bulletins table with the fields shown in Table 11.2.

Table 11.2   Bulletins Table Field Listing

Field Name	Data Type
Date	Date/Time
Description	Text
FileName	Text
Bulletin_Level	Text

Some typical entries are shown in Table 11.3.

Table 11.3   Bulletins Table Sample Records

Date	Description	FileName	Bulletin_Level
31/7/96	3 Series Prices	3series.xls	Prices
2/8/96	5 Series Prices	5series.xls	Prices
31/7/96	3 Series Options	3seropts.doc	Options

How It Works

The first lines declare the variables needed. They verify that a valid request is passed and that it has a topic field. If this is valid, the database is queried for the given topic, as follows:

```
Result = GetField(Request, "TOPIC")
Set rsBulletins = dbBulletins.OpenRecordset("SELECT date,
➥description,filename FROM Bulletins WHERE bulletin_level like '
➥" & Result & "*' ORDER BY date DESC", dbOpenSnapshot)
```

If the topic were Prices, the first two records would be returned, as shown previously in Table 11.3.

```
Result = GetField(Request, "BACK")
```

This line checks for a BACK parameter, which is used to set the URL for a Back button.

N O T E The full version of this code includes an image complete with a client-side image map. This is updated to include the BACK parameter if it is passed. This URL is also passed to subpages created by this DLL. But is not used in this example without the image map.

```
If InStr(UCase(Request), "START") <> 0 Then
```

This line checks for a START value in the request. If present, this value means that more than seven entries were retrieved last time and that the More option was selected.

The limitation of seven was chosen so as not to display scroll bars in the browser. It is not a limitation of the program.

The number of lines returned (seven) is set by a constant at the top of the listing. If a START value is found, the record set is advanced to the starting position.

```
Response = Response & "<TR><TD WIDTH=100><A HREF=/Bulletins/" &
➥rsBulletins!FileName & ">" & rsBulletins!Date & "</A></TD>"
➥& vbCrLf
Response = Response & "<TD WIDTH=1000><A HREF=/Bulletins/" &
➥rsBulletins!FileName & ">" & rsBulletins!Description &
➥"</A></TD></TR>" & vbCrLf & vbCrLf
```

These two lines form one line of a two-field table. Included are HREF links to the /Bulletins virtual directory and to the file name as it is in the database. Fixed table widths are used to suit the client browser.

```
If Counter = iNumberOfBulletins Then
```

This line checks to see if the current list of items has reached the maximum limit for the page. If it has, you may need to add a More... link. The following psuedocode explains the logic for this section:

```
if EndOfRecordset then
   if "START" <= MaximumNumber
         show "Previous..." with no "START"
   else
         show "Previous..." with "START" = "START" - MaximumNumber
   endif
else
   if "START" <= MaximumNumber
         show "Previous..." with no "START"
   else
         show "Previous..." with "START" = "START" - MaximumNumber
   endif
   show MANY_XX's in White (not visible) for spacing
   show "More..." with "START" = "START" + MaximumNumber
endif
```

If no START value is found, the code progresses in much the same way. But the pseudocode section shows a Previous... in white if a More... is needed. The More... includes the START parameter.

```
If Counter < iNumberOfBulletins Then
   For I = Counter To iNumberOfBulletins - 1
        Response = Response & "<TR><TD WIDTH=100>  </TD>" &
        ➥vbCrLf
        Response = Response & "<TD WIDTH=1000></TD></TR>" & vbCrLf
        ➥& vbCrLf
   Next
   Response = Response & "</TABLE>" & vbCrLf
   Response = Response & "<TABLE BORDER=0><TR><TD><FONT COLOR=
   ➥#FFFFFF>...Previous</TD>"
End If
```

This checks that if fewer than seven records are returned, the table is filled with blank lines to ensure that the layout is consistent.

Part
III

Ch

11

A number of the methods used for the HTML file returned were to ensure good visibility in IE 1.5 for Windows NT 3.51. They are not necessarily a good example of HTML layout.

Entering the URL

**http://localhost/scripts/oleisapi.dll/
TProject4.TClass4.GetBulletins?TOPIC=Prices**

returns the Web page shown in Figure 11.9, given the previous sample table data.

FIG. 11.9
The TProj4 Web page.

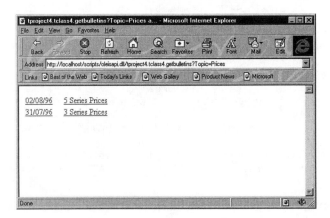

In the full version, the URL is hardcoded into another page that has links to Prices, Options, and so on. The URL also includes a link back to that page via the BACK parameter. This is because the previous page could be from anywhere:

```
&BACK=/somepage.htm
```

OLEISAPI 2.0 Version

Once again, the conversion for this project is the same as for the previous two. But the options don't stop there. With the extra features of OLEISAPI 2.0, you could add a lot more functionality.

The Request object enables you to retrieve server variables, upload files, and do other such things that are not possible with OLEISAPI. Using some of this functionality, you could expand this project to include, for example, submitting the documents as well as viewing them. I leave this for you to investigate.

From Here...

Building and running OLEISAPI applications is straightforward once you have all the components installed and configured. You must install and configure IIS, a browser, the OLEISAPI.DLL file and its files, and your OLE server application.

The complexity of your OLEISAPI application is limited only by your creativity and VB4 capabilities. These examples should give you a good grounding in OLEISAPI programming. You'll be able to produce bigger and better things in a very short time.

Topics covered in this chapter include:

- Returning a simple HTML formatted page.
- Processing simple requests from an URL.
- Processing information returned from a form.

From here, you can expand these basic samples for almost any application suitable for the Internet, for example:

- Creating a survey form and returning analyzed results.
- Marking a quiz form and returning the results to the user.

Part
III

Ch
11

ISAPI Filters

CHAPTER 12

Using ISAPI Filters

As we learn in Chapter 13, "Understanding ISAPI Filters," an Internet Server Application Programming Interface (ISAPI) filter is made up of 32-bit, dynamic link libraries (DLLs).

A filter is replaceable. A filter is put into server memory at startup and removed at shutdown. A filter can also be uninstalled by removing it from Windows NT Server's registry.

Instead of being called only in special instances, a filter is executed with every Hypertext Transport Protocol (HTTP) request.

A filter controls its own functions. A filter can ignore an HTTP request if the filter registers for an event notification. When that event occurs, the filter is called to process it. So the filter, once it is loaded into memory, controls its own functions instead of being controlled by the operating system.

Port management

Whether a port is secure or nonsecure, and the types of data to pass through a port.

Authentication of user IDs and passwords

Whether the user logging on to the network is authorized to use the network.

URL mapping or translation

Translating a Web resource's URL into a physical address.

Page generation

Building a Web page from scratch.

Page translation

Changing (customizing) the appearance of a received page or the received results of an ISAPI process.

Logging

Recording the administrative details of a number of server functions.

Encryption

When Secure Socket Layer (SSL) is running, all data sent to or from a client is encrypted.

> **CAUTION**
>
> Once a filter registers for a request, it gets that data regardless of whether the request is for a file, a Common Gateway Interface (CGI) application, or an ISAPI application.

In this chapter, we discuss how Windows NT Server and Microsoft's Internet Information Server (IIS) deal with several of the more common network functions. Included are examples of ISAPI code you can write to tailor some of these functions to your network's needs. ∎

Port Management

IIS 3.0 uses the Secure Socket Layer (SSL) security protocol. IIS enables and disables SSL through its Key Manager Tool, which can be executed from the Windows NT Start button or from the Internet Service Manager tool.

But there's more to the port security picture than that. Your network must be certified to use SSL. One certifying body is VeriSign.

Instructions are available online from VeriSign about getting an SSL certificate. Look for the SSL Certificates for IIS selection at the following Web address: **http://www.verisign.com/microsoft/index.html**.

> **CAUTION**
>
> Problems have been reported with installing VeriSign keys. Loading these keys has sometimes caused the error message:
>
> ```
>      Key check failed with error 0x........
> ```
>
> Retrace your attempts to install the key. If you can find no reason for the failure, check one last thing: Be sure that when you installed the key, you used the file sent to you by VeriSign and not the file you sent to it.
>
> Using the wrong file to install the key is a frequent cause of the error message.

 TIP SSL has also been reported to have trouble dealing with input from a form. One fix is to use the command GET instead of the more frequently used POST to send input from the form to the destination.

Apparently, when SSL is activated, IIS does not know where to send form input, so that input may as well have gone into a black hole. As far as your server's ability to process it is concerned, it disappears.

The IIS FAQ recently reported that both a Perl script and an ISAPI filter that used this fix worked successfully. The latest version of the IIS FAQ is available at

http://rampages.onramp.net/~steveg/iis.html.

Adding Further Security

SSL enables both data encryption and server authentication. When SSL is running, all data sent to or from a client is encrypted.

For instance, when HTTP basic authentication is configured and SSL is used, the user name and password are encrypted. Only then are they transmitted to the server for authentication.

To further ensure the security of selected services, you can write an ISAPI filter that causes an application to accept data only if that data originates from a secure port. Such a filter would involve the use of the SF_NOTIFY_SECURE_PORT notification or the testing of the HTTP_FILTER_CONTEXT *fIsSecurePort* member variable.

User Authentication

Part IV Ch 12

IIS can confirm the validity of attempts by users to access Web, Gopher, and FTP services. Such verification is fully integrated with user and file access permissions for Windows NT Server.

IIS by default enables anonymous connections. An anonymous connection is a user's attempt to access a Web, Gopher, or FTP service without supplying a user name and password. This is the typical access scenario for the Internet.

Access Control Lists

The Windows NT Server file system (NTFS) uses Access Control Lists (ACLs) to grant or deny certain Windows NT user accounts and groups of users access to files and directories.

continues

continued

An ACL is a list of files and directories. Associated with every file and directory on the list are the names of the users and groups allowed to use that item.

When an attempt to access the file or directory named in an ACL is denied, it is because the user or the group to which the user is assigned is not associated with that file or directory in the ACL.

How does an ISAPI filter handle anonymous connection attempts? IIS maintains a *fictitious user* account for each of its Internet services. This anonymous user account is intended solely to process anonymous requests.

Such an account is created and incorporated into Windows NT Server's domain user management scheme when IIS is installed. The user name for this account has the form

```
IUSR_<server_name>
```

For example, if the server on which IIS is being loaded is called Platform1, the anonymous user account has the name

```
IUSR_Platform1
```

IUSR_Platform1 is automatically made a member of the Guest domain user group at the time of the creation of this account. IIS can handle a number of domains or run from more than one server in a network, and still manage automatically created anonymous user accounts.

Each such account has the name of the computer on which it runs. Accounts created by domain-member servers are placed on the local computer. In this way, every account name created when IIS is installed is unique.

When an anonymous request is received, the service to which the request has been directed impersonates a user. It "pretends" that the request comes from the fictitious user identified in the anonymous user account. The request succeeds if the anonymous user has permission in Windows NT Server's ACL to access the resource.

Your ISAPI filter might be written to change the way IIS handles failed anonymous access attempts. In the next section, we discuss this possibility.

Changing Anonymous Access Handling

Suppose an anonymous user account does not have permission in the ACL to access a resource. Also suppose that IIS is configured to use basic HTTP authentication or Windows NT challenge and response authentication. In this case, most Web browsers respond by

- Popping up a dialog box that asks for a valid user name and password to be input.

- Reissuing the request for HTTP service under the user ID entered.

> **CAUTION**
>
> As of mid-November 1996, Web browsers that accept Windows NT native user authentication (NTLM) include Microsoft Internet Explorer (IE) versions 2.0 and later, and Netscape Navigator versions 2.0 and later.

Coding the Change to User Authentication   To change how IIS does user authentication by preventing the pop up of the dialog box described above, you could use the SF_NOTIFY_ACCESS_DENIED notification (available only in IIS 3.0 and later). This notifies an ISAPI filter whenever the server is about to return a status code of 401 Access Denied. This notification enables the filter to analyze the failure and return a custom message.

To request the access-denied event, the filter sets the SF_NOTIFY_ACCESS_DENIED flag when the GetFilterVersion method is called by IIS at the filter's initialization. Listing 12.1 is an example of how to request notification of the SF_NOTIFY_ACCESS_DENIED event.

Part

IV

Ch

12

Listing 12.1   LST12_1.CPP—*GetFilterVersion*: Access Denied

```
/*
        GetFilterVersion - An ISAPI/Win32 API method
        This method is required by IIS.  It is called
        following the process load to ensure that the
        filter is compatible with the server.
*/
```

continues

Listing 12.1   Continued

```
BOOL WINAPI GetFilterVersion(HTTP_FILTER_VERSION * pVer)
{
    pVer->dwFilterVersion = MAKELONG( 0, 1 );    // Version 1.0

    pVer->dwFlags = (SF_NOTIFY_ACCESS_DENIED ¦
                     SF_NOTIFY_ORDER_DEFAULT);
      /*
             A brief one line description of the filter
      */
    strcpy( pVer->lpszFilterDesc, TEXT("Sample Filter, v1.1"));

    return TRUE;
}
```

When the filter requests notification for an event, it gets a notification each time the event occurs. HttpFilterProc is called by the Web service just before it issues a status code of 401 Access Denied. This triggers the SF_NOTIFY_ACCESS_DENIED event. Listing 12.2 is an HttpFilterProc function to handle the SF_NOTIFY_ACCESS_DENIED event.

Listing 12.2   LST12_2CPP—*HttpFilterProc*: Access Denied

```
/*
        HttpFilterProc - ISAPI / Win32 API method
        This method is a required by IIS.  It is called
        for each notification event requested.  This is
        where the filter accomplishes its purpose in life.
*/
DWORD WINAPI HttpFilterProc(HTTP_FILTER_CONTEXT *pfc,
                                   DWORD NotificationType,
                                   VOID * pvData)
{
    DWORD dwRet;
    /*
               Direct the notification to the appropriate
               routine for processing.
    */
    switch ( NotificationType )
    {
    case SF_NOTIFY_ACCESS_DENIED:
        dwRet = OnAccessDenied(pfc, (PHTTP_FILTER_ACCESS_DENIED)
        ➥pvData );
```

```
            break;
    default:
        dwRet = SF_STATUS_REQ_NEXT_NOTIFICATION;
        break;
    }
    return dwRet;
}
```

When the `SF_NOTIFY_ACCESS_DENIED` event is received, the filter calls
`OnAccessDenied` to provide the custom processing necessary. Listing 12.3 is an
example of how to return a custom message to the client browser instead of the
standard error code message.

Listing 12.3 LST12_3CPP—*OnAccessDenied*: Access Denied

```
/*
    OnAccessDenied -
    The data returned at pvData->pvInData includes the
    header, types of data accepted and the browsers type
*/
DWORD OnAccessDenied(HTTP_FILTER_CONTEXT *pfc,
                        HTTP_FILTER_ACCESS_DENIED *pvData)
{
    char* pszBuffer;
    DWORD dwBufferSize=400;
    pszBuffer=(CHAR*)pfc->AllocMem(pfc, dwBufferSize, (DWORD)NULL);
    strcpy(pszBuffer, TEXT("<HTML><BODY><H1>Sorry this section is
    ➥closed!</H1></BODY></HTML>"));
    dwBufferSize = (DWORD) strlen(pszBuffer);
    pfc->WriteClient(pfc, (LPVOID)pszBuffer, &dwBufferSize,
    ➥(DWORD)NULL);
    return SF_STATUS_REQ_FINISHED;
}
/*
```

Part

IV

Ch

12

Monitoring and Logging the Server

When you install IIS, performance monitoring objects are added to the list of available objects in the Performance Monitor of Windows NT Server.

Tracking Your System with Performance Monitor

Performance Monitor is a graphical tool that charts the features of a number of network or station functions. Among these features are

- Processor usage
- Memory usage
- Cache usage
- Progress and status of threads
- Status of processes

Every object Performance Monitor reports on has associated with it a set of counters that track device usage, queue delays, and other vital statistics.

Performance Monitor can also be set up to provide administrator alerts and system log entries in certain conditions.

Some of the performance objects made available to the Performance Monitor offer statistics, as shown in Table 12.1.

Table 12.1   IIS Performance Monitoring Objects

Counter	Definition
BGI Requests	The number of requests to installed, custom DLLs that use the Binary Gateway Interface (BGI) and forms processing, or other dynamic data sources
Bytes Received/Sec	Bytes received per second by the server
Bytes Sent/Sec	Bytes sent per second by the server
Bytes Total/Sec	Total bytes received and sent by the server
CGI Requests	Number of requests to installed, custom EXE files compiled from CGI source code; these executables add forms processing or other dynamic data sources

Counter	Definition
Connection Attempts	Total number of connection attempts made to the HTTP server `Connections/Sec`; number of HTTP requests the server is handling per second
Current Anonymous Users	Number of connected anonymous users
Current BGI Requests	Number of current BGI requests being processed simultaneously by the server
Current CGI Requests	Number of current CGI requests being processed simultaneously by the server; includes WAIS index queries
Current Connections	Total number of active connections to the server
Current NonAnonymous Users	Total number of nonanonymous users connected to the server
Files Received	Total number of files received by the server
Files Sent	Total number of files sent by the server
Files Total	`Files Sent` plus `Files Received Get Requests Number` of current HTTP requests using the `GET` method (usually the retrieval of text or image files, but can be applied to form fill-in)
Read Requests	Number of current HTTP requests using the `READ` method (which usually indicates that a client is querying the condition of the current document to determine, for example, if it needs to be refreshed)
Logon Attempts	Total logon attempts made to the server
Maximum Anonymous Users	Maximum number of simultaneous anonymous user connections to the server

Part
IV

Ch
12

continues

Table 12.1   Continued

Counter	Definition
Maximum BGI Requests	Maximum number of simultaneous BGI requests being processed by the server
Maximum CGI Requests	Maximum number of simultaneous BGI requests being processed by the server; includes WAIS index queries
Maximum Connections	Maximum number of simultaneous user connections to the HTTP server
Maximum NonAnonymous Users	Maximum number of simultaneous nonanonymous user connections to the server
Not Found Errors	Total number of requests that could not be satisfied by the server because the document in question could not be found
Other Request Methods	Total number of requests to the server that do not use GET, POST, or READ; can include but are not limited to PUT, DELETE, and LINK
Post Requests	Total number of requests to the server that use the POST method (most commonly associated with forms fill-in or with gateway requests)
Total Anonymous Users	Total number of anonymous users who have ever connected to the server
Total NonAnonymous Users	Total number of users who have ever connected to the server

Custom Logging

You can construct a filter to change the IIS log file or produce a separate custom log file. The best place to produce a changed or custom log file is when the SF_NOTIFY_LOG event is triggered. When this event is triggered, a pointer to the HTTP_FILTER_LOG structure is available and provides the following information:

```
typedef struct _HTTP_FILTER_LOG
{
    const CHAR *    pszClientHostName;
    const CHAR *    pszClientUserName;
    const CHAR *    pszServerName;
    const CHAR *    pszOperation;
    const CHAR *    pszTarget;
    const CHAR *    pszParameters;
    DWORD           dwHttpStatus;
    DWORD           dwWin32Status;
} HTTP_FILTER_LOG, *PHTTP_FILTER_LOG;
```

The pointer to the HTTP_FILTER_LOG structure also includes these members:

- pszClientHostName—The client's host name.

- pszClientUserName—The client's user name.

- pszServerName—The server the client is connected to.

- pszOperation—The HTTP command.

- pszTarget—The target of the HTTP command.

- pszParameters—Parameters passed to the HTTP command.

- dwHttpStatus—The HTTP return status.

- dwWin32Status—The Win32 error code.

Coding the Log-Change Filter   To supply custom logging, your filter should request notification of the SF_NOTIFY_LOG event. To register for the logging event, the filter sets the SF_NOTIFY_LOG flag when the GetFilterVersion method is called by IIS at the filter's initialization, as shown in Listing 12.4.

Listing 12.4   LST12_4.CPP—*GetFilterVersion*: Change Log

```
/*
     GetFilterVersion - An ISAPI/Win32 API method
     This method is required by IIS.  It is called
     following the process load to ensure that the
     filter is compatible with the server.
*/
BOOL WINAPI GetFilterVersion(HTTP_FILTER_VERSION * pVer)
{
    pVer->dwFilterVersion = MAKELONG( 0, 1 );    // Version 1.0

    pVer->dwFlags = (SF_NOTIFY_LOG ¦
                     SF_NOTIFY_ORDER_DEFAULT);
        /*
             A brief one line description of the filter
        */
    strcpy( pVer->lpszFilterDesc, TEXT("Sample Filter, v1.1"));

    return TRUE;
}
```

Part
IV

Ch
12

When the filter requests notification of an event, it gets notification each time the event occurs. When `HttpFilterProc` is called by IIS, `SF_NOTIFY_LOG` is triggered, the function associated with the event is executed, and logging information can be changed or analyzed. Listing 12.5 and Listing 12.6 show you how to change the logging information.

Listing 12.5   LST12_5.CPP—*HttpFilterProc*: Change Log

```
/*

        HttpFilterProc - ISAPI / Win32 API method
        This method is a required by IIS.  It is called
        for each notification event requested.  This is
        where the filter accomplishes its purpose in life.
*/
DWORD WINAPI HttpFilterProc(HTTP_FILTER_CONTEXT *pfc,
                                    DWORD NotificationType,
                                    VOID * pvData)

{
    DWORD dwRet;
    /*
            Direct the notification to the appropriate
            routine for processing.
    */
    switch ( NotificationType )
    {
    case SF_NOTIFY_LOG:
        dwRet = OnLog(pfc, (PHTTP_FILTER_LOG) pvData );
        break;
    default:
        dwRet = SF_STATUS_REQ_NEXT_NOTIFICATION;
        break;
    }
    return dwRet;
}
```

Listing 12.6   LST12_6.CPP—*OnLog*: Change Log

```
/*

        OnLog -
        This routine is called following the data
        being sent to the browser.  The data within
        pvData includes the client host name,
        client username, server name, operation
        requested (e.g. GET, POST, etc.), target
```

```
        item (e.g. /default.htm), parameters passed
        with the target and the status returned to
        the browser.
*/
DWORD OnLog(HTTP_FILTER_CONTEXT *pfc,
                    HTTP_FILTER_LOG *pvData)
{
        char* pszBuffer;
        // Check for a username and if it is blank
        // then replace it with "Unknown User"
        if (strstr((char*) pvData->pszClientUserName,TEXT("")))
        {
                pszBuffer=(CHAR*)pfc->AllocMem(pfc, 100, (DWORD)NULL);
                memset(pszBuffer,'\0',100);
                strcpy(pszBuffer, TEXT("Unknown User"));
                pvData->pszClientUserName = pszBuffer;
        }
        return SF_STATUS_REQ_NEXT_NOTIFICATION;
}
/*
```

URL Mapping

Web servers have to map a Web resource's URL to a physical address. In this section, you learn how to customize URL mapping.

Manipulating URL Mapping

An ISAPI filter enables you to customize URL mapping. The filter does this using the HTTP_FILTER_URL_MAP structure, which is defined as follows:

```
typedef struct _HTTP_FILTER_URL_MAP
{
    const CHAR *    pszURL;
    CHAR *          pszPhysicalPath;
    DWORD           cbPathBuff;
} HTTP_FILTER_URL_MAP, *PHTTP_FILTER_URL_MAP;
```

Also defined are these members:

- pszURL—A pointer to the URL that is being mapped to a physical path.

- pszPhysicalPath—A pointer to the buffer where the physical path is stored.

- cbPathBuffThe— size of the buffer pointed to by pszPhysicalPath.

Part
IV

Ch
12

This structure is pointed to by pvData in the HttpFilterProc when Notification Type is SF_NOTIFY_URL_MAP. This is done when the server is about to map the specified URL to a physical path. Filters can change the physical path, or analyze the path or resource requested.

Coding the Filter   To register for physical directory mapping, the filter sets the SF_NOTIFY_URL_MAP flag when the GetFilterVersion method is called by IIS during the filter's initialization. This is shown in Listing 12.7.

Listing 12.7   LST12_7.CPP—*GetFilterVersion*: URL Map

```
/*
     GetFilterVersion - An ISAPI/Win32 API method
     This method is required by IIS.  It is called
     following the process load to ensure that the
     filter is compatible with the server.
*/
BOOL WINAPI GetFilterVersion(HTTP_FILTER_VERSION * pVer)
{
    pVer->dwFilterVersion = MAKELONG( 0, 1 );   // Version 1.0

    pVer->dwFlags = (SF_NOTIFY_URL_MAP |
                 SF_NOTIFY_ORDER_DEFAULT);
     /*
            A brief one line description of the filter
     */
    strcpy( pVer->lpszFilterDesc, TEXT("Sample Filter, v1.1"));

    return TRUE;
}
```

When the filter requests notification for an event, it gets notification each time the event occurs. When HttpFilterProc is called by IIS, SF_NOTIFY_URL_MAP is triggered, the function associated with the event is executed, and logging information can be changed or analyzed. Listing 12.8 and Listing 12.9 show you how to analyze a URL mapping.

Listing 12.8   LST12_8.CPP—*HttpFilterProc*: URL Map

```
/*
     HttpFilterProc - ISAPI / Win32 API method
     This method is a required by IIS.  It is called
```

```
        for each notification event requested.  This is
        where the filter accomplishes its purpose in life.
*/
DWORD WINAPI HttpFilterProc(HTTP_FILTER_CONTEXT *pfc,
                                        DWORD NotificationType,
                                        VOID * pvData)
{
    DWORD dwRet;
    /*
                Direct the notification to the appropriate
                routine for processing.
    */
    switch ( NotificationType )
    {
    case SF_NOTIFY_URL_MAP:
        dwRet = OnUrlMap(pfc, (PHTTP_FILTER_URL_MAP) pvData );
        break;
    default:
        dwRet = SF_STATUS_REQ_NEXT_NOTIFICATION;
        break;
    }
    return dwRet;
}
```

Listing 12.9   LST12_9.CPP—*OnUrlMap*: URL Map

```
/*
        OnUrlMap -
        The data returned within pvData includes the URL
        requested (pvData->pszURL) and the full path to
        the physical data (pvData->pszPhysicalPath.
*/
DWORD OnUrlMap(HTTP_FILTER_CONTEXT *pfc,
                        HTTP_FILTER_URL_MAP *pvData)
{
    // This example looks at the URL path and analyzes it
    // to see if it is a specific page.  If so performs some
    // special processing.
    if (!strcmp(pvData->pszURL, TEXT("/ads.htm"))) {
            // Do your special processing if the resource
            // requested is named "ads.htm"
    }
    return SF_STATUS_REQ_NEXT_NOTIFICATION;
}
```

Part
IV

Ch
12

Page Translation and Manipulation

You can write an ISAPI filter to develop custom HTML tags or text placeholders. The custom HTML tags or text placeholders can be developed to do date and time stamping of pages, make consistent headers or footers, or to add counters to a page as it is written back to the browser.

Changing a Raw Page

Changing the raw data sent back to the browser uses the HTTP_FILTER_RAW_DATA structure, which is defined as follows:

```
typedef struct _HTTP_FILTER_RAW_DATA
{
    PVOID    pvInData;
    DWORD    cbInData;
    DWORD    cbInBuffer;
    DWORD    dwReserved;
} HTTP_FILTER_URL_MAP, *PHTTP_FILTER_URL_MAP;
```

Also defined are these members:

- pvInData—A pointer to the buffer containing the data to be written back to the browser.

- cbInData—The length of the data in the buffer at pvInData.

- cbInBuffer—The total size of the buffer as defined by pvInData.

This structure is pointed to by the void pointer, pvData, in the HttpFilterProc when NotificationType is SF_NOTIFY_SEND_RAW_DATA. SF_NOTIFY_SEND_RAW_DATA is signaled when the server is about to send the raw data back to the browser.

For each HTML page sent to a browser, SF_NOTIFY_SEND_RAW_DATA is triggered twice: when the page headers are returned to the browser and when the page is returned to the browser.

T I P   When changing the size of a page, especially enlarging the page, you must also change the Content-Length: header. This is among the headers sent to the browser before the page.

See the AdFlipperFilter sample code on the companion CD to this book to learn how to change the content length in the header and the page.

Coding the Filter   To register for the raw data sent to the browser, the filter sets the SF_NOTIFY_SEND_RAW_DATA flag when the GetFilterVersion method is called by IIS at the filter's initialization. This is shown in Listing 12.10.

Listing 12.10   LST12_10.CPP—*GetFilterVersion*: Send Raw Data

```
/*
        GetFilterVersion - An ISAPI/Win32 API method
        This method is required by IIS.  It is called
        following the process load to ensure that the
        filter is compatible with the server.
*/
BOOL WINAPI GetFilterVersion(HTTP_FILTER_VERSION * pVer)
{
    pVer->dwFilterVersion = MAKELONG( 0, 1 );    // Version 1.0

    pVer->dwFlags = (SF_NOTIFY_SEND_RAW_DATA ¦
                     SF_NOTIFY_ORDER_DEFAULT);
        /*
                A brief one line description of the filter
        */
    strcpy( pVer->lpszFilterDesc, TEXT("Sample Filter, v1.1"));

    return TRUE;
}
```

When the filter requests notification for an event, it gets notification each time the event occurs. When `HttpFilterProc` is called by IIS, `SF_NOTIFY_SEND_RAW_DATA` is triggered twice for an HTML page.

Listing 12.11 and Listing 12.12 show you how to handle multiple calls for `SF_NOTIFY_SEND_RAW_DATA`.

Part
IV

Ch
12

Listing 12.11   LST12_11.CPP—*HttpFilterProc*: Send Raw Data

```
/*
        HttpFilterProc - ISAPI / Win32 API method
        This method is a required by IIS.  It is called
        for each notification event requested.  This is
        where the filter accomplishes its purpose in life.
*/
DWORD WINAPI HttpFilterProc(HTTP_FILTER_CONTEXT *pfc,
                                            DWORD NotificationType,
                                            VOID * pvData)
{
    DWORD dwRet;
        /*
                Direct the notification to the appropriate
                routine for processing.
        */
```

continues

Listing 12.11   Continued

```
    switch ( NotificationType )
    {
    case SF_NOTIFY_SEND_RAW_DATA:
        dwRet = OnSendRawData(pfc, (PHTTP_FILTER_RAW_DATA) pvData );
        break;
    default:
        dwRet = SF_STATUS_REQ_NEXT_NOTIFICATION;
        break;
    }
    return dwRet;
}
```

Listing 12.12   LST12_12.CPP—*OnSendRawData*: Send Raw Data

```
/*
    OnSendRawData -
    This routine is called twice for this event.
    The first time it is called is when it sends
    the browser a notification of the actual data
    it is about to transmit(e.g. text/html, image/gif,
    etc.)  The second time this routine is called
    is when the actual data (e.g. text, gif, etc.)
    is being transmitted to the browser.
*/
DWORD OnSendRawData(HTTP_FILTER_CONTEXT *pfc,
                            HTTP_FILTER_RAW_DATA *pvData)
{
    CHAR*   pszBuffer;
    CHAR          szTime[10];
    DWORD   i=0;
    DWORD   j=0;

    HTTP_FILTER_RAW_DATA* pRawData = (PHTTP_FILTER_RAW_DATA)
    ➥pvData;

    pszBuffer=pvData->pvInData;

    if (strstr((char*) pRawData->pvInData,"HTTP/1.0"))
    {
        // This is were HTML header manipulation takes place
    }
    else
    {
        // This is where the custom HTML tag <%TIME%> will be
        // replaced with the servers current system time.
        for (i = pvData->cbInData-10; i > 0; i--)
        {
```

```
                              if (!_memicmp(pszBuffer+i, TEXT("<%TIME%>"), 8))
                              {
                                      strtime(szTime);
                                      memcpy(pszBuffer+i, szTime, 8);
                                      break;
                              }
                      }
              }
              return SF_STATUS_REQ_NEXT_NOTIFICATION;
      }
```

Reasons for Using Filters

From the examples in this chapter, you can see that filters can change and customize how IIS works. Filters offer a lower level of access to HTTP data during its communication cycle.

When a filter requests notification for an event, it is called each time the event occurs. For this reason, you have to be careful not to request notification of events for which the filter won't do processing. In the next few sections, we outline some of the advantages of using filters.

Lower Level of Access than Extensions

Filters enable analysis and manipulation of raw data transmitted to the server and raw data sent back to the client; enable the change and redirection of URL mapping; enable the change or customization of an authentication process; and enable the analysis and change of logging information.

Access to and Control of Events and Data During the HTTP Communication Cycle

In this section, We discuss the setting of event notification flags for secure and nonsecure ports, and processing priority flags. These flags enable the filter to take control at certain predefined events and with a predefined priority relative to the other filters executed by the server.

Part
IV

Ch
12

Following the discussion of the flags, we discuss the order in which events occur in the HTTP communication cycle.

Filter Notification Flags   Filter notification flags are set in the `GetFilterVersion` function. Filter notification flags are defined in the SDK header file HTTPFILT.H. They can all be identified as beginning with `SF_NOTIFY_*`.

The three groups of notification flags are priorities, port, and events. An explanation of the three groups of flags is next.

Filter Priority Processing   The filter processing priority is set in the `GetFilterVersion` function by turning on an `SF_NOTIFY_ORDER_*` flag in the `HTTP_FILTER_VERSION` structure's member variable `dwFlags`. A filter can have one of four flags set to indicate to the Web service what priority level the filter should get when processing HTTP events.

The four flags signify a processing priority of low, medium, high, or default. A priority of default is the same as a priority of low. The syntax for the priority flags is shown in Table 12.2.

Table 12.2   Filter Priority Flags

Value	Description
SF_NOTIFY_ORDER_DEFAULT	Loads the filter at the default priority (recommended).
SF_NOTIFY_ORDER_LOW	Loads the filter at the low priority.
SF_NOTIFY_ORDER_MEDIUM	Loads the filter at a medium priority.
SF_NOTIFY_ORDER_HIGH	Loads the filter at a high priority.

If multiple filters are processing the same HTTP events, the filter with the highest priority gets the notification of the event first. Each priority gets the event notification in descending order (from highest to lowest).

If multiple filters are processing the same HTTP events and have the same priority, the order of the filters in the registry takes precedence. The key where filters are registered is

`HKEY_LOCAL_MACHINE\System\CurrentControlSet\Services\W3SCVC\Parameters`

with an entry name of filter DLLs.

T I P Unless you have a reason for setting a priority other the default setting, it is recommended that you set SF_NOTIFY_ORDER_DEFAULT as a priority. If no priority is set in the HTTP_FILTER_VERSION member dwFlags, the Web service assumes a priority of low.

Filter Port Processing

Filters can process HTTP events for a port that is secure, nonsecure, or both. A secure port request is a request to the Web service that is specified with the HTTP's protocol.

The port processing flags are set in the GetFilterVersion function by turning on either SF_NOTIFY_SECURE_PORT, SF_NOTIFY_NONSECURE_PORT, or both flags in the HTTP_FILTER_VERSION structure's member variable dwFlags. The syntax for the port flags is shown in Table 12.3

Table 12.3   Port Processing Flags

Value	Description
SF_NOTIFY_SECURE_PORT	Notifies the filter that it is passing data through a secure port
SF_NOTIFY_NONSECURE_PORT	Notifies the filter that it is passing data through a nonsecure port

N O T E If neither SF_NOTIFY_SECURE_PORT or SF_NOTIFY_NONSECURE_PORT are specified, the server defaults to both, which allows filter processing to occur through any port.

HTTP Communication Events

The HTTP communication event notification flags are set in the GetFilterVersion by turning on appropriate SF_NOTIFY_* flag in the HTTP_FILTER_VERSION structure's member variable dwFlags. A filter can have any number of the available event notification flags set in the filter. The syntax for the HTTP event notification flags is shown in Table 12.4.

Part
IV

Ch
12

Table 12.4   HTTP Event Notification Flags

Value	Description
SF_NOTIFY_READ_RAW_DATA	Allows the filter to see the raw data. The data returned will contain both headers and data.
SF_NOTIFY_PREPROC_HEADERS	The server has preprocessed the headers.
SF_NOTIFY_AUTHENTICATION	The server is authenticating the client.
SF_NOTIFY_ACCESS_DENIED	Allows the filter to be notified whenever the server is about to return a 401 Access Denied. This allows the filter to analyze the failure and return a custom message.
SF_NOTIFY_URL_MAP	The server is mapping a logical URL to a physical path.
SF_NOTIFY_SEND_RAW_DATA	The server is sending raw data back to the client.
SF_NOTIFY_LOG	The server is writing information to the server log.
SF_NOTIFY_END_OF_NET_SESSION	The session with the client is ending.

 T I P   Only specify the HTTP event notification flags in which the filter has requested notification of data available or if the filter is going to process at a certain point in the HTTP communication. Unnecessary use of HTTP event notification flags reduces the performance of the Web service.

The HTTP event-processing order is significant for determining which events to request for a filter solution. The order shown in Table 12.4 is the order of events for an HTTP communication cycle.

To monitor the HTTP communication cycle, set up the GenesisFilter project in debug mode and set breakpoints throughout the code to see the what, why, and how of the request flow. The GenesisFilter project on the companion CD is the tutorial for this chapter.

Review Chapter 17, "Troubleshooting and Debugging Extensions and Filters," to learn how to set up Microsoft Visual C++ in debug mode for the GenesisFilter.

Overhead

Be careful when you develop filters because they can be resource-intensive. When a filter requests notification for an event, it gets notification every time the event occurs.

Because filters are executed in an HTTP communication cycle, make sure that the filter's function code is as efficient as possible. Some techniques to avoid or to use in moderation include database accesses, unnecessary file reads and writes, and dynamic page creation.

If a process does not need access to the HTTP transaction information (such as authentication, logging, HTTP headers, and URL mapping), an ISAPI extension is preferable to an ISAPI filter.

Tutorial: Building the Genesis Filter

The GenesisFilter project is on the companion CD. GenesisFilter does nothing but request all the available HTTP communication events. It passes control to a worker function that returns control back to the Web server.

Why include such an unproductive example? The tutorial is a way to monitor the HTTP communication event process and analyze what data is available at each event in the cycle.

You should only use the GenesisFilter when in an interactive debugging mode. Review Chapter 17, "Troubleshooting and Debugging Extensions and Filters," for the steps to use Visual C++ for debugging ISAPI extensions.

While in debug mode, set breakpoints among the GetFilterVersion, HttpFilterProc, and worker functions to see what data is available at each event processed.

Part

IV

Ch

12

You can also use the GenesisFilter as the starting point for any new filter development since the backbone of the filter process is already coded. All you need to do is add the worker functions to do your processing and remove the events notification flags from GetFilterVersion to turn off specific notification processing.

Listing 12.13 is the source code for the GenesisFilter. This source code is on the companion CD.

Listing 12.13   GenesisFilter.C—*GenesisFilter* Source

```
/*

Copyright (c) 1996  ClearMind, Inc. and David A. Torres

Module Name:

    GenesisFilter.c

Abstract:

    This filter does NOTHING, but its a great place to
        observe how the IIS world works.  This filter
        requests notification of all IIS filter events
        and is the starting point for all of my filter
        development.

*/

#include <windows.h>
#include <httpfilt.h>
#include <string.h>
#include <stdio.h>
#include <stdarg.h>
#include <time.h>
/*
        DebugMsg() is used for debugging.
        Choose debugger output or log file.
*/
//#define TO_FILE            // uncomment out to use a log file
#ifdef TO_FILE
        #define DEST ghFile
        #define DebugMsg(x)    WriteToFile x;
        HANDLE ghFile;
        #define LOGFILE "c:\\GenesisFilter.log"
        void WriteToFile (HANDLE hFile, char *szFormat, ...) {
                char szBuf[1024];
                DWORD dwWritten;
                va_list list;
```

```
                va_start (list, szFormat);
                vsprintf (szBuf, szFormat, list);
                hFile = CreateFile (LOGFILE, GENERIC_WRITE,
                                            0, NULL, OPEN_ALWAYS,
                                            FILE_ATTRIBUTE_NORMAL, NULL);
            if (hFile != INVALID_HANDLE_VALUE) {
                    SetFilePointer (hFile, 0, NULL, FILE_END);
                    WriteFile (hFile, szBuf, lstrlen (szBuf),
                    ➥&dwWritten, NULL);
                    CloseHandle (hFile);
            }
            va_end (list);
    }
#else

    #define DEST               buff
    #define DebugMsg(x) {                              \
                        char buff[256];                          \
                        wsprintf x;                              \
                        OutputDebugString( buff );   \
                    }
#endif
/*
    Private prototypes
            These are the methods executed for each of
            the related filter events.
*/
DWORD OnAuthentication(HTTP_FILTER_CONTEXT *pfc,
                                HTTP_FILTER_AUTHENT *pvData);

DWORD OnAccessDenied(HTTP_FILTER_CONTEXT *pfc,
                                HTTP_FILTER_ACCESS_DENIED
                                ➥*pvData);

DWORD OnLog(HTTP_FILTER_CONTEXT *pfc,
                HTTP_FILTER_LOG *pvData);

DWORD OnUrlMap(HTTP_FILTER_CONTEXT *pfc,
                    HTTP_FILTER_URL_MAP *pvData);

DWORD OnPreprocHeaders(HTTP_FILTER_CONTEXT *pfc,
                                HTTP_FILTER_PREPROC_HEADERS
                                ➥*pvData);

DWORD OnEndOfNetSession(HTTP_FILTER_CONTEXT *pfc);

DWORD OnSendRawData(HTTP_FILTER_CONTEXT *pfc,
                                HTTP_FILTER_RAW_DATA *pvData);

DWORD OnReadRawData(HTTP_FILTER_CONTEXT *pfc,
```

continues

Listing 12.13   Continued

```
                                         HTTP_FILTER_RAW_DATA *pvData);

void WhatError(DWORD dwError);


/*
      Globals
*/
CRITICAL_SECTION gCS;        // A critical section handle
                                        // is used to protect
                                        // global
                                        // state properties
BOOL              gfHTML;


/*
      This is the entry and exit point for the filter
      it is called when the filter is loaded and unloaded
      by IIS.  This is where state properties need to be
      retrieved and store on persistant storage.
*/
BOOL APIENTRY DllMain( HANDLE hModule,
                       DWORD ul_reason_for_call,
                       LPVOID lpReserved )
{
    switch( ul_reason_for_call ) {
    case DLL_PROCESS_ATTACH:
              {
              InitializeCriticalSection(&gCS);
              gfHTML = FALSE;
              break;
              }
//    case DLL_THREAD_ATTACH:
//    case DLL_THREAD_DETACH:
    case DLL_PROCESS_DETACH:
              {
              DeleteCriticalSection(&gCS);
              break;
              }
    }
    return TRUE;
}

/*
      GetFilterVersion - An ISAPI/Win32 API method
      This method is required by IIS.  It is called
```

```
                    following the process load to ensure that the
                    filter is compatable with the server.
*/
BOOL WINAPI GetFilterVersion(HTTP_FILTER_VERSION * pVer)
{

    WORD wMajorVersion=0;
    WORD wMinorVersion=0;

    wMajorVersion = HIWORD( pVer->dwServerFilterVersion );
    wMinorVersion = LOWORD( pVer->dwServerFilterVersion );

    DebugMsg(( DEST,
            "[GetFilterVersion] Server version is %d.%d\n",
            HIWORD( pVer->dwServerFilterVersion ),
            LOWORD( pVer->dwServerFilterVersion ) ));
    /*
        This filter is intended for IIS version 2.0 or greater.
        This is an example of how to test the server version.
    */

    if (wMajorVersion < 2) return FALSE;

    pVer->dwFilterVersion = MAKELONG( 0, 2 );   // Version 1.0
    DebugMsg(( DEST,
            "[GetFilterVersion] Server version is %d.%d\n",
            HIWORD( pVer->dwFilterVersion ),
            LOWORD( pVer->dwFilterVersion ) ));
    /*
            Specify the security level of notifications
            (secured port, nonsecured port, or both), the
            types of events and order of notification for
            this filter (high, medium or low, default=low).
    */
    pVer->dwFlags = (
                            SF_NOTIFY_SECURE_PORT
                            SF_NOTIFY_NONSECURE_PORT
                            SF_NOTIFY_READ_RAW_DATA
                            SF_NOTIFY_PREPROC_HEADERS
                            SF_NOTIFY_URL_MAP
                            SF_NOTIFY_AUTHENTICATION
                            SF_NOTIFY_ACCESS_DENIED
                            SF_NOTIFY_SEND_RAW_DATA
                            SF_NOTIFY_LOG
```

Part

IV

Ch

12

continues

Listing 12.13 Continued

```
                                        SF_NOTIFY_END_OF_NET_SESSION  |
                                        SF_NOTIFY_ORDER_DEFAULT
                                        );
    /*
            A brief one line description of the filter
    */
    strcpy( pVer->lpszFilterDesc, "Genesis Filter, v1.0" );

    return TRUE;
}


/*
    HttpFilterProc - ISAPI / Win32 API method
    This method is a required by IIS.  It is called
    for each notification event requested.  This is
    where the filter accomplishes its purpose in life.
*/
DWORD WINAPI HttpFilterProc(HTTP_FILTER_CONTEXT *pfc,
                                            DWORD
                                            ➥NotificationType,
                                            VOID * pvData)
{
    DWORD dwRet;
    /*
            Direct the notification to the appropriate
            routine for processing.
    */
    switch ( NotificationType )
    {
    case SF_NOTIFY_READ_RAW_DATA:
        dwRet = OnReadRawData(pfc, (PHTTP_FILTER_RAW_DATA) pvData );
        break;
    case SF_NOTIFY_PREPROC_HEADERS:
        dwRet = OnPreprocHeaders(pfc, (PHTTP_FILTER_PREPROC_HEADERS)
        ➥pvData );
        break;
    case SF_NOTIFY_URL_MAP:
        dwRet = OnUrlMap(pfc, (PHTTP_FILTER_URL_MAP) pvData );
        break;
    case SF_NOTIFY_AUTHENTICATION:
        dwRet = OnAuthentication(pfc, (PHTTP_FILTER_AUTHENT)
        ➥pvData );
        break;
    case SF_NOTIFY_ACCESS_DENIED:
        dwRet = OnAccessDenied(pfc, (PHTTP_FILTER_ACCESS_DENIED)
        ➥pvData );
```

```
            break;
        case SF_NOTIFY_SEND_RAW_DATA:
            dwRet = OnSendRawData(pfc, (PHTTP_FILTER_RAW_DATA) pvData );
            break;
        case SF_NOTIFY_LOG:
            dwRet = OnLog(pfc, (PHTTP_FILTER_LOG) pvData );
            break;
        case SF_NOTIFY_END_OF_NET_SESSION:
            dwRet = OnEndOfNetSession(pfc);
            break;
        default:
            DebugMsg(( DEST,
                    "[HttpFilterProc] Unknown notification type,
                    ➥%d\r\n",
                        NotificationType ));
            dwRet = SF_STATUS_REQ_NEXT_NOTIFICATION;
            break;
    }
    return dwRet;
}
/*
    IIS Filter Event Routines
*/
/*
    OnReadRawData -
    The data returned at pvData->pvInData includes the
    header, types of data accepted and the browsers type
*/
DWORD OnReadRawData(HTTP_FILTER_CONTEXT *pfc,
                                    HTTP_FILTER_RAW_DATA *pvData)
{
    return SF_STATUS_REQ_NEXT_NOTIFICATION;
}
/*
    OnPreprocHeaders -
    The data returned within pvData includes three
    callback methods to get, set and/or add to the
    header
*/
DWORD OnPreprocHeaders(HTTP_FILTER_CONTEXT *pfc,
                                    HTTP_FILTER_PREPROC_HEADERS
                                        ➥*pvData)
{
    return SF_STATUS_REQ_NEXT_NOTIFICATION;
}
/*
    OnUrlMap -
    The data returned within pvData includes the URL
    requested (pvData->pszURL) and the full path to
```

continues

Part

IV

Ch

12

Listing 12.13   Continued

```
        the physical data (pvData->pszPhysicalPath).
*/
DWORD OnUrlMap(HTTP_FILTER_CONTEXT *pfc,
                        HTTP_FILTER_URL_MAP *pvData)
{
    return SF_STATUS_REQ_FINISHED;
}
/*
        OnAuthentication -
        The data returned within pvData includes
        User identification (pvData->pszUser) and
        the user's password (pvData->pszPassword).
*/
DWORD OnAuthentication(HTTP_FILTER_CONTEXT *pfc,
                                    HTTP_FILTER_AUTHENT *pvData)
{
        return SF_STATUS_REQ_NEXT_NOTIFICATION;
}
/*
        OnAccessDenied -
        The data returned at pvData->pvInData includes the
        header, types of data accepted and the browsers type
*/
DWORD OnAccessDenied(HTTP_FILTER_CONTEXT *pfc,
                                    HTTP_FILTER_ACCESS_DENIED *pvData)
{
        return SF_STATUS_REQ_FINISHED;
}
/*
        OnSendRawData -
        This routine is called twice for this event.
        The first time it is called is when it sends
        the browser a notification of the actual data
        it is about to transmit(e.g. text/html, image/gif,
        etc.)  The second time this routine is called
        is when the actual data (e.g. text, gif, etc.)
        is being transmitted to the browser.
*/
DWORD OnSendRawData(HTTP_FILTER_CONTEXT *pfc,
                                    HTTP_FILTER_RAW_DATA *pvData)
{
        return SF_STATUS_REQ_NEXT_NOTIFICATION;
}
/*
        OnLog -
        This routine is called following the data
        being sent to the browser.  The data within
        pvData includes the client host name,
        client username, server name, operation
```

```
        requested (e.g. GET, POST, etc.), target
        item (e.g. /default.htm), parameters passed
        with the target and the status returned to
        the browser.
*/
DWORD OnLog(HTTP_FILTER_CONTEXT *pfc,
                    HTTP_FILTER_LOG *pvData)
{
    return SF_STATUS_REQ_NEXT_NOTIFICATION;
}
/*
    OnEndOfNetSession -
    This routine is called following the
    transmission of all the data requested
    by the browser.
*/
DWORD OnEndOfNetSession(HTTP_FILTER_CONTEXT *pfc)
{
    return SF_STATUS_REQ_NEXT_NOTIFICATION;
}
void WhatError(DWORD dwError)
{
    switch ( dwError )
    {
    case ERROR_INVALID_PARAMETER:
        break;
    case ERROR_INVALID_INDEX:
        break;
    case ERROR_INSUFFICIENT_BUFFER:
        break;
    case ERROR_MORE_DATA:
        break;
    case ERROR_NO_DATA:
        break;
    }
}
```

Part

IV

Ch

12

Building the *GenesisFilter.dll*

To build the GenesisFilter.dll, perform the following steps:

1. Copy the project from the companion CD to an accessible drive.

2. Open a command window and navigate to the directory where the GenesisFilter project is stored.

3. Make sure *nmake.exe* is in a directory in the system's path.

4. From the GenesisFilter project's directory, execute:

```
nmake /f makefile CFG="GenesisFilter - Win32 Release"
```

Installing the *GenesisFilter.dll*

To install the `GenesisFilter.dll`, perform the following steps:

1. Copy `GenesisFilter.dll` into your IIS install directory on the server.

2. Run REGEDT32.EXE.

3. Go to the registry key:

   ```
   HKEY_LOCAL_MACHINE\System\CurrentControlSet\Services
   \W3SCVC\Parameters
   ```

4. Edit the Filter Dlls entry by double-clicking it.

5. Add `,c:\path\to\GenesisFilter.dll` to the end of the value.

6. Save the value.

7. Exit REGEDT32.EXE.

8. Stop and restart the World Wide Web Publishing Service.

From Here...

This chapter outlined some scenarios in which ISAPI filters play an important role. It gave you models for building a filter in each of the categories discussed. For more information about ISAPI filters, see the following chapters:

- Chapter 1, "Introducing ISAPI," explains the role of DLLs in Web server applications.

- Chapter 3, "Understanding Dynamic NT Web Sites," discusses how earlier versions of Windows NT Server and NT 4.0 Server work with Web interfaces. Also covered are programming languages for customizing those interfaces.

- Chapter 4, "CGI vs. ISAPI: Pros and Cons," describes the advantages of using ISAPI to build and manage the interaction of Web requests with your Windows NT 4.0 network.

- Chapter 13, "Understanding ISAPI Filters," gives you the rules for constructing an ISAPI filter.

- Chapter 14, "Creating an ISAPI Filter," is a step-by-step procedure for constructing an ISAPI filter using Visual C++ 4.x.

Understanding ISAPI Filters

ISAPI filters are a powerful way to extend your Web server. Because of the trend toward more complex Web sites, developers are asked to invent uses for the Web far beyond its original design.

You can use ISAPI filters to change or enhance the default processing of an HTTP request. Unlike ISAPI extensions, which you must specify in the requesting URL, ISAPI filters are executed by IIS in response to any request from a client.

Let's take a look at what filters are and how they can help you develop Web solutions. ■

What ISAPI filters are and how they work

Since they can examine and handle any client request, ISAPI filters are a powerful way to extend Microsoft's Internet Information Server (IIS).

How you create an ISAPI filter

You build a DLL with two entries and set one registry entry. Then the filter is ready to examine and process client requests.

What you can do with ISAPI filters

Custom logging and authentication are just some of the tasks you can do using ISAPI filters.

What happens when a request comes into the server

ISAPI filters give you a chance to examine and process a request before IIS does.

The rules of ISAPI filters

Follow a few basic rules and you can have an ISAPI filter up and running in a short time.

How ISAPI Filters Work

This section introduces the basics of what makes an ISAPI filter work. First, we'll explore the necessary entries for an ISAPI filter. Then look at some of the things you can do with filters.

DLL Gets Control on Every Request

The first thing to understand about an ISAPI filter is that it is a 32-bit DLL loaded by IIS at server startup. IIS calls filter DLLs at predefined times during the processing of an HTTP request.

At each one of these points, the filter can either add to or change the default processing done by IIS. This is what gives ISAPI filters their power. Imagine that you are on-site at Microsoft and can extend the Web server in any way you want.

Let's begin by breaking up the processing of a filter into two phases: registration and event processing. The phases are shown in Table 13.1.

Table 13.1   Phases in Filter Processing

Phase	What Happens
Registration	IIS loads the filter and calls the `GetFilterVersion()` entry.
Event processing	IIS calls the filter's `HttpFilterProc()` entry as it processes HTTP requests.

Each ISAPI filter has to have two entries defined: `GetFilterVersion()` and `HttpFilterProc()`. Let's take a look at these entries.

The *GetFilterVersion()* Entry

When the server starts up, it checks a special registry entry to find out which DLLs it should load as filters. As each DLL is loaded, the special-purpose `GetFilterVersion()` entry is called. `GetFilterVersion()` does the registration phase of the filter. It serves the following purposes:

- It specifies the filter's version information.

  Using the HTTP_FILTER_VERSION structure, GetFilterVersion returns a string to IIS with a version of ISAPI that the filter conforms to and a short description of the extension. This ensures that the filter and IIS are compatible. It also supplies descriptive information to identify a particular filter in the Web server or operating system (OS) event logs.

- It specifies the filter's priority.

  Each filter must show its priority. The priority sets the order in which the filter is called to handle the events that apply to it. IIS may have to call many filters, so this is how the filter assigns the processing importance of any applicable events.

  Table 13.2 shows the four priority levels. They are listed according to the priority by which IIS calls them.

Table 13.2 The Four Filter Priorities

Priority	What It Means
SF_NOTIFY_ORDER_HIGH	Will load the filter at a HIGH priority.
SF_NOTIFY_ORDER_MEDIUM	Will load the filter at a MEDIUM priority.
SF_NOTIFY_ORDER_DEFAULT	Will load the filter at the DEFAULT priority. This is recommended.
SF_NOTIFY_ORDER_LOW	Will load the filter at a LOW priority.

N O T E If two filters register to process the same event at the same priority level, IIS calls them in the order that they are listed in the registry. We'll explain more about registry entries later. ■

Part
IV

Ch
13

CAUTION

Only specify a higher priority when you know that your filter will process a majority of the events it is notified about. An example is a filter that logs all requests of a particular server. A high-priority filter that ignores most events can add significant overhead.

■ It tells the server what events it will process.

The filter has the option of processing a defined set of events. It must tell the server which event it will process. This saves on the overhead needed to call each filter for every request that comes in.

Imagine the performance penalties if IIS had to call every loaded filter for every event for every request! When GetFilterVersion() executes, IIS knows which events the filter will process and only calls it for one of those events.

Table 13.3 shows the notification event types.

Table 13.3   Notification Events and What They Mean

Notification	What It Means
SF_NOTIFY_SECURE_PORT	The server calls the filter about sessions over a secure port only.
SF_NOTIFY_NONSECURE_PORT	The server calls the filter about sessions over a nonsecure port only.
SF_NOTIFY_READ_RAW_DATA	The server calls the filter before it processes the incoming raw data.
SF_NOTIFY_PREPROC_HEADERS	The server calls the filter before it has preprocessed the headers coming from the client.
SF_NOTIFY_AUTHENTICATION	The server calls the filter when it is about to authenticate the client.
SF_NOTIFY_URL_MAP	The server calls the filter when it is about to map a logical URL to a physical path.
SF_NOTIFY_SEND_RAW_DATA	The server calls the filter when it is about to send raw data back to the client.
SF_NOTIFY_LOG	The server calls the filter when it is about to write data to the server log.
SF_NOTIFY_END_OF_NET_SESSION	The server calls the filter when it is about to end the session with the client. This gives the filter a chance to clean up any data specific to this client session.

Notification	What It Means
SF_NOTIFY_ACCESS_DENIED	The server calls the filter any time it is about to return a 401 Access Denied response. With this notification, a filter can return a custom message.

N O T E Even though the filter registers to get notifications for a particular event, it doesn't have to process every occurrence of that event. As we'll see shortly, you can limit the processing of the occurrences of an event in the filter's HttpFilterProc().

GetFilterVersion() is declared as follows. You must define it exactly as it appears here so that IIS can call it.

```
BOOL WINAPI GetFilterVersion( PHTTP_FILTER_VERSION pVer );
```

IIS passes only one parameter to GetFilterVersion(), a pointer to an HTTP_FILTER_VERSION structure. The structure is defined in Listing 13.1.

Listing 13.1   HTTPFILT.H—Definition of HTTP_FILTER_VERSION

```
typedef struct _HTTP_FILTER_VERSION {
    DWORD     dwServerFilterVersion;
    DWORD     dwFilterVersion;
    CHAR      lpszFilterDesc[SF_MAX_FILTER_DESC_LEN+1];
    DWORD     dwFlags;
} HTTP_FILTER_VERSION;
```

When the call to GetFilterVersion() returns, IIS uses the information that the filter put in the HTTP_FILTER_VERSION structure to determine when to call the filter. Table 13.4 shows which members of this structure are meaningful to the filter and how to populate them.

Part
IV

Ch
13

Table 13.4   Meaningful *HTTP_FILTER_VERSION* Members

Member	What It Means
dwFilterVersion	Gives the version of the filter.
lpszFilterDesc	Supplies a readable text description of the filter. Set this to something meaningful, as it may be used in administrative tools.
dwFlags	Sets the value of all of the notification events that your filter is to handle OR'ed together.

Listing 13.2 shows a simple use of GetFilterVersion() that completes the steps to register a filter DLL with IIS.

Listing 13.2   Steps to Register *GetFilterVersion()*

```
BOOL WINAPI GetFilterVersion( PHTTP_FILTER_VERSION pVer )
{
    // Set the version of your filter.
    pVer->dwFilterVersion = HTTP_FILTER_REVISION;

    // Set the description of your filter.
    lstrcpy( pVer->lpszFilterDesc, "Your Filter Description Here!" );

    // Set the notifications to handle. This filter will handle only
    // authentication events over the standard HTTP nonsecure port.
    pVer->dwFlags = SF_NOTIFY_AUTHENTICATION |
SF_NOTIFY_NONSECURE_PORT;

    return TRUE;
}
```

The *HttpFilterProc()* Entry

Once the filter is loaded and registered, it is ready to get notifications. This is done when the server calls the HttpFilterProc() entry in the filter. Once again, you must declare this entry exactly as IIS expects it. This is shown in Listing 13.3.

Listing 13.3   Declaring *HttpFilterProc()*

```
DWORD WINAPI HttpFilterProc( PHTTP_FILTER_CONTEXT pfc, DWORD
➥notificationType, LPVOID pvNotification );
```

The first parameter, `pfc`, is a pointer to an `HTTP_FILTER_CONTEXT` structure. This structure holds information about the HTTP request itself. See Appendix A, "ISAPI Reference," for the definition of this structure.

The second parameter, `notificationType`, is a `DWORD` that represents one of the notification events the filter registered with the server. Table 13.3 shows the possible values for this parameter.

The third parameter, `pvNotification`, is a void pointer to a server-supplied data area. This data area is the vehicle by which IIS shares the data to be processed with the filter. It is different for each notification type.

Table 13.5 summarizes the data type of this parameter for each notification type.

Table 13.5   *pvNotification*: Events and Data Types

When the Notification Type Is	*pvNotification* Points to a Structure of This Type
SF_NOTIFY_READ_RAW_DATA	HTTP_FILTER_RAW_DATA
SF_NOTIFY_SEND_RAW_DATA	HTTP_FILTER_RAW_DATA
SF_NOTIFY_PREPROC_HEADERS	HTTP_FILTER_PREPROC_HEADERS
SF_NOTIFY_AUTHENTICATION	HTTP_FILTER_AUTHENT
SF_NOTIFY_URL_MAP	HTTP_FILTER_URL_MAP
SF_NOTIFY_LOG	HTTP_FILTER_LOG
SF_NOTIFY_ACCESS_DENIED	HTTP_FILTER_ACCESS_DENIED

Part

IV

Ch

13

The declaration of `HttpFilterProc()` specifies a return type of `DWORD`. As you may have guessed, `HttpFilterProc()` is allowed to return a predefined set of values. IIS uses these values to determine how to continue processing the event.

Table 13.6 shows these possible values and when they should be used.

Table 13.6 Return Codes from the *HttpFilterProc()*

Monitor What Happens Return Code	When to Use It
SF_STATUS_REQ_FINISHED	Use this return code if the filter has handled the HTTP request. This tells the server to disconnect the session.
SF_STATUS_REQ_FINISHED_KEEP_CONN	Use this return code if the filter has handled the HTTP request and you want the server to keep the TCP session open if the option was negotiated.
SF_STATUS_REQ_NEXT_NOTIFICATION	Use this return code if you want the server to call the next filter in the notification chain.
SF_STATUS_REQ_HANDLED_NOTIFICATION	Use this return code if the filter has handled the notification and no other filters should be called for this notification.
SF_STATUS_REQ_ERROR	Use this return code to tell the server that an error occurred. The server will call GetLastError() and indicate the error to the client.
SF_STATUS_REQ_READ_NEXT	Use this return code for raw-read notification only. It is used when the filter is an opaque stream filter and the session parameters are being negotiated.

Filter Operations

Now that you have a basic understanding of ISAPI filters, you probably can't wait to use one! Well, before you do that, let's take a look at some of the useful things that filters can do.

An excellent use of ISAPI filters is advanced logging. IIS gives you some powerful logging options. But two of the things that IIS doesn't log are the user agent (HTTP_USER_AGENT) and the referring page (HTTP_REFERRER).

Does that mean that if you need this information you're out of luck? Absolutely not. A simple filter does the trick.

Let's start by defining the GetFilterVersion() entry. Listing 13.4 shows a sample use of this entry.

Listing 13.4   Sample Use of *GetFilterVersion()*

```
BOOL WINAPI GetFilterVersion( PHTTP_FILTER_VERSION pVer )
{
    // Set this filter's version.
    pVer->dwFilterVersion = HSE_FILTER_VERSION;

    // Set this filter's description.
    strcpy( pVer->lpszFilterDesc, "Advanced logging filter. " );

    // Set the notifications to handle. This filter will handle
    // only log events
    // over the standard HTTP nonsecure port.
    pVer->dwFlags = SF_NOTIFY_ORDER_HIGH ¦ SF_NOTIFY_LOG;

    return TRUE;
}
```

N O T E   The sample code in this section is for illustration only. For a complete use of advanced logging and other filters, see Chapter 16, "Extending Your Web Server with Filters." ▨

That was pretty easy, wasn't it? Now you just need to define HttpFilterProc(). This allows the filter to process notifications. Listing 13.5 shows a sample use of HttpFilterProc().

Part
IV

Ch
13

Listing 13.5   LST13_6.CPP—Sample Use of *HttpFilterProc()*

```
DWORD WINAPI HttpFilterProc( PHTTP_FILTER_CONTEXT pfc, DWORD
➥notificationType, LPVOID pvNotification   )
{
     switch(notificationType) {
          case SF_NOTIFY_LOG:
               // Cast the void pointer to the proper datatype for
               // this notification.
               PHTTP_FILTER_LOG logData =
               ➥(PHTTP_FILTER_LOG)pvNotification;

               // Perform specific processing on the log data
               // here...
               //

               // Even though we handled the notification, we
               // want to tell IIS to
               // allow normal processing of this notification.
               return SF_STATUS_REQ_NEXT_NOTIFICATION;
               break;
     };

     return SF_STATUS_REQ_NEXT_NOTIFICATION;
}
```

Remember that the pvNotification parameter is passed as an LPVOID because it varies based on the type of the current notification. This allows the same function to be called for all notifications. And it's why we must cast the pointer to the specific data type for a given event, as shown in the following line of code:

```
PHTTP_FILTER_LOG logData = (PHTTP_FILTER_LOG)pvNotification;
```

N O T E HttpFilterProc() is the entry IIS calls for every notification specified by the filter. Therefore, you must use a switch statement or some form of conditional logic to determine the current notification event. ▨

The previous example shows a filter that monitors some server function. Next, we'll look at a filter that changes the server's interaction with the client.

Customize Authentication   A good example of the power of ISAPI filters is a custom authentication filter. Imagine that your Web site needs a secure area to protect sensitive documents. You must have a user name and password combination to access this area.

Since IIS security is integrated with Windows NT, one option in granting select users access to this area is to set up a Windows NT user account for each user. This is a tedious process, especially if the potential user base is large.

Another option is to build an ISAPI filter to intercept the SF_NOTIFY_AUTHENTICATION event. When the filter is called, it can easily determine the URL requested. If it is a protected URL, the filter can access some external data source (such as a database or flat file) to validate the user name and password. See Chapter 16, "Extending Your Web Server with Filters," for a sample use of a custom authentication filter.

Balance Requests Among Multiple Web Servers   Yet another use of ISAPI filters is balancing requests among multiple Web servers. Imagine a setup where you have one server acting as the "load balancer" and any number of machines serving the pages.

You make the URL of the load balancer available to the public. The load balancer has an ISAPI filter that monitors the load on the other three servers. When it gets a request, it uses a round robin to redirect the requests evenly among the other three servers.

If you want to get really sophisticated, you could put an ISAPI filter on each server to communicate with the load balancer via an interprocess communication (IPC), giving it an exact count of how many connections it is processing. This would allow the load balancer to redirect requests to the servers with the least amount of traffic.

These examples should give you a feel for what you can accomplish with ISAPI filters. Let's look at how HTTP requests flow through IIS and how ISAPI filters fit into this flow.

Loaded at Startup, Kept in Memory Until Shutdown

ISAPI filters are loaded by IIS when it starts up and stay in memory until IIS is shut down. This makes calling them efficient. But if the code in HttpFilterProc() is *not* efficient, the performance of the server is affected.

Part

IV

Ch

13

See "ISAPI Filter Rules" later in this chapter for more information about how IIS loads ISAPI filters.

Filters must also be thread-safe. IIS maintains a pool of threads that it gives requests to process. The filter can be processing many requests on many different threads at any given time. Thread safety is discussed later in this chapter under "ISAPI Filter Rules."

Flow of a Filter

This section explains what happens when you add filters to your Web server. To understand the flow of a filter, let's first take a look at the steps that IIS takes when it gets a client request.

Information Flow

A server processes information from a client in seven steps:

1. Processes the incoming HTTP headers.
2. Processes the incoming HTTP data.
3. Maps the URL to a physical file.
4. Authenticates the user if needed.
5. Builds the HTTP headers and data to be sent back to the client.
6. Writes log data to the log file.
7. Ends the connection.

For a graphical representation of this flow, see Figure 13.1.

You can see that the IIS scenario works fine as long as you don't want to change the default processing of these HTTP requests through IIS. An ISAPI filter, however, allows us to change the default processing of an HTTP request. Figure 13.2 is a graphical representation of the IIS flow with filters added.

As you can see, IIS makes many calls to the registered filters as it is processing each HTTP request. This allows any ISAPI filter to change the default processing of a request.

FIG. 13.1
Flow of a request
through IIS.

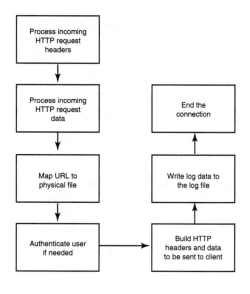

FIG. 13.2
Flow of a request with
filters.

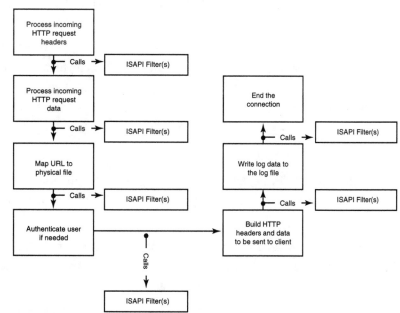

Part
IV

Ch
13

Each call is different in that it gives the filter a chance to process a different event
during the processing of the request. Each filter can choose to process the event
or to ignore it. If the filter ignores it, IIS processes the event.

Sample Registration and Information Flow

What if you need advanced logging or custom authentication? You might first try to do this with either an ISAPI extension or a CGI application. But for either choice to be effective, each request for a page from your site would have to come through either your extension or your CGI application—not feasible.

ISAPI filters are a much cleaner solution. Take a look at a sample interaction between IIS and a couple of ISAPI filters that do these functions.

Interaction During Filter Registration   As we have already seen, the first phase in the processing of a filter is registration. The following list shows the interaction between IIS and two filters during the registration phase:

1. IIS loads the DLL for filter 1 and calls GetFilterVersion().

2. Filter 1 sets its version, indicates that it wants to be notified when IIS is about to authenticate a client (SF_NOTIFY_AUTHENTICATION) and that it has a default priority (SF_NOTIFY_ORDER_DEFAULT).

3. IIS loads the DLL for filter 2 and calls GetFilterVersion().

4. Filter 2 sets its version, indicates that it wants to be notified when IIS is about to write data to the server log (SF_NOTIFY_LOG) and when it is about to authenticate a client (SF_NOTIFY_AUTHENTICATION). It also specifies that it has default priority (SF_NOTIFY_ORDER_DEFAULT).

Registration is now complete.

Interaction During Event Processing   Now imagine that a client requests a document from a secure area of our Web site. This happens to be the area that filter 2 is protecting.

Using the seven steps in "Information Flow" earlier in this chapter, let's see what the interaction between IIS and these two filters would look like. Remember, the filters are registered for authentication and logging, steps 4 and 6 of the flow.

1. IIS gets the request. It checks if any filters are to handle the incoming raw HTTP data and headers (SF_NOTIFY_READ_RAW_DATA). In this scenario, no filters are to handle the data and headers. IIS handles them.

2. Next, IIS checks to see if any filters are to do a task before it processes the headers (SF_NOTIFY_PREPROC_HEADERS). In this scenario, no filters are to do a task. IIS processes the headers.

3. Now IIS must map the URL to a physical path (SF_NOTIFY_MAP_URL). Before it does this, it checks if any filters are to map the path. In this scenario, no filters are to map the path. IIS maps the path.

Since neither of the filters registered for the first three steps of the information flow, the server handled them alone. Now we get to the first event that the filters registered for, step 4 under "Information Flow" earlier in this chapter.

1. The server sees that the document is in a secure area. It checks if any filters are to authenticate the client (SF_NOTIFY_AUTHENTICATION). It sees that both filter 1 and filter 2 registered to do this.

2. IIS calls HttpFilterProc() in filter 1.

3. Filter 1 looks at the path of the document and determines that it is not protecting this document. It tells IIS to pass the notification on to other filters.

4. IIS calls HttpFilterProc() in filter 2.

5. Filter 2 looks at the path of the document and determines that it is protecting this document. It does the processing to check if the user name and password are valid.

   In this scenario, the user name and password are valid. The filter tells IIS that it handled the request (SF_STATUS_REQ_HANDLED_NOTIFICATION).

6. IIS sees that it doesn't have to pass this notification down to any other filters because filter 2 handled it. So it checks if the authentication passed.

In this scenario, the user ID and password combination pass the test supplied by filter 2 in the authentication, step 4 under "Information Flow" earlier in this chapter. IIS is ready to process the raw data.

1. IIS prepares to send the data back to the client. Before it does this, it checks if any filters are to handle this (SF_NOTIFY_SEND_RAW_DATA).

2. In this scenario, no filters are to handle this. IIS sends the data back to the client.

Part
IV

Ch
13

The server is at step 6 under "Information Flow" earlier in this chapter, the logging event. Filter 2 registered for this event.

1. IIS prepares the data that will be written to the server log. Before it does this, it checks if any filters are to handle this (`SF_NOTIFY_LOG`).

2. IIS sees that filter 2 is to handle this. IIS calls the filter's `HttpFilterProc()` with the relevant data.

3. Filter 2 takes some data, logs it for itself, and returns to IIS, indicating that IIS should keep passing this notification down (`SF_STATUS_REQ_NEXT_NOTIFICATION`). Although the filter processed the event, it doesn't stop the default processing. Instead, it tells IIS to continue processing the event.

4. IIS sees that it should continue passing the notification to other filters. But in this scenario, there are no more filters. IIS writes the default log information.

IIS must end the connection with the client, the final step under "Information Flow" earlier in this chapter.

1. IIS checks if any filters are to be notified of the end of the network session with the client (`SF_NOTIFY_END_OF_NET_SESSION`).

2. In this scenario, no filters are to be notified. IIS ends the session.

This sample should give you a pretty clear picture of the interactions between IIS and ISAPI filters.

Information Flow Inside a Filter

Now let's take a quick look at what happens inside a filter's `HttpFilterProc()` when a request comes in. The steps for the `HttpFilterProc()` in most filters are listed below.

1. Determine the notification type (refer to Table 13.5).

2. Decide whether to process this occurrence.

3. If yes, process it.

4. Decide whether IIS should pass it on or not.

5. Return the proper status to IIS.

ISAPI Filter Rules

The previous sections describe what ISAPI filters are and how they work. Now we look into a few rules that each ISAPI filter must follow to work properly.

Must Be Registered Before IIS Starts

Because IIS loads all ISAPI filters at startup, you must know which DLLs to load. You can do this via the Windows NT registry. Unfortunately, at present there is no easier (or safer) way to do this. These are the steps to follow:

1. Run the Windows Registry Editor: REGEDT32.EXE

2. Edit the following key:

   ```
   HKEY_LOCAL_MACHINE\System\CurrentControlSet\Services\W3SVC
   ➥\Parameters\Filter DLLs
   ```

3. Add your filter's fully qualified path name to this key. Make sure you separate it from other filters with a comma.

Figure 13.3 shows what the registry screen should look like.

> **CAUTION**
>
> Be sure to separate filter DLLs by commas but only by commas. If you use any other character, such as semicolons, IIS ignores the entry and won't load your filter DLL. Also, be careful not to remove other entries that may already be there.

You should make editing the registry part of your filter's setup program, if it has one. If the filter doesn't have a setup program, you must do it manually.

After you have changed the registry, you must stop IIS (if it is already running) and restart it. This allows the server to load the filter.

Part
IV

Ch
13

To see if IIS has a problem loading your filter or any other filter, look in the Event Viewer. IIS writes an event to the event log when it encounters a failure loading a filter DLL.

FIG. 13.3
A snapshot of the
Windows NT registry.

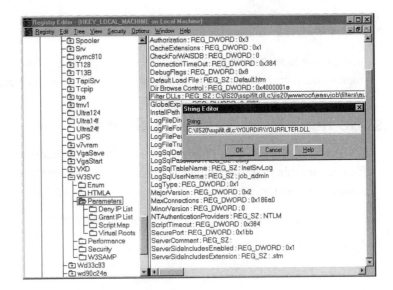

Must Be a 32-Bit DLL

Each ISAPI filter must be a 32-bit DLL. This is because IIS itself is a 32-bit program
and it must call entry points in your DLL.

Must Expose Defined Entry Points

As we have already discussed in this chapter, each filter DLL must have the
GetFilterVersion() and HttpFilterProc() entry points defined. Remember, this is
the only way IIS can communicate with your DLL. If these entry points are not
defined, IIS won't be able to load and use your filter DLL.

Must Be Thread-Safe

IIS makes extensive use of Windows NT's multithreading capabilities. It can respond to many requests simultaneously. This means that all ISAPI filters must be
thread-safe.

An in-depth discussion of threads is beyond the scope of this chapter. But
Figure 13.4 shows how IIS processes more than one request simultaneously.
The shaded area indicates periods of time that IIS is processing multiple requests
simultaneously.

FIG. 13.4
Multiple requests processed simultaneously.

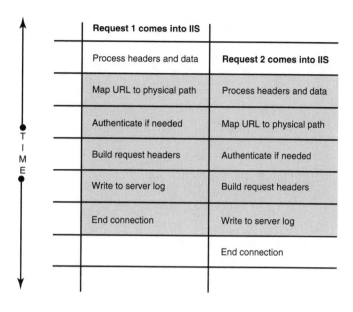

Request 1 comes into IIS	
Process headers and data	**Request 2 comes into IIS**
Map URL to physical path	Process headers and data
Authenticate if needed	Map URL to physical path
Build request headers	Authenticate if needed
Write to server log	Build request headers
End connection	Write to server log
	End connection

For more information about thread safety, see Chapter 18, "Making Your Extensions Thread-Safe."

From Here...

In this chapter, we learned how ISAPI filters work and what you need to make them work smoothly. We reviewed the priority levels and notifications used by filters.

We also looked at some practical uses for ISAPI filters. The following chapters give you good examples for building and using ISAPI filters:

- Chapter 14, "Creating an ISAPI Filter," takes you step-by-step through building an ISAPI filter.
- Chapter 15, "Building Filters with MFC ISAPI Classes," gives you in-depth information about the ISAPI filter capabilities and how to use them.
- Chapter 16, "Extending Your Web Server with Filters," illustrates how to build a custom authentication filter and a logging filter.

Part
IV

Ch
13

Creating an ISAPI Filter

In this chapter, you learn how to create an Internet Server Application Programming Interface (ISAPI). We begin by creating a dynamic-link library (DLL) in Microsoft Visual C++ (MSVC++) 4.x.

We outline the filter's initializations and termination, the entry points, the hypertext transport protocol (HTTP) flow events, and the API function calls. A tutorial shows you how to create a filter that does customized text replacement in an HTML page.

If you need a refresher, see Chapter 13, "Understanding ISAPI Filters," and review the rules for creating a filter. ■

Creating a DLL in MSVC++ 4.x

ISAPI extensions and filters are 32-bit DLLs—or they are called by 32-bit DLLs, as with OLEISAPI.DLL.

Outlining the filter's initialization and terminations

We outline the filter's initialization and terminations, entry points, Hypertext Transport Protocol (HTTP) flow events, and API function calls.

Creating a filter that does customized text replacement

In a tutorial, you learn how to create a filter that does customized text replacement in an HTML page.

Step 1: Create a 32-Bit DLL

In this section, we follow the steps to create an ISAPI filter DLL. We use the MSVC++ version 4.x development environment, running on Windows NT server 4.0, with Microsoft's Internet Information Server (IIS) 3.0 to serve the Web requests.

Create a 32-Bit DLL Project Workspace

To begin a new project with MSVC++, open Microsoft Developer Studio from the Microsoft Visual C++ programs folder. If you have a subscription to Microsoft Developer Network (MSDN) and it is integrated with the Microsoft Developer Studio, you see a window like the one in Figure 14.1.

FIG. 14.1
Microsoft Developer
Studio—ready to go.

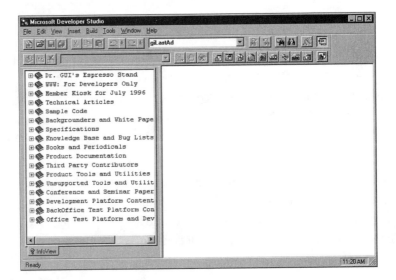

Microsoft Published Resources

Time is money and knowledge is power. Microsoft publishes two CDs and offers both via MSDN and Microsoft TechNet. These are invaluable tools for the busy and the beginning developer.

MSDN is produced quarterly and is the official source from Microsoft for comprehensive programming information, development toolkits, and testing platforms.

TechNet, with over 150,000 pages of in-depth technical information on each CD, is produced monthly and is the comprehensive information resource for evaluating, using, and supporting Microsoft business products.

Additional ordering and pricing is at Microsoft's Web site: **http://www.microsoft.com/ msdn** and **http://www.microsoft.com/technet**.

When you have an empty palette to work with, you are ready to create a DLL project workspace. From the File menu, select New. You see the New dialog box (see Figure 14.2).

FIG. 14.2
New dialog box—
select an object to
create.

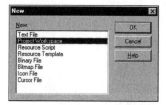

Select Project Workspace and click the OK button. You see the New Project Workspace dialog box (see Figure 14.3).

FIG. 14.3
New Project
Workspace—select
a project type to
create.

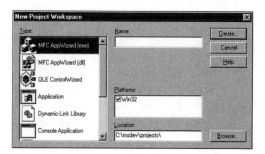

From the Type list box, select Dynamic-Link Library. In the Name text box, enter the name of the DLL to be created. Notice that in the Location text box, the project name is appended to the path where the Developer Studio projects are stored.

Make sure that Win32 is checked in the Platforms group. When you finish the New Project Workspace dialog box as shown in Figure 14.4, you are ready to click the Create button. We have a new project workspace and we are ready to begin adding code.

Part
IV

Ch
14

FIG. 14.4
New project work-
space ready for the
sample project.

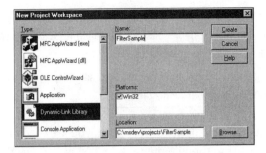

Add *DllMain()* for Startup/Shutdown

DllMain is the first function we use when creating a new ISAPI filter. DllMain is normally the entry point for 32-bit DLLs. This single function replaces LibMain and WEP in the Win32 model.

DllMain is optional but highly recommended. The name DllMain is also optional but it is the de facto standard. A DllMain function allows the server to notify your filter when per-process, and per-thread initialization and clean-up, are needed.

DllMain has a specific function prototype that you must adhere to so it works properly. This prototype is as follows:

```
BOOL WINAPI DllMain (
  HINSTANCE hinstDLL,
  DWORD fdwReason,
  LPVOID lpvReserved
  );
```

DllMain is called when the filter is loaded and unloaded from the server's address space. DllMain can determine why it is being called by checking the value of *fdwReason*.

The four possible values for *fdwReason* are DLL_PROCESS_ATTACH, DLL_PROCESS_DETACH, DLL_THREAD_ATTACH, and DLL_THREAD_DETACH. We use DLL_PROCESS_ATTACH to do filter initialization and DLL_PROCESS_DETACH to do filter clean-up.

An example of an initialization process is to read data from persistent storage to initialize the filter's global variables—for example, a Web-site visit counter.

An example of clean-up processing is writing global variables to persistent storage to save the state of the variables between the termination and restarting of the World Wide Web publishing service.

Listing 14.1 is an example of how to retrieve and store state variables in the DllMain function.

Listing 14.1 LST14_1.C—Retrieving and Storing State Variables

```
/*
      Globals
*/
CRITICAL_SECTION gCS;           // A critical section handle
                                // is used to protect global
                                // state properties
unsigned int  giCurrentAd;

/*
      This is the entry and exit point for the filter
      it is called when the filter is loaded and unloaded
      by IIS.  This is where state properties need to be
      retrieved and store on persistant storage.
*/
BOOL APIENTRY DllMain( HANDLE hModule,
                       DWORD fdwReason,
                       LPVOID lpReserved )
{
      char szLastAd[4];
      switch( fdwReason ) {
      case DLL_PROCESS_ATTACH:
      {
      /*
            On process attach we will set the state
            variables for the filter.  This entails
            counting the number of advertisers we're
            flipping ads for.
      */
      InitializeCriticalSection(&gCS);
      EnterCriticalSection(&gCS);
      gbHTML=FALSE;
      giCurrentAd = GetPrivateProfileInt(TEXT("Info"), TEXT("LastAd"),
                            1, TEXT("ads.ini"));
      LeaveCriticalSection(&gCS);
      break;
      }
```

continues

Part

IV

Ch

14

Listing 14.1   Continued

```
//      case DLL_THREAD_ATTACH:
//      case DLL_THREAD_DETACH:
        case DLL_PROCESS_DETACH:
        {
        sprintf(szLastAd, "%d", giCurrentAd);
        WritePrivateProfileString(TEXT("Info"), TEXT("LastAd"),
                                szLastAd, TEXT("ads.ini"));
        DeleteCriticalSection(&gCS);
        break;
        }
    }
    return TRUE;
}
```

N O T E   Listing 14.1 includes an example of using critical-section code to make your filter thread-safe. For information on making your extension thread-safe, see Chapter 18, "Making Your Extensions Thread-Safe."

To add a new source file and create a DllMain function for your new filter project in MSVC++, from the File menu, select New. You see the New dialog box shown in Figure 14.2 earlier in this chapter.

Select Text File from the New list box and click the OK button. You see an empty window that is ready for your DllMain function. With the DllMain function added, your development environment should look something like Figure 14.5.

The last task is to add the new code to the filter project. From the File menu, select Save As and save the file under an appropriate source file name in the same directory as the other project files.

After you save the file to disk, from the Insert menu, select Files into Project. You see the Insert Files into Project dialog box shown in Figure 14.6.

With the source file selected, click the Add button. The new source file is added to the new filter project and displayed in the project workspace tree view. The single source file is normally all you need for a basic filter.

Now we are ready to move on to the function calls that enable an ISAPI filter to be recognized and to work as an extension of the Web service.

FIG. 14.5
Workspace with new
DllMain function
added.

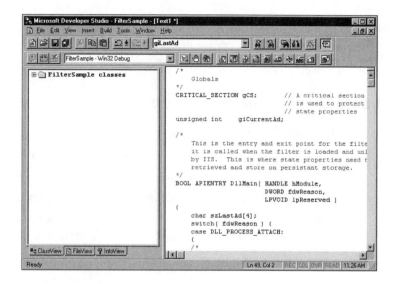

FIG. 14.6
The Insert Files into
Project dialog box.

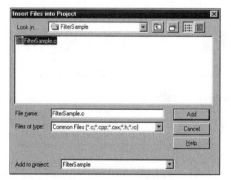

Step 2: Define *GetFilterVersion()*

GetFilterVersion is one of two necessary functions for every ISAPI filter. It is the
initial entry point called by IIS. GetFilterVersion receives a pointer to the structure, HTTP_FILTER_VERSION, which must be completed by the function.

Items to be completed in the structure include the filter's version information, the
events that the filter is to process, and the priority of these events in terms of other
registered filters.

TIP Register the filter only for events that the filter will process. Registering extraneous events can reduce the Web service's performance and scalability.

The *GetFilterVersion* Prototype

The prototype for GetFilterVersion is

```
BOOL WINAPI GetFilterVersion (PHTTP_FILTER_VERSION pVer)
```

The *pVer* parameter points to the HTTP_FILTER_VERSION structure and provides the communication channel between IIS and the filter. The structure holds version information for the server and fields for the client to denote the version, event notifications, filter priority, and a text description of the filter.

The structure is defined as

```
typedef struct _HTTP_FILTER_VERSION
{
 DWORD dwServerFilterVersion;
 DWORD dwFilterVersion;
 CHAR lpszFilterDesc[SF_MAX_FILTER_DESC_LEN+1];
 DWORD dwFlags;
} HTTP_FILTER_VERSION, *PHTTP_FILTER_VERSION;
```

The structure members are as follows:

dwServerFilterVersion [in]   The version of the specification used by the server. The version of the current header file is HTTP_FILTER_REVISION.

dwFilterVersion [out]   The version of the specification used by the server. The version of the current header file is HTTP_FILTER_REVISION.

lpszFilterDesc [out]   The location in which to store a short string description of the ISAPI filter.

dwFlags [out]   The combination of SF_NOTIFY_* flags to specify which events this application is to process. Table 14.1 lists the valid SF_NOTIFY_* flags for IIS version 3.0.

Table 14.1   Valid *SF_NOTIFY_* * Flags for IIS Version 3.0

Flag	Description
SF_NOTIFY_SECURE_PORT	Notifies application only for sessions over a secure port.
SF_NOTIFY_NONSECURE_PORT	Notifies application only for sessions over a nonsecure port.
SF_NOTIFY_READ_RAW_DATA	Allows the application to see the raw data. The data returned holds both headers and data.
SF_NOTIFY_PREPROC_HEADERS	Server has reprocessed the headers.
SF_NOTIFY_AUTHENTICATION	Server is authenticating the client.
SF_NOTIFY_URL_MAP	Server is mapping a logical URL to a physical path.
SF_NOTIFY_SEND_RAW_DATA	Server is sending raw data back to the client.
SF_NOTIFY_LOG	Server is writing information to the server log.
SF_NOTIFY_END_OF_NET_SESSION	Session with the client is ending.
SF_NOTIFY_ACCESS_DENIED	Allows a filter to be notified when the server is about to return a 401 Access Denied. This allows the filter to analyze the failure and return a custom message.
SF_NOTIFY_ORDER_DEFAULT	Loads the filter at the default priority (recommended).
SF_NOTIFY_ORDER_LOW	Loads the filter at the low priority.
SF_NOTIFY_ORDER_MEDIUM	Loads the filter at a medium priority.
SF_NOTIFY_ORDER_HIGH	Loads the filter at a high priority.

Part
IV

Ch

14

Set the ISAPI Version Number and Description

As we said earlier, GetFilterVersion holds key information that must be set before the server begins notifying the filter of events. The first two items to be set in the HTTP_FILTER_VERSION structure are *dwFilterVersion* and *lpszFilterDesc*. These items give the Web service version information for the filter and a text description that can be displayed in processing logs.

TIP You should test the HTTP_FILTER_VERSION *dwServerFilterVersion* member if you are developing the filter for a specific version of IIS. Use the HIWORD and LOWORD macros to extract the major version and minor version numbers of the Web service.

Listing 14.2 is an example of how to test the server's version information. When you set the filter's version number, use the MAKELONG macro to set the high and low word that make up the HTTP_FILTER_VERSION structure *dwFilterVersion* member.

Set the Event Notifications

The most important data element to set in the HTTP_FILTER_VERSION structure is *dwFlags*. This member tells the Web service which events the filter is to process.

Table 14.1 lists the event notification flags to set for IIS version 3.0. Typically, you can copy this example of a GetFilterVersion function and use it for each new filter. You need to change only the description and events notification flags.

Listing 14.2 LST14_2.C—*GetFilterVersion* Function

```
/*
        GetFilterVersion - An ISAPI/Win32 API method
        This method is required by IIS.  It is called
        following the process load to ensure that the
        filter is compatible with the server.
*/
BOOL WINAPI GetFilterVersion(HTTP_FILTER_VERSION * pVer)
{

    WORD wMajorVersion=0;
    WORD wMinorVersion=0;
```

```
wMajorVersion = HIWORD( pVer->dwServerFilterVersion );
wMinorVersion = LOWORD( pVer->dwServerFilterVersion );

/*
    This filter is intended for IIS version 2.0 or greater.
    This is an example of how to test the server version.
*/

if (wMajorVersion < 2) return FALSE;

pVer->dwFilterVersion = MAKELONG( 0, 1 );   // Version 1.0

/*
        Specify the security level of notifications
        (secured port, nonsecured port, or both), the
        types of events and order of notification for
        this filter (high, medium or low, default=low).
*/
pVer->dwFlags = (
                        SF_NOTIFY_SECURE_PORT
                        SF_NOTIFY_NONSECURE_PORT
                        SF_NOTIFY_READ_RAW_DATA
                        SF_NOTIFY_PREPROC_HEADERS
                        SF_NOTIFY_URL_MAP
                        SF_NOTIFY_AUTHENTICATION
                        SF_NOTIFY_ACCESS_DENIED
                        SF_NOTIFY_SEND_RAW_DATA
                        SF_NOTIFY_LOG
                        SF_NOTIFY_END_OF_NET_SESSION
                        SF_NOTIFY_ORDER_DEFAULT
                                );
    /*
            A brief one line description of the filter
     */
strcpy( pVer->lpszFilterDesc, "Sample Filter, v1.0" );

    return TRUE;
}
```

N O T E IIS makes assumptions if certain notification flags are not specified.

   If a port notification flag is not specified, IIS assumes that the filter
is to get notifications for both secure (`SF_NOTIFY_SECURE_PORT`) and nonsecure
(`SF_NOTIFY_ NONSECURE_PORT`) port requests.

If a priority order is not specified, IIS assumes the default priority
(`SF_NOTIFY_ORDER_ DEFAULT`). This is the same as specifying a low priority
(`SF_NOTIFY_ORDER_LOW`). ▤

Part

IV

Ch

14

Step 3: Define *HttpFilterProc()*

HttpFilterProc is the callback function that gets the event notification from the Web service. HttpFilterProc is to IIS what WindowProc is to the Windows operating system: the main event message loop. This is where the event messages are parceled out to the worker functions to do the task at hand.

The *HttpFilterProc* Prototype

The HttpFilterProc prototype is

```
DWORD WINAPI HttpFilterProc(
 PHTTP_FILTER_CONTEXT pfc,
 DWORD notificationType,
 LPVOID pvNotification
 );
```

The parameters for HttpFilterProc include a pointer, *pfc*, to the HTTP_FILTER_CONTEXT structure that can be used by the filter to associate any context information with the HTTP request. The HttpFilterProc parameters also include pointers to callback functions in the Web service for two-way communications.

The other two parameters, *notificationType* and *pvNotification*, have a direct correlation. The data pointed to by the void pointer, *pvNotification*, can take the shape of several structures, based on the event notification type, *notificationType*.

Table 14.2 shows the correlation between *notificationType* and the structures pointed to by *pvNotification*.

Table 14.2   Notification Types and Structures

Notification Type	Structure Name
SF_NOTIFY_READ_RAW_DATA	HTTP_FILTER_RAW_DATA
SF_NOTIFY_SEND_RAW_DATA	HTTP_FILTER_RAW_DATA
SF_NOTIFY_PREPROC_HEADERS	HTTP_FILTER_PREPROC_HEADERS
SF_NOTIFY_AUTHENTICATION	HTTP_FILTER_AUTHENT

Notification Type	Structure Name
SF_NOTIFY_URL_MAP	HTTP_FILTER_URL_MAP
SF_NOTIFY_LOG	HTTP_FILTER_LOG
SF_NOTIFY_ACCESS_DENIED	HTTP_FILTER_ACCESS_DENIED

A filter's HttpFilterProc serves as a traffic director for routing events to the right worker function. Listing 14.3 is an example of a typical HttpFilterProc set up to accept all the possible HTTP communication events.

Listing 14.3 LST14_3.C—*HttpFilterProc* Example

```
/*
      HttpFilterProc - ISAPI / Win32 API method
      This method is required by IIS.  It is called
      for each notification event requested.  This is
      where the filter accomplishes its purpose in life.
*/
DWORD WINAPI HttpFilterProc(HTTP_FILTER_CONTEXT *pfc,
                            DWORD NotificationType,
                            VOID * pvData)
{
    DWORD dwRet;
    /*
       Direct the notification to the appropriate
       routine for processing.
    */
    switch ( NotificationType )
    {
    case SF_NOTIFY_READ_RAW_DATA:
        dwRet = OnReadRawData(pfc, (PHTTP_FILTER_RAW_DATA) pvData );
        break;
    case SF_NOTIFY_PREPROC_HEADERS:
        dwRet = OnPreprocHeaders(pfc, (PHTTP_FILTER_PREPROC_HEADERS)
        ➥pvData );
        break;
    case SF_NOTIFY_URL_MAP:
        dwRet = OnUrlMap(pfc, (PHTTP_FILTER_URL_MAP) pvData );
        break;
    case SF_NOTIFY_AUTHENTICATION:
        dwRet = OnAuthentication(pfc, (PHTTP_FILTER_AUTHENT) pvData );
        break;
    case SF_NOTIFY_ACCESS_DENIED:
        dwRet = OnAccessDenied(pfc, (PHTTP_FILTER_ACCESS_DENIED) pvData );
        break;
```

Part
IV

Ch
14

continues

Listing 14.3   Continued

```
    case SF_NOTIFY_SEND_RAW_DATA:
        dwRet = OnSendRawData(pfc, (PHTTP_FILTER_RAW_DATA) pvData );
        break;
    case SF_NOTIFY_LOG:
        dwRet = OnLog(pfc, (PHTTP_FILTER_LOG) pvData );
        break;
    case SF_NOTIFY_END_OF_NET_SESSION:
        dwRet = OnEndOfNetSession(pfc);
        break;
    default:
        dwRet = SF_STATUS_REQ_NEXT_NOTIFICATION;
        break;
    }
    return dwRet;
}
```

Filter Context Structure and Key Members

pfc is a pointer to the HTTP_FILTER_CONTEXT structure for all request notification types. It keeps a consistent state between HTTP communication events and has this layout:

```
typedef struct _HTTP_FILTER_CONTEXT
{
DWORD cbSize;  // structure size
DWORD Revision;       // revision level
PVOID ServerContext;  // context info for the server
DWORD ulReserved;     // for future use
BOOL fIsSecurePort;   // TRUE=request from secure port
PVOID pFilterContext; // context info for the filter
//
//  Server callbacks
//
BOOL (WINAPI * GetServerVariable) (
 struct _HTTP_FILTER_CONTEXT *      pfc,
 LPSTR    lpszVariableName,
 LPVOID   lpvBuffer,
 LPDWORD  lpdwSize
);

BOOL (WINAPI * AddResponseHeaders) (
 struct _HTTP_FILTER_CONTEXT *      pfc,
 LPSTR    lpszHeaders,
 DWORD    dwReserved
);
```

```
BOOL (WINAPI * WriteClient) (
   struct _HTTP_FILTER_CONTEXT *        pfc,
   LPVOID   Buffer,
   LPDWORD  lpdwBytes,
   DWORD    dwReserved
);

VOID * (WINAPI * AllocMem) (
   struct _HTTP_FILTER_CONTEXT *        pfc,
   DWORD    cbSize,
   DWORD    dwReserved
);

BOOL (WINAPI * ServerSupportFunction) (
   struct _HTTP_FILTER_CONTEXT *        pfc,
   enum SF_REQ_TYPE sfReq,
   PVOID    pData,
   DWORD    ul1,
   DWORD    ul2
);

} HTTP_FILTER_CONTEXT, *PHTTP_FILTER_CONT
```

fIsSecurePort   The filter context structure has a member named fIsSecurePort, which is a Boolean flag that indicates whether the HTTP request was made over a secured port using the secure socket layer (SSL) encryption protocol. If the request did originate from the client requesting a secure port, this flag is set to TRUE or a nonzero value.

pFilterContext   The pFilterContext member of the filter context structure is a void pointer. It can be replaced with a pointer to data that is relevant in the context of the HTTP request.

Use the filter-context AllocMem callback function or a standard memory-allocation method to allocate memory and set pFilterContext to the allocated memory and data structure.

 Since the SF_NOTIFY_END_OF_NET_SESSION is the last event in the HTTP communication flow, you can request it in the GetFilterVersion function. This allows the release of resources requested during the context of a single HTTP request.

If memory is allocated using the AllocMem callback function, resources are automatically released at the end of the HTTP communication.

Part
IV
Ch
14

Filter Context Callback Functions

In the HTTP_FILTER_CONTEXT structure are five callback functions, all for two-way communication between the filter and the Web service. These functions are detailed next.

***GetServerVariable* Callback Function**   The first callback function found in HTTP_FILTER_CONTEXT is GetServerVariable. This function retrieves information about a connection or about the Web service. The function prototype and parameters are as follows:

```
BOOL WINAPI GetServerVariable (
 PHTTP_FILTER_CONTEXT  pfc,
 LPSTR  lpszVariableName,
 LPVOID lpvBuffer
 LPDWORD       lpdwSizeofBuffer
);
```

The parameters for GetServerVariable include the following:

- *pfc*, a pointer to the filter context structure.

- *lpszVariableName*, a null-terminated string that indicates which server variable is requested (see Table 14.3 for a list of server variables).

- *lpvBuffer* is a void pointer to a memory buffer used to return the contents of the information requested.

- *lpdwSizeofBuffer* is a pointer to a DWORD that indicates the size of the buffer sent to the server and the size of the returned information transferred into *lpvBuffer* once the callback is completed.

Table 14.3   Possible Server Variables

Variable Name	Description
AUTH_TYPE	Holds the type of authentication used. For example, if basic authentication is used, the string is Basic. For NT challenge-response, it is NTLM. Other authentication schemes have other strings.
CONTENT_LENGTH	Number of bytes the script can expect to receive from the client.
CONTENT_TYPE	Content type of the information supplied in the body of a POST request.

Variable Name	Description
PATH_INFO	Additional path information, as given by the client. This consists of the trailing part of the URL after the script name but before the query string, if any.
PATH_TRANSLATED	Value of PATH_INFO but with any virtual path name expanded into a directory specification.
QUERY_STRING	Information that follows the "?" in the URL that referenced this script.
REMOTE_ADDR	IP address of the client or agent of the client (for example, a gateway or firewall) that sent the request.
REMOTE_HOST	Host name of the client or agent of the client (for example, a gateway or firewall) that sent the request.
REMOTE_USER	Holds the user name supplied by the client and authenticated by the server. This comes back as an empty string when the user is anonymous (but authenticated).
UNMAPPED_REMOTE_USER	User name before a filter maps the user making the request to an NT user account (which appears as REMOTE_USER).
REQUEST_METHOD	HTTP request method.
SCRIPT_NAME	Name of the script program executed.
SERVER_NAME	Server's host name or IP address as it should appear in self-referencing URLs.
SERVER_PORT	TCP/IP port on which the request was received.
SERVER_PORT_SECURE	String of either 0 or 1. If the request is handled on the secure port, this is 1. Otherwise, it is 0.
SERVER_PROTOCOL	Name and version of the information-retrieval protocol relating to this request. This is normally HTTP/1.0.
SERVER_SOFTWARE	Name and version of the server under which the ISAPI filter DLL program is running.

continues

Part

IV

Ch

14

Table 14.3   Continued

Variable Name	Description
ALL_HTTP	All HTTP headers not already parsed into one of the previous variables. These variables are of the HTTP_<header field name> form. The headers consist of a null-terminated string with the individual headers separated by line feeds.
HTTP_ACCEPT	Special-case HTTP header. Values of the Accept: fields are concatenated and separated by a comma (","). For example, if the following lines are part of the HTTP header:
| | ```
accept: */*; q=0.1
accept: text/html
accept: image/jpeg
``` |
| | the HTTP_ACCEPT variable has a value of: */*; q=0.1, text/html, image/jpeg. |
| URL | Gives the base portion of the URL. |

If GetServerVariable returns successfully, the return value is TRUE. If the function fails, you can use the Win32 GetLastError function to determine why the function call failed.

Table 14.4 lists the errors that can be returned by GetLastError, following a failed return from GetServerVariable.

Table 14.4   *GetServerVariable*: Possible Errors

Value	Description
ERROR_INVALID_PARAMETER	Bad connection handle.
ERROR_INVALID_INDEX	Bad or incompatible variable identifier
ERROR_INSUFFICIENT_BUFFER	Buffer too small. The necessary buffer size is lpdwSize.
ERROR_MORE_DATA	Buffer too small. Only part of the data is returned. The total size of the data is not known.
ERROR_NO_DATA	The data requested is not available.
```

Listing 14.4 is an example of how to access the Web service variables using
`GetServerVariables`.

Listing 14.4   LST14_4.C—*GetServerVariable* Example

```
/*
The following is an example of how to use GetServerVariable to
retrieve information concerning the web server or the communication
in process.  In this example pfc is a pointer to the
HTTP_FILTER_CONTEXT structure.
*/

CHAR   achUserAgent[4182];
DWORD  cbUserAgent= 4182;

// Execute the server callback function GetServerVariable
if ( !pfc->GetServerVariable(pfc,"HTTP_USER_AGENT",achUserAgent,
➥&cbUserAgent ))
{
/*
There was an error in processing the request. This is an example
of checking the error type using the Win32 function GetLastError.
*/
        if (ERROR_INVALID_INDEX != GetLastError()) (
                return SF_STATUS_REQ_ERROR;
        }
}
```

***AddResponseHeaders* Callback Function**   The `AddResponseHeaders` callback
function allows the server to add response header information to the HTTP
communication response to the client. The function prototype for `AddResponse`
`Headers` is

```
BOOL WINAPI AddResponseHeaders) (
 PHTTP_FILTER_CONTEXT pfc,
 LPSTR lpszHeaders,
 DWORD dwReserved
 );
```

The parameters for `AddResponseHeaders` include the following:

■ *pfc*, a pointer to the filter context structure.

■ *lpszHeaders*, a pointer to a null-terminated string that holds the response
header to be included in the HTTP response to the client.

■ *dwReserved*, a double word (DWORD) reserved for future use, which should be
set to NULL.

AddResponseHeaders is normally used with the WriteClient callback function, which allows HTTP or binary data to be written directly to the client. Response headers supply information to the client about the data to be transmitted.

You can formulate a complete communication reply by using AddResponseHeader to notify the client of a data type to be sent to a client and WriteClient to write the data to the client.

Listing 14.5 is an example of how to add response headers to an HTTP request using AddResponseHeaders.

Listing 14.5   LST14_5.C—*AddResponseHeaders* Example

```
/*
The following is an example of how to use AddResponseHeaders to inform
the client browser of the content length of the data about to be
transmitted.
*/
// Execute the server callback function AddResponseHeaders
if ( !pfc->AddResponseHeaders( pfc, "Content-Length = 100", NULL))
{
/*
      There was an error in processing the request so
      do error processing here
*/
}
```

***WriteClient* Callback Function**   The WriteClient callback function sends data to the client from a buffer provided by the filter. WriteClient enables the transfer of binary data because it does not assume that a null-terminated string is passed back to the client.

The function prototype for WriteClient is

```
BOOL WINAPI WriteClient (
 PHTTP_FILTER_CONTEXT pfc,
 LPVOID lpvBuffer,
 LPDWORD lpdwSizeofBuffer,
 DWORD dwReserved
 );
```

The parameters for WriteClient include the following:

- ■ *pfc*, a pointer to the filter context structure.

- *lpvBuffer*, a void pointer to a memory buffer that holds the data to be passed to the client.

- *lpdwSizeofBuffer*, a pointer to a double word (DWORD) used to indicate the size of the buffer sent to the client.

- *dwReserved*, a double word (DWORD) reserved for future use, which should be set to NULL.

WriteClient is often used with AddResponseHeaders to complete an HTTP request. If *lpvBuffer* points to a null-terminated string and the whole string is to be sent, *lpdwSizeofBuffer* should be set to the length of the string.

On its return from the call, *lpdwSizeofBuffer* is equal to the number of bytes transferred. This number is less than the original amount only if the original call returns FALSE.

Listing 14.6 is an example of how to transfer data to the client using WriteClient.

Listing 14.6   LST14_6.C—*WriteClient* Example

```
/*
The following is an example of how to use WriteClient to transfer
data to the client browser.
*/
char szResponse[100];
char szTime[20];
DWORD dwRespLen=0;
DWORD dwError=0;

// Create a forced response string
_strtime(szTime);
sprintf(szResponse,
        "<HTML><BODY><H1>Forced Response at %s</H1></BODY></HTML>",
        szTime);
dwRespLen=strlen(szResponse);

// Execute the server callback function WriteClient
if ( !pfc->WriteClient( pfc, (LPVOID)&szResponse,(LPDWORD)&dwRespLen,NULL))
{
        dwError = GetLastError();
}
```

***AllocMem* Callback Function**   The `AllocMem` callback function allocates a generic memory buffer that is automatically freed at the end of the HTTP request. The function prototype for `AllocMem` is

```
LPVOID AllocMem (
 DWORD cbSize,
 DWORD dwReserved
);
```

The parameters for `AllocMem` include the following:

- *cbSize*, a double word (`DWORD`) used to indicate the size of the buffer to be allocated.

- *dwReserved*, a double word (`DWORD`) reserved for future use, which should be set to `NULL`.

The return value is a void pointer (`LPVOID`) to a memory buffer that was allocated by the function call.

N O T E   You can't manage memory blocks allocated with `AllocMem` with the normal C runtime or Windows API memory management functions. ▪

T I P   Calls to `AllocMem` can reduce performance because the burden of memory management is on the Web service. You might increase the filter's performance by allowing the filter to manage its own memory allocations.

Allocate memory as needed and then release it at the end of the HTTP communication request. The last event in the HTTP request is `SF_NOTIFY_END_OF_NET_SESSION`.

The filter has to register for this event in the `GetFilterVersion` function to get a notification of the end-of-net-sessions event.

Listing 14.7 is an example of how to allocate a block of memory with a call to `AllocMem`.

Listing 14.7   LST14_7.C—*AllocMem* Example

```
/*
The following is an example of how to use AllocMem to
allocate a block of memory.
*/
char* pszBuffer;
```

```
pszBuffer=(CHAR*)pfc->AllocMem(pfc, 400, (DWORD)NULL);
memset(pszBuffer,'\0',sizeof(pszBuffer));
```

***ServerSupportFunction* Callback Function**   The `ServerSupportFunction` callback function gives the filter general-purpose functions, plus methods specific to the Web service. The function prototype for `ServerSupportFunction` is

```
BOOL WINAPI ServerSupportFunction (
 PHTTP_FILTER_CONTEXT pfc,
 enum SF_REQ_TYPE sfRequest,
 PVOID pvData,
 LPDWORD lpdwSizeofBuffer,
 LPDWORD lpdwDataType
);
```

The parameters for `ServerSupportFunction` include

- *pfc*, a pointer to the filter context structure.

- *sfRequest*, a server request type used to indicate the type of request being made (see Table 14.5 for a list of possible values).

- *pData*, a void pointer to a null-terminated string, normally used for an optional status message.

- *lpdwSizeofBuffer*, a pointer to a double word (DWORD) that normally indicates the size of *pData*.

- *lpdwSizeofBuffer*, a double word (DWORD) that is a pointer to a null-terminated string. *lpdwSizeofBuffer* is used for optional headers or for data appended and sent with the HTTP response header *lpdwDataType*.

Table 14.5   *SF_REQ_* * Options

Value	Description
SF_REQ_SEND_RESPONSE_HEADER	Sends a complete HTTP server response header, including the status, server version, message time, and Content-type MIME version. Server extensions should append other information at the end, followed by an extra \r\n.

continues

Table 14.5   Continued

Value	Description
SF_REQ_ADD_HEADERS_ON_DENIAL	If the server denies the HTTP request, add the specified headers to the server error response. This allows an authentication filter to advertise its services without filtering every request.
	Generally, the headers are WWW-Authenticate headers with custom authentication schemes but no restriction on what headers can be specified.
SF_REQ_SET_NEXT_READ_SIZE	Used only by raw-data filters that return SF_STATUS_READ_NEXT *lpdwSizeofBuffer* size in bytes for the next read.

Listing 14.8 is an example of one of the possible function calls using ServerSupportFunction.

Listing 14.8   LST14_8.C—*ServerSupportFunction* Example

```
/*
The following is an example of how to use ServerSupportFunction to read
additional data from the client browser.
*/
char szBuffer[100];
DWORD dwBufferLen=0;

dwszBufferLen=sizeof(szBuffer);
pfc->ServerSupportFunction(pfc,
             SF_REQ_SET_NEXT_READ_SIZE,
             (PVOID)&szBuffer,
             dwBufferLen,
             (DWORD)NULL );
```

Do the Processing

When the necessary functions are in your filter and the notification events have been requested, you're ready to do your processing. But when and where does the code get written?

Chapter 12, "Using ISAPI Filters," outlines the sequence of events in the HTTP request. Chapter 12 also gives you ideas for the kinds of filters you can create.

Listing 14.3 earlier in this chapter is the backbone for HTTP request event processing. Worker functions are called from the `switch/case` statement or processing is done in the case statement.

The tutorial at the end of chapter brings together all the pieces we discussed with an example of how to change the raw data sent back to the browser.

Return Status Code

When the filter's processing is done, the right return code has to be passed back to the Web service. The return code tells the Web service how the event was handled and what process is needed next.

Table 14.6 lists the valid return codes and their meanings for the `HttpFilterProc` function.

Table 14.6   *HttpFilterProc* Return Codes

Value	Description
SF_STATUS_REQ_FINISHED	The filter has handled the HTTP request. The server should disconnect the session.
SF_STATUS_REQ_FINISHED_KEEP_CONN	This is the same as SF_STATUS_REQ_FINISHED, except that the server should keep the TCP session open if the option was negotiated.
SF_STATUS_REQ_NEXT_NOTIFICATION	The next filter in the notification chain should be called.
SF_STATUS_REQ_HANDLED_NOTIFICATION	This filter handled the notification. No other handlers should be called for this notification type.
SF_STATUS_REQ_ERROR	An error occurred. The server should call GetLastError and indicate the error to the client.

Part

IV

Ch

14

continues

Table 14.6   Continued

Value	Description
SF_STATUS_REQ_READ_NEXT	The filter is an opaque stream filter and the session parameters are being negotiated. This is valid only for raw-read notification.

Tutorial: Building the AdFlipperFilter

The AdFlipperFilter project is on the companion CD to this book. AdFlipperFilter replaces a text string in an HTML page to create advertisement graphics with hyperlinks to the advertiser's Web site.

The filter uses a DllMain function to initialize filter-wide parameters. When DllMain is called with the flag, DLL_PROCESS_ATTACH, a critical-section handle is created for thread-safe processing.

The contents of a configuration file are loaded into global variables to be used throughout the filter. When DllMain is called with DLL_PROCESS_DETACH, clean-up processing is done by deleting the critical section handle.

AdFlipperFilter's GetFilterVersion function requests notifications for two specific events, SF_NOTIFY_URL_MAP and SF_NOTIFY_SEND_RAW_DATA. The URL map event is requested to analyze the name of the HTML page requested. The send raw data event is requested because that is where the raw data being sent to the client browser can be manipulated.

By default, IIS assumes that a filter will be used for processing on both secure and nonsecure ports. IIS also assumes that the filter will process at a default priority, which is defined as low priority. For our tutorial, the SF_NOTIFY_* flags are requested specifically to ensure proper processing.

AdFlipperFilter's HttpFilterProc function directs the event traffic to the proper worker function. The function's switch/case statement directs notification events of SF_NOTIFY_URL_MAP to the OnUrlMap function and SF_NOTIFY_SEND_RAW_DATA to the OnSendRawData function. All other extraneous events are bypassed.

The OnUrlMap function analyzes the URL resource that is requested. In this example, we want to do processing only for resources that end with the ads.htm string. So URLs like **http://www.yoursite.com/ads.htm** and **http://www.yoursite.com/HOMads.htm** are valid for processing.

When a URL passes the test for AdFlipperFilter processing, the filter-context callback function AllocMem is called to create a memory buffer to hold the image and link string. The InsertAd function is called with the memory buffer just created.

The InsertAd function uses the filter's global variables and configuration file to determine which advertisement is next in the rotation. The function then constructs the image-and-link strings to be inserted into the body of the HTML page at the special tag placeholder.

NOTE The image-and-link string that is created in the InsertAd function also calls an ISAPI ClickThruExtension.dll extension. This extension is on the companion CD in the AdFlipperFilter project directory.

The ClickThruExtension.dll extension tallies the number of times a user clicks an advertisement that passes control to the advertiser's Web site. Click-thru statistics can be reviewed by placing a request with the ISAPI SiteStatsExtension.dll extension (also on the companion CD in the AdFlipperFilter project directory).

A request to the **http://www.yoursite.com/scripts/SiteStatsExtension.dll?ClickThrus** resource produces an HTML page with the number of click thrus and the first date a click thru occurred by URL. You should put the supplemental extensions mentioned above in the IIS scripts directory before you try to use them. ▤

The OnSendRawData function is called twice in the HTTP communication flow. It's first called with the response headers to be passed back to the client browser.

These headers include the Content-Length header, which tells the browser how much data to expect. Since AdFlipperFilter expands the HTML page size, the Content-Length header needs to be increased to include the number of bytes added by the image-and-link string.

The second call to the OnSendRawData function is just before the server passes the HTML page to the browser. This is when the function inserts the image-and-link string into the page.

Part

IV

Ch

14

Listing 14.9 is the source code for the AdFlipperFilter.

```
/*

Copyright  1996  ClearMind, Inc.

Module Name:

    AdFlipperFilter.c

Abstract:

    This filter checks HTML pages accessed at the server for
       the special advertisement tags.  Then it looks into its
       database for the next ad to run on the page.  It then
       inserts the hyperlink, graphic and alternate text for the
       advertiser.
*/

#include <windows.h>
#include <httpfilt.h>
#include <string.h>
#include <stdio.h>
#include <stdarg.h>

#define ADINI                   "d:\\inetsrv\\scripts\\filters\\Ad.INI"
#define ADLINKS                     "AdLinks"
#define ADGRAPHICS              "AdGraphics"
#define ADHEIGHTS               "AdHeights"
#define ADWIDTHS                "AdWidths"
#define ADTARGETS               "AdTargets"
/*
       Private prototypes
*/
DWORD OnUrlMap(HTTP_FILTER_CONTEXT *pfc,
                        HTTP_FILTER_URL_MAP *pvData);

DWORD OnSendRawData(HTTP_FILTER_CONTEXT *pfc,
                                HTTP_FILTER_RAW_DATA *pvData);

//void InsertAd(char* pszBuffer, char* pszAdBuffer, int b);
void InsertAd(char* pszAdBuffer);
/*
       Globals
*/
```

```
CRITICAL_SECTION gCS;          // A critical section handle
                                               // is used to protect
                                               // global
                                               // state properties

char              gszAdLinks[2048];
char*             gpszAdLink;
char*             gpszNewBuffer;
char*             gpszAdBuffer;
unsigned int  giCurrentAd;
unsigned int  giLastAd;
unsigned int  giExpandedLen;


/*
     This the the entry and exit point for the filter
     it is called when the filter is loaded and unloaded
     by IIS.  This is where state properties need to be
     retrieved and stored on persistent storage.
*/
BOOL APIENTRY DllMain( HANDLE hModule,
                       DWORD ul_reason_for_call,
                       LPVOID lpReserved )
{
     unsigned int i = 0;
     switch( ul_reason_for_call ) {
   case DLL_PROCESS_ATTACH:
      {
              /*
                      On process attach we will set the state
                      variables for the filter.  This entails
                      counting the number of advertisers we're
                      flipping ads for.
              */
              InitializeCriticalSection(&gCS);
              EnterCriticalSection(&gCS);
              giCurrentAd=1;
              giLastAd=1;
              GetPrivateProfileString(ADLINKS, NULL, TEXT(" "),
                                      gszAdLinks, sizeof(gszAdLinks),
                                      ADINI);
              gpszAdLink = (char*)gszAdLinks;
              while (gszAdLinks[i])
              {
                      giLastAd++;
                      i+=strlen(gpszAdLink)+1;
                      gpszAdLink+=strlen(gpszAdLink)+1;
              }
```

Part

IV

Ch

14

continues

Listing 14.9   Continued

```
                gpszAdLink = (char*)gszAdLinks;
                LeaveCriticalSection(&gCS);
                break;
        }
//    case DLL_THREAD_ATTACH:
//    case DLL_THREAD_DETACH:
     case DLL_PROCESS_DETACH:
                {
                DeleteCriticalSection(&gCS);
                break;
                }
     }
     return TRUE;
}


/*
     GetFilterVersion - An ISAPI/Win32 API method
     This method is required by IIS.  It is called
     following the process load to ensure that the
     filter is compatible with the server.
*/
BOOL WINAPI GetFilterVersion(HTTP_FILTER_VERSION * pVer)
{
     pVer->dwFilterVersion = MAKELONG( 0, 1 );   // Version 1.0

     /*
                Specify the security level of notifications
                (secured port, nonsecured port, or both), the
                types of events and order of notification for
                this filter (high, medium or low, default=low).
     */
     pVer->dwFlags = (
                                    SF_NOTIFY_SECURE_PORT           |
                     SF_NOTIFY_NONSECURE_PORT           |
                                    SF_NOTIFY_URL_MAP                    |
                                    SF_NOTIFY_SEND_RAW_DATA         |
                     SF_NOTIFY_ORDER_DEFAULT
                                    );
        /*
                A brief one line description of the filter
        */
     strcpy( pVer->lpszFilterDesc, TEXT("Ad Flipper Filter, v1.1"));

     return TRUE;
}

/*
```

```
        HttpFilterProc - ISAPI / Win32 API method
        This method is required by IIS.  It is called
        for each notification event requested.  This is
        where the filter accomplishes its purpose in life.
*/
DWORD WINAPI HttpFilterProc(HTTP_FILTER_CONTEXT *pfc,
                                              DWORD NotificationType,
                                              VOID * pvData)
{
    DWORD dwRet;
    /*
              Direct the notification to the appropriate
              routine for processing.
    */
    switch ( NotificationType )
    {
case SF_NOTIFY_URL_MAP:
    dwRet = OnUrlMap(pfc, (PHTTP_FILTER_URL_MAP) pvData );
    break;
    case SF_NOTIFY_SEND_RAW_DATA:
        dwRet = OnSendRawData(pfc, (PHTTP_FILTER_RAW_DATA) pvData );
        break;
    default:
        dwRet = SF_STATUS_REQ_NEXT_NOTIFICATION;
        break;
    }
    return dwRet;
}
/*
      IIS Filter Event Routines
*/
/*
      OnUrlMap -
      The data returned within pvData includes the URL
      requested (pvData->pszURL) and the full path to
      the physical data (pvData->pszPhysicalPath.
*/
DWORD OnUrlMap(HTTP_FILTER_CONTEXT *pfc,
                      HTTP_FILTER_URL_MAP *pvData)
{
    /*
        In this routine we will check to see if the page begin
        requested ends with "ads.htm".  This will signify an
        advertisement page.  Then we will create the text link
        and image line that will create the ad...
    */
    if (strstr(pvData->pszURL, TEXT("ads.htm"))) {
            gpszAdBuffer=(CHAR*)pfc->AllocMem(pfc, 400, (DWORD)NULL);
            memset(gpszAdBuffer,'\0',sizeof(gpszAdBuffer));
```

continues

Part

IV

Ch

14

Listing 14.9 Continued

```
                InsertAd(gpszAdBuffer);
                pfc->pFilterContext = (void*)gpszAdBuffer;
        }
    return SF_STATUS_REQ_NEXT_NOTIFICATION;
}
/*
    OnSendRawData -
    This routine is called twice for this event.
    The first time it is called is when it sends
    the browser a notification of the actual data
    it is about to transmit(e.g. text/html, image/gif,
    etc.)  The second time this routine is called
    is when the actual data (e.g. text, gif, etc.)
    is being transmitted to the browser.
*/
DWORD OnSendRawData(HTTP_FILTER_CONTEXT *pfc,
                                    HTTP_FILTER_RAW_DATA *pvData)

{
        CHAR*   pszBuffer;
        DWORD   cbNewInData=0;
        BOOL    bAdPage=FALSE;
        DWORD   i=0;
        DWORD   j=0;

        char*   pcBefore;
        char*   pcBetween;
        char*   pcAfter;
        char    cCurrentLen[5];
        int             c=0;
        HTTP_FILTER_RAW_DATA* pRawData = (PHTTP_FILTER_RAW_DATA) pvData;

        pszBuffer=pvData->pvInData;
        if (pfc->pFilterContext)    // Is this an ad?
        {
          /*  This first call to OnSendRawData are the response
              headers.  Since we are expanding the page size, we
              need to alter the "Content-Length" header.
          */
              if (strstr((char*) pRawData->pvInData,"HTTP/1.0"))
              {
                      giExpandedLen=strlen((char*) pfc->pFilterContext);
                      memset(cCurrentLen, '\0', sizeof(cCurrentLen));
                      pcBefore=(char*)pRawData->pvInData;
                      pcBetween=strstr(pcBefore,"Content-Length:");
                      if (pcBetween)
                      {
                          pcAfter=pcBetween;
```

```
                        while (*pcAfter>=' ')
                        {
                                if (*pcAfter>='\x30' && *pcAfter
                                ➥<='\x39')
                                        cCurrentLen[c++]=*pcAfter;
                                pcAfter++;
                        }
                        c = atoi((char*)cCurrentLen);
                        giExpandedLen+=c;
                        *pcBetween='\0';
                        sprintf((char*) pRawData->pvInData,
                                "%sContent-Length: %i%s",
                                pcBefore,giExpandedLen,pcAfter);
                        pRawData->cbInData=(DWORD) strlen((char*)
                        ➥pRawData->pvInData);
                }
        }
        else
        {
/*  This is the second call to OnSendRawData, this call
    contains the actual html page.  This section checks
    for the special tag we're using. "<!ADIN>" as a place
    holder for the link and image line.
*/
        if (strstr((char*)pvData->pvInData,"<!%ADIN%>"))
                {
                        gpszNewBuffer=(CHAR*)pfc->AllocMem(pfc,
                        ➥giExpandedLen+1, (DWORD)NULL);
                        memset(gpszNewBuffer,'\0',giExpandedLen+1);
                        pcBefore=(char*)pRawData->pvInData;
                        pcBetween=strstr(pcBefore,"<!%ADIN%>");
                        if (pcBetween)
                        {
                                pcAfter=pcBetween;
                                while (*pcAfter!='>') { pcAfter++; }
                                pcAfter++;
                                *pcBetween='\0';

                                sprintf(gpszNewBuffer,"%s%s%s",
                                ➥pcBefore,gpszAdBuffer,pcAfter);
                                ➥pRawData>pvInData=(void*)
                                ➥gpszNewBuffer;
                                pRawData->cbInData=giExpandedLen;
                        }
                }
        }
}
        return SF_STATUS_REQ_NEXT_NOTIFICATION;
}
```

Part

IV

Ch

14

continues

Listing 14.9 Continued

```
/*
    The following #define defines all the possible string
    combinations that may inserted into the html page
*/
#define LINK_STRING "<A HREF=\"http:/scripts/
➥ClickThruExtension.dll?http://
%s\"><IMG SRC=\"/images/%s\"
ALT=\"%s\" BORDER=0></A>"
#define LINK_STRING2 "<A HREF=\"http:/scripts/
➥ClickThruExtension.dll?http://
%s\"><IMG
SRC=\"/images/%s\" ALT=\"%s\" BORDER=0 height=\"%s\" width=\"%s\"></A>"
#define LINK_STRING3 "<A HREF=\"http:/scripts/
➥ClickThruExtension.dll?http://
%s\" target=\"%s\"><IMG SRC=\"/images/%s\"
ALT=\"%s\" BORDER=0 height=\"%s\" width=\"%s\"></A>"
/*
    InsertAd -
    The routine gets the graphic and alternate text from
    the database and creates the graphic link HTML line
    and inserts it into the HTML page.
*/
void InsertAd(char* pszAdBuffer){
    char    szGraphic[100];
    char    szAltText[100];
    char    szHeight[7];
    char    szWidth[7];
    char    szTarget[20];
    unsigned int i=0;
    GetPrivateProfileString(ADGRAPHICS, gpszAdLink,
                                        TEXT("clearmind.gif"),
                                        ➥szGraphic,
                                        sizeof(szGraphic),
                                        ➥ADINI);
    GetPrivateProfileString(ADLINKS, gpszAdLink,
                                        TEXT("ClearMind
                                        ➥Inc."), szAltText,
                                        sizeof(szAltText),
                                        ➥ADINI);
    GetPrivateProfileString(ADHEIGHTS, gpszAdLink,
                                        TEXT("\0"), szHeight,
                                        sizeof(szHeight),
                                        ➥ADINI);
    GetPrivateProfileString(ADWIDTHS, gpszAdLink,
                                        TEXT("\0"), szWidth,
                                        sizeof(szWidth),
                                        ➥ADINI);
```

```
GetPrivateProfileString(ADTARGETS, gpszAdLink,
                                    TEXT("\0"), szTarget,
                                    sizeof(szTarget),
                                ➥ADINI);

if (szHeight[0] == '\0' ¦¦ szWidth[0] == '\0') {
        wsprintf(pszAdBuffer, LINK_STRING,
                        gpszAdLink, szGraphic, szAltText);
} else {
        if (szTarget[0] =='\0') {
                wsprintf(pszAdBuffer, LINK_STRING2,
                                gpszAdLink, szGraphic, szAltText,
                            ➥szHeight, szWidth);
        } else {
                wsprintf(pszAdBuffer, LINK_STRING3,
                                gpszAdLink,  szTarget, szGraphic,
                            ➥szAltText, szHeight, szWidth);
        }
}
giCurrentAd++;
if (giLastAd==giCurrentAd){
        giCurrentAd = 1;
        gpszAdLink=(char*)gszAdLinks;
}
else {
        gpszAdLink+=strlen(gpszAdLink)+1;
}
return;
}
```

To Build the AdFlipperFilter.dll

Use the following instructions to built the AdFlipperFilter.dll:

1. Copy the project from the companion CD to an accessible drive.

2. Open a command window and navigate to the directory where the AdFlipperFilter project is stored.

3. Make sure nmake.exe is in a directory in the system's path.

   From the AdFlipperFilter project's directory execute the following:

   ```
   nmake /f makefile CFG="AdFlipperFilter - Win32 Release
   ```

To Install the AdFlipperFilter.dll

Use the following instructions to install the AdFlipperFilter.dll:

1. Copy AdFlipperFilter.dll into your IIS install directory on the server.

2. Run REGEDT32.EXE.

3. Go to the following registry key:

   ```
   HKEY_LOCAL_MACHINE\System\CurrentControlSet\Services\W3SCVC
   ➥\Parameters
   ```

4. Edit the filter DLL's entry by double-clicking it.

5. Add **,c:\path\to\AdFlipperFilter.dll** to the end of the value.

6. Save the value.

7. Exit REGEDT32.EXE.

8. Stop and restart the Web service.

From Here...

ISAPI filters enable you to interact with the request event data and Web server data at a low level. The following chapters tell you more about how to construct filters and how filters interact with the Web service and the HTTP communication flow:

- Chapter 12, "Using ISAPI Filters," gives you an overall understanding of the kinds of filters you can construct and the HTTP communication flow.

- Chapter 13, "Understanding ISAPI Filters," gives you the rules for constructing an ISAPI filter.

- Chapter 18, "Making Your Extensions Thread-Safe," gives you practical advice on how to use some of the thread-safe techniques available in the Win32 environment.

Building Filters with MFC ISAPI Classes

If you're familiar with Microsoft Foundation Classes (MFC) and if you're relatively new to client/server computing, the MFC ISAPI classes are a great way to get started writing ISAPI filters. You'll be working with a programming paradigm that you're familiar with, and you'll be writing code that adds value to your filter.

If you have Microsoft Visual C++ (MSVC) version 4.1+, you'll be using the ISAPI Extension Wizard to get started quickly. This chapter tells you how to do that. Then we focus on how MFC works so that you can apply what you learn in other chapters to your MFC ISAPI filter. ■

Use the Extension Wizard to create a project

You'll use the Extension Wizard to create an MFC ISAPI filter that serves as a starting point for exploring the capabilities of MFC ISAPI.

Explore MFC

You'll explore MFC ISAPI in detail so that you understand the relationship between the code you are writing and what you learn in other chapters.

Log all events as they occur

You'll change your filter to log all events as they occur. This way, you can see what the filter does when the server processes a request from a client browser.

Learn to avoid some potential problems

You'll learn about some common sources of trouble for MFC developers new to ISAPI.

Creating a Filter with the Extension Wizard

MSVC version 4.1+ supplies a wizard to generate MFC ISAPI extensions and filters. This wizard generates the skeleton code that is the framework for your ISAPI extension or filter. As in other MFC applications, the wizard enables you to concentrate on the functionality of your program.

Using the Extension Wizard

To start the Extension Wizard, run MSVC and select File, New, Project Workspace. From the New Project Workspace dialog box, shown in Figure 15.1, select the ISAPI Extension Wizard. Name the project **Example** and click Create.

FIG. 15.1
Starting the Extension Wizard.

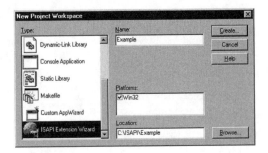

Step 1: Define the Filter   In Step 1, you indicate whether you want your ISAPI project to have an extension, a filter, or both. Select Generate a Filter Object, and deselect Generate a Server Extension Object, as shown in Figure 15.2. You can also choose whether to use MFC in a dynamic link library (DLL) or in a static library.

Using MFC in a DLL or in a Static Library

Linking to MFC via a static library decreases the load time of your program and means you do not need to install other files with your program. But this performance boost does come with a penalty. Since each program would have its own copy of MFC, several ISAPI extensions or filters would need more memory than if you were to link to MFC dynamically.

FIG. 15.2
ISAPI Extension
Wizard, Step 1.

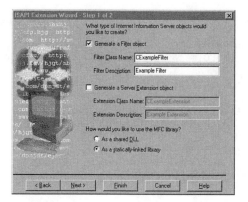

Step 2: Choose the Notifications

In Step 2, shown in Figure 15.3, you select the notifications. Normally, you only select the notifications you need to use for your filter. But for this example, choose all notifications.

FIG. 15.3
Extension Wizard,
Step 2.

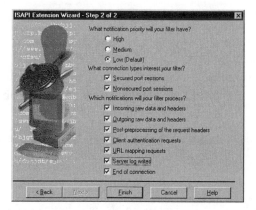

TIP The OnLog() method is not automatically generated by the Extension Wizard. To add this method, open Class Wizard. Under the Messages list box, scroll until you see OnLog. Click OnLog and click Add Function (see Listing 15.1).

NOTE In object-oriented programming, a procedure providing access to an object's data is called a *method*. For example, in CExampleFilter, OnLog can also be called a method because it's a public member function (see Listing 15.2). ■

Listing 15.1   EXAMPLE.H—Add *OnLog()* Declaration to *CExampleFilter*

```
// ClassWizard generated virtual function overrides
        // NOTE - the ClassWizard will add and remove member functions
        // here.
        //    DO NOT EDIT what you see in these blocks of generated
        //    code !
//{{AFX_VIRTUAL(CExampleFilter)
public:
...
virtual DWORD OnLog(CHttpFilterContext* pCtxt, PHTTP_FILTER_LOG pLog);
//}}AFX_VIRTUAL
```

Listing 15.2   EXAMPLE.CPP—Add *OnLog()* to *CExampleFilter*

```
DWORD CExampleFilter::OnLog(CHttpFilterContext*, PHTTP_FILTER_LOG)
{
        return SF_STATUS_REQ_NEXT_NOTIFICATION;
}
```

Chapter 14, "Creating an ISAPI Filter," describes the steps to create an ISAPI filter: create a 32-bit DLL, define `GetFilterVersion()`, and define `HttpFilterProc()`. The Extension Wizard does these steps in their most minimal form. Now you have a filter project named EXAMPLE that holds the files listed in Table 15.1.

Table 15.1   Files Generated by the Wizard to Complete the ISAPI Project

Name	Description
EXAMPLE.MAK	Project make file, which makes EXAMPLE.DLL
EXAMPLE.H	Definition of the `CExampleFilter` class
EXAMPLE.CPP	Implementation of the `CExampleFilter` class
EXAMPLE.DEF	Exports for EXAMPLE.DLL
EXAMPLE.RC	Resource file
EXAMPLE.RC2	Resource file
STDAFX.H	Common header for the project
STDAFX.CPP	Precompiling source file

Look at \MSDEV\MFC\INCLUDE\ISAPI.H and \MSDEV\MFC\SRC\ISAPI.CPP. ISAPI.H holds the definition of the CHttpFilter and CHttpFilterContext classes. ISAPI.CPP holds the implementation of the CHttpFilter class. It also holds the implementation of the GetFilterVersion() and HttpServerContext() functions exported from the DLL.

Building and Testing EXAMPLE.DLL

With EXAMPLE.MAK open as the current project in MSVC, select Project, Build. Before the filter can be used, we'll need to make a change in the Windows NT Registry. Open REGEDT32.EXE, which should be in your WINNT\SYSTEM32 folder.

ISAPI filter DLLs are registered under the HKEY_LOCAL_MACHINE\SYSTEM\ CurrentControlSet\Services\W3SVC\FilterDLLs key. Type the full path and file name of your new filter. Separate multiple filters with commas.

Because changing the registry settings can have detrimental effects on your server, you should only use REGEDT32.EXE if you are familiar with the Windows NT Registry.

An alternative way to register your filters is to use Microsoft's Internet Information Server (IIS) Hypertext Transport Protocol (HTTP) Configuration Utility. This is on the companion CD to this book in the IISCFG.ZIP file.

Start the World Wide Web Publishing Service using Internet Services Manager. Or look at the section on debugging in Chapter 17, "Troubleshooting and Debugging Extensions and Filters," for information on how to run the filter in the debugger.

When building the EXAMPLE filter, you may want to change the linker settings to generate the filter DLL in the directory where it will be used by the Web service. Typically, this is \WINNT\SYSTEM32\INSTSRV.

If you do this, you'll have to stop the service before trying to link the filter DLL. Filter DLLs are loaded when the Web service starts and are not unloaded until it stops.

The MFC ISAPI Filter Class

Your filter uses the CExampleFilter class, which is derived from CHttpFilter. As described in Chapter 14, "Creating an ISAPI Filter," this is the first entry point called by your server.

The properties returned by the GetFilterVersion() method determine which notifications are received by the filter. The properties also determine the order in which these notifications are called, according the filter's priority flag.

Each of these notifications is received as a call to the HttpFilterProc() function, which passes the notification on to CExampleFilter::HttpFilterProc(). This method initializes the CHttpFilterContext object, checks the notification type, and calls the appropriate notification handler methods.

The CHttpFilterContext object and the notification-specific data are passed as arguments to the notification handler method.

The CHttpFilterContext class provides the GetServerVariable(), AddResponseHeaders(), WriteClient(), AllocMem(), and ServerSupportFunction() methods, which are wrappers for the API calls of the same name.

This class exists separately from CHttpFitler, allowing multiple threads in your CExampleFilter. It is the reason your ISAPI classes must be thread-safe. See Chapter 14 for details. Figure 15.4 illustrates these concepts.

NOTE   A wrapper is essentially an alternative interface to a function, group of functions, or class. ▨

CHttpFilter and *CExampleFilter*

CHttpFilter is the MFC-defined class that is the base class for your filter. It provides an implementation of HttpFilterProc().

Your class, CExampleFilter, provides an implementation of GetFilterProc() and one or more of the notification handler methods: OnPreprocHeaders(), OnAuthentication(), OnUrlMap(), OnSendRawData(), OnReadRawData(), OnLog(), and OnEndOfNetSession().

FIG. 15.4
ISAPI calls are processed by the exported DLL functions, which pass the calls to the MFC ISAPI object.

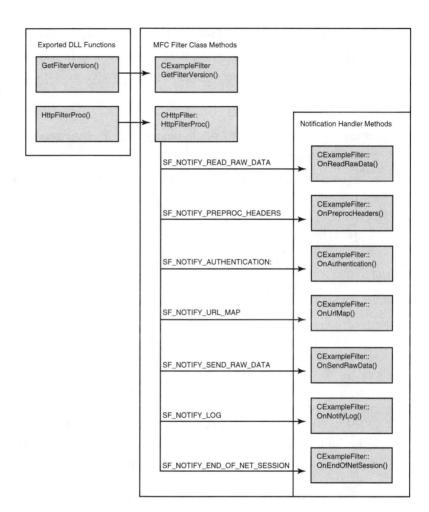

A single instance of this class is created when the DLL is loaded. Remember, all registered filter DLLs are loaded when the Web service is started. As your filter receives requests, CHttpFilter creates a CHttpFilterContext object for each request. This permits simultaneous calls from multiple clients (see Listing 15.3).

Listing 15.3   FLTREX1.CPP—Filter Declared as Global Object

```
CExampleFilter theFilter;
```

GetFilterVersion() Your MFC ISAPI filter DLL, like a non-MFC ISAPI filter DLL, has an exported `GetFilterVersion()` function. In your MFC ISAPI DLL, the function calls the filter object's `GetFilterVersion()` method, as shown in Listing 15.4.

> **Listing 15.4 ISAPI.CPP—Exported *GetFilterVersion()* Passes Call to Filter Object**

```
extern "C" BOOL WINAPI GetFilterVersion(PHTTP_FILTER_VERSION pVer)
{
#ifdef _AFXDLL
        AFX_MANAGE_STATE(AfxGetStaticModuleState());
#endif

        BOOL bRet;

        ISAPIASSERT(pFilter != NULL);
        if (pFilter == NULL)
                bRet = FALSE;
        else
                bRet = pFilter->GetFilterVersion(pVer);

        return bRet;
}
```

The `GetFilterVersion()` method used by your filter class specifies the priority of the filter, tells whether secure and nonsecure ports are filtered, and determines which notifications your filter handles, as shown in Listing 15.5. See Chapter 14 for details.

> **Listing 15.5 EXAMPLE.CPP—*GetFilterVersion()* Implementation Handles Notifications**

```
BOOL CExampleFilter::GetFilterVersion(PHTTP_FILTER_VERSION pVer)
{
        // Call default implementation for initialization
        CHttpFilter::GetFilterVersion(pVer);

        // Clear the flags set by base class
        pVer->dwFlags &= ~SF_NOTIFY_ORDER_MASK;

        // Set the flags we are interested in
        pVer->dwFlags |= SF_NOTIFY_ORDER_LOW | SF_NOTIFY_SECURE_PORT |
        ➥SF_NOTIFY_NONSECURE_PORT
```

```
            ¦ SF_NOTIFY_LOG ¦ SF_NOTIFY_AUTHENTICATION ¦
            // SF_NOTIFY_PREPROC_HEADERS
            ¦ SF_NOTIFY_READ_RAW_DATA ¦ SF_NOTIFY_SEND_RAW_DATA ¦
            // SF_NOTIFY_URL_MAP
            ¦ SF_NOTIFY_END_OF_NET_SESSION;

        // Load description string
        TCHAR sz[SF_MAX_FILTER_DESC_LEN+1];
        ISAPIVERIFY(::LoadString(AfxGetResourceHandle(),
                    IDS_FILTER, sz, SF_MAX_FILTER_DESC_LEN));
        _tcscpy(pVer->lpszFilterDesc, sz);
        return TRUE;
}
```

To learn what the MFC ISAPI classes do, we use all the notification handler methods in this chapter. If you decide to change your sample filter to create a production filter, you'll change the pVer->dwFlags settings so that only the necessary notifications are processed by the filter. You can also remove the declarations and implementations of the unused methods from the filter class.

HttpFilterProc()   Your MFC ISAPI filter DLL has an exported HttpFilterProc() function consistent with the non-MFC ISAPI filter DLLs. In the MFC filter DLL, this function passes the call to the CHttpFilter::HttpFilterProc() method (see Listing 15.6).

This method is where the bulk of your filter's work is done. HttpFilterProc() is what in turn calls the various notification handlers you specified in GetFilterVersion().

The PHTTP_FILTER_CONTEXT structure holds information on the specific request being processed. The second parameter, NotificationType, is the type of event that has occurred. The last parameter, pvNotification, contains a notification-specific structure that gives HttpFilterProc() the notification handler to use.

Listing 15.6   ISAPI.CPP—Exported *HttpFilterProc()* Passes Call to Filter Object

```
extern "C" DWORD WINAPI HttpFilterProc(PHTTP_FILTER_CONTEXT pfc,
    DWORD dwNotificationType, LPVOID pvNotification)
{
#ifdef _AFXDLL
        AFX_MANAGE_STATE(AfxGetStaticModuleState());
#endif
```

continues

Listing 15.6   Continued

```
        DWORD dwRet;

        ISAPIASSERT(pFilter != NULL);
        if (pFilter == NULL)
                dwRet = SF_STATUS_REQ_NEXT_NOTIFICATION;
        else
                dwRet = pFilter->HttpFilterProc(pfc,
                        dwNotificationType, pvNotification);

        return dwRet;
 }
```

Most of the notifications get notification data. This data is typecast by the
CHttpFilter::HttpFilterProc() method to structures that conform to the data
type sent with that notification (see Listing 15.7).

**Listing 15.7   ISAPI.CPP—*HttpFilterProc()* Calls Notification Handler
Method**

```
DWORD CHttpFilter::HttpFilterProc(PHTTP_FILTER_CONTEXT pfc,
    DWORD dwNotificationType, LPVOID pvNotification)
{
        DWORD dwRet = SF_STATUS_REQ_NEXT_NOTIFICATION;
        CHttpFilterContext callCtxt(pfc);

        switch (dwNotificationType)
        {
        case SF_NOTIFY_READ_RAW_DATA:
                dwRet = OnReadRawData(&callCtxt,
                ➥(PHTTP_FILTER_RAW_DATA) pvNotification);
                break;

        case SF_NOTIFY_PREPROC_HEADERS:
                dwRet = OnPreprocHeaders(&callCtxt,
                        (PHTTP_FILTER_PREPROC_HEADERS)
                        ➥pvNotification);
                break;

        case SF_NOTIFY_AUTHENTICATION:
                dwRet = OnAuthentication(&callCtxt,
                        (PHTTP_FILTER_AUTHENT) pvNotification);
                break;

        case SF_NOTIFY_URL_MAP:
                dwRet = OnUrlMap(&callCtxt, (PHTTP_FILTER_URL_MAP
                ➥pvNotification);
```

```
                break;

        case SF_NOTIFY_SEND_RAW_DATA:
                dwRet = OnSendRawData(&callCtxt,
                ➥(PHTTP_FILTER_RAW_DATA) pvNotification);
                break;

        case SF_NOTIFY_LOG:
                dwRet = OnLog(&callCtxt, (PHTTP_FILTER_LOG)
                ➥pvNotification);
                break;

        case SF_NOTIFY_END_OF_NET_SESSION:
                dwRet = OnEndOfNetSession(&callCtxt);
                break;

        default:
                ISAPITRACE1("Warning: unrecognized HTTP filter
                ➥notification code %d\n", dwNotificationType);
                break;
        }

        return dwRet;
}
```

Notification Handler Methods There are seven notification handler methods. As mentioned earlier, you should normally use only the ones you need. In this example, we use all the methods to see what each does. Table 15.2 shows how each notification type is mapped to a notification handler method.

Table 15.2 Notification Handler Methods

Notification	Handler Method
SF_NOTIFY_PREPROC_HEADERS	OnPreprocHeaders()
SF_NOTIFY_AUTHENTICATION	OnAuthentication()
SF_NOTIFY_URL_MAP	OnUrlMap()
SF_NOTIFY_SEND_RAW_DATA	OnSendRawData()
SF_NOTIFY_LOG	OnLog()
SF_NOTIFY_READ_RAW_DATA	OnReadRawData()
SF_NOTIFY_END_OF_NET_SESSION	OnEndOfNetSession()

CExampleFilter

CExampleFilter supplies dummy implementations of the notification handler methods. As in other C++ programs, before you can use a class, it must be declared.
The class declaration for CExampleFilter is shown in Listing 15.8.

Listing 15.8   EXAMPLE.H—*CExampleFilter* Class Definition

```
// EXAMPLE.H - Header file for your Internet Server
//     Example Filter

#include "resource.h"


class CExampleFilter : public CHttpFilter
{
public:
        CExampleFilter();
        ~CExampleFilter();

// Overrides
        // ClassWizard generated virtual function overrides
                // NOTE - the ClassWizard will add and remove member
                // functions here.
                //     DO NOT EDIT what you see in these blocks of
                //       generated code !
        //{{AFX_VIRTUAL(CExampleFilter)
        public:
        virtual BOOL GetFilterVersion(PHTTP_FILTER_VERSION pVer);
        virtual DWORD OnPreprocHeaders(CHttpFilterContext* pCtxt,
        ➥PHTTP_FILTER_PREPROC_HEADERS pHeaderInfo);
        virtual DWORD OnAuthentication(CHttpFilterContext* pCtxt,
        ➥PHTTP_FILTER_AUTHENT pAuthent);
        virtual DWORD OnUrlMap(CHttpFilterContext* pCtxt,
        ➥PHTTP_FILTER_URL_MAP pMapInfo);
        virtual DWORD OnSendRawData(CHttpFilterContext* pCtxt,
        ➥PHTTP_FILTER_RAW_DATA pRawData);
        virtual DWORD OnReadRawData(CHttpFilterContext* pCtxt,
        ➥PHTTP_FILTER_RAW_DATA pRawData);
        virtual DWORD OnEndOfNetSession(CHttpFilterContext* pCtxt);
        virtual DWORD OnLog(CHttpFilterContext* pCtxt,
        ➥PHTTP_FILTER_LOG pLog);
        //}}AFX_VIRTUAL

        //{{AFX_MSG(CExampleFilter)
        //}}AFX_MSG
};
```

Once `CExampleFilter` is declared, we use it in the EXAMPLE.CPP file (see Listing 15.9). This file is where you add the code to respond to individual events as they occur. You use these functions to do the filter's work.

Listing 15.9   EXAMPLE.CPP—*CExampleFilter* Implementation

```
// EXAMPLE.CPP - Implementation file for your Internet Server
// Example Filter

#include "stdafx.h"
#include "Example.h"


/////////////////////////////////////////////////////////////////////
// The one and only CExampleFilter object

CExampleFilter theFilter;


/////////////////////////////////////////////////////////////////////
// CExampleFilter implementation

CExampleFilter::CExampleFilter()
{
}

CExampleFilter::~CExampleFilter()
{
}

BOOL CExampleFilter::GetFilterVersion(PHTTP_FILTER_VERSION pVer)
{
        // Call default implementation for initialization
        CHttpFilter::GetFilterVersion(pVer);

        // Clear the flags set by base class
        pVer->dwFlags &= ~SF_NOTIFY_ORDER_MASK;

        // Set the flags we are interested in
        pVer->dwFlags |= SF_NOTIFY_ORDER_LOW | SF_NOTIFY_SECURE_PORT |
        ➡SF_NOTIFY_NONSECURE_PORT
                        | SF_NOTIFY_LOG |
        ➡SF_NOTIFY_AUTHENTICATION | SF_NOTIFY_PREPROC_HEADERS |
        SF_NOTIFY_READ_RAW_DATA | SF_NOTIFY_SEND_RAW_DATA |
        ➡SF_NOTIFY_URL_MAP | SF_NOTIFY_END_OF_NET_SESSION;

        // Load description string
        TCHAR sz[SF_MAX_FILTER_DESC_LEN+1];
```

continues

Listing 15.9   Continued

```
            ISAPIVERIFY(::LoadString(AfxGetResourceHandle(),
                        IDS_FILTER, sz, SF_MAX_FILTER_DESC_LEN));
        _tcscpy(pVer->lpszFilterDesc, sz);
        return TRUE;
}

DWORD CExampleFilter::OnPreprocHeaders(CHttpFilterContext* pCtxt,
        PHTTP_FILTER_PREPROC_HEADERS pHeaderInfo)
{
        // TODO: React to this notification accordingly and
        // return the appropriate status code
        return SF_STATUS_REQ_NEXT_NOTIFICATION;
}

DWORD CExampleFilter::OnAuthentication(CHttpFilterContext* pCtxt,
        PHTTP_FILTER_AUTHENT pAuthent)
{
        // TODO: React to this notification accordingly and
        // return the appropriate status code
        return SF_STATUS_REQ_NEXT_NOTIFICATION;
}

DWORD CExampleFilter::OnUrlMap(CHttpFilterContext* pCtxt,
        PHTTP_FILTER_URL_MAP pMapInfo)
{
        // TODO: React to this notification accordingly and
        // return the appropriate status code
        return SF_STATUS_REQ_NEXT_NOTIFICATION;
}

DWORD CExampleFilter::OnSendRawData(CHttpFilterContext* pCtxt,
        PHTTP_FILTER_RAW_DATA pRawData)
{
        // TODO: React to this notification accordingly and
        // return the appropriate status code
        return SF_STATUS_REQ_NEXT_NOTIFICATION;
}

DWORD CExampleFilter::OnReadRawData(CHttpFilterContext* pCtxt,
        PHTTP_FILTER_RAW_DATA pRawData)
{
        // TODO: React to this notification accordingly and
        // return the appropriate status code
        return SF_STATUS_REQ_NEXT_NOTIFICATION;
}

DWORD CExampleFilter::OnLog(CHttpFilterContext* pCtxt,
        PHTTP_FILTER_LOG pLog)
{
```

```
        // TODO: React to this notification accordingly and
        // return the appropriate status code
        return SF_STATUS_REQ_NEXT_NOTIFICATION;
}

DWORD CExampleFilter::OnEndOfNetSession(CHttpFilterContext* pCtxt)
{
        // TODO: React to this notification accordingly and
        // return the appropriate status code
        return SF_STATUS_REQ_NEXT_NOTIFICATION;
}

// Do not edit the following lines, which are needed by ClassWizard.
#if 0
BEGIN_MESSAGE_MAP(CExampleFilter, CHttpFilter)
        //{{AFX_MSG_MAP(CExampleFilter)
        //}}AFX_MSG_MAP
END_MESSAGE_MAP()
#endif          // 0
```

CHttpFilterContext

The CHttpFilterContext class wraps the HTTP_FILTER_CONTEXT structure and provides methods that deal with the data in that structure. Table 15.3 shows how the standard ISAPI calls are mapped to your filter's notification handler methods. As mentioned earlier, the MFC wrapper functions are named the same way as the ISAPI functions.

Table 15.3   *CHttpFilterContext* Methods Are Wrappers for ISAPI Functions

API Function	Wrapper Method
GetServerVariable()	CHttpFilterContext::GetServerVariable()
AddResponseHeaders()	CHttpFilterContext::AddResponseHeaders()
WriteClient()	CHttpFilterContext::WriteClient()
AllocMem()	CHttpFilterContext::AllocMem()
ServerSupportFunction()	CHttpFilterContext::ServerSupportFunction()

Add Logging to EXAMPLE

In this section, you'll add logging to the MFC ISAPI filter that you've already created. You can use this filter to do your own research into what each notification is doing.

In EXAMPLE, we declare private member functions to build the output string for each of the notification handler methods. OnReadRawData() and OnSendRawData() share the same string-building function, as shown in Listing 15.10.

Listing 15.10   EXAMPLE.H—*CExampleFilter* Adds Private Data and Methods for Logging

```
// EXAMPLE.H - Header file for your Internet Server
//    Example Filter

#include "resource.h"


class CExampleFilter : public CHttpFilter
{
public:
        CExampleFilter();
        ~CExampleFilter();

// Overrides
        // ClassWizard generated virtual function overrides
                // NOTE - the ClassWizard will add and remove member
                // functions here.
                //    DO NOT EDIT what you see in these blocks of
                //      generated code !
        //{{AFX_VIRTUAL(CExampleFilter)
        public:
        virtual BOOL GetFilterVersion(PHTTP_FILTER_VERSION pVer);
        virtual DWORD OnPreprocHeaders(CHttpFilterContext* pCtxt,
        ➡PHTTP_FILTER_PREPROC_HEADERS pHeaderInfo);
        virtual DWORD OnAuthentication(CHttpFilterContext* pCtxt,
        ➡PHTTP_FILTER_AUTHENT pAuthent);
        virtual DWORD OnUrlMap(CHttpFilterContext* pCtxt,
        ➡PHTTP_FILTER_URL_MAP pMapInfo);
        virtual DWORD OnSendRawData(CHttpFilterContext* pCtxt,
        ➡PHTTP_FILTER_RAW_DATA pRawData);
        virtual DWORD OnReadRawData(CHttpFilterContext* pCtxt,
        ➡PHTTP_FILTER_RAW_DATA pRawData);
        virtual DWORD OnEndOfNetSession(CHttpFilterContext* pCtxt);
        virtual DWORD OnLog(CHttpFilterContext* pCtxt,
        ➡PHTTP_FILTER_LOG pLog);
```

```
        //}}AFX_VIRTUAL

        //{{AFX_MSG(CExampleFilter)
        //}}AFX_MSG

private:
        CString BuildString(LPCTSTR pszFunctionName,
        ➡PHTTP_FILTER_PREPROC_HEADERS pHeaderInfo);
        CString BuildString(LPCTSTR pszFunctionName,
        ➡PHTTP_FILTER_AUTHENT pAuthent);
        CString BuildString(LPCTSTR pszFunctionName,
        ➡PHTTP_FILTER_URL_MAP pMapInfo);
        CString BuildString(LPCTSTR pszFunctionName,
        ➡PHTTP_FILTER_RAW_DATA pRawData);
        CString BuildString(LPCTSTR pszFunctionName, PHTTP_FILTER_LOG
        ➡pLog);
        CString BuildString(LPCTSTR pszFunctionName);

        CCriticalSection m_criticalSection;
};
```

Each of the notification handler methods is changed to log the data it gets.
OnAuthentication() is shown in Listing 15.11 with its string-building function.
See the companion CD to this book for the source code for logging events.

**Listing 15.11 EXAMPLE.CPP—*OnAuthentication()* Changed to Log
Notification**

```
DWORD CExampleFilter::OnAuthentication(CHttpFilterContext* pCtxt,
        PHTTP_FILTER_AUTHENT pAuthent)
{
        try
        {
                CString csOutput = BuildString("OnAuthentication",
                ➡pAuthent);
                CSingleLock lock(&m_criticalSection, TRUE);
                CFile cfLog(csLogFilename, FILE_MODES);
                cfLog.Seek(0, CFile::end);
                cfLog.Write(csOutput, csOutput.GetLength());
                cfLog.Close();
                lock.Unlock();
        }
        catch(CException* e)
        {
```

continues

Listing 15.11   Continued

```
                    ISAPIASSERT(FALSE);
                    e->Delete();
        }
        catch(...) // catch structured (hardware) exceptions
        {
                        ISAPIASSERT(FALSE);
        }
        return SF_STATUS_REQ_NEXT_NOTIFICATION;
}

CString CExampleFilter::BuildString(LPCTSTR pszFunctionName,
➥PHTTP_FILTER_AUTHENT pAuthent)
{
        CString csVal("BEGIN LOG ENTRY for ");
        csVal += pszFunctionName;
        csVal += "\r\n";

        // Add the username
        csVal += "Username: ";
        csVal += pAuthent->pszUser;
        csVal += "\r\n";

        // Add the password
        csVal += "Password: ";
        csVal += pAuthent->pszPassword;
        csVal += "\r\n";

        csVal += "END LOG ENTRY for ";
        csVal += pszFunctionName;
        csVal += "\r\n\r\n\r\n";

        return csVal;
}
```

A global CString is used to hold the log file name. This is valid only because the value doesn't change. The CString variable could have been declared as a member of the CExampleFilter class, again only because its value doesn't change.

The CCriticalSection and CSingleLock classes are used to force operations on the log file to wait until any existing operation completes. In this case, the CCriticalSection object is declared as a member variable of the CExampleFilter class.

In each of the methods that work on the log file, a CSingleLock object is declared and used to lock the CCriticalSection object.

The data in an HTTP_FILTER_RAW_DATA structure is not necessarily null-terminated, so the filter has to handle this when logging the raw data, as shown in Listing 15.12.

Listing 15.12   EXAMPLE.CPP—*BuildString()* Handles HTTP_FILTER_RAW_DATA

```
CString CExampleFilter::BuildString(LPCTSTR pszFunctionName,
➥PHTTP_FILTER_RAW_DATA pRawData)
{
        CString csVal;
        char* pszBuffer = NULL;

        do
        {
                // Start the string
                csVal = "BEGIN LOG ENTRY for ";
                csVal += pszFunctionName;
                csVal += "\r\n";

                // Add NULL termination to the raw data
                if(pRawData->cbInData < pRawData->cbInBuffer)
                {
                        // There's room in the buffer for the NULL
                        // terminator
                        ((char*)pRawData->pvInData)[pRawData-
                        ➥>cbInData] = 0x0;
                        pszBuffer = (char*)pRawData->pvInData;
                }
                else
                {
                        // There's no room in the buffer for the
                        // NULL terminator
                        pszBuffer = (char*)malloc(pRawData-
                        ➥>cbInData + 1);
                        if(! pszBuffer) { ISAPIASSERT(FALSE);
                        ➥break; }

                        memcpy(pszBuffer, pRawData->pvInData,
                        ➥pRawData->cbInData);
                        pszBuffer[pRawData->cbInData] = 0x0;
                }

                // Add the raw data to the string
                csVal += "pvInData = ";
                csVal += (char*)pszBuffer;
                csVal += "\r\n";
```

continues

Listing 15.12   Continued

```
                       // Finish the string
                       csVal += "END LOG ENTRY for ";
                       csVal += pszFunctionName;
                       csVal += "\r\n\r\n\r\n";
        } while(0);

        if(pszBuffer && (pszBuffer != pRawData->pvInData))
        {
                       free(pszBuffer);
        }
        return csVal;
}
```

Avoiding Problems

If you are coming into ISAPI development from a traditional MFC background, some important differences may not be obvious. We look at these next.

Storing State Data in the Class

Your filter class cannot store state data as member data because the class handles multiple notifications concurrently. A good rule of thumb is to use member data only if it is initialized in the constructor and never changed while the service is running.

Using Classes That Are Not Thread-Safe

For the same reason that you can't store member data, you can't use classes that are not thread-safe without gaining access to them yourself. CString and CFile are examples of MFC classes that can be used in a filter because they are thread-safe.

The data access object (DAO) class is not thread-safe. It is not suitable for use in ISAPI unless it is protected from concurrent access through a mechanism, such as critical sections of code.

Dealing with an Unknown Client

If you're using a filter for a Web server, you don't know what the client application will be. Over time, your filter will probably act on requests from all the major client browsers.

Each of these browsers may send different information or they may send the same information differently. They are constrained only by the HTTP specification.

The HTTP specification is vague because its version differs from browser to browser. In addition, the major browsers use their own nonstandard extensions.

Spend some time looking at what your filter gets from each of the major browsers to understand how these differences affect your filter. Even different versions of the same browser can change what your filter gets with a notification.

Protecting File I/O

Even though the CFile class is thread-safe, you need to code any file input/output (I/O) not to allow concurrent writes to the same file. One way to do this is by using the CFile::shareExclusive mode.

But this mode by itself causes the second open to fail. If you put your file I/O inside critical sections of code, though, the thread waits until it gains access to the critical section. If you use the critical section appropriately, it guarantees the success of the open operation because no other opens are pending. This is the method used in EXAMPLE.

Handling Exceptions

An exception is an error that occurs during the execution of a program. C++ provides built-in support for exception handling through its try and catch statements. Generally, sections you want to monitor for exceptions are in a try block:

```
try
{
         //              some section of code
}
```

If an exception takes place, it is caught in the `try` block's corresponding `catch` handler:

```
catch(Cexception* pEX)
{
            // do something
}
```

This is an orderly and efficient way to deal with errors. Although a detailed discussion of exception handling is beyond the scope of this chapter, let's take a moment for this important topic.

MSVC has supported C++ exceptions since version 2.0. C++ handling is now the preferred method for exceptions in both standard C++ and MFC programs. The short example we discussed earlier was a C++ exception handler. For a more thorough investigation, see Microsoft Visual C++ *Books Online*.

In Win32, another method for exceptions is *structured exception handling* (SEH). SEH enables developers to catch exceptions generated by the operating system. SEH has two types of handlers: exception handlers and termination handlers. The names of these handlers represent what they are and when you should use them.

Since MFC 1.0, Microsoft has provided macros to help developers deal with exceptions. These macros are still included with MSVC 4.2 but are primarily for backward compatibility. Although leaving the MFC macros in legacy code should not cause any harm, for new MFC programs, Microsoft recommends using C++ exception handling.

ASSERTing

MFC programmers should be familiar with the ASSERT and TRACE macros. These macros help developers find bugs in their programs. For ISAPI developers, Microsoft introduced ISAPIASSERT and ISAPITRACE.

ISAPIASSERT and ISAPITRACE call ASSERT and TRACE if MFC is being used. But you can also use these two new macros in non-MFC ISAPI applications. In a program's debug build, you can use ASSERT or ISAPIASSERT to evaluate an expression for a particular situation.

For example, in the following expression, ASSERT ensures that i is not equal to 0 before the program tries division:

```
ASSERT(i != 0);
z = y/i;
```

When you're testing the debug build, if i equals 0 right before the program tries division, the program stops executing and a message appears with the line number of the ASSERT macro.

TRACE and ISAPITRACE are a way to send messages to a dump device. You can use this to track the values of variables as the program executes. Each of these macros functions only in debug builds. For more information, see Microsoft Visual C++ *Books Online*.

Handling Multiple Notifications

What you might expect to be a single notification often results in multiple notifications. For example, mapping an URL may trigger more than one SF_NOTIFY_URL_MAP notification as the URL is deciphered.

Notifications are detailed in Chapters 14, "Creating an ISAPI Filter," and 16, "Extending Your Web Server with Filters." The EXAMPLE filter with logging should help you understand when notifications occur.

From Here...

In this chapter, we discuss the MFC ISAPI filter classes and how they do the work of an ISAPI filter. With this understanding, you can use what you learn in other chapters for your MFC ISAPI filter. For more information on this and related topics, see the following chapters:

- Review Chapter 12, "Using ISAPI Filters," and Chapter 13, "Understanding ISAPI Filters," for a basic understanding of what ISAPI filters do and how they work.

- See Chapter 14, "Creating an ISAPI Filter," for details on using your filter.

- See Chapter 16, "Extending Your Web Server with Filters," to learn how to build a custom authentication filter and a logging filter. You can apply what you learn in Chapter 15 and build those filters using the MFC classes.

- Chapter 17, "Troubleshooting and Debugging Extensions and Filters," and Chapter 18, "Making Your Extensions Thread-Safe," give you more advanced information about ISAPI filters. You can apply this information to your MFC ISAPI filter.

Extending Your Web Server with Filters

After learning about the different types of ISAPI filters you can create, you are probably anxious to see some of these concepts come to life. This chapter gives you two sample ISAPI filter applications.

The first sample is a custom authentication scheme that is used with the standard Windows NT Internet Information Server (IIS) authentication.

The second sample shows how you can use an ISAPI filter to add a few custom pieces of information to your log files.

Both examples touch on key points that you can use to build many different types of ISAPI filters. ■

How to create an authentication filter

You'll get a step-by-step tutorial on creating the CustomAuth authentication filter.

When and how to use thread synchronization

The CustomAuth filter provides examples of using the Microsoft Foundation Classes (MFC) thread synchronization objects.

How to connect to an ODBC data source

The CustomAuth filter also connects to any data source compatible with using the thread-safe ODBC application program interface (API).

How to build a custom logging filter

You can use the CustomLog sample provided here as a basis for your own customized logging filter.

How to properly allocate memory in a filter

The CustomLog sample shows methods of allocating and freeing memory that will exist throughout the time a browser is connected to your Web server.

Building a Custom Authentication Filter

Have you ever visited a Web site and your browser pops up a dialog box asking for a user name and password? That Web site has asked your browser for credentials to ensure that you have access to the document you have requested.

Figure 16.1 shows an example of Microsoft's Internet Explorer (IE) browser prompting the user for authentication credentials.

FIG. 16.1

Microsoft's Internet Explorer Authentication dialog box.

The default authentication scheme used by Microsoft's IIS uses file security based on Windows NT to determine access privileges for documents. When a browser requests a document, IIS first checks the credentials given by the browser.

Most browsers do not provide credentials when first requesting a document. In this case, IIS authenticates the document using the security context specified in the Anonymous Logon section of the properties dialog box in the Microsoft Internet Service Manager, as shown in Figure 16.2.

FIG. 16.2

Service properties dialog box from Internet Service Manager.

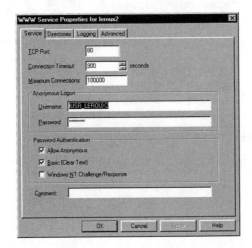

Also pay close attention to the Password Authentication frame shown in Figure 16.2. You need to have the Allow Anonymous check box set if you have pages on your Web site that do not need authentication.

The Basic (Clear Text) check box needs to be set if you plan to provide standard Internet authentication, as shown in this chapter. The Windows NT Challenge/ Response check box applies only to Microsoft's Internet Explorer (IE).

A browser that can use the Microsoft Windows NT Challenge/Response authentication does not prompt the user to enter credentials when connecting to a secured Web site with this kind of authentication scheme. Instead, the browser automatically authenticates using the credentials of the currently logged on account.

If you have this check box set and your clients will be connecting with Microsoft's IE, the client is never prompted to enter an alternative set of credentials. In other words, if you are writing your own authentication filter, you probably don't want this check box set.

All documents on your Web site should have read-only privileges assigned to the anonymous logon. If, however, this account does not have security privileges to read the document requested, IIS tells the browser that authentication is needed. The browser, in turn, presents the user with a dialog box that prompts for a user name and password, as shown previously in Figure 16.1.

After the user enters a user name and password, the browser again requests the same document, but this time includes the authentication credentials in the header of its request. IIS tries to read the document using the new credentials as its security context.

If security is sufficient, the document is returned to the browser. If not, IIS tells the browser that authentication failed.

Most browsers usually cache, by Web site, the last successfully authenticated credentials entered by the user. Therefore, it may seem as if a browser is not supplying credentials when it really is. Keep this in mind when you build your own authentication scheme.

The built-in IIS security system works well for restricting parts of your Web site to a few users. What if you have a few thousand users who need secure access to a section of your Web site?

One solution, albeit a bad one, is to add a few thousand user accounts to your NT domain. Although Windows NT can handle many times more users than this, think of the nightmare it would be to administer all of these accounts.

Another rather poor solution is to create only one account for a restricted area and let all the users share the same user name and password for this account. There are a couple of problems with this solution.

First, you lose the ability to revoke access from only one user without informing all the others that you have changed the account. Second, and more important, each user looks the same. You've lost the ability to distinguish the identity of individual users.

Let's say you are designing a Web site for a bank. Wouldn't it be great to have the user enter his or her own account number and PIN, upon which an ISAPI filter would authenticate the customer, and an ISAPI extension would dynamically put together a Web page with the customer's account information?

You probably would not want to add all the bank customers into an NT domain. It's just not practical. However, there is probably a data source available with the customer's account number and PIN.

The ideal solution would be to have one Windows NT user account that secures a section of your Web site. You would have a process transparently transform a customer's user name and password into the generic account with the privilege to read a secure section of your site.

Any extension you then write could use the UNMAPPED_REMOTE_USER server variable to get the credentials originally used to request authentication. This is the solution presented in the following ISAPI filter application.

In this example we use an ODBC data source to do the translation from a logical user name and password to a physical Windows NT user name and password. Since a database hit can be resource-intensive, I've also supplied a class that caches authenticated credentials for a period of time.

In addition, since you may not want this translated at all sections of your Web site, I've also supplied a mechanism to selectively invoke this custom authentication scheme.

Before you see the steps to create the CustomAuth filter, here are a few implementation details. CustomAuth was compiled using Microsoft Visual C++ 4.1. I did not use the ISAPI Application Wizard that comes with Visual C++ 4.1, nor did I use the MFC ISAPI filter classes.

Although there's absolutely nothing wrong with using the MFC ISAPI classes, they are explained elsewhere in the book and they tend to hide what is really happening behind the scenes. As you will soon see, I used MFC for some utility functions for strings, maps, and thread synchronization.

Part
IV
Ch
16

Adding the Filter Entry Points

First, you create a new project workspace. Your target is a dynamic link library (DLL). Figure 16.3 shows how the Microsoft Developer Studio should look when you first create the CustomAuth filter.

FIG. 16.3

Creating a new DLL.

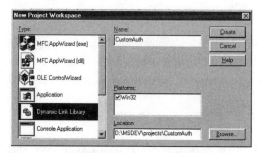

Next, we add the standard ISAPI entry points. Every ISAPI filter must have two exported functions, which are defined in Listing 16.1.

Only two functions are ever called by the Web server. The first function, GetFilterVersion, is called only once when the Web server starts and the filter is first loaded. The second, HttpFilterProc, is called for every filter event. These two functions will be explained in detail a bit later.

Listing 16.1   LST16_1.CPP—Declaring the Exported Functions

```
extern "C" {
    BOOL    WINAPI GetFilterVersion(PHTTP_FILTER_VERSION pVer);
    DWORD    WINAPI HttpFilterProc(HTTP_FILTER_CONTEXT* pfc,
                DWORD NotificationType, VOID* pvNotification);
}
```

First, we'll discuss the *extern "C"* block. Since we are writing C++ code that is compiled by a C++ compiler, we tell the compiler that these two functions will be called using the "C" calling convention. If you omit this keyword, the compiler uses the default C++ naming convention, and the Web server can't find your exported functions.

Before we start writing code for these functions, we tell the compiler that these two functions will be exported. The normal method for exporting DLL functions is to declare them using the declspec(dllexport) attribute—but not in this case.

As you can see in Listing 16.1, these two functions have already been declared using the WINAPI macro, which expands to stdcall. You can't declare a function using both declspec(dllexport) and stdcall. The only other way to export a function is to include the exported functions in the contents of a .DEF file.

Including the file in Listing 16.2 into your project ensures that these two functions are properly exported.

 You can use the DUMPBIN.EXE utility supplied with Visual C++ to show you the exported functions of a DLL. Use the DUMPBIN YourFile.DLL /EXPORTS syntax. When a filter does not load, it is often because you have improperly exported the GetFilterVersion function.

Listing 16.2   LST16_2.DEF—The CustomAuth.DEF File

```
LIBRARY "CustomAuth"

EXPORTS
    GetFilterVersion
    HttpFilterProc
```

Writing the *GetFilterVersion* Function

When Microsoft's IIS first starts, it opens the following registry key and reads the data stored in the Filter DLLs value.

```
HKEY_LOCAL_MACHINE\SYSTEM\CurrentControlSet\Services\W3SVC\Parameters
```

You must put all ISAPI filters, separated by commas, in this registry value. Next, IIS calls the GetFilterVersion function for each filter DLL in this list.

It is each filter's responsibility to fill out the HTTP_FILTER_VERSION structure passed to it in the GetFilterVersion function. This structure informs IIS of the name of the filter, the version of the filter, the events of which this filter should be notified, and the priority of the filter.

The code in Listing 16.3 tells the Web server that we respond only to SF_NOTIFY_AUTHENTICATION events and that our filter should have the default SF_NOTIFY_ORDER_DEFAULT priority.

We also tell IIS that our filter is version 1.0 and its name is CustomAuth filter. The return of TRUE from GetFilterVersion tells IIS that our filter initialization was successful.

Part
IV
Ch
16

Listing 16.3   LST16_3.CPP—The *GetFilterVersion* Function

```cpp
#define MAJOR_VERSION 1
#define MINOR_VERSION 0
#define MY_FILTER_VERSION MAKELONG(MINOR_VERSION,MAJOR_VERSION)

BOOL WINAPI GetFilterVersion(PHTTP_FILTER_VERSION pVer)
{
    pVer->dwFilterVersion =    MY_FILTER_VERSION;
    strcpy(pVer->lpszFilterDesc,"CustomAuth Filter");
    pVer->dwFlags =    SF_NOTIFY_ORDER_DEFAULT |
    ➡SF_NOTIFY_AUTHENTICATION;

    return TRUE;
}
```

Later, we add more tasks to this function, which read the registry and create a cache object. The GetFilterVersion function is a good place to put any other initialization code, since you can tell the Web server whether or not your initialization completed successfully.

Writing the *HttpFilterProc* Function

The last needed function of a filter is the HttpFilterProc. This function is the entry point for all filter events. We've already told IIS that we're interested in authentication events, so this function is called by IIS whenever a browser's credentials need to be validated (see Listing 16.4).

Listing 16.4 LST16_4.CPP—The *HttpFilterProc* Function

```
DWORD WINAPI HttpFilterProc(HTTP_FILTER_CONTEXT* pfc,
                                DWORD NotificationType,
                                VOID* pvNotification)
{
    // Even though we should only get authentication events,
    // you may wish to add your own events later.

    switch (NotificationType)
    {

    case SF_NOTIFY_AUTHENTICATION:
        {
            // Pull the URL out of the ServerVariables

            char pszURL[MAX_URL_SIZE];
            DWORD dLen = MAX_URL_SIZE;
            pfc->GetServerVariable(pfc,"SCRIPT_NAME",pszURL,&dLen);

            // Should we even bother authenticating?

            if (CheckFilterList(pszURL))
            {
                // Cast the filter data to the correct type.
                // In this case it's PHTTP_FILTER_AUTHENT

                PHTTP_FILTER_AUTHENT pAuthInfo =
                    (PHTTP_FILTER_AUTHENT)pvNotification;

                CString strUser(pAuthInfo->pszUser,
                                pAuthInfo->cbUserBuff);
                CString strPassword(pAuthInfo->pszPassword,
                    pAuthInfo->cbPasswordBuff);

                //
                // perform validation here
                //

                strcpy(pAuthInfo->pszUser, (LPCSTR)strUser);
                strcpy(pAuthInfo->pszPassword, (LPCSTR)strPassword);

            }
        }
        break;
```

```
    } // switch

    return SF_STATUS_REQ_NEXT_NOTIFICATION;

}
```

As a parameter to the HttpFilterProc function, we are given a pointer to HTTP_FILTER_CONTEXT. This structure has a reference to a function named GetServerVariable.

In Listing 16.4, we call this function to get the server variable SCRIPT_NAME, which has the logical path to the document requested by the browser. For example, if the browser requests the URL **http://www.leroux.com/secured/nona.htm**, the variable SCRIPT_NAME would be /secured/nona.htm.

In the middle of Listing 16.4, we call a function named CheckFilterList and pass in as a parameter the value obtained from SCRIPT_NAME. As you'll see in the next section, this function informs the CustomAuth filter that the document should be authenticated using our custom authentication scheme.

If this document should not be authenticated using this new scheme, we'll pass control back to IIS with a return of SF_STATUS_REQ_NEXT_NOTIFICATION and without touching the authentication credentials.

To get the credentials supplied by the browser, we'll have to examine pvNotification. The pvNotification variable passed into HttpFilterProc is a void pointer to a structure that corresponds to the NotificationType.

In this instance, the NotificationType is SF_NOTIFY_AUTHENTICATION, so we should cast pvNotification to the correct data type of PHTTP_FILTER_AUTHENT. The HTTP_FILTER_AUTHENT structure is defined in Listing 16.5.

Listing 16.5   LST16_5.CPP—The *HTTP_FILTER_AUTHENT* Structure

```
typedef struct _HTTP_FILTER_AUTHENT
{
    CHAR * pszUser;            // IN/OUT
    DWORD  cbUserBuff;         // OUT

    CHAR * pszPassword;        // IN/OUT
    DWORD  cbPasswordBuff;     // OUT

} HTTP_FILTER_AUTHENT, *PHTTP_FILTER_AUTHENT;
```

We extract the user and password text from this structure and put them into two CStrings. At this point, a database check, explained later, translates the browser user name and password to an NT user name and password.

After this new authentication, the data in the CStrings is copied back into the HTTP_FILTER_AUTHENT structure, where IIS uses the new user name and password as the security context to retrieve the document.

 T I P If a filter returns an invalid user name and password to IIS in the HTTP_FILTER_AUTHENT structure, an error is written to the NT application event log.

Filtering on Part of the URL

Since you probably won't want to use CustomAuth.DLL to authenticate every browser request, we add a simple routine to check the requested SCRIPT_NAME against a list of strings. If one of these strings appears in the SCRIPT_NAME, CustomAuth invokes its database authentication process.

Whenever the CustomAuth filter loads, the registry setting HKEY_LOCAL_MACHINE\SOFTWARE\CustomAuth is opened and the URLFilterList value is queried. You need to add this value manually by using the REGEDT32.EXE utility.

This value is of type REG_MULTI_SZ, meaning that it has multiple strings in one registry entry. If the value in any of these strings is in the SCRIPT_NAME server variable, our custom authentication scheme is invoked.

You'll probably add strings like /secured and /private to this registry entry. Then, if a browser requests an URL like **http://vicki.shippen.com/secured/special.htm**, the CustomAuth filter takes over and does its own authentication.

The first step in providing this type of function is to get a list of "validation" strings from the registry. The LoadFilterParams function, as shown in Listing 16.6, opens the registry, gets the REG_MULTI_SZ value from UrlFilterList, and stores it in the UrlFilterList global variable.

To save time when comparing strings and because IIS is case-insensitive, we immediately convert all strings in UrlFilterList to lowercase.

N O T E When a `REG_MULTI_SZ` is queried from the registry and put in a buffer, each
string in the list is separated by a null, and the final string in the list is ended
with two nulls. ▨

Listing 16.6   LST16_6.CPP—The *LoadFilterParams* Function

```cpp
char* UrlFilterList = 0;

void LoadFilterParams()
{
    HKEY hKey;
    DWORD dwResult;

    if (RegCreateKeyEx(HKEY_LOCAL_MACHINE, "SOFTWARE\\CustomAuth", 0,
    ➥NULL,
        REG_OPTION_NON_VOLATILE, KEY_ALL_ACCESS, NULL, &hKey,
        ➥&dwResult)
            == ERROR_SUCCESS)
    {
        DWORD dwRegLength;
        DWORD dwType;

        // UrlFilterList - List of strings to check against URL's

        // First, get the length of the data so we can allocate space
        RegQueryValueEx(hKey,"UrlFilterList", 0, &dwType, NULL,
        ➥&dwRegLength);
        if (dwRegLength > 0 && dwType == REG_MULTI_SZ)
        {
            // Allocate space
            UrlFilterList = new char[dwRegLength];
            RegQueryValueEx(hKey, "UrlFilterList", 0, &dwType,
                (LPBYTE)UrlFilterList, &dwRegLength);

            // convert to lower case
            char* pszBigCheck = UrlFilterList;
            while (!(*pszBigCheck == 0 && *(pszBigCheck+1) == 0))
            {
                if (*pszBigCheck >= 'A' && *pszBigCheck <= 'Z')
                    *pszBigCheck = *pszBigCheck - 'A' + 'a';
                pszBigCheck++;
            }

        }

        RegCloseKey(hKey);
    }
}
```

At this point, we add a line to GetFilterVersion to call LoadFilterParams. Therefore, whenever the CustomAuth filter is loaded, the filter immediately queries the registry to get a list of strings to use for SCRIPT_NAME comparison. The next step is to provide the functions to compare the SCRIPT_NAME to the list of strings in UrlFilterList.

The CheckFilterList function, as shown in Listing 16.7, takes a const char* to the SCRIPT_NAME as a parameter and returns a TRUE if any of the strings in UrlFilterList are in it. This function is called in our HttpFilterProc, as shown earlier in Listing 16.4.

Listing 16.7   LST16_7.CPP—The *CheckFilterList* Function

```
BOOL CheckFilterList(const char* pcszCheckMe)
{
    char *pszCheckList =      UrlFilterList;
    int nCheckListLen =       0;
    BOOL bStringFound =       FALSE;

    while (!bStringFound && (nCheckListLen = strlen(pszCheckList)))
    {
        if (strstr(pcszCheckMe, pszCheckList) != 0)
            bStringFound = TRUE;

        pszCheckList += nCheckListLen + 1;
    }

    return bStringFound;
}
```

Now that we know when to use the custom authentication scheme, we add code for the user validation against an ODBC data source.

Adding an ODBC Database Check

The idea behind using an ODBC data source to provide our customized authentication scheme is obvious. Instead of maintaining a list of users in a text file or hardcoded into your filter, you can now keep a mapping of user names to NT user accounts in a database.

You may have a list of valid user names in a database already. In that case, you'll just need a stored procedure or static Structured Query Language (SQL) to get that data and pass it back to the CustomAuth filter.

As I wrote CustomAuth, I envisioned a database table called UserTranslation with four columns: Username, Password, TranslatedUsername, and TranslatedPassword. The SQL to get the data from this table would be simple:

```
SELECT TranslatedUsername, TranslatedPassword
FROM UserTranslation
WHERE Username = <user> and Password = <password>
```

In this case, the <user> and <password> values would be dynamically inserted into the SQL or, preferably, passed as parameters into a stored procedure. If the user name is on the table and the password is valid, the translated NT user name and password would be passed back to CustomAuth.

If there is no valid entry, no data is passed back. In this case, the translated user and password are blank, simulating an anonymous logon and failing authentication.

The database routine using the ODBC API was written for two reasons. First, nothing beats the speed of straight ODBC function calls. Second, the MFC supplied with Visual C++ 4.1 does not provide thread-safe ODBC classes.

Writing straight ODBC is guaranteed to be safe in a multithreaded environment. Microsoft's Visual C++ 4.2 supposedly uses thread-safe ODBC, but using CDatabase and CRecordset objects may be a bit awkward.

You can also forget about using the data access object (DAO) classes supplied with MFC. They don't work at all in an ISAPI filter.

Notice that in Listing 16.8, we reference m_strDataSource, m_strDataUser, and m_strDataPassword. For now, you can assume that these three variables are CStrings with a global scope. You will soon see, however, that the DatabaseCheck is going to be a member function of a class and that these variables are protected member variables.

Listing 16.8   LST16_8.CPP—The *CheckDatabase* Function

```
void DatabaseCheck(const CString& strUser,
               const CString& strPassword,
               CString& strTranslatedUser,
               CString& strTranslatedPassword)
{
    HENV henv;
    RETCODE retcode = SQLAllocEnv(&henv);

    if (retcode == SQL_SUCCESS)
    {
        HDBC hdbc;
        retcode = SQLAllocConnect(henv, &hdbc);

        SQLSetConnectOption(hdbc, SQL_LOGIN_TIMEOUT, 5);

        retcode = SQLConnect(hdbc,(UCHAR*)(LPCSTR)m_strDataSource,
        ➥SQL_NTS,
                        (UCHAR*)(LPCSTR)m_strDataUser, SQL_NTS,
                        (UCHAR*)(LPCSTR)m_strDataPassword,
                        ➥SQL_NTS);

        if (retcode == SQL_SUCCESS ¦¦ retcode ==
        ➥SQL_SUCCESS_WITH_INFO)
        {
            HSTMT hstmt;
            retcode = SQLAllocStmt(hdbc, &hstmt);

            if (retcode == SQL_SUCCESS)
            {
                CString strSQL;
                strSQL.Format("execute TranslateUser '%s','%s'",
                            strUser, strPassword);

                retcode = SQLExecDirect(hstmt,
                ➥(UCHAR*)(LPCSTR)strSQL,
                            strSQL.GetLength());

                if (retcode == SQL_SUCCESS)
                {
                    SDWORD cbUser(0), cbPassword(0);

                    SQLBindCol(hstmt, 1, SQL_C_CHAR,
                                    strTranslatedUser.
                                    ➥GetBuffer(255), 255,
                                    &cbUser);

                    SQLBindCol(hstmt, 2, SQL_C_CHAR,
                        strTranslatedPassword.GetBuffer(255), 255,
                        &cbPassword);
```

```
                retcode = SQLFetch(hstmt);

                if (retcode == SQL_SUCCESS ||
                    retcode == SQL_SUCCESS_WITH_INFO)
                {
                    strTranslatedUser.ReleaseBuffer(cbUser);
                                        strTranslatedPassword.
                                        ➥ReleaseBuffer(
                                        cbPassword);
                } else {
                    strTranslatedUser.ReleaseBuffer(0);
                    strTranslatedPassword.ReleaseBuffer(0);
                }
            }
            SQLFreeStmt(hstmt, SQL_DROP);
        }
        SQLDisconnect(hdbc);
    }
    SQLFreeConnect(hdbc);
}
SQLFreeEnv(henv);
}
```

In the DatabaseCheck function, we take the user name and password as input, and return the translated user name and password. These translated values are from the SQL stored procedure TranslateUser.

This stored procedure would have a SQL like the one shown in the beginning of this section. If rows are retrieved from this function, they are bound to the strTranslatedUser and strTranslatedPassword parameters, which are returned to the calling function.

You can make the call to DatabaseCheck directly from HttpFilterProc. This, however, is not a great idea. If a browser is mucking about in the /secured section of your site, every document that is requested with the /secured string will make this user translation.

Remember that most browsers cache authenticated credentials. Even though the authentication dialog box does not pop up, authentication is still happening behind the scenes.

A browser requesting 20 documents under a secured directory would, in this case, make 20 database hits. A query to a database, especially one needing a connect and a disconnect, is fairly resource-intensive.

One possibility might be to keep the database connection open, but then you must deal with asynchronous queries and additional thread-synchronization problems.

What we really need is a cache of previously translated authentication requests. A successful authentication would add an item to the cache. Future requests for the same credentials would authenticate via the cache instead of the database.

Then we would need a way to kick items out of the cache if they are outdated or the cache is full. In the next section, you see how to use just such a class.

Building a Cache Class

Before we set out to build a cache that holds a history of previously authenticated users, we should probably step back and do a little object-oriented design. So far, our custom authentication scheme has fit into a few small C functions. It would be nice to have a class that would do database validation and caching, and provide a simple interface to call from our `HttpFilterProc` function.

Here's a simple two-class approach. The first class is a cache item and the second is the cache class. The cache item is responsible for storing the user name, password, translated user name, and translated password of a previously authenticated request.

The cache item would also be responsible for keeping track of how long the request has existed. Since items should not stay in the cache forever, we must provide a mechanism for their expiration. Listing 16.9 shows the declaration for the `CacheItem` class.

Listing 16.9 LST16_9.H—The *CacheItem* Class

```
class CacheItem {

public:

    CacheItem(CString& strUser, CString& strPassword,
            CString& strTranslatedUser, CString&
            ➥strTranslatedPassword,
            const int nExpireMins);

    ~CacheItem() {};
```

```
CString&         GetUser()                  { return m_strUser; }
CString&         GetPassword()              { return m_strPassword; }
CString&         GetTranslatedUser()        { return
➥m_strTranslatedUser; }
CString&         GetTranslatedPassword()      { return
➥m_strTranslatedPassword;}
COleDateTime&    GetTimeAdded()             { return m_dtTimeAdded; }
COleDateTime&    GetTimeExpired()             { return
➥m_dtTimeExpired; }

BOOL             IsExpired();

private:

    CString m_strUser;
    CString m_strPassword;

    CString m_strTranslatedUser;
    CString m_strTranslatedPassword;

    COleDateTime m_dtTimeAdded;
    COleDateTime m_dtTimeExpired;
    BOOL m_bDoNotExpire;

};
```

There's really no rocket science behind the CacheItem. It keeps track of the time it was added and the time it should expire. In its constructor, we tell the CacheItem how long it will take before it should be considered expired. The IsExpired function returns whether or not the CacheItem should be considered valid.

Our next step is to build a container to hold CacheItems. A MFC Map class would work well in this situation. We could map the untranslated user name to a pointer to a CacheItem.

One way to do this would be to use a CMapStringToPtr map. However, a better way would be to derive our own map class from a templated map class like this:

```
typedef CMap<CString, LPCSTR, CacheItem*, CacheItem*> THE_CACHE;
```

Now we can derive from THE_CACHE and give ourselves a nice, type-safe CString to CacheItem map. The declaration for our new cache class is simple, as shown in Listing 16.10.

Listing 16.10   LST16_10.H—The *CCache* Class

```
class CCache : public THE_CACHE
{

public:

    CCache(int nMaxCacheSize, int nKeepCacheMinutes,
            CString strDataSource,     CString strDataUser,
                        CString strDataPassword);
    ~CCache() {};

    void TranslateUser(CString& strUser, CString& strPassword);

protected:

    void DeleteOldest();
    void DatabaseCheck(const CString& strUser, const CString&
    ➥strPassword,
                        CString& strTranslatedUser,
                                CString& strTranslatedPassword);

    int m_nMaxCacheSize;
    int m_nKeepCacheMinutes;

    CString m_strDataSource;
    CString m_strDataUser;
    CString m_strDataPassword;

    CCriticalSection m_csMap;

};
```

The only section of this class that may need a bit of explaining is the
CCriticalSection member variable m_csMap. Remember that since there will be
only one cache for our filter, we'll need to protect all data that will be stored in this
map from the feet of stomping threads.

Using the MFC CCriticalSection class is a simple way to ensure that only
one thread reads and writes to the cache at a time. You'll soon see how we use
the CSingleLock class with the CCricitalSection class to provide thread
synchronization.

The only public interface to the CCache class is through the TranslateUser member function. This function takes references to two CStrings as parameters: the
user name and the password to be validated.

The TranslateUser function translates these credentials into an NT user name and a password. First, the cache (map) is checked to see if this user has been authenticated recently.

If this user name is in the cache but is no longer valid because it has reached its expiration time, the CacheItem is removed from the CCache. If the user name has not expired, the password is compared to the password in the cache. If the password matches, the translated user name and password are taken from the cache and passed back into the return parameters.

Listing 16.11 shows how the CCache::TranslateUser function works.

Listing 16.11   LST16_11.CPP—The *CCache::TranslateUser* Function

```cpp
void CCache::TranslateUser(CString& strCheckUser, CString&
➥strCheckPassword)
{
    if (strCheckUser != "") // don't bother with the empty guys
    {
        CacheItem* pCItem;
        BOOL bFoundInCache(FALSE);
        CString strTranslatedUser("");
        CString strTranslatedPassword("");

        // First, check to see if it's in the cache yet...

        if (Lookup(strCheckUser, pCItem))
        {
            // User found in cache
            if (!pCItem->IsExpired())
            {
                bFoundInCache = TRUE;

                // If password is not ok, they shouldn't be allowed
                // in
                if (strCheckPassword == pCItem->GetPassword())
                {
                    // User entered ok password
                    strTranslatedUser = pCItem-
                    ➥>GetTranslatedUser();
                    strTranslatedPassword =
                                        pCItem->GetTranslatedPassword();
                }

            } else {
```

continues

Listing 16.11 Continued

```
                          // expired! remove from cache and re-check user
                          RemoveKey(strCheckUser);
                          delete pCItem;
                  }
          }

          if (!bFoundInCache) // then we must perform a database check..
          {
                  DatabaseCheck(strCheckUser, strCheckPassword,
                      strTranslatedUser, strTranslatedPassword);

                  if (strTranslatedUser != "")
                  {
                          // if cache is full, delete the oldest item and
                          // clean up

                          CSingleLock lockMap(&m_csMap, TRUE);

                          if (GetCount() >= m_nMaxCacheSize)
                              DeleteOldest();

                          // Add item into cache
                          pCItem = new CacheItem(strCheckUser,
                          ➡strCheckPassword,
                              strTranslatedUser, strTranslatedPassword,
                              m_nKeepCacheMinutes);

                          SetAt(strCheckUser, pCItem);
                          lockMap.Unlock();
                  }
          }

          // Return translated stuff back to the user..
          strCheckUser = strTranslatedUser;
          strCheckPassword = strTranslatedPassword;
      }
  }
```

If the user name cannot be found in the cache (or the password entered is different from the one found in the cache), the database must be checked to validate the user name. You can see in Listing 16.11 that the DatabaseCheck function is called. We've basically taken the code from Listing 16.8 and turned it into a protected member function of CCache.

If the DatabaseCheck function returns a blank as the translated user name, you can assume that the credentials did not pass validation and that this item should not be added to the cache. On the other hand, if the DatabaseCheck returns a translated user name, a CacheItem object is created on the heap and added to the cache.

The only tricky part here is if the CCache is full. Listing 16.12 shows what happens if the cache is full when we need to add a new CacheItem.

Listing 16.12   LST16_12.CPP—The CCache::DeleteOldest Function

```cpp
void CCache::DeleteOldest()
{

    POSITION    pos;
    CString     key;
    CacheItem*  pCacheItem              = NULL;
    CacheItem*  pOldestCacheItem        = NULL;
    BOOL            bAlreadyDeletedOne   = FALSE;

    for (pos = GetStartPosition(); pos != NULL; )
    {
        GetNextAssoc(pos, key, pCacheItem);

        if (pCacheItem->IsExpired())
        {
            // If expired, delete it...
            bAlreadyDeletedOne = TRUE;
            RemoveKey(pCacheItem->GetUser());
            delete pCacheItem;
        }

        if (!bAlreadyDeletedOne)
            // If we deleted one already, we don't need to go through
            // this
            if (pOldestCacheItem == NULL)
                pOldestCacheItem = pCacheItem;
        else
            if (pCacheItem->GetTimeAdded() <
                                pOldestCacheItem->GetTimeAdded())
                pOldestCacheItem = pCacheItem;
    }

    if (!bAlreadyDeletedOne && (pOldestCacheItem != NULL))
    {
        RemoveKey(pCacheItem->GetUser());
        delete pOldestCacheItem;
    }
}
```

The DeleteOldest function does more than delete the oldest item in the cache. Since it already searches the entire cache looking for the oldest CacheItem, it also deletes every CacheItem it finds that has expired. If an expired CacheItem is found, we are guaranteed space to add our new entry into the cache.

Let's take a moment to talk about thread synchronization. Notice how the TranslateUser CCache member function uses the CSingleLock object. Since it is likely that multiple threads will be executing through the CustomAuth filter concurrently, we need to make sure that only one thread is manipulating the cache at a time.

We also need to make sure that if a CacheItem is deleted because the cache is full, other threads wait until the new CacheItem has been added before doing any operations on the cache. The m_csMap CCriticalSection member variable of CCache is passed into the CSingleLock constructor at the start of all cache operations.

At that point, the CSingleLock has locked the CCricitalSection object. No other thread can enter this section of code until the CSingleLock has called its Unlock member function.

In fact, a thread waits indefinitely until the CSingleLock has unlocked the CCriticalSection. After the cache operations have completed, the lock on the critical section is released.

As you may have noticed, the constructor to CCache takes five parameters. The first two, nMaxCacheSize and nKeepCacheMinutes, define our cache behavior. The nMaxCahceSize parameter specifies the maximum number of CacheItems that can exist before we should start purging the cache.

The nKeepCacheMinutes parameter specifies the number of minutes that a CacheItem should be considered "valid" (that is, before it expires). A CacheItem that has been around longer than nKeepCacheMinutes can be deleted.

The last three parameters passed into CCache are ODBC connection parameters. The first, strDataSource is the ODBC data source that will be opened.

The second and third, strDataUser and strDataPassword, are the credentials used to log into the ODBC data source. All of these parameters will be stored in the registry and passed to the cache on instantiation.

N O T E All ODBC data sources that will be used by ISAPI filters and extensions must be defined as a "system" data source. This has the effect of making the ODBC data source visible to all users and system processes. You can do this by clicking the System DSN button from the ODBC Administrator Control Panel applet. ▨

Our `CCache` is instantiated in the `GetFilterVersion` function. In our call to `LoadFilterParams`, we get the `CCache` constructor parameters from the registry and put them into global variables.

Then we create a `CCache` object on the heap with these parameters. Last, we put a call to the `CCache::TranslateUser` function in the `HttpFilterProc`. Our cache is now connected to the ISAPI authentication filter.

Completing CustomAuth Application

That takes care of all of the major pieces of our CustomAuth filter DLL. We are left with gluing all of the pieces together and compiling our filter into a DLL. A full listing of the CustomAuth filter application can be found on the CD.

We have taken a few shortcuts here and there when writing the CustomAuth filter. You may want to add the following new features to make CustomAuth a more durable application:

▨ Add error handling and logging

We have not included any error handling. You'll probably want to write events out to the Windows NT application error log (or at least into a text file). This is especially important for all ODBC errors.

▨ Add registry security or encryption

We've stored the ODBC data source password as straight text in the registry. This is definitely a no-no. Either add security to the registry key or encrypt the password.

▨ Pass the URL into the ODBC authentication procedure

You may have multiple users who need different security, depending on the document they are trying to access. If so, you'll want to build logic into your authentication stored procedure to return a different translated user and translated password, depending on the URL the user is trying to access.

In the next section, you learn how to process the ISAPI log event that gives your Web site an audit log with custom information.

Building a Custom Logging Filter

As you may know, three styles of logging are built into Microsoft's IIS version 3.0. The first is standard file logging. This means that log data is saved to a file, with all fields separated by commas.

The second format for logging is also to a file but in the NCSA standard format. The third style of logging is to an ODBC data source table.

You can use the Logging property sheet of the Microsoft Internet Service Manager, as shown in Figure 16.4, to change the active logging style.

FIG. 16.4
The Logging property sheet of Microsoft's Internet Service Manager.

If you select standard file logging or ODBC table logging, the data recorded is exactly the same. Table 16.1 lists the fields, in the order they occur, in the standard log file and the ODBC log table.

The NCSA-style logging has a subset of the information listed in Table 16.1 but in a format that many log-analysis programs can read. Microsoft, however, has supplied CONVLOG.EXE, a log-conversion program with IIS that translates a Microsoft-style log file into an NCSA-style log file.

NOTE The filter we are building in this chapter adds columns to the Microsoft-style log file. As a result, the CONVLOG.EXE utility supplied with IIS that converts Microsoft-style logs to NCSA-style logs won't work.

To convert the new-style log file to NCSA style, you first strip out the new fields and then run the resulting file through the CONVLOG.EXE utility. Of course, the other solution is just to write your own CONVLOG application. ■

Part

IV

Ch

16

Table 16.1   The Log File Format—Standard Log File and ODBC Log Table

Name	Description
Client host	IP address of the client
User name	User name of the client (post-authentication)
Log date	Date the log record was written
Log time	Time the log record was written
Service	Service (W3SVC, MSFTPSVC, or GOPHERSVC)
Machine	WINS computer name of the server
Server IP	Server's IP address
Processing time	Elapsed time, in milliseconds, to send the document
Bytes received	Number of bytes received from the client
Bytes sent	Number of bytes sent from the server to the client
HTTP return status	Return status of the service
Win32 status	Win32 error code
Operation	Operation requested (POST or GET)
Target	Document and path requested
Parameters	Any parameters sent after the target

As you will soon see, you can replace the contents of some of the items in the log with other pieces of information (usually obtained via queries to the Web server). Unfortunately, the ISAPI hooks into the logging event are not flexible, and adding new data to the logs is not pretty.

The ISAPI filter, CustomLog, does a good job of "pseudo-adding" columns to the standard log file without adding an entirely new logging process.

Understanding How CustomLog Works

The ISAPI filter event, SF_NOTIFY_LOG, occurs immediately before the Web server writes its information to the logs (no matter what style of logging you have enabled). When your ISAPI filter registers to receive this event and a browser requests a document from your Web site, your filter is given the HTTP_FILTER_LOG data structure, which looks like Listing 16.13.

Listing 16.13   LST16_13.H—The *HTTP_FILTER_LOG* Structure

```
typedef struct _HTTP_FILTER_LOG
{
    const CHAR * pszClientHostName;  // Client's host name
    const CHAR * pszClientUserName;  // Client's user name
    const CHAR * pszServerName;      // Name of the server the client
                                     // connected to
    const CHAR * pszOperation;       // HTTP command
    const CHAR * pszTarget;          // Target of HTTP command
    const CHAR * pszParameters;      // Parameters passed to HTTP command

    DWORD   dwHttpStatus;            // HTTP Return status
    DWORD   dwWin32Status;           // Win32 Error code

} HTTP_FILTER_LOG, *PHTTP_FILTER_LOG;
```

You can't copy data on top of any of the member variables (hence the const before the CHAR) in the HTTP_FILTER_LOG structure. You can, however, replace the pointer in the structure with a pointer to memory that you have allocated.

At first it may look ridiculous. Why would you want to replace any of these columns with your own data? The elements supplied in this structure are all important pieces of information that you want to keep in the logs.

Well, the answer is that you wouldn't. Believe it or not, we are going to squeeze four fields into one variable. Sound a bit messy? It is. Let me explain.

First off, if you are using an ODBC data source or NCSA-style logging as the format for your logs, you are not going to like this solution. It is impossible with version 3.0 of Microsoft's IIS to add additional columns in a log table without using a new logging process from scratch (which I wouldn't recommend).

The CustomLog solution presented in this chapter works only with the standard log file format. Since the standard log file format consists of comma-delimited log elements, we are going to replace the first field, the client's IP address (pszClientHostName) with four fields that were previously unlogged (three were previously unlogged—the fourth is the client's IP address that will be stuck at the end of the string).

We do this by comma-delimiting the four fields during the SF_NOTIFY_LOG event— that is, before IIS puts them in the logs. Here are three new fields that we are adding:

■ User Agent

When a browser connects to a server, it sends a User-Agent header with the name (and usually the version) of the browser software connecting to your site. This information could help you decide whether to use browser-specific features on your Web site.

■ Referer

Most browsers also send the Referer header, which has the link from which the browser was sent. You may want to analyze this field to see which Web sites are referring clients to your server.

■ Unmapped Remote User Name

If you are using your own authentication scheme, you'll want this information. The UNMAPPED_REMOTE_USER server variable has the name that was sent to your authentication filter before it was translated into Windows NT user credentials.

Without the unmapped user, you don't know which client has hit your site. If you are not using your own custom authentication scheme, this value is the same as the user name (pszClientUserName).

Before you start writing code for the CustomLog filter, you need to set up a new C++ project. As explained in the CustomAuth filter, you need to prototype your two filter entry point functions and create a .DEF file to export these functions from your DLL.

As with the CustomAuth filter, we do not use the ISAPI Extension Wizard or any of the MFC ISAPI classes. By contrast, we use no MFC classes at all. This is probably a good idea, since you'll want to streamline this code as much as possible. Let's begin.

Allowing Only the Standard Log File

Since CustomLog only works when you log to a standard log file, there is no need for our filter to load if NCSA style logging is active, ODBC style logging is active, or no logging is active. All information about Microsoft's IIS is stored in the registry under the following key:

```
HKEY_LOCAL_MACHINE\CurrentControlSet\Services\W3SVC\Parameters
```

Two entries under this key tell us the type of logging selected: LogType and LogFileFormat. Table 16.2 illustrates the type of logging that corresponds to values in each of these registry entries.

Table 16.2 Possible Registry Entries for *LogType* and *LogFileFormat*

LogType	LogFileFormat	Description
0	0	Logging has been disabled
1	0	Logging to file, standard format
1	3	Logging to file, NCSA format
2	0	Logging to ODBC

We'll start by writing a function that opens the registry, queries the LogType and LogFileFormat entries, and returns TRUE if the Web server is indeed using standard format logging. The code to perform this procedure is shown in Listing 16.14.

Listing 16.14 LST16_14.CPP—The *IsStandardLogFile* Function

```
BOOL IsStandardLogFile()
{
    HKEY hKey;
    DWORD dwResult;
    DWORD dwLogFileFormat;
    DWORD dwLogType;
```

```
if (RegCreateKeyEx(HKEY_LOCAL_MACHINE,
        "SYSTEM\\CurrentControlSet\\Services\\W3SVC\\Parameters",
        0, NULL, REG_OPTION_NON_VOLATILE, KEY_READ, NULL,
        &hKey, &dwResult) == ERROR_SUCCESS)
{
    DWORD dwRegLength;
    DWORD dwType;

    RegQueryValueEx(hKey, "LogFileFormat", 0, &dwType,
        (LPBYTE)&dwLogFileFormat, &dwRegLength);

    RegQueryValueEx(hKey, "LogType", 0, &dwType,
        (LPBYTE)&dwLogType, &dwRegLength);

    RegCloseKey(hKey);
}

return (dwLogFileFormat == 0 && dwLogType == 1);
}
```

This procedure is straightforward. If the registry key is opened successfully, the values for the two registry entries are queried. If the LogType is 1 and the LogFileFormat is 0, this function returns TRUE. Any other values for these entries return FALSE. As you see in the next section, this function is called by the GetFilterVersion ISAPI function.

Writing the *GetFilterVersion* Function

As with all ISAPI filters, the CustomLog filter must have a GetFilterVersion function. The two events we are interested in trapping are the SF_NOTIFY_LOG event and the SF_NOTIFY_END_OF_NET_SESSION event.

The first, SF_NOTIFY_LOG, is the event in which the logic to change the log data occurs. The second, SF_NOTIFY_END_OF_NET_SESSION, is used to clean up memory that was allocated during the log event. This event is discussed later in the chapter.

Listing 16.15 shows how the GetFilterVersion function works.

Listing 16.15 LST16_15.CPP—The *GetFilterVersion* Function

```
BOOL WINAPI GetFilterVersion(PHTTP_FILTER_VERSION pVer)
{
    pVer->dwFilterVersion =      MY_FILTER_VERSION;
    strcpy(pVer->lpszFilterDesc,"CustomLog Filter");
    pVer->dwFlags =      SF_NOTIFY_ORDER_DEFAULT | SF_NOTIFY_LOG |
        SF_NOTIFY_END_OF_NET_SESSION;

    return IsStandardLogFile();
}
```

Notice the call to the IsStandardLogFile function in the last line of our GetFilterVersion function in Listing 16.15. If we are indeed logging to a standard format file, we tell the Web server that our filter should be loaded. Returning FALSE from GetFilterVersion tells the Web server that there is a problem and our filter should not be loaded.

Writing the *HttpFilterProc* Function

Logically, the first step in building our HttpFilterProc is to determine where we get the data for our new logging columns. Microsoft's IIS takes all headers supplied by the browser and turns them into server variables that can be queried using the filter context's GetServerVariable function.

IIS just slaps an HTTP_prefix in front of the header name. Therefore, the User-Agent header becomes the HTTP_USER_AGENT server variable and the Referer header becomes the HTTP_REFERER server variable. The unmapped remote user variable is aptly named UNMAPPED_REMOTE_USER. You'll have to hunt around in the documentation to find that one.

We'll copy the result of each of these variables into a temporary buffer. For instance, Listing 16.16 is used to get the HTTP_USER_AGENT server variable. This data is then put in the pszUserAgent buffer and the length is put in the cbUserAgentLen DWORD.

Listing 16.16 LST16_16.CPP—Getting the *HTTP_USER_AGENT*

```
char pszUserAgent[MAX_USER_AGENT] = {0};
DWORD cbUserAgentLen(MAX_USER_AGENT);
```

```
if (!pfc->GetServerVariable(pfc,"HTTP_USER_AGENT",
        pszUserAgent,&cbUserAgentLen))
    if (GetLastError() == ERROR_INVALID_INDEX)
    {
        pszUserAgent[0] = '-';
        pszUserAgent[1] = 0;
        cbUserAgentLen = 1;
    }
```

Notice that if the GetServerVariable function fails and the last error is ERROR_INVALID_INDEX, we know that the Referer header was not supplied with the request. In this case, we put a "-" character in the buffer to differentiate from a Referer header that was supplied without data.

Also remember that since the UNMAPPED_REMOTE_USER server variable does not come from the header (well, it really does, but it's encoded and handled differently by IIS), it will always exist.

The HTTP_FILTER_LOG member that we commandeer is the pszClientHostName pointer. Since we are not allowed to copy our own strings into any of the HTTP_FILTER_LOG pointer variables themselves, we allocate another buffer big enough to hold our three new variables, the pszClientHostName, and our comma separators, spaces, and null terminator.

The ISAPI documentation says that if we replace the pointer to a data member in HTTP_FILTER_LOG, the data pointed to by the new member must be valid until either (a) the next SF_NOTIFY_LOG event or (b) the SF_NOTIFY_END_OF_NET_SESSION event. To satisfy this need, we allocate a buffer on the heap using the new[] operator.

N O T E The ISAPI HTTP_FILTER_CONTEXT structure provides a function named AllocMem. This function allocates memory on the heap that is guaranteed to be freed at the end of a client's session.

If we were to use this function, we would not need to keep track of our buffers and we would not need to trap the SF_NOTIFY_END_OF_NET_SESSION event to free our memory. However, I am not partial to other processes' memory-allocation functions and I would rather use the C++ new[] and delete[] operators to allocate and free my buffer space.

continues

Part
IV
Ch
16

continued

To really boost performance, Microsoft's documentation suggests starting your filter with a pool of buffers, and dynamically enlarging and shrinking this pool according to Web site activity. This lessens the time wasted by allocating and freeing buffer space. ▨

We can determine the size of our buffer by adding the length of each of our four strings and then adding 7 to account for the commas and the null terminator:

```
char* pszNewData = new char[cbUserAgentLen +
    cbRefererLen +
    cbUnmappedUserLen +
    strlen(pLogInfo->pszClientHostName) +
    7]; // for the commas, spaces and null
```

Next, we copy our four strings into the new buffer:

```
sprintf(pszNewData, "%s, %s, %s, %s", pszReferer, pszUserAgent,
    pszUnmappedUser, pLogInfo->pszClientHostName);
```

And then, we put the pointer to our buffer in the HTTP_FILTER_LOG structure:

```
pLogInfo->pszClientHostName = pszNewData;
```

And that's it, right? Not quite. When are we going to delete the pszNewData buffer? And more important, since the ISAPI HttpHeaderProc can be called many times for each client request, how are we going to keep track of our new buffer? It's actually quite easy.

The HTTP_FILTER_CONTEXT structure has a member variable pFilterContext. This pointer is given to the filter for just such an occasion. At the start of a client session, the pFilterContext is guaranteed to be null. It is also guaranteed to be unchanged for each event in a client's session.

Therefore, if we put a pointer in pFilterContext in the SF_NOTIFY_LOG event, the pFilterContext should have the same pointer for the same client session's SF_NOTIFY_END_OF_NET_SESSION event. If that's the case, we just put a delete[] in the SF_NOTIFY_END_OF_NET_SESSION event and that's it, right? Again, not quite.

The SF_NOTIFY_LOG event can't be called multiple times before the SF_NOTIFY_END_OF_NET_SESSION event. Therefore, before we do any writing to pFilterContext in the SF_NOTIFY_LOG event, we should make sure that pFilterContext does not already have a valid pointer. If it does, we should delete[] it.

Our completed HttpFilterProc appears in Listing 16.17. We should now be ready to compile our CustomLog filter.

Listing 16.17   LST16_17.CPP—The *HttpFilterProc* Function

```
DWORD WINAPI HttpFilterProc(HTTP_FILTER_CONTEXT* pfc,
                               DWORD NotificationType,
                               VOID* pvNotification)
{

    switch (NotificationType)
    {

    case SF_NOTIFY_LOG:
        {
            // Cast the filter data to the correct type.
            //    In this case, it's PHTTP_FILTER_LOG

            PHTTP_FILTER_LOG pLogInfo =
                (PHTTP_FILTER_LOG)pvNotification;

            // Delete any previous items in the filter context
            // if they've stuck around

            if (pfc->pFilterContext)
                delete[] pfc->pFilterContext;

            // HTTP_USER_AGENT
            // Set to '-' if it does not exist
            char pszUserAgent[MAX_USER_AGENT] = {0};
            DWORD cbUserAgentLen(MAX_USER_AGENT);
            if (!pfc->GetServerVariable(pfc,"HTTP_USER_AGENT",
                            pszUserAgent,&cbUserAgentLen))
                if (GetLastError() == ERROR_INVALID_INDEX)
                {
                    pszUserAgent[0] = '-';
                    pszUserAgent[1] = 0;
                    cbUserAgentLen = 1;
                }

            // HTTP_REFERER
            // Set to '-' if it does not exist
            char pszReferer[MAX_REFERER] = {0};
            DWORD cbRefererLen(MAX_REFERER);
            if (!pfc->GetServerVariable(pfc,"HTTP_REFERER",
                            pszReferer,&cbRefererLen))
                if (GetLastError() == ERROR_INVALID_INDEX)
                {
```

Part

IV

Ch

16

continues

Listing 16.17 **Continued**

```
                            pszReferer[0] = '-';
                            pszReferer[1] = 0;
                            cbRefererLen = 1;
                    }

            // UNMAPPED_REMOTE_USER
            // (this one will always exist)
            char pszUnmappedUser[MAX_UNMAPPED] = {0};
            DWORD cbUnmappedUserLen(MAX_UNMAPPED);
            pfc->GetServerVariable(pfc,"UNMAPPED_REMOTE_USER",
                                    pszUnmappedUser,&cbUnmappedUserLen);
            if (cbUnmappedUserLen == 0)
                    {
                            pszUnmappedUser[0] = '-';
                            pszUnmappedUser[1] = 0;
                            cbUnmappedUserLen = 1;
                    }

            // Build the big string
            char* pszNewData = new char[cbUserAgentLen +
                    cbRefererLen +
                    cbUnmappedUserLen +
                    strlen(pLogInfo->pszClientHostName) +
                    7]; // for the commas, spaces and null
                                            ;
            // tack them on to the beginning of the log record
            sprintf(pszNewData, "%s, %s, %s, %s", pszReferer,
            ➥pszUserAgent,
                    pszUnmappedUser, pLogInfo->pszClientHostName);

            pLogInfo->pszClientHostName = pszNewData;
            pfc->pFilterContext = pszNewData;

        }
        break;

    case SF_NOTIFY_END_OF_NET_SESSION:
        {
            // delete the string if it's valid
            if (pfc->pFilterContext)
                    delete[] pfc->pFilterContext;
        }
        break;

    } // switch

    return SF_STATUS_REQ_NEXT_NOTIFICATION;
}
```

After you install the CustomLog filter and activate standard logging, you should see the three new columns prepended to each line of the log file. As mentioned before, you may need to write a utility to convert this file to NCSA file format to use tools that provide Web site statistics.

A better solution would be to insert the log files into a database. At that point, your database can compile statistics, or you can export the log table from your database into the NCSA formatted file.

Completing the CustomLog Filter

Now that our CustomLog filter is complete, here are a few ideas that you can use to further extend this filter.

- Add error handling and error logging

  As with CustomAuth, we have omitted a lot of important error checking and handling. Since an ISAPI filter can't pop up an information message in a dialog box, you'll probably want to write errors to the Windows NT application event log.

- Allocate a buffer pool

  Instead of allocating a buffer every time the log filter is called, allocate a pool of buffers when your filter starts. Each filter event can then grab a buffer from the pool, fill it, and give it back when it's done. Using a CMap MFC collection class would work well. This solution can greatly increase performance during the log event.

From Here...

As shown in this chapter, providing additional features to your Web site using ISAPI filters isn't hard. In fact, you can use the CustomAuth and CustomLog filters as a foundation for building additional functionality to your Web site. These two examples also touch on important concepts, such as thread safety and memory allocation, that you need to be familiar with when building your own custom filters.

While you are building these filters, check out the following chapters for reference and guidance:

- Chapter 9, "Building Extensions with MFC," shows you how to use the MFC ISAPI classes and the ISAPI Extension Wizard to build custom filters and extensions.

- Chapter 15, "Building Filters with MFC ISAPI Classes," illustrates the different events that an ISAPI filter can trap. See this chapter when deciding the best way to design your ISAPI filter.

- Chapter 17, "Troubleshooting and Debugging Extensions and Filters," provides insight and instruction when your ISAPI filter does not load or behave properly.

Advanced ISAPI Topics

Troubleshooting and Debugging Extensions and Filters

Developing ISAPI extensions and filters can be frustrating. Many of the debugging tips and tricks you've used in the past don't work for ISAPI. Even the most basic features of your debugger have to be changed or customized to step through your ISAPI code.

This chapter gives you tips, techniques, and debugging hints to build extensions and filters into your Web server. Even if you have built ISAPI applications in the past, this chapter gives you the insight to make future ISAPI applications solid, safe, and durable. ■

Common ISAPI Errors

Many problems with ISAPI filters and extensions can be traced back to a few common problems. For example, a filter that doesn't load is usually the result of incorrectly declaring the ISAPI functions or forgetting to put a few needed libraries in the search path of the server.

So before you go crazy trying to attach your debugging environment to your Web server, you may want to read this section to find out if you have forgotten something obvious.

Improperly Declaring Entry Points

Let's say you've just compiled a fancy ISAPI extension and put it into your scripts directory. You're all ready to try it out so you fire up your browser and enter the URL that should give you the results from your extension. Instead of your results, your browser gives you the message in Figure 17.1.

FIG. 17.1
A server message resulting from bad extension exports.

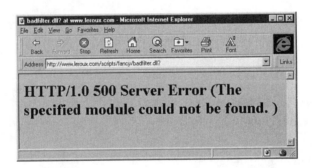

Maybe you've created an ISAPI filter. You've registered it and now you start your Web server. Everything seems okay since your Web server started, but you suddenly realize that your filter is not really loaded.

You check the Windows NT system event log and see the following message: The HTTP Filter DLL badfilter.dll failed to load. The data is the error. (By the way, you get a similar message when an ISAPI extension fails to load.)

Your Web server is trying to load your DLL but it can't find the function it is looking for. The function responsible for this error is usually GetExtensionVersion(), in the case of extensions, or GetFilterVersion(), in the case of filters.

This problem is usually in one (or more) of the following three categories:

- Improper calling convention used for your ISAPI entry point functions.
- Improper exportation of your ISAPI entry-point functions.
- Missing files that are needed by your ISAPI extension or filter.

Using the Wrong Calling Convention   One reason that your ISAPI extension or filter is not working may be your use of the wrong calling convention. Since the designers of ISAPI do not know the language your application will be programmed in, they must make a few assumptions about the way your function appears in your DLL.

The first assumption, the way parameters are expected on the stack, is provided to you in the function declarations in the ISAPI header files. Below are the two declarations for the DLL entry points of an ISAPI extension:

```
BOOL  WINAPI    GetExtensionVersion(HSE_VERSION_INFO  *pVer);
DWORD WINAPI    HttpExtensionProc(EXTENSION_CONTROL_BLOCK *pECB);
```

The keyword WINAPI is a macro expanded as stdcall. As you may have guessed, this is the default calling convention for all Win32 functions. See your handy compiler reference to learn more about how the stdcall calling convention puts parameters on the stack.

The only trick to calling conventions is when you are programming in C++. By default, C++ uses its own name decoration. Name decoration is the way a function is declared in the object file by the compiler before it is linked with the right library files.

Since Win32 functions use C, not C++, name decoration, you need to enclose your ISAPI entry-point functions with the extern "C" block. Therefore, the prototypes for an ISAPI extension when programming in C++ should look like this:

```
extern "C" {
BOOL  WINAPI    GetExtensionVersion(HSE_VERSION_INFO  *pVer);
DWORD WINAPI    HttpExtensionProc(EXTENSION_CONTROL_BLOCK *pECB);
}
```

Once you've declared your ISAPI entry points, your Web site should have no problem finding its functions.

Part

V

Ch

17

Forgetting to Export Your ISAPI Functions   Another common error that results in an extension giving your browser the "procedure not found" message or a filter not loading is when you forget to export your DLL's functions. Your compiler has not found any problems with the way you have declared your ISAPI entry-point functions.

But you have not told it that these functions should be visible to processes outside your library. Functions that are expected to be called from outside your library are called *exported* functions.

The normal way to export a function in C++ is to use the __declspec(dllexport) keyword in front of your function declaration. However, the ISAPI functions are already declared as __stdcall and the compiler won't let you have both.

The way around this is to export your functions using a .DEF file. This is the standard way of exporting functions from a library when programming in C. Listing 17.1 shows a typical .DEF file for an ISAPI extension. The function names after the EXPORTS keyword tell the linker to export these functions, no matter how they are declared.

Listing 17.1   LST17_1.DEF—Sample ISAPI Extension .DEF File

```
LIBRARY "Sample"

DESCRIPTION "Sample ISAPI Extension"

EXPORTS
      GetExtensionVersion
      HttpExtensionProc
```

After compiling and linking your ISAPI DLL, you may want to see if the two ISAPI entry-point functions have indeed been exported. Microsoft Visual C++ users can use the DUMPBIN.EXE utility in the \MSDEV\BIN directory.

Using the DUMPBIN myfilter.dll /EXPORTS command lists all the exported functions in the myfilter.dll library. The absence of your functions from the output of this program tell you that you have probably forgotten to include the .DEF file when linking your ISAPI DLL.

Missing Files Needed by Your ISAPI DLL   Another reason that your ISAPI extension or filter does not load may be that your library can't find dependent files. For instance, if you write an ISAPI filter that uses MFC, your filter automatically needs the runtime MFC DLLs.

Put all dependent files in the same directory as your extension or filter, or put them in the system32 directory. Older versions of Microsoft's Internet Information Server (IIS) used LoadLibrary() to load your extension or filter and would not search your DLL's path for any dependent libraries or files.

Version 3.0 of IIS uses LoadLibraryEx() with the LOAD_WITH_ALTERED_SEARCH_PATH flag. This causes the operating system to first search the directory of the loading library for any dependent files.

Improper file or directory permissions may also cause your DLL's load to fail. Remember that a thread running an ISAPI extension always impersonates an account on your system. Also remember that anonymous requests from a browser impersonate the default anonymous account on your Web server.

A thread running an ISAPI filter always runs under the context of the system account. Therefore, if your DLL is not loading, make sure your library, all dependent files, and the directory holding the files have the appropriate permissions.

One way to see if file or directory permissions are causing problems is to go into User Manager on your server (USRMGR.EXE), choose Policies, Audit, and select the Failure check box of File and Object Access, as shown in Figure 17.2.

FIG. 17.2
How to set audit policies in User Manager.

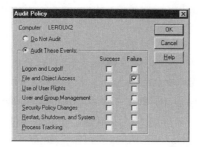

TIP Any process trying to access a file with insufficient security causes an event to appear in the Windows NT security event log. The error tells you which file is failing security and the user account that is trying to access it.

One last note: Any thread running under the security context of the system account has no privileges over the network. So make sure your filter DLL and all dependent files are located on the same machine as your Web server.

Improperly Registering a Filter

Let's say you know that your ISAPI filter has properly exported its ISAPI entry-point functions and that all dependent files your filter uses are in the search path. Now you want to register your ISAPI DLL with your Web server so that it loads when you restart your filter. You open the following registry key:

```
\HKEY_LOCAL_MACHINE\SYSTEM\CurrentControlSet\Services\W3SVC\
➡Parameters
```

You examine the `FilterDLLs` entry and see that there is already a filter DLL in this key. By default, the `sspifilt.dll` secured sockets filter is placed in this registry key when IIS is installed. Where should you put your filter?

Unfortunately, Microsoft did not make the `FilterDLLs` registry value of the `REG_MULTI_SZ` type (a multilined text entry). Therefore, you'll need to string your filter names together. How you delimit them makes a world of difference.

The bottom line is: separate file names in the `FilterDLLs` registry entry with a comma. Using anything else either causes only the first filter DLL to load or causes no filter DLLs to load. In either case, there is no entry in the Windows NT system event log explaining the problem.

NOTE Remember that the order in which you specify your DLLs in the registry makes a difference. Your Web server calls your filter DLLs using the `SF_NOTIFY_ORDER` specified in each filter's `GetFilterVersion()` function. Then it uses the order specified in this registry entry to determine the priority for DLLs that have the same `SF_NOTIFY_ORDER`.

To guarantee that your filter gets called first, use `SF_NOTIFY_ORDER_HIGH` and make sure it is the first DLL in the `FilterDLLs` list. Conversely, to guarantee that your filter gets called last, use `SF_NOTIFY_ORDER_LOW` and make sure it is the last DLL in the `FilterDLLs` list.

Programming Tips

Before you start coding your ISAPI extension or filter, you may want to read through this section to get a few tips and suggestions.

Since you probably do not have the source code to your Web server, you have to debug your ISAPI DLL using more creative methods. This section should give you a few ideas and some precautions you can take to minimize the amount of debugging you need to do later on in the development process.

Develop on the Same Machine as Your Web Server

Although this may be more of a debugging tip, I'm telling you this now to save you frustration later on. Before you start coding, make sure that your development machine is running Windows NT Server as well as Microsoft's IIS. This allows you to easily set up certain scenarios that may need phone calls to system administrators, or worse, long walks to other computers.

For example, you may want to change the security permissions for a particular document without affecting other Web users. Also, when you are developing ISAPI filters, you tend to take the server up and down a lot. Depending on your situation, this may be a nuisance for other users.

If you plan on doing a lot of database work, I'd recommend that you not place a development database server on your machine unless, of course, your production database will be on the same computer as your Web server. Most problems when you are developing against a database server on another computer have to do with security.

This is especially true if you are using Microsoft SQL Server with integrated security turned on. You can work out many of these problems early on if you start development with your database on another computer.

Although I probably already sound like a Microsoft salesman, I'll give you a piece of advice: You can buy from Microsoft the developer's network that gives you a "limited" version of BackOffice, including Windows NT Server and SQL Server.

This version usually limits you to a total of 10 server connections. But that should be plenty when you are testing your ISAPI applications. You can then effectively simulate the platform for which you are developing.

Use an Alternate Heap

I got this idea and a few others from a technical article in Microsoft's Knowledge-Base, which I recommend reading as a supplement to this chapter. The article is "Tips for Debugging ISAPI DLLs" and the Article ID is Q152054. You can get this article from Microsoft's Web site or from the Developer's Network CD.

Since all DLLs use the heap of the calling process (in this case, the Web server), a memory problem in your ISAPI extension or filter may seem to be coming from your Web server. For example, an error in your routine that fills a dynamically allocated character buffer may overwrite pieces of data used internally by your Web server.

These problems may go undetected for quite some time before you track them down. Tracking memory leaks in your ISAPI DLL is even harder since you can't step through your Web server's source code.

A good way to ensure that your ISAPI extension filter does not overwrite your Web server's heap is to create your own heap. Creating your own heap has the following advantages:

- Memory protection. When using its own heap, your DLL can't allocate memory in any other process's heap.

- Memory allocation size. A heap populated with classes or structures of identical size does not become fragmented.

- Memory allocation performance. Keeping frequently accessed objects in a small heap lessens the chances that the memory you are trying to access has been swapped out to the paging file.

Since you know your data needs best, you should decide how to manage them. If you are doing a lot of allocating and freeing of identically sized blocks of memory, you'll definitely want to create your own heap.

The Win32 `HeapCreate()` and `HeapDestroy()` functions, as their names imply, create and destroy a heap that is used only by your application. Once created, the `HeapAlloc()` and `HeapFree()`functions can be used to allocate and free memory in your new heap.

By default, all these heap functions are serialized. This means you don't have to worry about one thread allocating a block of memory in your heap while another thread is deleting it. The code behind these functions makes sure that this never happens.

Using your own heap also allows you to contain and detect memory leaks. You may find it advantageous to wrap the `HeapAlloc()` and `HeapFree()` functions with your own thread- safe functions that keep track of the amount of memory you have allocated. When your application terminates, you can check your heap size to see if you have forgotten to clean up any memory.

For those of you programming in C++, you can build new heap functions right into your classes. A class that is frequently allocated and deallocated is a good candidate for its own heap.

Your class keeps a pointer to its own heap in a private static data member. You override the `new` and `delete` operators to allocate memory in your class's own private heap.

Always remember that even though the Win32 heap functions are serialized, you still need to make your `new` and `delete` functions thread-safe. One tip is to have a static data member keep track of the number of instances of your class that are allocated, then put a debug message in the `destructor` to inform you of this value.

Remember that building "smart" memory allocation routines up-front may take you a bit of time. But it is well worth the effort when you are trying to nail down memory leaks in your ISAPI extension filter.

Always Check the Return Status

You should always check the return value of ISAPI functions (and of all Win32 functions). Almost all ISAPI functions return a TRUE or a FALSE, indicating their success. It is up to you, however, to call the Win32 `GetLastError()` function to retrieve the reason that the ISAPI function failed.

One of the more common ISAPI functions you'll call is `GetServerVariable()`. The pointer to this function is both the `EXTENSION_CONTROL_BLOCK` for ISAPI extensions and the `HTTP_FILTER_CONTEXT` for ISAPI filters.

Here is a list of possible error codes, as specified in `WINERROR.H`, that can be returned by `GetServerVariable()`:

■ `ERROR_INVALID_PARAMETER`

The pointer to either the control block or the filter context is invalid.

■ `ERROR_INVALID_INDEX`

The variable passed to `GetServerVariable()` does not exist. This variable was probably not supplied by the client.

■ `ERROR_INSUFFICIENT_BUFFER`

The buffer supplied to `GetServerVariable()` was not big enough and no attempt was made to fill it. The size of the needed buffer is passed back from the function in the `lpdwSize` parameter of `GetFilterVersion()`.

■ `ERROR_MORE_DATA`

The buffer supplied to `GetServerVariable()` was not big enough. The buffer was filled, but the size of the needed buffer is not returned.

■ `ERROR_NO_DATA`

The data requested is not available from the server. In other words, the variable exists but is not associated with any data.

C++ developers should take notice that although ISAPI functions do not throw their own exceptions, Microsoft's IIS does catch any exceptions that you may throw. If IIS catches an unhandled exception, it writes an error to the Windows NT application event log.

Be Thread-Aware

When writing ISAPI DLLs, you should always be aware that you are composing a multithreaded application. You need to protect all global and static data so that it is not corrupted by updates from separate threads.

Detecting problems from thread synchronization can be tricky. Most errors are not obvious and are hard to reproduce.

TIP

It is recommended that you stress-test all your applications with both an automated stress-testing tool and heavy user testing. To stress-test a multithreaded application, you probably need to write another multithreaded application. Spending a little time configuring a testing tool or building a custom stress-testing application is worth it in the long run.

The new Win32 Internet functions like `InternetOpen()` and `HttpOpenRequest()` make it easy to program custom tools that access your Web server. You may even find it worthwhile to build an application that takes a log file as input. Then open a variable number of threads to reproduce all the commands in the log.

Knowing when and where to provide thread synchronization may not be obvious at first. Here are a few hints for writing multithread-safe ISAPI extensions and filters:

Part
V

Ch
17

- ODBC (open database connectivity) API calls are multithread-safe, but the ODBC classes provided in MFC may not be. Only versions of MFC after 4.1 provide multithread-safe `CRecordset` and `CDatabase` classes. My recommendation, however, is to write all ODBC calls using the native ODBC API.

- Use critical sections to protect global and static data elements. The MFC `CCriticalSection`, `CSingleLock`, and `CMultiLock` classes offer easy ways to ensure that multiple threads do not concurrently access sections of your code.

- Watch out for container classes. Even if a container class is said to be thread-safe, it may take a few lines of code to add or delete an item from the container. Code that manipulates container classes should almost always be contained in critical sections.

- When writing filters, remember that the `pFilterContext` member of `HTTP_FILTER_CONTEXT` is there for you to use. This function makes it easier to program thread-safe code. If you are storing a copy of the `pServerContext` somewhere, you are probably doing something wrong.

After a bit of practice, programming a multithreaded application will become second nature. Remember, threads are your friends. When used properly, they can make your application much more efficient. For more information on thread safety, see Chapter 18, "Making Your Extensions Thread-Safe."

Debugging Extensions and Filters

The hardest thing about writing any DLL is debugging. You might even say that debugging an ISAPI DLL is twice as hard as debugging any other DLL.

The following problems come to mind when debugging an ISAPI filter or extension:

- You probably do not have access to the Web server's source code. So you may not be able to understand all of its nuances and stepping into your code using a debugger becomes a chore.

- Since ISAPI filters and extensions execute under a different security context from your development environment, you will undoubtedly run into problems with file and directory permissions.

- Even though ISAPI DLLs are designed to run on remote machines, you have to put your development environment on the same machine as your server. This can be a problem if you are designing in one operating system (Windows 95) but running your DLL in another (Windows NT Server).

- ISAPI DLLs have no window or desktop. You have to write error messages and debug information to more creative destinations.

In this section, I describe a number of different techniques to help you with development and debugging. Following them will save you many hours of frustration.

Turning Off Extension Caching

When debugging an ISAPI extension, the first thing you want to do is to turn off extension caching. By default, Microsoft's IIS constantly analyzes the usage of ISAPI extensions.

If the server determines that a particular extension is called frequently, it keeps the extension in memory. This is great for performance but bad for debugging.

To have IIS unload your DLL after every call, open the registry key:

```
HKEY_LOCAL_MACHINE\SYSTEM\CurrentControlSet\Services\W3SVC\
➥Parameters
```

The CacheExtensions registry is by default set to 1, which means all ISAPI extension DLLs can be cached. Change this setting to 0 when you are debugging an ISAPI extension.

Do not leave this value set to 0 for your production Web server. If you do, you'll have a severe performance penalty as your filter is constantly loaded, unloaded, and reloaded. Obviously, this wouldn't be much better than writing a CGI application.

Running IIS Interactively

Normally, when you debug a DLL, you can inform your development environment of the executable that will be calling your DLL. Then, when you debug your DLL, the development environment runs the executable and stops at any break points you have put in the DLL.

The trouble with this scenario is obvious. The process that calls your ISAPI DLL is not a "normal" executable. It is a service. The difference between running an application as a service and running an application from the command line of a user account is as follows:

■ A service normally runs under the local system account. The system account has no user context and usually has no authority over the network. It does, however, have special privileges on the local computer that allow it to access parts of the operating system that are off limits to user accounts.

When running as a service, Microsoft's IIS can only run under the local system account. This cannot be changed.

■ A service does not have a desktop. This means that message boxes and windows generated by a process running under the local system account are not displayed. Although you can change this behavior so that the local system account interacts with the currently logged-on desktop, it's usually better to display output using a different method.

I mentioned earlier that when running as a service, Microsoft's IIS must use the local system account. This is true. But you can also run the server from the command line of a logged-in account. Great! Then it should be no problem to debug your DLL without leaving the development environment, right?

By now you should know that things are not that easy. First, we'll explain a couple of ways you can do this. Then we'll show you a few problems with running Microsoft's IIS interactively.

Part
V

Ch
17

Configuring Visual C++ for Local Debugging   Running Microsoft's IIS from the Visual C++ development environment or from the command shell is easy. Begin by setting certain permissions on the user account that will be running the server.

Users in the administrator group by default have all the necessary user rights except two. You need to make sure that the two advanced user rights listed below are set before you try to run the service from your account. You set the check box marked Show Advanced User Rights to make these settings visible in User Manager.

The two advanced user rights allow the user to

- Act as Part of the Operating System
- Generate Security Audits

Once these advanced user rights are set, your account should have the permissions to run Microsoft's IIS. If you are logged into an account that is affected by these changes, you need to log off and log back on for these changes to take effect.

Next, you need to tell the Visual C++ development environment which executable should be run to invoke your DLL. To do this, go into the Build, Settings dialog box.

Select the Debug property sheet and enter the path to your inetinfo.exe file in the Executable for debug session: edit box. Enter the -e W3SVC string in the Program Arguments edit box.

Figure 17.3 shows the settings to run IIS on my machine for interactive debugging.

N O T E   The inetinfo.exe application is usually installed in the inetsvc directory. This executable is just a stub program that loads the appropriate Internet service. By specifying the -e W3SVC string on the command line, you are telling the inetinfo application to load only the Web server. The inetinfo application loads the W3SVC.DLL library, which holds the HTTP service.

FIG. 17.3
Debug options for running IIS interactively.

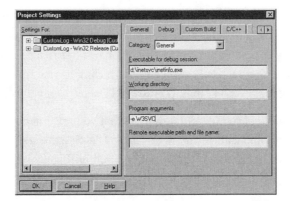

Of course, you should also make sure that your Web server is loading your debugged image. If you are writing a filter, the FilterDLL's registry setting should point to the DLL in your development directory.

If you are writing an extension, the logical path that the browser is accessing must map to the physical path of the development directory holding your DLL. If this is not possible, see "Attaching the Debugger to the Service" later in this chapter.

Before you start the debugger, you should also make sure that all services started by the inetinfo application (Web server, ftp server, and gopher server) are not running. Since this involves stopping the Web server, debugging your extension interactively may not be suitable for your test environment.

You can now put break points in your code and execute the debugger from within the Visual C++ development environment with the normal Build, Debug, Go menu command. It may take a few seconds for your debugger to start the Web server and load your DLL, its symbols, and all the dependent files.

Configuring Visual C++ for Remote Debugging   Remote debugging is like local debugging. The only difference is that your debugger sends data to the debugged process over the network via the TCP/IP protocol. So you need an application supplied with Visual C++ for debugging tasks, such as starting and stopping the application, on the remote computer.

The advantage of remote debugging is that your development environment can be on a separate machine from your Web server. You can develop on a computer running Windows 95, copy your ISAPI extension or filter to a remote Windows NT server, and debug your application without having to visit the server. This is great for those of you who can't run a Windows NT server on your desktop.

The disadvantage of remote debugging is that you are still running the Web server as an interactive application and not as a service. See the section "Potential Problems" to learn what problems arise out of running IIS as an interactive application.

Since there are quite a few steps in setting up a remote debugging session, I break it into two sections: configuring the remote computer and configuring the local (development) computer.

Setting Up the Remote Computer

1. Make sure that you have stopped all services using the inetinfo application (Web server, ftp server, and gopher server).

2. Make sure that the DLL you are going to debug and all dependent files are on the remote computer. You should never tell IIS to load an ISAPI filter or extension that is on another computer.

3. You need an administrator account to be logged on to the remote computer. This account must have the Act as Part of the Operating System and Generate Security Audits advanced user rights, as described in the section "Configuring Visual C++ for Local Debugging." If you make a change to user rights, make sure that your account logs off and logs back on before you continue.

4. Copy the following files from your local machine into a directory on the remote machine:

   MSVCMON.EXE

   MSVCRT40.DLL (or the appropriate runtime library for MSVC++)

   TLN0COM.DLL

   TLN0T.DLL

   DMN0.DLL

5. Run the MSVCMON.EXE application that you just copied on the remote computer. Choose the Network (TCP/IP) setting as shown in Figure 17.4 and press the Settings button.

FIG. 17.4

The Visual C++ debug monitor.

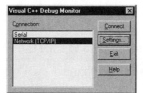

6. When prompted for the remote machine name as shown in Figure 17.5, enter either the host name or the IP address of the local (development) machine. You can also enter an optional password that prevents unauthorized access to your debugged process.

Pressing the Connect button from the MSVCMON main dialog box causes the remote computer to start "listening" for debugging instructions. You must now instruct the development debugger to communicate with the remote machine. Since the MSVCMON application controls the debugging process on the remote machine, the account currently executing this program must remain logged in.

Part

V

Ch

17

FIG. 17.5

TCP/IP Settings for Remote Debugging.

Setting Up the Local Computer

1. Start the Microsoft Visual C++ development environment. Choosing the menu option Tools, Remote Connection brings up a dialog box similar to the one shown in Figure 17.4. Choose TCP/IP, and then choose the Settings button. Now enter the host name or IP address of the remote computer. If you need a password to connect to the remote debugging process, enter that too.

2. Next, select the Build, Settings menu option and choose the Debug property sheet. A dialog box appears similar to Figure 17.3. Fill out the dialog box as follows:

- Executable for Debug Session

  Enter the path to the inetinfo.exe application in relation to your own machine. In other words, you probably need a network share. Enter the path relative to that share in this edit box.

- Program Arguments

  Enter **-e W3SVC** to instruct inetinfo to start the Web server.

- Remote Executable Path and File Name

  Enter the path to inetinfo.exe in relation to the remote computer. If the remote computer has this application on the "c" drive, you would most likely enter c:\inetsvc\inetinfo.exe.

3. From the same dialog box and property sheet, change the drop-down list box labeled Category to Additional DLLs. If you are set up for remote debugging, this dialog box should look like Figure 17.6. In the edit box captioned Local Name, enter the path and file name to your ISAPI DLL on the local machine.

FIG. 17.6

Additional DLLs for remote debugging.

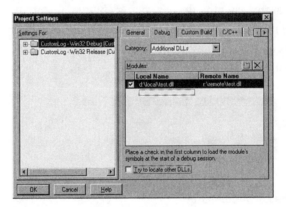

In the edit box captioned Remote Name, enter the path and file name to your ISAPI DLL on the remote machine. Make sure you clear the check box labeled Try to Locate Other DLLs.

4. Now put in your break points and start the debugger. The local debugger tells the remote debugger to start the process. Whenever a break point occurs in the remote process, the local debugger is told. Stopping the local debugger stops the process being debugged on the remote machine.

Setting up remote debugging can be a hassle at first. But once set up, it is a power-ful tool that allows you to debug from different operating systems on different computers. Now that I've explained how to interactively debug Microsoft's IIS, I'll discuss a few problems that may make you think twice about debugging this way.

Potential Problems   There are a couple of problems with running Microsoft's IIS interactively. Running the Web server from the command line is close to but not exactly like running the Web server on the local system account.

First off, you are running your Web server on an account that is different from the one normally used. Your account may have permissions to access a file, whereas the local system account does not.

This is especially true for network connections. Since the local system account has no authority over the network, it can't access files that are not on the local computer.

ODBC data sources are another tricky area. Since ODBC data sources by default are registered for a specific user, your Web server has access to that data source when running interactively but not when running as a service.

You can easily rectify this by specifying that your ODBC data source be set up as a System data source. Notice the button on the bottom of Figure 17.7, which is la-beled System DSN. This sets up a data source that any user, including the local system account, can use.

Part
V

Ch
17

FIG. 17.7
Notice the System
DSN button.

The Microsoft KnowledgeBase also says that authentication filters do not work properly when you run IIS interactively this way. Although I have had success debugging an authentication filter this way, I would nevertheless be wary about running IIS from your account to debug authentication filters.

Since there are probably a few other quirks that you'll only discover when running IIS as a service, I recommend that you do the initial phase of your development using interactive debugging. Then start attaching your debugger to the inetinfo application (see the next section) as the development process for your DLL winds down. This ensures that your development environment closely mirrors that of a production system.

Attaching the Debugger to the Service

As I have just discussed, running your Web server interactively from the debugger is a quick way to step through your ISAPI extension or filter DLL. Debugging this way, however, does not provide a real-life representation of how your Web server works.

To closely mimic a "production" system, have your Web server running as a service when you debug your code. The Win32 API and today's debuggers offer simple ways to debug an application that is executing.

In the next few sections, I describe how to use tools provided with the operating system, Visual C++, and assembly code to debug a running process. Each method attaches the debugger to a particular process and yields control to your debugger whenever a thread hits a break point in your code. The only requirement for this type of debugging is that your Web server be running on the same machine as your debugger.

Since the first two methods involve first starting your Web server and then attaching the debugger to the Web server process, it is impractical for debugging a filter's GetFilterVersion() function. This function is called before the Web server finishes its initialization. You have to use the third debugging method, hardcoding break points, to debug a filter's GetFilterVersion() function.

All the following debugging methods allow you to step through your source code as your code is executed. A debugger can do this only after your linker generates a program database file (.PDB file).

This file cross-references your DLL's executable code with lines of source code. It also lets you keep track of variables and the call stack. The file usually needs to reside in the same directory as your DLL.

Using *TASKMGR* The first method for attaching your debugger to your Web server's process uses the Task Manager application supplied with Windows NT version 4.0. The Task Manager takes care of starting your debugger and attaching the process.

First, start your Web server. Next, run the Task Manager application (TASKMGR.EXE is in the Windows NT system32 directory) and select the Processes property sheet. You see a list of all processes that are executing on your machine. Right-clicking the inetinfo.exe application shows you a pop-up menu. Task Manager should now look like Figure 17.8.

FIG. 17.8
Using Task Manager to debug inetinfo.exe.

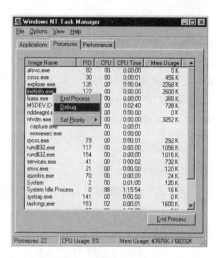

Choosing the Debug menu command launches your debugger and attaches the inetinfo.exe application to it. After your debugger has started, you can load your ISAPI DLL's source file and put break points in your code.

The debugger monitors the running process and pauses when it reaches a break point. If you have trouble setting break points, you may want to try one of the following:

- In the Build, Settings, Debug property sheet of the Visual C++ development environment, choose Additional DLLs from the Category drop-down list box. Then enter the path to your ISAPI DLL in the Local Name edit box.

- Use the hardcoding break-points debugging solution described in this chapter. This involves placing lines of code that tell the operating system you have hit a break point.

Note that once the debugger is attached to your Web server's process, there is no way to detach it short of stopping the server. This is usually not a problem, but keep it in mind when you have several people using your test Web server.

Running *MSDEV*   Another alternative for attaching the debugger to the Web server process is to use the Microsoft Visual C++ development environment executable command-line parameters. Starting with Visual C++ 4.0, the development environment executable is MSDEV.EXE and is found by default in the \MSDEV\BIN directory. The command-line parameter -p is an undocumented switch that tells the development environment to attach to a certain process.

The syntax is

```
MSDEV -p pid
```

where *pid* is the process ID for the process you want to debug. This can be in decimal format (for instance, 155) or in hexadecimal format (for instance, 0x9B). When debugging ISAPI extensions or filters, you need to get the process ID of the inetinfo.exe application using one of the following tools:

■ Task Manager (TASKMGR.EXE)

This utility is supplied with Windows NT 4.0. Tabbing to the Process property sheet lists all executing processes and the associated process ID in decimal format.

■ Process Viewer (PVIEW.EXE)

The Process Viewer utility is supplied with Visual C++. It is also supplied in the Windows NT 3.5 and 3.51 resource kit. This utility, too, gives you a list of active processes. The process ID is the hexadecimal number in parentheses next to the inetinfo.exe application.

■ TLIST (TLIST.EXE)

This command-line application is in the Windows NT 3.5 and 3.51 resource kit. It lists each active process and process ID.

Once you start MSDEV using the -p command line argument, the development environment attaches itself to the inetinfo.exe application. You can now open your source code files and put in break points. If your break points are not triggering, read the preceding section about entering your DLL file name in the development environment.

You may also find it useful to know that attaching the Microsoft Visual C++ development environment generates an .MDP file for every debugged application. For instance, attaching the debugger to inetinfo.exe creates the inetinfo.mdp file.

This file holds development environment information, including a list of source code files that have been opened, break points in these files, and project settings. If you save the .MDP file after you attach your debugger to the process, it loads automatically whenever you debug the same application.

Hardcoding Break Points   When all other alternatives to debugging have failed, you can always count on hardcoding a break-point statement into your code. This is not a flexible solution, because you obviously can't place a new break point while the code is executing. But it's guaranteed to work.

Just put the following line into your source code:

```
#ifdef _DEBUG
  #define DEBUG_BREAK _asm int 3
#else
  #define DEBUG_BREAK
#endif
```

Now all you need to do when you want to hardcode a break point into your application is to put the DEBUG_BREAK keyword into your code. If you are running in debug mode, this embeds the int 3 assembly language command into your application.

When executed, this command causes software interrupt 3. When the operating system learns that this interrupt has occurred, Windows NT pops up the dialog box shown in Figure 17.9.

FIG. 17.9

Entering the debugger from a user break-point dialog box.

Pressing the OK button halts the Web server process. But pressing the Cancel button from this dialog box invokes your debugger and attaches it to the Web server process. If everything is configured properly, your debugger should put the cursor directly on the DEBUG_BREAK line in your source code file.

N O T E In case you were browsing through the Win32 reference and noticed the `DebugBreak()` function, forget about it. Using the `DebugBreak()` function from your ISAPI extension does indeed stop execution of the Web server.

But the debugger thinks that the break occurred in the operating system kernel and not in your source code. Therefore, you won't able to look at variables or the call stack of your DLL. Stick with the method outlined in this section. ▨

Running ISAPI Extensions and Filters by Hand

You may want to debug your ISAPI extension or filter without using a Web server or a browser for two reasons:

- Debugging ease

  As shown earlier in this chapter, debugging an ISAPI DLL is not easy. It would be nice if your ISAPI extension were called from an application that you control and not from a Web service.

- Customization

  Writing an application to call your ISAPI extension gives you control over the client header variables and server variables that are passed into your extension. For instance, if your extension does different tasks depending on the browser used by the client, you can "fake" this information to see how your extension reacts.

  You can also easily send all output from your extension to a destination other than the browser. For example, you may want output data sent to a file or to a window.

In this section, I give you a few hints on writing your own stub application. I also talk about the one provided with this book: EyeSAPI. I am sure you'll find that developing ISAPI extensions is much easier when you can control all input to your application via a stub application.

Writing a Stub Application   There are quite a few things to consider before you write a stub application. For instance, your stub application must have the same interface as your Web server. Return codes must be the same, functions must be the same, and the function-calling sequence must be the same as your Web server's.

N O T E Writing a stub application for an ISAPI filter is harder than writing one for an extension. ISAPI filters are called with a "filter context" to achieve a browser session. Remember that the filter entry point is called numerous times during one browser request.

This means that your filter may depend on the calling process (normally the Web server but in this case the stub program) to keep state information that is consistent between function calls. Also, ISAPI filters have data parameters that are passed into the filter entry point. These parameters are associated with the notification type. ■

You'll be writing an application that does the following:

- Load library. Your stub application maps your ISAPI DLL to its own address space by calling the LoadLibrary() function.

- Fill data structures. Your application needs to populate the appropriate data structures: either HTTP_FILTER_CONTEXT and its associated filter data for filters or EXTENSION_CONTROL_BLOCK for extensions.

  You have to provide your own functions for the callback functions in both of these structures. Remember that your use of these functions must be exactly the same as your Web server's!

- Call DLL function. You call the filter or extension entry-point function with your data structure(s) passed as parameters.

- Capture results. The results of the function should be put in a log file or written to a window.

- Unload library. Use the FreeLibrary() function to unload your ISAPI DLL.

Only after you have programmed all these steps into an executable (and debugged it) can you finally debug your ISAPI application. Was it worth it? Probably not. Don't you wish this was already done for you? Probably yes.

Well, the EyeSAPI application on the CD-ROM does exactly what I described above for ISAPI extensions. For now, you need to debug ISAPI filters using the methods discussed earlier in this chapter, or use your own stub application.

Using EyeSAPI The EyeSAPI application gives you an alternate interface to your ISAPI extension. Testing different browser scenarios against your ISAPI extension is easy since all browser header fields can be manipulated directly from the EyeSAPI application. Once you start EyeSAPI, the main dialog box looks like Figure 17.10.

FIG. 17.10
The EyeSAPI
application.

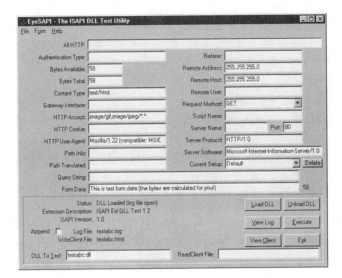

As you can see, many edit boxes allow you to customize the call to your extension. Using EyeSAPI allows you to simulate almost any type of browser action that your extension is faced with. Specifically, you can:

■ Enter header contents

There is an edit box for every standard Hypertext Transport Protocol (HTTP) client header. You can easily change pieces of data such as User-Agent from the EyeSAPI main dialog box.

■ Simulate different actions

You can simulate either a GET or a POST action. You can enter data into the query string and into the form data for each respective action. The size of your form data is automatically calculated for you and sent to your application.

■ Log output to a file

Two output files are generated by EyeSAPI. One consists of the HTML output by your ISAPI extension. The other is a log file that gives you results from all functions requested from your extension.

Providing Debug Output from Your DLL

As a developer, you often output variables and messages that tell you the status of your application. While your application runs in debug mode, it might be a good idea to dump the contents of things like collection classes, or to print messages when objects are allocated or deallocated.

This proactive debugging reduces the amount of time you spend doing just-in-time debugging. And as I've already emphasized in this chapter, debugging an ISAPI DLL using a just-in-time debugger can be a real hassle.

You may also need to communicate errors and informational messages to whoever will be maintaining your ISAPI DLL. For instance, a user should be notified of memory exceptions or error results returned by your Web server.

Since your ISAPI extension or filter is loaded by a process without a desktop, much less a main window, finding ways to output messages can be quite a challenge. The three places where you may want to put messages relating to the status of your ISAPI DLL are log files, a debug window, and the Windows NT application event log.

Depending on the type of message, you'll probably want to display the output at a different destination. Table 17.1 gives you a guideline for the best place to output your information.

Table 17.1   Appropriate Places to Write ISAPI Informational Messages

Message Type	Log File	Debug Window	Event Log
Debug Messages	X		X
Object/Variable Dumps	X		
Status Messages	X	X	X
Error Messages			X

In the rest of this section I explain some of the advantages and disadvantages of using each output type.

Part

V

Ch

17

Writing to a Log File The obvious place to write debugging information and messages is to a log file. I'm sure you're familiar with opening up a log file and appending messages to it using commands like `fopen` and `fprintf`. A log file may seem like a great place to write messages. But it has two problems: serialization and location.

■ Serialization

The problem with log files is that there is only one of them. Things get messy when multiple threads are writing to the same file. You can overcome such problems with thread synchronization, but do this only when you have no other place to log information.

■ Location

Writing important messages to a log file hides the significance of the message. For example, if you write a message to log file when your ISAPI extension can't allocate enough memory for a certain operation, you or a system administrator don't see such a message until the file is opened and inspected.

This message should probably be written to the Windows NT application event log where it would be more easily noticed. The event log should be your central repository for administrative messages.

Although you probably shouldn't be writing messages to files in a production system, it is a great time-saver to write messages to files for debug information. For instance, a failed assertion should not pop up a dialog box in your ISAPI extension. Since a failed assertion would never happen in a release version of your code, you may not want to write it to the Windows NT event log but to write such events to a debug file.

Another good candidate for file logging is an object dump. If you dump the contents of a container class whenever an item is added or deleted, you probably want this information in a file.

Displaying Info in a Debug Window The next best thing to writing information to a file is to write it to a debug window. Notice that when I say *window*, I don't mention whose window.

Since you're aware that ISAPI extensions and filters are loaded by a process that does not own a window, you need to write to the window of another process. Fortunately, the Win32 API gives you functions to do this.

The Win32 OutputDebugString() function is declared as follows:

```
VOID OutputDebugString(LPCTSTR lpOutputString);
```

The *lpOutputString* is a pointer to a string, which, as you've probably guessed, holds the message to be displayed in a debug window. What is a debug window, you ask? It's an application that waits for certain operating system events indicating that another process has generated a debug message.

The debug window application gets the string for this message from the operating system and displays it in a window. The debugger provided with most compilers has the same function.

But you probably don't have your development environment on every test Web server. Luckily, the DBMON application supplied in the Win32 SDK has the same function. The DBMON application looks like a "blank" console application until a another process calls the OutputDebugString() function.

When this happens, DBMON displays the ID of the process that generated the message, followed by the text of the message. Figure 17.11 shows how DBMON displays the messages generated by my authentication filter.

Using the OutputDebugString() function is a simple way to have your application display debug messages—without running your ISAPI extension or filter in the debugger.

FIG. 17.11

Sample debug output from DBMON.EXE.

Recording to the Windows NT Application Event Log   By far the best destination for displaying informational messages to an administrator or Web server operator is the Windows NT event log. Writing to the event log is harder than writing to a file. But you get these benefits:

- Remote access

    You can connect to the Windows NT event log from remote computers via RPC. Win32 functions allow you to open a remote event log. Or you can use your event viewer to open a remote computer's event log.

- Central repository

    All informational and error messages generated by your ISAPI application are stored in a central location. Most Windows NT applications, including Microsoft's IIS, write messages to the event log. Since the first place anyone looks when your Web server starts acting strangely is the event log, you're best off writing error messages there.

- Secure access

    You can write events that can be viewed only by administrators of your Web server.

- Management

    You can set up the Windows event log to grow to a certain size before it starts to overwrite itself. You no longer need to contend with 100-M log files.

The only downside to writing to the Windows NT event log is setting up your messages. Although Microsoft created the Win32 event log functions for portability and internationalization, setting up the messages to put into the log is a hassle at first.

You might think that you can use the `RegisterEventSource()` and `ReportEvent()` functions right out of the box. But you need to do the following first:

1. Register your application. Update the EventLog registry settings to register your application with the event log. Registering tells the event log which application (or DLL) holds the event messages.

2. Build the message file. Enter all messages your application will display into a message resource file. Don't confuse this resource with the string resource: They are two different things. A message file is usually compiled separately from the rest of your resources.

3. Include the message file. The resulting compiled message file should be included in your application's .RC file. Many large applications build a resource library that holds only messages.

Only after you do these steps can you start writing to the Windows NT event log. You'll want to refer to the Win32 and message compiler documentation to learn the exact steps.

From Here...

The goal of this chapter is to give you information that makes the development of an ISAPI extension or filter easier. Some of the information in this chapter took days to figure out. Let's hope that these are debugging tips and techniques that you would normally only learn from trial and error.

From here, you can explore the following chapters to learn more about ISAPI extensions and filters:

- Chapter 10, "Extending Your Web Server with Extensions," supplies code you can reference when writing your own ISAPI extension.

- Chapter 16, "Extending Your Web Server with Filters," supplies code you can reference when writing an ISAPI filter.

- Chapter 18, "Making Your Extensions Thread-Safe," gives you valuable insight into one of the more difficult areas of ISAPI development: thread safety.

Making Your Extensions Thread-Safe

The Internet Information Server (IIS) can serve multiple client requests simultaneously. If the IIS were not able to handle multiple clients simultaneously, users of your Web site would have severe delays when accessing the information they need.

ISAPI (Internet Server Application Programming Interface) extensions must also be able to handle requests from multiple clients simultaneously. This allows clients faster access to information and prevents user frustration. IIS and other information servers that support ISAPI extensions can handle multiple clients, in part, because of the multithreading capabilities of Windows NT.

At this point you may be asking yourself why you need to know about threads if you are writing an

What threads are and how threads enhance the performance of ISAPI extensions

The information server creates separate threads for clients using your extensions.

How Windows NT schedules threads for execution

The Win32 Software Development Kit (SDK) provides functions that allow you to alter the priority of your thread.

How to use critical sections in your ISAPI extensions

A critical section is a Win32 synchronization object that protects resources from being simultaneously accessed from multiple threads.

How to use Windows NT synchronization mechanisms to protect access to shared resources

The Win32 API provides a variety of objects that can be used for synchronization, including semaphores, events, and mutexes.

ISAPI extension. After all, the server simply calls your extension with input data and you return the correct output.

The answer is simple: You don't know how a server handles client requests. So you must protect common resources and information from being changed or accessed by simultaneous requests.

A server can handle separate client requests by different threads of execution. This means that your extension may be called from multiple places at the same time. Your extension must provide safeguards for thread synchronization to prevent data corruption.

N O T E To illustrate the use of thread synchronization and creating multiple threads in an ISAPI extension, we look at the lottery extension provided as part of the ISAPI developers SDK. The complete source code and make files for the extension are on the accompanying CD-ROM in the CHAP18 directory.

The lottery extension provides clients with a lucky lottery number. This example shows how to create a thread, and how to use critical sections and semaphores to provide synchronized access to the extension's resources.

What Are Threads?

A *thread* is a path of code execution in a process. When a process such as a server is initialized, the operating system creates a primary thread for the process. The primary thread continues until the process ends.

N O T E A *process* is an executable program. This is typically an *.exe file. Although tasking in Windows NT is controlled at the thread level, the process has a main thread of execution when started. This main thread can then start other threads as needed.

A process may need to start other threads that handle specific tasks to increase the performance of the application. For example, a server might handle each client request in a separate thread. This allows each client to access the Web sites without being affected by requests from other clients.

Threads are an important concept because the Windows NT operating system schedules code for execution on a thread basis. Each thread is scheduled for execution according to its class and priority.

In a preemptive operating system like Windows NT, each thread is guaranteed CPU time. This is in direct contrast to Windows 3.x in which the multitasking capabilities depend on the cooperation of each running process.

Threads can increase the performance of your applications and the use of your CPU. But you need a thorough understanding of threads and the new errors that can result from faulty design. Otherwise, threads can make a software engineer's life very hard.

How Windows NT Schedules Threads

Windows NT schedules threads based on priority levels. Each thread is assigned a priority level. Priority levels range from 0 (lowest) to 31 (highest).

Part

V

Ch

18

N O T E   A thread cannot be assigned a priority level of 0, even though 0 is a valid priority level. This is because priority level 0 is assigned to a special thread called the *zero page* thread.

The zero page thread is responsible for zeroing free pages in memory. Since the zero page thread is at priority level 0, it only runs when no other threads are executing. ■

Figure 18.1 illustrates these concepts.

NT segments each thread according to its priority level. All threads in a priority level are treated equally. The Windows NT scheduler starts by assigning all level-31 threads to the CPU.

After each level-31 thread executes, if there are no more level-31 threads waiting to execute, the level-30 threads are assigned. This assignment continues through all thread levels until the scheduler reaches level 0. Then the process starts back at level 31.

If, during the progression down the thread priority levels, a higher-priority thread than the one currently running needs to run, it immediately interrupts the currently executing thread and starts running. For example, if a level-20 thread is executing but a level-25 thread needs to execute, the level-20 thread is suspended and the level-25 thread starts executing.

FIG. 18.1

The Process Viewer can be used to show the relative thread class and thread priorities of any thread in a Win32 process.

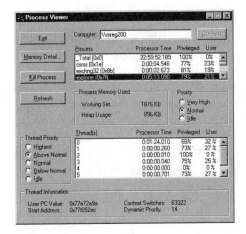

At first the scheduling algorithm may seem unfair. In fact, it may even look as if thread starvation could set in. But the reality is that threads do not need to run very often.

For example, a server may be sitting idle waiting for client requests most of the time. User interface threads sit idle unless messages are placed in the processes queue.

Windows NT also places applications in a sleep state. For example, when an application calls GetMessage to get its messages, if the message queue is empty, the application is put in an efficient sleep state.

N O T E   Thread starvation occurs when a thread never gets a time slice from the processor. In other words, the thread never executes. Windows NT scheduling guarantees that starvation never occurs.   ▪

Thread Priority Classes   Windows NT does not allow you to change a thread's priority based on the priority levels discussed in the previous section. Instead, a thread's priority level is set by a two-step classification.

The first step is to assign a priority class to a process. Windows NT compares the priority class of each process in the system. The second step is to assign relative priority levels to each thread owned by the process.

The Win32 API allows four priority classes: Idle, Normal, High, and Realtime. Table 18.1 shows the priority classes and the default thread priority level for each class.

Table 18.1   Win32 Default Thread Priority Level

Priority Class	Priority Level
Idle	4
Normal	7 – 9
High	13
Realtime	24

The default thread priority level is assigned to each thread created in the process.

The Normal priority class has a default priority level shown as a range of 7 to 9 rather than a definite level like the other priority classes. This is because the priority class for normal processes can be changed depending on the tasking mode of the NT computer. As shown in Figure 18.2, the user can set the tasking mode of normal processes.

To change the performance of Windows NT applications, do the following:

1. Select Control Panel from the Settings option of the Windows NT Start menu.
2. Select the System icon from the Control Panel.
3. Choose the Performance tab from the System Properties dialog box.
4. Adjust the Application Performance slider to the proper positions and click the OK button when finished.

Use these guidelines to change the thread priority of normal Windows NT processes:

- Positioning the Application Performance slider in the Maximum position provides the best foreground-application response time. This means that normal processes running in the foreground have a thread priority level of 9.

- Positioning the slider in the Middle position makes the foreground application more responsive than background applications. This means that normal processes running in the foreground have a thread priority level of 8.

Part
V

Ch
18

■ Positioning the slider to the None position causes foreground and background applications to be equally responsive. This means that normal processes in the foreground have a thread priority level of 7.

■ For machines such as a Windows NT server running the IIS, positioning the Application Performance slider at the None position yields the best results because all processes have equal access to the CPU.

FIG. 18.2

Changing the thread priority level of normal Windows NT processes.

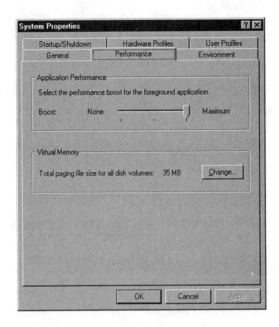

Most processes, including IIS, run at normal priority. Normal priority level provides the best overall results for system performance.

A process can change its priority class through the SetPriorityClass function. The prototype for this function is shown in Listing 18.1.

Listing 18.1   Prototype for the *SetPriorityClass* Function

```
#define NORMAL_PRIORITY_CLASS      0x00000020
#define IDLE_PRIORITY_CLASS        0x00000040
#define HIGH_PRIORITY_CLASS        0x00000080
#define REALTIME_PRIORITY_CLASS    0x00000100
BOOL SetPriorityClass( HANDLE hProcess, DWORD fdwPriority );
```

The `SetPriorityClass` function takes two parameters. The first is the handle of the process whose priority you are going to change. The second is the priority class that the process is being changed to. All the priority class definitions are shown on the accompanying CD.

Thread Priority Levels   When a thread is created, it gets the default priority level in the class it is assigned to. For a process in the idle priority class, the default priority level is 4. You can change the priority of a thread through the `SetThreadPriority` function. The prototype of this function is

```
BOOL SetThreadPriority( HANDLE hThread, int nPriority);
```

The first parameter, `hThread`, is the handle of the thread to be changed. The second parameter, `nPriority`, can be one of the values shown in Table 18.2.

Table 18.2   Priority Values and What They Mean

nPriority Values	Description
THREAD_PRIORITY_LOWEST	Changes the thread's priority level to 2 less than the priority class default.
THREAD_PRIORITY_BELOW_NORMAL	Changes the thread's priority level to 1 less than the priority class default.
THREAD_PRIORITY_NORMAL	Changes the thread's priority level to the priority class default.
THREAD_PRIORITY_ABOVE_NORMAL	Changes the thread's priority level to 1 more than the priority class default.
THREAD_PRIORITY_HIGHEST	Changes the thread's priority level to 2 more than the priority class default.
THREAD_PRIORITY_IDLE	Changes the thread's priority level to 1 unless the process priority class is realtime. If the process priority class is realtime, the thread's priority level is set to 16.
THREAD_PRIORITY_TIME_CRITICAL	Changes the thread's priority level to 15 unless the process priority class is realtime. If the process priority class is realtime, the thread's priority level is set to 31.

Part
V

Ch
18

You are probably wondering how Windows NT uses priority levels when the
Win32 API deals with process priority classes and relative thread priority levels.
Table 18.3 shows a mapping of the process priority class and relative thread prior-
ity level to the Windows NT priority level.

Table 18.3   How Windows NT Determines a Thread's Priority Level

Relative Thread Priority	Idle	Normal, in Background	Normal, in Foreground (Boost+1)	Normal, in Foreground (Boost+2)	High	Real-time
Time Critical	15	15	15	15	15	31
Highest	6	9	10	11	15	26
Above Normal	5	8	9	10	14	25
Normal	4	7	8	9	13	24
Below Normal	3	6	7	8	12	23
Lowest	2	5	6	7	11	22
Idle	1	1	1	1	1	16

Rather than limiting a thread to the 32 priority levels, the priority class/level
mechanism provides logical performance barriers that can be used to affect the
performance of applications and threads.

From Table 18.3, we can see that the process priority class directly affects the
thread's absolute priority level. For a thread running at the normal priority level,
the absolute priority level changes as the process class changes from idle to
realtime. The two-step mechanism allows across-the-board changes to all threads
of a process, as well as to individual threads.

When to Change a Thread's Priority Level   There are a few reasons for increasing
a thread's priority level in an ISAPI extension. You may decide that the performance of an ISAPI extension could be enhanced by changing the priority level of
the thread that is calling your extension.

You may choose to boost the priority level of your extension when processing a server request. This improves the response time to the waiting client if a time-consuming operation is running. When the results are being returned, the extension can reset the priority level of the calling thread back to its original value.

If your extension creates its own thread, it may improve the performance of the extension and the system to increase or decrease the thread's priority, depending on the function of the new thread.

> **CAUTION**
>
> Since your extension is used as a dynamic link library (DLL), it would not be good practice to change the priority class of the process. Changing the priority class of a process could adversely affect the overall performance of your system.

If you are increasing the performance of your thread, avoid the time-critical priority level. It is rarely necessary to raise a priority level much.

Thread Synchronization Objects

Programming in a multithreaded environment is vastly different from programming in an environment that is not multithreaded. For example, several HTTP page requests may be in your ISAPI extension at the same time. If the requests are accessing shared data, you must supply some sort of thread synchronization to protect the data from corruption.

If your extension accesses data that is global to the extension, you must protect this data by a synchronization object. Likewise, if your extension shares resources such as an open database connectivity (ODBC) database access handle, these resources must be protected so that multiple threads are not accessing the resource simultaneously.

Fortunately, Windows NT provides thread synchronization objects, such as *critical sections*, *mutexes*, *semaphores*, and *events*. Each of these objects is used for different purposes and is explained in the following sections.

Part
V

Ch
18

Creating a New Thread

Creating a new thread of execution is relatively easy. The two steps are

1. Create a thread function.

2. Call the CreateThread function, passing a pointer to the thread function that you created as one of the parameters.

Let's take a look at the lottery extension. In the lottery extension, a separate thread is created to receive incoming requests for new lottery numbers. As the requests are received, a new lucky lottery number is generated and returned to the client. The function shown in code Listing 18.2 is called PoolThread and can be found in the lottery.c file on the accompanying CD.

Listing 18.2   The *PoolThread* Function

```
DWORD WINAPI PoolThread( LPDWORD lpParams )
{
    WORK_QUEUE_ITEM * pwqi;
    DWORD             res;

    while ( TRUE )
    {
        res = WaitForSingleObject( hWorkSem, INFINITE );
        if ( res == WAIT_OBJECT_0 )
        {
            //
            //  There's work to do, grab the queue lock and get the next
            //  work item
            //

            EnterCriticalSection( &csQueueLock );
            if ( WorkQueueList.Flink != &WorkQueueList )
            {
                pwqi = CONTAINING_RECORD( WorkQueueList.Flink,
                                          WORK_QUEUE_ITEM,
                                          ListEntry );
                pwqi->ListEntry.Flink->Blink = &WorkQueueList;
                WorkQueueList.Flink          = pwqi->ListEntry.Flink;
                cQueueItems--;
            }
            else
            {
                pwqi = NULL;
            }
```

```
                    LeaveCriticalSection( &csQueueLock );
                    if ( !pwqi )
                        continue;

                    //
                    //  Impersonate the specified user so security is maintained
                    //  accessing system resources
                    //
                    ImpersonateLoggedOnUser( pwqi->hImpersonationToken );
                    SendLotteryNumber( pwqi->pecb );

                    RevertToSelf();
                    //
                    //  Cleanup this work item
                    //
                    pwqi->pecb->ServerSupportFunction( pwqi->pecb->ConnID,
                                                       HSE_REQ_DONE_WITH_SESSION,
                                                       NULL,
                                                       NULL,
                                                       NULL );

                    CloseHandle( pwqi->hImpersonationToken );
                    FreeWorkItem( pwqi );
                }
            }
        return 0;
    }
```

Part
V

Ch

18

Once the thread function is created, the next step is to call the `CreateThread` function.

```
HANDLE CreateThread( LPSECURITY_ATTRIBUTES lpThreadAttributes,
    DWORD dwStackSize,
    LPTHREAD_START_ROUTINE lpStartAddress,
    LPVOID lpParameter,
    DWORD dwCreationFlags,
    LPDWORD lpThreadId
    );
```

The lottery extension creates all its worker threads during the extension initialization, as shown in code Listing 18.3. The lottery extension creates two instances of the `PoolThread` for each processor on the computer, with a maximum of eight threads allowed.

When the lottery extension calls `CreateThread`, it passes in the following parameters. NULL is passed in for the first parameter, indicating thread security attributes. NULL means that the thread will inherit the security parameters of the parent process.

dwStackSize is set to zero, indicating the use of the system default stack size for the thread. The address of the PoolThread function is the third parameter. The fourth parameter is a pointer to any parameters that are to be passed into the thread.

Lottery sets this to NULL, indicating no parameters. The dwCreationFlags parameter is set to 0, and the last parameter is the address of a DWORD that gets the thread ID of the newly created thread.

Listing 18.3   *DllMain* **Function—Entry Point for All DLLs**

```
BOOL WINAPI DllMain( IN HINSTANCE hinstDll,
IN DWORD fdwReason, IN LPVOID lpvContext OPTIONAL
        )
/*++
 Routine Description:

    This function DllLibMain() is the main initialization function for
      this DLL. It initializes local variables and prepares it to be
      invoked subsequently.

 Arguments:

    hinstDll           Instance Handle of the DLL
    fdwReason          Reason why NT called this DLL
    lpvReserved        Reserved parameter for future use.

 Return Value:

    Returns TRUE is successful; otherwise FALSE is returned.
--*/
{
    BOOL        fReturn = TRUE;
    SYSTEM_INFO si;
    DWORD       i;
    DWORD       dwThreadId;

    switch (fdwReason )
    {
    case DLL_PROCESS_ATTACH:

        //
        // Initialize various data and modules.
        //

        if ( !InitializeLottery() )
```

```
{
    fReturn = FALSE;
    break;
}

WorkQueueList.Flink = WorkQueueList.Blink = &WorkQueueList;
FreeQueueList.Flink = FreeQueueList.Blink = &FreeQueueList;

hWorkSem = CreateSemaphore( NULL,
                            0,           // Not signalled
                                         // initially
                            0x7fffffff, // Max reference count
                            NULL );

if ( !hWorkSem )
{
    return FALSE;
}

InitializeCriticalSection( &csQueueLock );

//
// We don't care about thread attach/detach notifications
//

DisableThreadLibraryCalls( hinstDll );

//
// Do an extra LoadLibrary on ourselves so we get terminated
// when the process gets terminated (avoids worrying about
// thread cleanup issues on dll detach).
//

LoadLibrary( MODULE_NAME );

//
// Create our thread pool, two times the number of processors
//

GetSystemInfo( &si );

for ( i = 0;
      i < THREADS_PER_PROCESSOR * si.dwNumberOfProcessors &&
      i < MAX_THREADS;
      i++ )
{
    HANDLE hThread;
```

Part
V

Ch
18

continues

Listing 18.3   Continued

```
                    hThread = CreateThread( NULL,
                                            0,
                                            (LPTHREAD_START_ROUTINE) PoolThread,
                                            NULL,
                                            0,
                                            &dwThreadId );

              if ( !hThread )
              {
                  CloseHandle( hWorkSem );
                  DeleteCriticalSection( &csQueueLock );
                  return FALSE;
              }

                  //
                  //  We don't use the thread handle so close it
                  //

              CloseHandle( hThread );
          }
          break;

      case DLL_PROCESS_DETACH:
          {

              //
              //  Note we should never get called because we did an extra
              //  LoadLibrary in our initialization
              //

              if ( lpvContext != NULL)
              {
                  TerminateLottery();
                  DeleteCriticalSection( &csQueueLock );
                  CloseHandle( hWorkSem );
              }

              break;
          } /* case DLL_PROCESS_DETACH */

      default:
          break;
      }   /* switch */

      return ( fReturn);
  } /* DllLibMain() */
```

Using Critical Sections

One of the simplest yet most effective forms of thread synchronization is the *critical section*. A critical section is a small section of code that needs exclusive access to a shared data object or resource before the code can execute. A critical section allows only one thread at a time to gain access to a shared resource.

A critical section can only be used to synchronize threads in a single process. Since ISAPI extensions are used as DLLs that are loaded into the server's process space, the critical section works very well for thread synchronization.

Creating a Critical Section Object

Creating a critical section is easy enough. The first step is to allocate a CRITICAL_SECTION data structure globally in the ISAPI extension. This allows access to the critical section by the different threads calling the extension.

Typically, the CRITICAL_SECTION data structure is declared as a global variable. The complete code for the lottery extension is shown in Listing 18.4 (lottery.c) and in Listing 18.5 (worker.c). These examples illustrate the declaration of the critical section csQueueLock as a global variable for the extension.

> **CAUTION**
>
> The CRICITAL_SECTION data structure has member variables in the structure. These variables are initialized and used by Windows NT, and should *not* be accessed or changed by your extension.

Once the CRITICAL_SECTION data structure is declared, the critical section must be initialized before it can be used by your extension. Since the data structure is global, it should be initialized in the DllMain function for your extension.

> **N O T E** DllMain is the function called by the Windows NT operating system whenever it loads, initializes, or unloads a DLL from memory. Since ISAPI extensions are used as DLLs, this is the logical place for initializing or destroying all variables global to the extension.

Listing 18.4   Code for the Lottery Extension

```c
typedef struct _WORK_QUEUE_ITEM
{
    LIST_ENTRY                  ListEntry;
    HANDLE                      hImpersonationToken;
    EXTENSION_CONTROL_BLOCK * pecb;
} WORK_QUEUE_ITEM;

CRITICAL_SECTION csQueueLock;

LIST_ENTRY WorkQueueList;

LIST_ENTRY FreeQueueList;

DWORD cQueueItems = 0;

HANDLE hWorkSem = NULL;

//
// Functions
//

BOOL WINAPI DllMain(
    IN HINSTANCE hinstDll,
    IN DWORD     fdwReason,
    IN LPVOID    lpvContext OPTIONAL
    )
/*++

  Routine Description:

    This function DllLibMain() is the main initialization function for
    this DLL. It initializes local variables and prepares it to be
    invoked subsequently.

  Arguments:

    hinstDll        Instance Handle of the DLL
    fdwReason       Reason why NT called this DLL
    lpvReserved     Reserved parameter for future use.

  Return Value:

    Returns TRUE is successful; otherwise FALSE is returned.
--*/
{
    BOOL        fReturn = TRUE;
    SYSTEM_INFO si;
    DWORD       i;
    DWORD       dwThreadId;
```

```
switch (fdwReason )
{
case DLL_PROCESS_ATTACH:

    //
    // Initialize various data and modules.
    //

    if ( !InitializeLottery() )
    {
        fReturn = FALSE;
        break;
    }

    WorkQueueList.Flink = WorkQueueList.Blink = &WorkQueueList;
    FreeQueueList.Flink = FreeQueueList.Blink = &FreeQueueList;

    hWorkSem = CreateSemaphore( NULL,
                                0,          // Not signalled
                                            // initially
                                0x7fffffff, // Max reference count
                                NULL );

    if ( !hWorkSem )
    {
        return FALSE;
    }

    InitializeCriticalSection( &csQueueLock );

    //
    // We don't care about thread attach/detach notifications
    //

    DisableThreadLibraryCalls( hinstDll );

    //
    // Do an extra LoadLibrary on ourselves so we get terminated
    // when the process gets terminated (avoids worrying about
    // thread cleanup issues on dll detach).
    //

    LoadLibrary( MODULE_NAME );

    //
    // Create our thread pool, two times the number of processors
    //

    GetSystemInfo( &si );
```

Part
V

Ch
18

continues

Listing 18.4 Continued

```
        for ( i = 0;
              i < THREADS_PER_PROCESSOR * si.dwNumberOfProcessors &&
              i < MAX_THREADS;
              i++ )
        {
            HANDLE hThread;

            hThread = CreateThread( NULL,
                                    0,
                                    (LPTHREAD_START_ROUTINE) PoolThread,
                                    NULL,
                                    0,
                                    &dwThreadId );

            if ( !hThread )
            {
                CloseHandle( hWorkSem );
                DeleteCriticalSection( &csQueueLock );
                return FALSE;
            }

                //
                //  We don't use the thread handle so close it
                //

            CloseHandle( hThread );
        }
        break;

    case DLL_PROCESS_DETACH:
        {

            //
            //  Note we should never get called because we did an extra
            //  LoadLibrary in our initialization
            //

            if ( lpvContext != NULL)
            {
                TerminateLottery();
                DeleteCriticalSection( &csQueueLock );
                CloseHandle( hWorkSem );
            }

            break;
        } /* case DLL_PROCESS_DETACH */

    default:
        break;
    }    /* switch */
```

```
    return ( fReturn);
}  /* DllLibMain() */

BOOL WINAPI GetExtensionVersion ( HSE_VERSION_INFO * pver )
/*++

Routine Description:
    This is the first function that is called when this ISAPI DLL is
    ➥loaded.
    We should fill in the version information in the structure passed in.

Arguments:
    pVer - pointer to Server Extension Version Information structure.

Returns:
    TRUE for success and FALSE for failure.
    On success the valid version information is stored in *pVer.
--*/
{
    pver->dwExtensionVersion = MAKELONG( HSE_VERSION_MINOR,
    ➥HSE_VERSION_MAJOR );

    strcpy( pver->lpszExtensionDesc,
            "Multi-threaded ISAPI Application example, v 1.0" );

    return TRUE;
}

DWORD WINAPI HttpExtensionProc( EXTENSION_CONTROL_BLOCK * pecb )
/*++

Routine Description:
    This is the main function that is called for this ISAPI Extension.
    This function processes the request and sends out appropriate
    ➥response.

Arguments:
    pecb  - pointer to EXTENSION_CONTROL_BLOCK, which contains most of the
            required variables for the extension called. In addition,
            it contains the various callbacks as appropriate.

Returns:
    HSE_STATUS code indicating the success/failure of this call.
--*/
{
    WORK_QUEUE_ITEM * pwqi;
    DWORD             cb;
    BOOL              fRet;
    HANDLE            hImpersonationToken;
```

Part
V

Ch
18

continues

Listing 18.4 Continued

```
//
//  Is the list too long?  If so, tell the user to come back later
//

if ( cQueueItems + 1 > MAX_WORK_QUEUE_ITEMS )
{
    //
    //  Send a message back to client indicating we're too busy,
    //  they should try again later.
    //

    fRet = SendError( pecb,
                      "503 Server too busy",
                      SERVER_TOO_BUSY_TEXT );

    pecb->dwHttpStatusCode = 503;

    return fRet ? HSE_STATUS_SUCCESS : HSE_STATUS_ERROR;
}

//
//  Capture the current impersonation token so we can impersonate
//  this user in the other thread
//

if ( !OpenThreadToken( GetCurrentThread(),
                       TOKEN_QUERY | TOKEN_IMPERSONATE,
                       TRUE,          // Open in unimpersonated
                                      // context
                       &hImpersonationToken ))
{
    fRet = SendError( pecb,
                      "500 Failed to open thread token",
                      "Failed to open thread token" );
    pecb->dwHttpStatusCode = 500;

    return fRet ? HSE_STATUS_SUCCESS : HSE_STATUS_ERROR;
}
//
//  Take the queue lock, get a queue item and put it on the queue
//

EnterCriticalSection( &csQueueLock );

pwqi = AllocateWorkItem();
```

```
        if ( !pwqi )
        {
            fRet = SendError( pecb,
                              "500 Not enough memory",
                              "Failed to allocate work queue item" );

            pecb->dwHttpStatusCode = 500;

            LeaveCriticalSection( &csQueueLock );
            CloseHandle( hImpersonationToken );
            return fRet ? HSE_STATUS_SUCCESS : HSE_STATUS_ERROR;
        }

        //
        //  Initialize the work queue item and put it at the end of the list
        //

        pwqi->pecb = pecb;
        pwqi->hImpersonationToken = hImpersonationToken;

        pwqi->ListEntry.Flink = &WorkQueueList;
        pwqi->ListEntry.Blink = WorkQueueList.Blink;

        WorkQueueList.Blink->Flink = &pwqi->ListEntry;
        WorkQueueList.Blink        = &pwqi->ListEntry;

        cQueueItems++;

        LeaveCriticalSection( &csQueueLock );

        //
        //  Signal the pool threads there is work to be done
        //

        ReleaseSemaphore( hWorkSem, 1, NULL );

        return HSE_STATUS_PENDING;
    }
```

Listing 18.5   Code for the Lottery Extension

```
//
// This global variable maintains the current state about the
// the lottery number generated.
//
// The lottery number is generated using a combination
// of the sequence number and a random number generated on the fly.
//
```

continues

Listing 18.5 Continued

```
DWORD g_dwLotteryNumberSequence = 0;

//
//  Critical section to protect the global counter.
//

CRITICAL_SECTION  g_csGlobal;

BOOL
InitializeLottery(
    VOID
    )
/*++

Routine Description:

    Sets up the initial state for the lottery number generator

Returns:

  TRUE on success, FALSE on failure

--*/
{
    time_t pTime;

    //
    //  Seed the random number generator
    //

    srand(time(&pTime));
    g_dwLotteryNumberSequence = rand();

    InitializeCriticalSection( &g_csGlobal );

    return TRUE;
}

BOOL
SendLotteryNumber(
  EXTENSION_CONTROL_BLOCK  * pecb
  )
/*++

  Routine Description:

    This function sends a randomly generated lottery number back to the
    ➥client
```

```
    Arguments:

      pecb  - pointer to EXTENSION_CONTROL_BLOCK for this request

    Returns:
      TRUE on success, FALSE on failure

--*/
{
    BOOL fRet;
    char rgBuff[2048];

    //
    //  Send the response headers and status code
    //

    fRet = pecb->ServerSupportFunction(
            pecb->ConnID,                   /* ConnID */
            HSE_REQ_SEND_RESPONSE_HEADER,   /* dwHSERRequest */
            "200 OK",                       /* lpvBuffer */
            NULL,                           /* lpdwSize. NULL=> send
                                              ➥string */
            (LPDWORD ) RESPONSE_HEADERS);   /* header contents */

    if ( fRet )
    {
        CHAR   rgchLuckyNumber[40];
        DWORD dwLotNum1, dwLotNum2;
        DWORD cb;

        CHAR   rgchClientHost[200] = "LT";
        DWORD cbClientHost = 200;

        if ( !pecb->GetServerVariable(pecb->ConnID,
                                      "REMOTE_HOST",
                                      rgchClientHost,
                                      &cbClientHost))
        {
            // No host name is available.
            // Make up one

            strcpy(rgchClientHost, "RH");
        }
        else
        {

            // terminate with just two characters
            rgchClientHost[2] = '\0';
        }
```

continues

Part

V

Ch

18

Listing 18.5   Continued

```
        //
        // Generate a lottery number, generate the contents of body and
        // send the body to client.
        //

        GenerateLotteryNumber( &dwLotNum1, &dwLotNum2);

        //  Lottery Number format is:  Number-2letters-Number.

        wsprintf( rgchLuckyNumber, "%03d-%s-%05d",
                dwLotNum1,
                rgchClientHost,
                dwLotNum2);

        //
        // Body of the message sent back.
        //

        cb = wsprintf( rgBuff,
                    "<head><title>Lucky Number</title></head>\n"
                    "<body><center><h1>Lucky Corner </h1></
                    ➥center><hr>"
                    "<h2>Your lottery number is: "
                    " <i> %s </i></h2>\n"
                    "<p><hr></body>",
                    rgchLuckyNumber);

        fRet = pecb->WriteClient (pecb->ConnID,        /* ConnID */
                                (LPVOID ) rgBuff,    /* message */
                                &cb,                 /* lpdwBytes */
                                0 );                 /* reserved */
    }


    return ( fRet ? HSE_STATUS_SUCCESS : HSE_STATUS_ERROR);

} /* SendLotteryNumber */

VOID
GenerateLotteryNumber(
    LPDWORD pLotNum1,
    LPDWORD pLotNum2
    )
{
    DWORD dwLotteryNum;
    DWORD dwModulo;

    //
    // Obtain the current lottery number an increment the counter
```

```
    // To keep this multi-thread safe use critical section around it
    //

    EnterCriticalSection( &g_csGlobal);

    dwLotteryNum = g_dwLotteryNumberSequence++;

    LeaveCriticalSection( &g_csGlobal);

    // obtain a non-zero modulo value

    do {
        dwModulo = rand();
    } while ( dwModulo == 0);

    // split the lottery number into two parts.

    *pLotNum1 = (dwLotteryNum / dwModulo);
    *pLotNum2 = (dwLotteryNum % dwModulo);

    return;
} // GenerateLotteryNumber()
```

For developers using the Microsoft foundation classes (MFC) to build extensions, MFC does not provide direct access to the DllMain function. Instead, the Application object of the extension has a virtual method that can be overwritten. This method is MyApp::InitAplication.

The InitApplication method is called when the extension is first loaded into memory. The CriticalSection object can be initialized in this method.

To initialize a critical section, call the InitializeCriticalSection function. The prototype for this function is

```
    VOID InitializeCriticalSection( LPCRITICAL_SECTION lpCriticalSection );
```

As shown in the prototype, a pointer to a CRITICAL_SECTION structure is passed in as the only parameter to the function.

Protecting a Code Block with a Critical Section

Once the critical section is initialized, it is easy to protect your code with a critical section. Two functions control the entrance and exit to a block of code protected by a critical section: EnterCriticalSection and LeaveCriticalSection. The prototypes for these functions are shown below.

Part
V

Ch
18

```
VOID LeaveCriticalSection(LPCRITICAL_SECTION lpCriticalSection );
VOID EnterCriticalSection(LPCRITICAL_SECTION lpCriticalSection );
```

Both LeaveCriticalSection and EnterCriticalSection take only one parameter, a pointer to a CRITICAL_SECTION object.

Destroying a Critical Section

Only destroy a critical section in the exit routine of the extension. This ensures that the process that loaded the extension has finished using the extension. It also ensures that there are no threads from the process using the variables in the extension.

Destroy a critical section object in the DllMain function. This function is called when a process is finished using the extension with the parameter of DLL_PROCESS_DETACH.

N O T E   For MFC users, the application framework provides a virtual method, MyApp::ExitApplication, that can be overwritten by the extension developer. This method is called when the extension is unloaded from memory. ■

You destroy a critical section by calling the DeleteCriticalSection function. The prototype for this function is

```
VOID DeleteCriticalSection(LPCRITICAL_SECTION lpCriticalSection );
```

Like the initialization function, DeleteCriticalSection takes a pointer to a CRITICAL_SECTION structure as its only parameter. Once the critical section is destroyed, it should not be used again without reinitialization.

Protecting Multiple Code Blocks with a Critical Section

In the previous sections, you have seen how to protect a block of code using a critical section. What if there are multiple blocks of code to be protected from simultaneous access? Two options are available: create another critical section or use an existing critical section.

If you create another critical section, you must follow the procedures under "Protecting a Block of Code with a Critical Section" earlier in this chapter. You can also use the came critical section for protecting multiple blocks of code.

Let's look at the sample code in Listing 18.6, which illustrates the use of a single critical section to protect multiple code blocks.

Listing 18.6 Single Critical Section Protecting Multiple Blocks

```
CRITICAL_SECTION gh_GlobalCriticalSection;
long gl_GlobalTime[20];
  .
  .
  .
DWORD WINAPI ExampleThread( LPVOID lpvParameter )
{
    int li_Index = (int)lpvParameter;
    EnterCriticalSection(&gh_GlobalCriticalSection);
    if ( gl_GlobalTime[li_Index] < time(NULL)
        UpdateTimeSlot(li_Index);
    LeaveCriticalSection(&gh_GlobalCriticalSection);
    return(0);
}
void UpdateTimeSlot(int vi_Index )
{
EnterCriticalSection(&gh_GlobalCriticalSection);
// increment the time index by one hour
gl_GlobalTime[vi_Index] = time(NULL) + (60 * 60);
LeaveCriticalSection(&gh_GlobalCriticalSection);
}
```

In Listing 18.6, the ExampleThread function gets the critical section when it first starts to execute. After it gets the critical section, the thread tests the value of the time stored in an index of time values against the current time. In this example, the array of time indexes is protected by the critical section. This way, no value in the array can be updated while the thread is testing the value.

If the current time is equal to the value in the index being tested, the UpdateTimeSlot function is called. UpdateTimeSlot is an independent function that can be called without knowledge of what functions call it. The global critical section is used to protect the array while the function updates a slot in the array.

In Listing 18.6, ExampleThread is calling UpdateTimeSlot while the thread is in possession of the critical section. This is a perfectly legal operation.

Windows NT knows that the thread that is in possession of the critical section is again requesting the critical section. So NT simply increments the internal reference count of the critical section and the function proceeds.

The thread only relinquishes possession of the critical section after LeaveCriticalSection has been called twice, once for the UpdateTimeSlow function and once for the ExampleThread function.

Thus, multiple code blocks are protected using the same critical section.

Other Thread-Control Options

For ISAPI extensions, critical sections are the most logical choices for protecting resources from simultaneous access. Critical sections provide fast access for serializing data access in a single process.

However, depending on the function of the extension, you may need to use other synchronization objects. Windows NT offers the developer many synchronization objects that can be used in different circumstances. Windows NT also offers events, semaphores, and mutexes as other choices for thread and process synchronization.

Events, semaphores, and mutexes all run on the same premise: each object can be in one of two states at any time. Valid object states are signaled and nonsignaled.

An object can be accessed by a thread when in the signaled state. A thread is put into an efficient wait state while waiting for an object to be signaled. Once the object is signaled, the thread begins to execute.

Two functions are used by threads to wait for an object to be signaled: WaitForSingleObject and WaitForMultipleObjects. These two functions are polymorphic in nature because they work with all of the Win32 synchronization objects. The prototypes for these functions are

```
DWORD WaitForSingleObject( HANDLE hObject, DWORD dwTimeout);
DWORD WaitForMultipleObjects( DWORD dwObjects, LPHANDLE lpHandles,

BOOL bWaitAll, DWORD dwTimeout);
```

The first function, WaitForSingleObject, takes two parameters. The first parameter, hObject, is a handle to a synchronization object that could be an event, a mutex, or a semaphore. The second parameter, dwTimeout, specifies, in milliseconds, how long to wait for the object to become signaled.

When a thread calls `WaitForSingleObject`, the thread waits for the object to be signaled. Once the object state is signaled or if the wait time expires, the function returns and the thread continues to execute.

The action that the thread takes should be based on the return value. `WaitForSingleObject` returns one of the following values:

Return Value	Description
WAIT_OBJECT_0	The object's state is signaled.
WAIT_TIMEOUT	The object did not reach the signaled state in the time specified in the timeout parameter.
WAIT_ABANDONED	This value is returned for mutex objects. This value specifies that the mutex was abandoned by another thread so its state is signaled.
WAIT_FAILED	This value indicates that an error has occurred. The `GetLastError` function can be called to retrieve additional information.

Two special values can be passed in as the timeout parameter to `WaitForSingleObject`. A value of 0 specifies that the operating system should return the current state of the object without waiting.

A return value of `WAIT_OBJECT_0` indicates that the object's state is signaled. A return value of `WAIT_FAILED` indicates that the object's state is not signaled.

Conversely, a value of `INFINITE` can be passed in as the timeout parameter. This value indicates that the operating system should wait forever until the object's state is signaled. If the object never reaches a signaled state, the thread remains suspended indefinitely until the process exits.

The second function, `WaitForMultipleObjects`, is like `WaitForSingleObject` except that it can wait for one or more objects to be signaled. `WaitForMultipleObjects` takes four parameters.

The first parameter, `dwObjects`, specifies how many objects are being passed into the function. This parameter cannot exceed `MAXIMUM_WAIT_OBJECTS`, which is 64. The second parameter, `lpHandles`, is a pointer to an array of object handles.

> **N O T E** An error occurs if `WaitForMultipleObjects` is called with the same object
> appearing more than once in the list. This error occurs even if the same object
> is referenced through different handles. ▪

The third parameter, `bWaitAll`, indicates whether the function should wait for all objects in the list to be signaled (`TRUE`) or wait for any object in the list to be signaled (`FALSE`). Like `WaitForSingleObject`, the last parameter, `dwTimeout`, specifies how long to wait for all objects on the list to be signaled or a single object to be signaled.

For mutex, semaphore, and event objects, one function call destroys or invalidates the object: `CloseHandle`.

```
BOOL CloseHandle( HANDLE hObject );
```

`CloseHandle` is a generic function that closes any Win32 handle such as mutexes, events, semaphores, and communication ports.

Mutexes

Mutex objects are like critical sections except that mutexes can be used to synchronize resource access across multiple processes. Unlike critical sections, which are declared variables that are initialized, mutex objects must be created by the operating system.

To create a mutex object, you call the `CreateMutex` function. The prototype is

```
HANDLE CreateMutex(LPSECURITY_ATTRIBUTES lpSecurity,
BOOL bInitialOwner, LPTSTR lpzMutexName );
```

When the `CreateMutex` function is called successfully, a handle of a mutex object is returned. The first parameter to `CreateMutex`, `lpSecurity`, is a pointer to a `SECURITY_ATTRIBUTES` structure.

Passing `NULL` in creates a mutex with the default security settings of the current user. The second parameter, `bInitialOwner`, indicates if the thread creating the mutex should gain ownership—place the object in a nonsignaled state so other threads cannot access it.

If `TRUE` is passed in, the thread creating the mutex has ownership, which means that the mutex is in a nonsignaled state. If `FALSE` is passed in, the mutex is not owned and its state is signaled.

The third parameter, `lpzMutexName`, is a pointer to a string used for naming the mutex. The mutex name is used to identify a common mutex object to be shared between multiple threads or processes.

The most common method for using a mutex is for each thread that needs access to the mutex to call `CreateMutex`, passing the same string in the `lpzMutexName` parameter. The first thread calling `CreateMutex` creates the mutex object.

As subsequent calls are made to `CreateMutex`, the operating system determines that a mutex with an identical name already exists. If the mutex already exists, the operating system creates a new handle to the existing mutex object.

To use the mutex, the calling thread calls `WaitForSingleObject`, passing in the handle to the mutex returned from `CreateMutex`. When `WaitForSingleObject` sees that the mutex has reached a signaled state, the waiting thread immediately gets ownership of the mutex. The mutex is placed back in a nonsignaled state, and the thread continues to execute.

When a thread is finished accessing the resources protected by the mutex, it can release the mutex. Releasing the mutex puts the mutex back into a signaled state. The mutex can be released by calling the `ReleaseMutex` function. The prototype for `ReleaseMutex` is

```
BOOL ReleaseMutex( HANDLE hMutex );
```

The `ReleaseMutex` function takes a handle to the mutex as its only parameter.

Mutex objects have different characteristics from other synchronization objects. Mutex objects are owned by a thread, not a process, and have two states, signaled or nonsignaled. But they also remember which thread has ownership of the mutex. Other synchronization objects such as events or semaphores also have two states, signaled or nonsignaled.

This is significant because a thread can gain ownership of a mutex and then terminate, either normally or abnormally, without releasing the mutes. Such a mutex is assumed to be abandoned.

When the operating system sees an abandoned mutex, it automatically switches the state of the mutex to signaled, allowing other threads waiting for the mutex to continue executing.

Like events or semaphores, mutexes are destroyed by calling the `CloseHandle` function.

Semaphores

Semaphores represent a different type of synchronization object from events, critical sections, or mutexes. Semaphores are used to keep track of the number of available resources.

A semaphore allows a thread to query for the availability of a resource. If the resource is available, the count of available resources is decremented.

A semaphore is created by calling the CreateSemaphore function.

```
HANDLE CreateSemaphore( LPSECURITY_ATTRIBUTE lpSecurity,
LONG cInitialCount, LONG cMaxCount, LPTSTR lpszSemName);
```

CreateSemaphore takes four parameters. The first parameter, lpSecurity, is a pointer to a SECURITY_ATTRIBUTE structure. NULL can be used to specify the default security attributes of the current user.

The second parameter, cInitialCount, specifies the initial number of resources available. Typically, this is set to cMaxCount. cInitialCount indicates how many of the resources are currently available.

cMaxCount specifies the maximum number of resources available. This parameter indicates how many threads can simultaneously access the resource(s) associated with the semaphore.

For example, if your extension maintains two ODBC database handles that can be used to process HTTP requests, 2 is passed in as the value of cInitialCount. This indicates that two handles are available and that 2 is the value for cMaxCount.

lpszSemName is a string used to name the semaphore. The name identifies the semaphore so that other processes or threads can get a handle to the semaphore.

When a semaphore is created, a process calls WaitForSingleObject, passing in the handle of the semaphore to determine if the resource protected by the semaphore is protected. If WaitForSingleObject returns a code of WAIT_OBJECT_0, the resource is available. WaitForSingleObject decrements the semaphore count before it returns to the calling thread.

The operating system works on a semaphore without interruption. When a resource is requested from a semaphore, the operating system tests to see if the resource is available.

If so, the operating system decrements the count without letting another thread use the semaphore. Only after the count is decremented can another thread access the semaphore.

A semaphore can be released (count incremented) by calling the ReleaseSemaphore function.

```
BOOL ReleaseSemaphore( HANDLE hSemaphore, LONG dwRelease, LPLONG
➥lpPrevious);
```

The first parameter, hSemaphore, is a handle to a semaphore. The second parameter, dwRelease, is a count that indicates how much to increment the semaphore count by.

This is typically set to 1. But if WaitForSingleObject is called multiple times, the semaphore can be reset by setting dwRelease to a number equal to the number of times the WaitForSingleObject is called. This feature allows ReleaseSemaphore to be called once.

The last parameter, lpPrevious, is a pointer to a long integer. ReleaseSemaphore fills this parameter with the resource count of the semaphore before adding dwRelease to it.

Unlike a mutex or a critical section, a semaphore is not owned by a thread. This means that a semaphore can be released by any thread, as long as the thread has a valid handle to the semaphore.

N O T E Even though any thread can release a semaphore, it is not good programming practice for a thread other than the calling thread to release the semaphore.

Events

Another synchronization object, events, are different from mutex or semaphores. Events are generally used to indicate that an operation has completed. This is in contrast to semaphores, mutexes, and critical sections, which are generally used to control resource access.

The two kinds of events are *manual-reset* and *auto-reset*. Manual-reset events are typically used to signal several threads simultaneously that an operation has completed. Auto-reset events are typically used to signal a single thread that an operation has completed.

Events are most often used in situations where one thread does some kind of initialization work. Then one or more threads can do some work after the initialization is completed.

For example, if your extension needs to read in a large file or get database information before any requests can be accepted, the extension can start a thread to get the necessary data. The initialization thread sets the event to a nonsignaled state.

Other threads trying to execute are blocked when waiting for the event to be signaled. After the data is obtained, the initialization thread sets the event to a signaled state, releasing any threads waiting for the event.

To create an event, the `CreateEvent` function is called.

```
HANDLE CreateEvent( LPSECURITY_ATTRIBUTES lpSecurity,
BOOL bManualReset, BOOL bInitialState, LPTSTR lpszEventName);
```

The first parameter, `lpSecurity`, is a pointer to a `SECURITY_ATTRIBUTES` structure. `NULL` can be passed in to get the security attributes of the current user.

The second parameter, `bManualReset`, indicates if the event is to be reset manually (`TRUE`) or if the event is auto-reset (`FALSE`). The third parameter, `bInitialState`, can set the initial state of the event to signaled (`TRUE`) or nonsignaled (`FALSE`).

The fourth parameter, `lpszEventName`, is a pointer to a string that can be used to name the event. If the event is named, other threads and other processes can get a handle to the event by passing in the same string to `CreateEvent`.

Like mutexes and semaphores, threads waiting for an event to be signaled must call either the `WaitForSingleObject` function or the `WaitForMultipleObjects` function. The effect these functions have on an event varies, depending on whether the event is manual-reset or auto-reset.

Using Manual-Reset Events   When a thread calls `WaitForSingleObject` or `WaitForMultipleObjects` on a manual-reset event, the event is not automatically reset to a nonsignaled state. This action is important because if multiple threads are waiting for the event to occur, all of the threads can execute when the event occurs. In other words, when a manual-reset event is signaled, all threads waiting on the event are allowed to run.

A thread sets an event object to signaled by calling the SetEvent function.

    BOOL SetEvent(HANDLE hEvent);

This function takes a handle of an event as its only parameter and returns TRUE if successful. When a manual-reset event is signaled, it remains signaled until the event is explicitly reset to a nonsignaled state. An event can be reset by calling the ResetEvent function.

    BOOL ResetEvent(HANDLE hEvent);

One more function that is useful when using manual-reset events is PulseEvent.

    BOOL PulseEvent(HANDLE hEvent);

PulseEvent has an equivalent function to calling SetEvent to release any waiting threads and then calling ResetEvent to reset the event to a nonsignaled state.

Using Auto-Reset Events   An auto-reset event behaves differently from manual-reset events. If multiple threads are waiting for an event to occur, only *one* thread is released when the event is set to a signaled state.

When you use auto-reset events, both WaitForSingleObject and WaitForMultipleObjects reset the event back to a signaled state before returning to their calling thread. This action enables the operating system to allow only one thread to execute when the event is signaled.

In other words, after a thread calls SetEvent to set the event to a signaled state, the thread does not have to call ResetEvent. The event is reset by either WaitForSingleObject or WaitForMultipleObjects before the function returns to the calling thread.

From Here...

In this chapter we learn how Windows NT schedules threads, how to add multithreaded capabilities to ISAPI extensions, and how to provide synchronization to resources in ISAPI extensions.

Part
V

Ch
18

- For more information on ISAPI extensions, see Chapter 6, "Understanding ISAPI Extensions." This chapter gives you a clear picture of how ISAPI extensions are constructed and used.

- For information on debugging extensions, see Chapter 17, "Troubleshooting and Debugging Extensions and Filters," to learn how to maximize the use of runtime debuggers.

Appendixes

ISAPI Reference

Appendix A is a complete Internet Server Application Programming Interface (ISAPI) reference. It describes the structures and functions that make up the API. ▪

ISAPI Extensions

This section describes the ISAPI structures and functions that apply to extensions. There are two sets of functions:

> The ISAPI extension exports three functions that are called by the server. These are described in "Entry Point Functions."

> The server passes four callback functions to the ISAPI extension using the EXTENSION_CONTROL_BLOCK (ECB) structure. These are described under "ISAPI Server Functions" later in this appendix.

Structures

This section describes the structures used in an ISAPI extension.

HTTP_EXTENSION_VERSION   This structure (shown in Listing A.1) holds the extension version information. It is passed to GetExtensionVersion().

Listing A.1   HTTPEXT.H—The Extension Control Block

```
typedef struct   _HSE_VERSION_INFO {
    DWORD   dwExtensionVersion;
    CHAR    lpszExtensionDesc[HSE_MAX_EXT_DLL_NAME_LEN];
} HSE_VERSION_INFO, *LPHSE_VERSION_INFO;
```

---

dwExtensionVersion

Form: DWORD

Value: [out] The version of the HTTP specification. The high and low words are the major and minor versions. The version can be set using MAKELONG.

> dwExtensionVersion = MAKELONG(HSE_VERSION_MINOR, HSE_VERSION_
> ➥MAJOR);

lpszExtensionDesc

Form: Pointer to a null-terminated string.

Value: [out] A description of the extension.

EXTENSION_CONTROL_BLOCK   The ECB holds frequently used information about a request and callback functions to get additional information. This structure is passed to HttpExtensionProc() (see Listing A.2).

Listing A.2   HTTPEXT.H—The Extension Control Block

```
typedef struct _EXTENSION_CONTROL_BLOCK {
    DWORD      cbSize;
    DWORD      dwVersion;
    HCONN      ConnID;
    DWORD      dwHttpStatusCode;
    CHAR       lpszLogData[HSE_LOG_BUFFER_LEN];
    LPSTR      lpszMethod;
    LPSTR      lpszQueryString;
    LPSTR      lpszPathInfo;
    LPSTR      lpszPathTranslated;
    DWORD      cbTotalBytes;
    DWORD      cbAvailable;
    LPBYTE     lpbData;
    LPSTR      lpszContentType;
    BOOL (WINAPI * GetServerVariable) ( HCONN        hConn,
                                        LPSTR        lpszVariableName,
                                        LPVOID       lpvBuffer,
                                        LPDWORD      lpdwSize );
    BOOL (WINAPI * WriteClient)  ( HCONN        ConnID,
                                   LPVOID       Buffer,
                                   LPDWORD      lpdwBytes,
                                   DWORD        dwReserved );
    BOOL (WINAPI * ReadClient)  ( HCONN        ConnID,
                                  LPVOID       lpvBuffer,
                                  LPDWORD      lpdwSize );
    BOOL (WINAPI * ServerSupportFunction)( HCONN        hConn,
                                           DWORD        dwHSERRequest,
                                           LPVOID       lpvBuffer,
                                           LPDWORD      lpdwSize,
                                           LPDWORD      lpdwDataType );
} EXTENSION_CONTROL_BLOCK, *LPEXTENSION_CONTROL_BLOCK;
```

---

cbSize

Form: DWORD

Value: [in] The size in bytes of the ECB.

dwVersion

Form: DWORD

Value: [in] The version of the HTTP specification. The high and low words hold the major and minor version numbers.

ConnID

Form: HCONN

Value: [in] A unique context number assigned by the server. It is not to be changed by the extension.

dwHttpStatusCode

Form: DWORD

Value: [out] The status code returned by the extension, as shown in Table A.1.

Table A.1   HTTP Status Code

Status Code	Meaning
HSE_STATUS_SUCCESS	The request was handled successfully. The server can terminate the session.
HSE_STATUS_SUCCESS_AND_KEEP_CONN	The request was handled successfully. The server should wait for the next HTTP request if the client supports keep-alive connections. Use this only when also returning a keep-alive connection header.
HSE_STATUS_PENDING	The ISAPI extension will notify the server when it has finished processing the request using ServerSupportFunction().
HSE_STATUS_ERROR	An error occurred while processing the request.

lpszLogData

Form: An array of HSE_LOG_BUFFER_LEN bytes holding a null-terminated string.

Value: [out] Log data that is specific to this extension.

lpszMethod

Form: Pointer to a null-terminated string.

Value: [in] The request method.

lpszQueryString

Form: Pointer to a null-terminated string.

Value: [in] The query data.

lpszPathInfo

Form: Pointer to a null-terminated string.

Value: [in] Additional path data provided by the client.

lpszPathTranslated

Form: Pointer to a null-terminated string.

Value: [in] The path after translation.

cbTotalBytes

Form: DWORD

Value: [in] The number of bytes to be received from the client. When there are 4G or more of available data, the value is 0xffffffff. In this case, use ReadClient() to read the data until no more is available.

cbAvailable

Form: DWORD

Value: [in] The number of bytes of data transferred to the buffer lpbData. If this is less than cbTotalBytes, use ReadClient() to get the rest of the data.

lpbData

Form: Pointer to the data buffer.

Value: [in] The client data buffer.

lpszContentType

Form: Pointer to a null-terminated string.

Value: [in] The content type of the data sent by the client.

Entry-Point Functions

An ISAPI extension DLL must use two entry points: `GetExtensionVersion()` and `HttpExtensionProc()`. The extension can also use an optional entry point : `TerminateExtentsion()`. The server communicates with the extension through these functions.

GetExtensionVersion() This function is called when the extension is started. It returns the version of the extension DLL to the server.

```
BOOL WINAPI GetExtensionVersion( HSE_VERSION_INFO  *pVer);
```

The ISAPI specification lists the following source code as the recommended implementation of `GetExtensionVersion()`:

```
BOOL WINAPI GetExtensionVersion( HSE_VERSION_INFO  *pVer )
{
    pVer->dwExtensionVersion = MAKELONG( HSE_VERSION_MINOR,
                                         HSE_VERSION_MAJOR );
    lstrcpyn( pVer->lpszExtensionDesc,
              "This is a sample Web Server Application",
              HSE_MAX_EXT_DLL_NAME_LEN );
    return TRUE;
}
```

Return Value: Return TRUE if successful, FALSE otherwise.

pVer

Form: Pointer to an `HTTP_EXTENSION_VERSION` structure.

Value: [out] The extension version and description.

HttpExtensionProc()   The server calls this function when a request for the extension is received. `HTTPExtensionProc` processes the request.

```
DWORD HttpExtensionProc(EXTENSION_CONTROL_BLOCK *pECB)
```

Return Value: Return `HSE_STATUS_SUCCESS` if successful. On error, return an appropriate error condition, such as `HSE_STATUS_ERROR` or `HTTP_STATUS_SERVER_ERROR`.

pECB

Form: Pointer to an `EXTENSION_CONTROL_BLOCK` structure.

Value: [in/out] The extension control block.

TerminateExtension()   `TerminateExtension()` is an optional entry point that enables shutdown of activities.

```
BOOL WINAPI TerminateExtension( DWORD dwFlags );
```

Return Value: TRUE or FALSE. See the description of the flags in Table A.2 for the meaning of the return code.

dwFlags

Form: `DWORD`

Value: [in] Flags (described in Table A.2) that indicate whether the server is requesting or mandating that the extension terminate.

Table A.2   *TerminateExtension* Flags

Flag	Meaning
HSE_TERM_ADVISORY_UNLOAD	The server is requesting that the extension be terminated. Return TRUE to enable the server to unload the extension. Return FALSE to indicate that the server is not to unload the extension.
HSE_TERM_MUST_UNLOAD	The server is notifying the extension that it will be unloaded unconditionally.

ISAPI Server Functions

The server provides the GetServerVariable(), ReadClient(), WriteClient(), and ServerSupportFunction()callback functions.

GetServerVariable()   This function can be used to get variables for this request that are not otherwise included in the ECB.

```
BOOL GetServerVariable(HCONN hConn, LPSTR lpszVariableName,
    LPVOID lpvBuffer, LPDWORD lpdwSize);
```

Return Value: TRUE if successful, FALSE otherwise. On error, use GetLastError() to get the specific error condition, as shown in Table A.3.

Table A.3   Possible Error Conditions

Error Code	Meaning
ERROR_INVALID_PARAMETER	The connection handle hConn is invalid.
ERROR_INVALID_INDEX	This lpszVariableName variable name is bad or not compatible.
ERROR_INSUFFICIENT_BUFFER	The buffer is too small to return the minimal information. lpdwSize has been changed to indicate the minimum buffer size needed.
ERROR_MORE_DATA	Only part of the data has been returned, and the total size is not known.
ERROR_NO_DATA	There is no data available to fulfill the request.

hConn

Form: HCONN

Value: [in] The context number.

lpszVariableName

Form: Pointer to a null-terminated string.

Value: [in] The name of the server variable requested. Valid variable names are shown in Table A.4.

Table A.4   Server Variable Names

Name	Meaning
AUTH_TYPE	The type of authentication, such as NTLM for challenge-response authentication, or Basic for basic authentication.
CONTENT_LENGTH	The number of bytes of content to be received.
CONTENT_TYPE	The type of information provided in the body of a POST request.
PATH_INFO	The path information after the script name (the name of the extension DLL) and before the query string, if any.
PATH_TRANSLATED	The path information from PATH_INFO after virtual paths are translated into directory paths.
QUERY_STRING	The information from the URL following the "?".
REMOTE_ADDR	The IP address of the client that sent the request. This can be an agent, such as a firewall, rather than the client's IP address.
REMOTE_HOST	The host name of the client (or its agent).
REMOTE_USER	The user name that is supplied by the client and authenticated by the server. When the user name is anonymous, the REMOTE_USER string is empty.

continues

Table A.4   Continued

Name	Meaning
UNMAPPED_REMOTE_USER	The user name before it is mapped to the user account on the server. (The mapping occurs in an ISAPI filter, for example.)
REQUEST_METHOD	The request method.
SCRIPT_NAME	The name of the script (the ISAPI extension).
SERVER_NAME	The name or IP address of the server.
SERVER_PORT	The TCP/IP port used for the request.
SERVER_PORT_SECURE	If the request is handled on a secure port, the value is "1". Otherwise it is "0".
SERVER_PROTOCOL	The protocol name and version, usually HTTP/1.0.
SERVER_SOFTWARE	The name and version of the server that is running the ISAPI extension.
ALL_HTTP	All server variables that have not been parsed into one of the variables in this table. The variables names are prefixed with HTTP.

Each variable is in the form of a header, with each header separated by a line feed. The string is null-terminated. |
| HTTP_ACCEPT | All the values of the accept headers on this request are concatenated into a comma- separated string. For example, the headers accept: text/html and accept: image/jpeg become an HTTP_ACCEPT. |
| URL | The base portion of the URL. This is new in HTML 2.0. |

lpvBuffer

Form: Pointer to the buffer in which the value of the server variable will be placed.

Value: [out] The value of the server variable requested.

lpdwSize

Form: Pointer to a DWORD.

Value: [in] The size of the buffer. [out] The length of the value of the server variable, including the null-termination character.

ReadClient()　　This function is used to read data from the client that was not included in the extension control block.

```
BOOL ReadClient(HCONN ConnID, LPVOID lpvBuffer, LPDWORD lpdwSize );
```

Return Value: TRUE if successful, FALSE otherwise. On error, use GetLastError() to get the specific error condition.

ConnID

Form: HCONN

Value: [in] The context number.

lpvBuffer

Form: Pointer to the client data buffer.

Value: [out] The client data.

lpdwSize

Form: Pointer to a DWORD.

Value: [in] The size of the buffer. [out] The length of the returned client data. If the length of the client data exceeds the length of the buffer, the server returns only as many bytes as are in the buffer. The size variable indicates the number of bytes returned.

WriteClient()　　This function can be used to write data to the client.

```
BOOL WriteClient(HCONN ConnID, LPVOID lpvBuffer, LPDWORD lpdwBytes,
    DWORD dwReserved );
```

Return Value: TRUE if successful, FALSE otherwise. On error, use GetLastError() to get the specific error condition.

ConnID

Form: HCONN

Value: [in] The context number.

lpvBuffer

Form: Pointer to the data buffer.

Value: [in] The data to write to the client.

lpdwBytes

Form: Pointer to a DWORD

Value: [in] The length in bytes of the data to be written to the client.

dwReserved

Form: DWORD

Value: This is reserved for future use.

ServerSupportFunction()   The ServerSupportFunction() supplies a function not otherwise provided by the other callbacks. The value of dwHSERRequest determines what this callback function is doing, as shown in Table A.5.

```
BOOL ServerSupportFunction(HCONN hConn, DWORD dwHSERRequest,
    LPVOID lpvBuffer, LPDWORD lpdwSize, LPDWORD lpdwDataType );
```

Return Value: TRUE if successful, FALSE otherwise. On error, use GetLastError() to get the specific error condition.

hConn

Form: HCONN

Value: [in] The context number.

dwHSERRequest

Form: DWORD

Value: [in] The HTTP Server extension request type. Table A.5 shows the meaning of the request types.

Table A.5   Extension Request Type

Request Type	Meaning
HSE_REQ_SEND_URL_REDIRECT_RESP	This sends an URL redirect message (302) to the client. Set lpvBuffer to point to the buffer holding the new URL (which must be a null-terminated string). Set lpdwSize to the address of a DWORD, and set the DWORD to the size of lpvBuffer. lpdwDataType is ignored.
	The extension does no additional processing after calling ServerSupportFunction() with this request type.
HSE_REQ_SEND_URL	This informs the server to send the data specified by the new URL to the client as if the client had requested that URL. Set lpvBuffer to an URL that is on the same server and does not include protocol information. The URL must be a null-terminated string.
	Set lpdwSize to the address of a DWORD, and set the DWORD to the size of lpvBuffer. lpdwDataType is ignored. The extension does no additional processing after calling ServerSupportFunction() with this request type.
HSE_REQ_SEND_RESPONSE_HEADER	This sends a complete HTTP server response header including the status, server version, message time, and MIME version. The extension adds additional HTTP headers, such as the content type and content length.

continues

Table A.5 Continued

Request Type	Meaning
	The headers are separated by carriage-return and line-feed pairs ("\r\n") with an extra "\r\n" at the end. Only text is valid with this response, and it is terminated when a null-termination character ("\0") is encountered.
HSE_REQ_MAP_URL_TO_PATH	This method is used to map a URL to a path. lpvBuffer points to the buffer that holds the physical path when called. The server uses the buffer to return the physical path.
	lpdwSize points to a DWORD holding the size of the buffer passed in lpvBuffer. The server returns the number of bytes placed in the buffer in lpdwSize. lpdwDataType is ignored.
HSE_REQ_DONE_WITH_SESSION	This request type is used to notify the server that the extension is done processing. It is used when a request has been left in a pending state— when HttpExtensionProc returns HSE_STATUS_PENDING. lpvBuffer, lpdwSize, and lpdwDataType are ignored.

lpvBuffer

Form: Pointer to the buffer holding the primary argument.

Value: [in] The primary argument needed for the support function requested.

lpdwSize

Form: Pointer to a DWORD.

Value: [in] The number of bytes of data passed in lpvBuffer.

lpdwDataType

Form: Pointer to a DWORD.

Value: [in] An additional argument needed by the support function request type. This can be a pointer, a set of flags, or a value, depending on the request type.

ISAPI Filters

This section describes the structures and functions used in an ISAPI filter.

Structures

This section describes the structures used in an ISAPI filter.

HTTP_FILTER_VERSION   This structure holds the filter version information and additional flags. It is passed to GetFilterVersion() (see Listing A.3).

Listing A.3   HTTPFILT.H—The Filter Version Structure

```
typedef struct _HTTP_FILTER_VERSION
{
    DWORD   dwServerFilterVersion;
    DWORD   dwFilterVersion;
    CHAR    lpszFilterDesc[SF_MAX_FILTER_DESC_LEN];
    DWORD   dwFlags;
} HTTP_FILTER_VERSION, *PHTTP_FILTER_VERSION;
```

dwServerFilterVersion

Form: DWORD

Value: [in] The version of the HTTP specification. The high and low words are the major and minor versions.

dwFilterVersion

Form: DWORD

Value: [out] The version of the HTTP specification. The high and low words are the major and minor versions. The version can be set using MAKELONG:

```
dwExtensionVersion = MAKELONG( HSE_VERSION_MINOR, HSE_VERSION_
➥MAJOR );
```

lpszFilterDesc

Form: A buffer of SF_MAX_FILTER_DESC_LEN bytes in which to place a null-terminated string.

Value: [out] The filter description.

dwFlags

Form: DWORD

Value: [out] The SF_NOTIFY_* flags that determine which notifications are processed by the filter, the priority of the filter, and whether the filter processes secure notifications, nonsecure notifications, or both. These are shown in Table A.6, Table A.7, and Table A.8.

Table A.6   Filter Notification Flags

Flag	Meaning
SF_NOTIFY_READ_RAW_DATA	Handles READ_RAW_DATA notifications.
SF_NOTIFY_PREPROC_HEADERS	Handles PREPROC_HEADERS notifications.
SF_NOTIFY_AUTHENTICATION	Handles AUTHENTICATION notifications.
SF_NOTIFY_ URL_MAP	Handles URL_MAP notifications.
SF_NOTIFY_ SEND_RAW_DATA	Handles SEND_RAW_DATA notifications.
SF_NOTIFY_ LOG	Handles LOG notifications.

Flag	Meaning
SF_NOTIFY_ END_OF_NET_SESSION	Handles END_OF_NET_SESSION notifications.
SF_NOTIFY_ ACCESS_DENIED	Handles ACCESS_DENIED notifications.

Table A.7 Filter Security Flags

Flag	Meaning
SF_NOTIFY_SECURE_PORT	Handles notifications on secure ports.
SF_NOTIFY_NONSECURE	Handles notifications on nonsecure ports.

Table A.8 Filter Priority Flags

Flag	Meaning
SF_NOTIFY_ORDER_DEFAULT	Loads the filter at the default priority.
SF_NOTIFY_ ORDER_LOW	Loads the filter at low priority.
SF_NOTIFY_ ORDER_MEDIUM	Loads the filter at medium priority.
SF_NOTIFY_ ORDER_HIGH	Loads the filter at high priority.

HTTP_FILTER_CONTEXT HTTP_FILTER_CONTEXT holds size and revision fields, data fields that are for use by the server, and callbacks (see Listing A.4).

Listing A.4 HTTPFILT.H—The Filter Context Structure

```
typedef struct _HTTP_FILTER_CONTEXT
{
    DWORD        cbSize;
    DWORD        Revision;
    PVOID        ServerContext;
    DWORD        ulReserved;
```

continues

Listing A.4   Continued

```
BOOL            fIsSecurePort;
PVOID           pFilterContext;

// Server callbacks
BOOL (WINAPI * GetServerVariable) (
    struct _HTTP_FILTER_CONTEXT * pfc,
    LPSTR                         lpszVariableName,
    LPVOID                        lpvBuffer,
    LPDWORD                       lpdwSize
    );
BOOL (WINAPI * AddResponseHeaders) (
    struct _HTTP_FILTER_CONTEXT * pfc,
    LPSTR                         lpszHeaders,
    DWORD                         dwReserved
    );
BOOL (WINAPI * WriteClient)  (
    struct _HTTP_FILTER_CONTEXT * pfc,
    LPVOID                        Buffer,
    LPDWORD                       lpdwBytes,
    DWORD                         dwReserved
    );
VOID * (WINAPI * AllocMem) (
    struct _HTTP_FILTER_CONTEXT * pfc,
    DWORD                         cbSize,
    DWORD                         dwReserved
    );
BOOL (WINAPI * ServerSupportFunction) (
    struct _HTTP_FILTER_CONTEXT * pfc,
    enum SF_REQ_TYPE              sfReq,
    PVOID                         pData,
    DWORD                         ul1,
    DWORD                         ul2
    );
} HTTP_FILTER_CONTEXT, *PHTTP_FILTER_CONTEXT;
```

cbSize

Form: DWORD

Value: [in] The size of this structure.

Revision

Form: DWORD

Value: [in] The version of this structure. The high and low words hold the major
and minor version numbers.

ServerContext

Form: Pointer

Value: Reserved for use by the server.

ulReserved

Form: DWORD

Value: [in] Reserved for use by the server.

fIsSecurePort

Form: BOOL

Value: [in] If this notification is on a secure port, this value is TRUE.

pFilterContext

Form: Pointer to filter context information.

Value: [in/out] A pointer used by the filter to associate context information with this request. The filter can set the pointer to memory allocated by the filter and free that memory when it gets the SF_NOTIFY_END_OF_NET_SESSION notification.

HTTP_FILTER_RAW_DATA   This structure holds the raw data of a request or the response to a request. It is passed to HttpFilterProc() for SF_NOTIFY_READ_RAW_DATA and SF_NOTIFY_SEND_RAW_DATA notifications.

Listing A.5   HTTPFILT.H—The Raw Data Structure

```
typedef struct _HTTP_FILTER_RAW_DATA
{
    PVOID        pvInData;
    DWORD        cbInData;
    DWORD        cbInBuffer;
    DWORD        dwReserved;
} HTTP_FILTER_RAW_DATA, *PHTTP_FILTER_RAW_DATA;
```

pvInData

Form: Pointer to the raw data buffer.

Value: [in] The raw data of the request.

cbInData

Form: DWORD

Value: [in] The number of bytes of data in the raw data buffer.

cbInBuffer

Form: DWORD

Value: [in] The size in bytes of the raw data buffer.

dwReserved

Form: DWORD

Value: This field is reserved for future use.

HTTP_FILTER_PREPROC_HEADERS   This structure provides access to the server callback functions. It is passed to HttpFilterProc() for SF_NOTIFY_PREPROC_HEADERS notification.

Listing A.6   HTTPFILT.H—The Preprocess Headers Structure

```
typedef struct _HTTP_FILTER_PREPROC_HEADERS
{
    BOOL (WINAPI * GetHeader) (
        struct _HTTP_FILTER_CONTEXT * pfc,
        LPSTR                         lpszName,
        LPVOID                        lpvBuffer,
        LPDWORD                       lpdwSize
        );
    BOOL (WINAPI * SetHeader) (
        struct _HTTP_FILTER_CONTEXT * pfc,
        LPSTR                         lpszName,
        LPSTR                         lpszValue
        );
    BOOL (WINAPI * AddHeader) (
        struct _HTTP_FILTER_CONTEXT * pfc,
        LPSTR                         lpszName,
        LPSTR                         lpszValue
        );
    DWORD dwReserved;
} HTTP_FILTER_PREPROC_HEADERS,*PHTTP_FILTER_PREPROC_HEADERS;
```

HTTP_FILTER_AUTHENT   This structure holds the authorization user name and password (see Listing A.7). It is passed to `HttpFilterProc()` for `SF_NOTIFY_AUTHENTICATION` notifications.

Listing A.7   HTTPFILT.H—The Authentication Structure

```
typedef struct _HTTP_FILTER_AUTHENT
{
    CHAR * pszUser;
    DWORD  cbUserBuff;
    CHAR * pszPassword;
    DWORD  cbPasswordBuff;
} HTTP_FILTER_AUTHENT, *PHTTP_FILTER_AUTHENT;
```

pszUser

Form: Pointer to a string.

Value: [in/out] The authentication user name. If the user name is anonymous, the string is empty.

cbUserBuff

Form: DWORD

Value: [in] The length of the `pszUser` buffer, which is always at least `SF_MAX_USERNAME`.

pszPassword

Form: Pointer to a string.

Value: [in/out] The authentication password.

cbPasswordBuff

Form: DWORD

Value: [in] The length of the `pszPassword` buffer, which is always at least `SF_MAX_PASSWORD`.

HTTP_FILTER_URL_MAP   This structure holds the URL and the physical path to which it is mapped (see Listing A.8). It is passed to `HttpFilterProc()` for `SF_NOTIFY_URL_MAP` notifications.

Listing A.8 HTTPFILT.H—The URL Map Structure

```
typedef struct _HTTP_FILTER_URL_MAP
{
    const CHAR * pszURL;
    CHAR *       pszPhysicalPath;
    DWORD        cbPathBuff;
} HTTP_FILTER_URL_MAP, *PHTTP_FILTER_URL_MAP;
```

pszURL

Form: Pointer to a string.

Value: [in] The URL that is mapped to a physical path.

pszPhysicalPath

Form: Pointer to a string.

Value: [in/out] The physical path.

cbPathBuff

Form: DWORD

Value: [in] The size of the pszPhysicalPath buffer.

HTTP_FILTER_LOG This structure holds information that is recorded in the server log (see Listing A.9). It is passed to HttpFilterProc() for SF_NOTIFY_LOG notifications.

Listing A.9 HTTPFILT.H—The Filter Log Structure

```
typedef struct _HTTP_FILTER_LOG
{
    const CHAR * pszClientHostName;
    const CHAR * pszClientUserName;
    const CHAR * pszServerName;
    const CHAR * pszOperation;
    const CHAR * pszTarget;
    const CHAR * pszParameters;
    DWORD  dwHttpStatus;
    DWORD  dwWin32Status;
} HTTP_FILTER_LOG, *PHTTP_FILTER_LOG;
```

pszClientHostName

Form: Pointer to a null-terminated string.

Value: [in/out] The host name of the client.

pszClientUserName

Form: Pointer to a null-terminated string.

Value: [in/out] The user name of the client.

pszServerName

Form: Pointer to a null-terminated string.

Value: [in/out] The name of the server to which the client is connected.

pszOperation

Form: Pointer to a null-terminated string.

Value: [in/out] The HTTP command.

pszTarget

Form: Pointer to a null-terminated string.

Value: [in/out] The HTTP command target.

pszParameters

Form: Pointer to a null-terminated string.

Value: [in/out] The HTTP command parameters.

dwHttpStatus

Form: DWORD

Value: [in/out] The return status.

dwWin32Status

Form: DWORD

Value: [in/out] The Win32 error code.

HTTP_FILTER_ACCESS_DENIED   This structure provides information about requests for which access was denied (see Listing A.10). This was introduced in IIS 3.0. It is passed to HttpFilterProc() for SF_NOTIFY_ACCESS_DENIED notifications.

Listing A.10   HTTPFILT.H—The Filter Log Structure

```
typedef struct _HTTP_FILTER_ACCESS_DENIED
{
    const CHAR * pszURL;
    const CHAR * pszPhysicalPath;
    DWORD        dwReason;
} HTTP_FILTER_ACCESS_DENIED, *PHTTP_FILTER_ACCESS_DENIED;
```

pszUrl

Form: Pointer to a null-terminated string.

Value: [in] The URL to which access was denied.

pszPhysicalPath

Form: Pointer to a null-terminated string.

Value: [in] The physical path from the translation of the requested URL.

dwReason

Form: DWORD

Value: [in] The reason the request was denied (see Table A.9).

Table A.9   Reasons for Denied Access

Name	Meaning
SF_DENIED_LOGON	Denied because of a logon failure.
SF_DENIED_RESOURCE	Denied because of a resource.
SF_DENIED_FILTER	Denied by an ISAPI filter.
SF_DENIED_APPLICATION	Denied by an ISAPI or CGI application.
SF_DENIED_BY_CONFIG	This can be set when SF_DENIED_LOGON is set if the logon failure was because of the server configuration.

Entry-Point Functions

There are two entry points to an ISAPI filter DLL: `GetFilterVersion()` and `HttpFilterProc()`.

GetFilterVersion() This function is called when the filter is loaded. It returns to the server the version of the filter DLL, the priority of the filter, and the notifications that the filter is to receive.

```
BOOL GetFilterVersion(PHTTP_FILTER_VERSION pVer)
```

Return Value: Returns TRUE if successful, FALSE otherwise. If the filter returns FALSE, it is unloaded. The server will process requests without using the filter.

pVer

Form: Pointer to an `HTTP_FILTER_VERSION` structure.

Value: [out] The extension version information.

HttpFilterProc() This function is called to notify the filter of the events it registered for in `GetFilterVersion()`.

```
DWORD HttpFilterProc(PHTTP_FILTER_CONTEXT pfc,
        DWORD dwNotificationType, LPVOID pvNotification)
```

Return Value: Returns `SF_STATUS_REQ_NEXT_NOTIFICATION` if the server is to continue processing the request. Table A.10 shows the return values.

Table A.10 *HttpFilterProc()* **Return Codes**

Return Code	Meaning
SF_STATUS_REQ_FINISHED	The filter has handled the HTTP request. The server should disconnect the session.
SF_STATUS_REQ_FINISHED_KEEP_CONN	The filter handled the HTTP request. The server should end the session but keep the TCP session open if it negotiated to do so.

continues

Table A.10   Continued

Return Code	Meaning
SF_STATUS_REQ_NEXT_NOTIFICATION	The next filter in the notification chain should be called.
SF_STATUS_REQ_HANDLED_NOTIFICATION	This filter handled the notification. No other handles should be called for this notification type.
SF_STATUS_REQ_ERROR	An error occurred. The server should use GetLastError() and indicate the error to the client.
SF_STATUS_REQ_READ_NEXT	The filter is an opaque stream filter, and the session parameters are being negotiated. This is only valid for raw read notification.

pfc

Form: Pointer to an HTTP_FILTER_CONTEXT structure.

Value: [in] The filter context information.

dwNotificationType

Form: DWORD

Value: One of the notification types described in Table A.11.

Table A.11 Notification Types

Name	Meaning
SF_NOTIFY_READ_RAW_DATA	The filter can act on data that is read from the client.
SF_NOTIFY_SEND_RAW_DATA	The filter can act on data that is written to the client.
SF_NOTIFY_PREPROC_HEADERS	The filter can preprocess the request headers.
SF_NOTIFY_AUTHENTICATION	The filter can participate in the authentication of the client user.
SF_NOTIFY_URL_MAP	The filter can participate in the mapping of the URL to a physical path.
SF_NOTIFY_LOG	The filter can participate in logging the request.
SF_NOTIFY_ACCESS_DENIED	The filter can handle cases in which access is denied. This is new in IIS 3.0.
SF_NOTIFY_END_OF_NET_SESSION	The filter can act when the client is about to disconnect.

pvNotification

Form: Pointer to a structure of a type appropriate for the notification type.

Value: [in/out] See the description of the structure associated with the notification type in Table A.12.

Table A.12   Notification Structures

Notification Type	Structure
SF_NOTIFY_READ_RAW_DATA	HTTP_FILTER_RAW_DATA
SF_NOTIFY_SEND_RAW_DATA	HTTP_FILTER_RAW_DATA
SF_NOTIFY_PREPROC_HEADERS	HTTP_FILTER_PREPROC_HEADERS
SF_NOTIFY_AUTHENTICATION	HTTP_FILTER_AUTHENT
SF_NOTIFY_URL_MAP	HTTP_FILTER_URL_MAP
SF_NOTIFY_LOG	HTTP_FILTER_LOG
SF_NOTIFY_ACCESS_DENIED	HTTP_FILTER_ACCESS_DENIED
SF_NOTIFY_END_OF_NET_SESSION	None

Resources

This appendix lists various resources on the Internet that you refer to in addition to this book. ∎

Web Resources

URL	Description
http://rampages.onramp.net/~steveg/isapi.html	The definitive site for ISAPI information, including the latest source code, developer tools, ISAPI FAQs, and more
http://www.valley.net/~tpozzy/iisvcdb.html	Theo Pozzy on debugging ISAPI interactively
http://rampages.onramp.net/~steveg/iis.html	FAQs about Microsoft IIS
http://www.w3c.org/	World Wide Web Consortium (W3C)
http://www.ntresearch.com/	NT security white papers and information
http://www.w3.org/pub/WWW/Protocols/	HTTP protocol specifications
http://www.w3.org/pub/WWW/MarkUp/	HTML specifications
http://www.mcp.com/306622191284704/general/workshop/	MCP's HTML Workshop
http://ds.internic.net/ds/dspg1intdoc.html	A searchable index of RFCs
http://hoohoo.ncsa.uiuc.edu/cgi/	CGI specification
http://website.ora.com/wsdocs/s/32demo/windows-cgi.html	WinCGI specification

ISAPI Developer's Tools

URL	Description
http://rampages.onramp.net/~steveg/eyesapi1.zip	The EyeSAPI extension spy logging and debugging tool.

URL	Description
http://rampages.onramp.net/~steveg/ ispy.zip	I-Spy, the latest version of the HTTP spy filter. I-Spy captures the raw HTTP transactions between client and server to help you debug your programs.
http://rampages.onramp.net/~steveg/ iiscfg.zip	IISCFG, a tool that helps you configure Microsoft IIS. It's useful for ISAPI developers using IIS.
http://rampages.onramp.net/~steveg/ websbt.htm	WebSBT, a framework for ISAPI, CGI, and WinCGI extensions using Delphi.
http://www.eudev.com/tornado.htm	Tornado for Visual Basic, an improved OLE-ISAPI implementation.
http://www.west-wind.com/wwcgi.htm	Web Connection for Visual FoxPro.
http://www.microsoft.com/visualc/	Visual C++.
http://www.microsoft.com/vbasic/	Visual Basic.
http://www.microsoft.com/msdn	MSDN, a subscription program that increases your productivity and makes it easier for you to take advantage of the latest Microsoft technologies.
http://www.microsoft.com/technet	Microsoft TechNet, the comprehensive information resource for anyone who evaluates, uses, or supports Microsoft business products.
http://www.borland.com	Delphi 2.0.
http://www.perl.hip.com/PerlIS.htm	Perl ISAPI.
http://w4.lns.cornell.edu/~pvhp/perl/ ntperl.html	NT Perl security information.

Part

VI

App

B

Important Internet RFCs

RFC	Location	Description
1808	http://ds.internic.net/rfc/rfc1808.txt	Relative URLs
1630	http://ds.internic.net/rfc/rfc1630.txt	URIs in WWW
1738	http://ds.internic.net/rfc/rfc1738.txt	URLs
1736	http://ds.internic.net/rfc/rfc1736.txt	Functional recommendations for Internet resource locators
1866	http://ds.internic.net/rfc/rfc1866.txt	Hypertext Markup Language 2.0
1980	http://ds.internic.net/rfc/rfc1980.txt	A proposed extension to HTML: client-side image maps
1867	http://ds.internic.net/rfc/rfc1867.txt	Form-based file upload in HTML
1942	http://ds.internic.net/rfc/rfc1942.txt	HTML tables
1945	http://ds.internic.net/rfc/rfc1945.txt	HTTP 1.0
1738	http://ds.internic.net/rfc/rfc1738.txt	URLs
822	http://ds.internic.net/rfc/rfc822.txt	Standard for the format of ARPA Internet text messages
1341	http://ds.internic.net/rfc/rfc1341.txt	MIME
1896	http://ds.internic.net/rfc/rfc1896.txt	The text-enriched MIME content type
1872	http://ds.internic.net/rfc/rfc1872.txt	The MIME multipart-related content type
1180	http://ds.internic.net/rfc/rfc1180.txt	A TCP/IP tutorial
1034	http://ds.internic.net/rfc/rfc1034.txt	Domain names, concepts, and facilities
1035	http://ds.internic.net/rfc/rfc1035.txt	Domain names, implementation, and specification

RFC	Location	Description
1794	**http://ds.internic.net/rfc/rfc1794.txt**	DNS support for load balancing
1983	**http://ds.internic.net/rfc/rfc1983.txt**	Internet user's glossary
1796	**http://ds.internic.net/rfc/rfc1796.txt**	Not all RFCs are standards

Web Servers

Resource Name	Resource Information
Microsoft IIS	Microsoft Corporation **http://www.microsoft.com** 10500 NE 8th Street Suite 1300 Bellevue, WA 98004 Phone: 800-426-9400 Fax: 206-635-1049
Process Purveyor	Process Software Corporation **http://www.process.com** 959 Concord St. Framingham, MA 01701 Phone: 800-722-7770 Fax: 508-879-0042 E-mail: sales@process.com
Cyber Presence Server	Cyber Presence International, Inc. **http://www.cyberpi.com** 622 EdgeWater Blvd., Suite 211 San Mateo, CA 94404 Phone : 415-638-2582 Fax : 415-638-2582
Alibaba	Computer Software Manufaktur - USA **http://www.csm-usa.com** P.O. Box 1105 Layton, Utah 84041 Phone: 801-547-0914 Fax: 801-546-0716 E-mail: sales@csm-usa.com

Part
VI

App
B

continues

Table B.4   Continued

Resource Name	Resource Information
Web Site	O'Reilly & Associates, Inc. **http://website.ora.com/** 101 Morris St. Sebastopol, CA 95472 Phone: 800-998-9938 Fax: 707-829-0104 E-mail: software@ora.com
Spyglass Software Server SDK 2.0	Spyglass, Inc. **http://www.spyglass.com/** 1240 E. Diehl Road Naperville, IL 60563 Phone: 708-505-1010 Fax: 708-505-4944
Commerce Builder	The Internet Factory, Inc. **http://www.aristosoft.com/** 6654 Koll Center Parkway, Suite 150 Pleasanton, CA 94566 Phone: 510-426-7763 Fax: 510-426-9538 E-mail: sales@ifact.com
Web Commander	Luckman Interactive **http://www.luckman.com/wc/** **webcom.html** Phone: 800-711-2676

Installing from the CD-ROM

The companion CD to this book holds the source code, programming tools, and reference materials mentioned in the book. This enables you to cut and paste code examples so you can quickly reuse them. ■

From the Index.htm page in the root directory, you can easily access the numerous features provided on this CD.

- ISAPI Source Code, Programs, and Developers Resources including: source code from the book, ISAPI C++ Header Files, EyeSAPI, I-Spy, and IISCFG
- Que Electronic Books: *Special Edition Using ISAPI* (this book in HTML format), *Special Edition Using Windows NT Server 4.0, Special Edition Using Visual C++*, and a sneak preview of Que's upcoming title, *Active Server Pages*. (The information provided is draft and maybe slightly different in the final publication.)
- Microsoft Internet Explorer 3.0
- ISAPI Programming Language and Resources including: ISAPI examples written in Borland's Delphi and OLEISAPI examples written with Microsoft VB
- Source Code from The ISAPI Developer's Site
- Web-Related Resources
- Important Internet RFCs for Web Developers
- ISAPI Web Server Vendors

The CD holds several subdirectories off of the root directory. The directories on the CD are listed next.

Directory	Structure on the CD
\Code	The source code from the book. For each chapter with sample files or source code, a subdirectory named for the chapter it references is in the \Code directory.
\Contrib	Source code from the ISAPI Developer's Site
\ebooks	*Special Edition Using ISAPI, Special Edition Using Windows NT Server 4.0, Special Edition Using Visual C++,* and a sneak preview of *Active Server Pages*
\ie30	Internet Explorer 3.0
\Include	ISAPI C++ header files
\Tools	EyeSAPI, IISCFG, I-spy, Mapdir and WebSBT
\index.htm	CD Index page (Start Here)

Index

G

X-Y-Z

Check out Que® Books on the World Wide Web
http://www.mcp.com/que

As the biggest software release in computer history, Windows 95 continues to redefine the computer industry. Click here for the latest info on our Windows 95 books

Make computing quick and easy with these products designed exclusively for new and casual users

Examine the latest releases in word processing, spreadsheets, operating systems, and suites

The Internet, The World Wide Web, CompuServe®, America Online®, Prodigy®—it's a world of ever-changing information. Don't get left behind!

Find out about new additions to our site, new bestsellers and hot topics

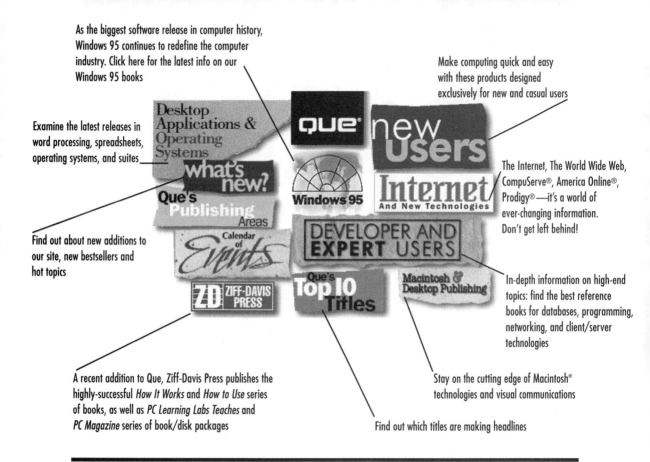

In-depth information on high-end topics: find the best reference books for databases, programming, networking, and client/server technologies

A recent addition to Que, Ziff-Davis Press publishes the highly-successful *How It Works* and *How to Use* series of books, as well as *PC Learning Labs Teaches* and *PC Magazine* series of book/disk packages

Stay on the cutting edge of Macintosh® technologies and visual communications

Find out which titles are making headlines

With 6 separate publishing groups, Que develops products for many specific market segments and areas of computer technology. Explore our Web Site and you'll find information on best-selling titles, newly published titles, upcoming products, authors, and much more.

- Stay informed on the latest industry trends and products available
- Visit our online bookstore for the latest information and editions
- Download software from Que's library of the best shareware and freeware

Complete and Return this Card
for a *FREE* Computer Book Catalog

Thank you for purchasing this book! You have purchased a superior computer book written expressly for your needs. To continue to provide the kind of up-to-date, pertinent coverage you've come to expect from us, we need to hear from you. Please take a minute to complete and return this self-addressed, postage-paid form. In return, we'll send you a free catalog of all our computer books on topics ranging from word processing to programming and the internet.

Mr. ☐   Mrs. ☐   Ms. ☐   Dr. ☐

Name (first) ☐☐☐☐☐☐☐☐☐☐☐☐ (M.I.) ☐ (last) ☐☐☐☐☐☐☐☐☐☐☐☐☐☐☐☐

Address ☐☐☐☐☐☐☐☐☐☐☐☐☐☐☐☐☐☐☐☐☐☐☐☐☐☐☐☐☐☐☐☐

☐☐☐☐☐☐☐☐☐☐☐☐☐☐☐☐☐☐☐☐☐☐☐☐☐☐☐☐☐☐☐☐

City ☐☐☐☐☐☐☐☐☐☐☐☐☐☐☐☐☐☐ State ☐☐ Zip ☐☐☐☐☐ ☐☐☐☐

Phone ☐☐☐ ☐☐☐ ☐☐☐☐ Fax ☐☐☐ ☐☐☐ ☐☐☐☐

Company Name ☐☐☐☐☐☐☐☐☐☐☐☐☐☐☐☐☐☐☐☐☐☐☐☐☐☐☐☐☐☐

E-mail address ☐☐☐☐☐☐☐☐☐☐☐☐☐☐☐☐☐☐☐☐☐☐☐☐☐☐☐☐☐☐

1. Please check at least (3) influencing factors for purchasing this book.

Front or back cover information on book .... ☐
Special approach to the content .... ☐
Completeness of content .... ☐
Author's reputation .... ☐
Publisher's reputation .... ☐
Book cover design or layout .... ☐
Index or table of contents of book .... ☐
Price of book .... ☐
Special effects, graphics, illustrations .... ☐
Other (Please specify): _____ ☐

2. How did you first learn about this book?

Saw in Macmillan Computer Publishing catalog .... ☐
Recommended by store personnel .... ☐
Saw the book on bookshelf at store .... ☐
Recommended by a friend .... ☐
Received advertisement in the mail .... ☐
Saw an advertisement in: _____ ☐
Read book review in: _____ ☐
Other (Please specify): _____ ☐

3. How many computer books have you purchased in the last six months?

This book only .... ☐   3 to 5 books .... ☐
2 books .... ☐   More than 5 .... ☐

4. Where did you purchase this book?

Bookstore .... ☐
Computer Store .... ☐
Consumer Electronics Store .... ☐
Department Store .... ☐
Office Club .... ☐
Warehouse Club .... ☐
Mail Order .... ☐
Direct from Publisher .... ☐
Internet site .... ☐
Other (Please specify): _____ ☐

5. How long have you been using a computer?

☐ Less than 6 months   ☐ 6 months to a year
☐ 1 to 3 years   ☐ More than 3 years

6. What is your level of experience with personal computers and with the subject of this book?

	With PCs	With subject of book
New	☐	☐
Casual	☐	☐
Accomplished	☐	☐
Expert	☐	☐

Source Code ISBN: 0-7897-0913-9

7. Which of the following best describes your job title?

Administrative Assistant .... ☐
Coordinator .... ☐
Manager/Supervisor .... ☐
Director .... ☐
Vice President .... ☐
President/CEO/COO .... ☐
Lawyer/Doctor/Medical Professional .... ☐
Teacher/Educator/Trainer .... ☐
Engineer/Technician .... ☐
Consultant .... ☐
Not employed/Student/Retired .... ☐
Other (Please specify): _____ ☐

8. Which of the following best describes the area of the company your job title falls under?

Accounting .... ☐
Engineering .... ☐
Manufacturing .... ☐
Operations .... ☐
Marketing .... ☐
Sales .... ☐
Other (Please specify): _____ ☐

9. What is your age?

Under 20 .... ☐
21-29 .... ☐
30-39 .... ☐
40-49 .... ☐
50-59 .... ☐
60-over .... ☐

10. Are you:

Male .... ☐
Female .... ☐

11. Which computer publications do you read regularly? (Please list)

_____
_____
_____
_____
_____
_____
_____
_____
_____
_____

Comments: _____
_____
_____

Fold here and scotch-tape to mail.

Licensing Agreement

By opening this package, you are agreeing to be bound by the following: